COMBAT INFANTRY KOREA

COMBAT INFANTRYMENS ASSOCIATION

TURNER PUBLISHING COMPANY
Nashville, Tennessee • Paducah, Kentucky

The first home of the Association was in the home of Richard E. Soesbee, the National Adjutant. The Combat Infantrymen's Association moved to 428 Haywood Road in 1993, then on to our present location, 70 Woodfin Place, Suite 323, Asheville, NC 28801-2466, on June 30, 1997.

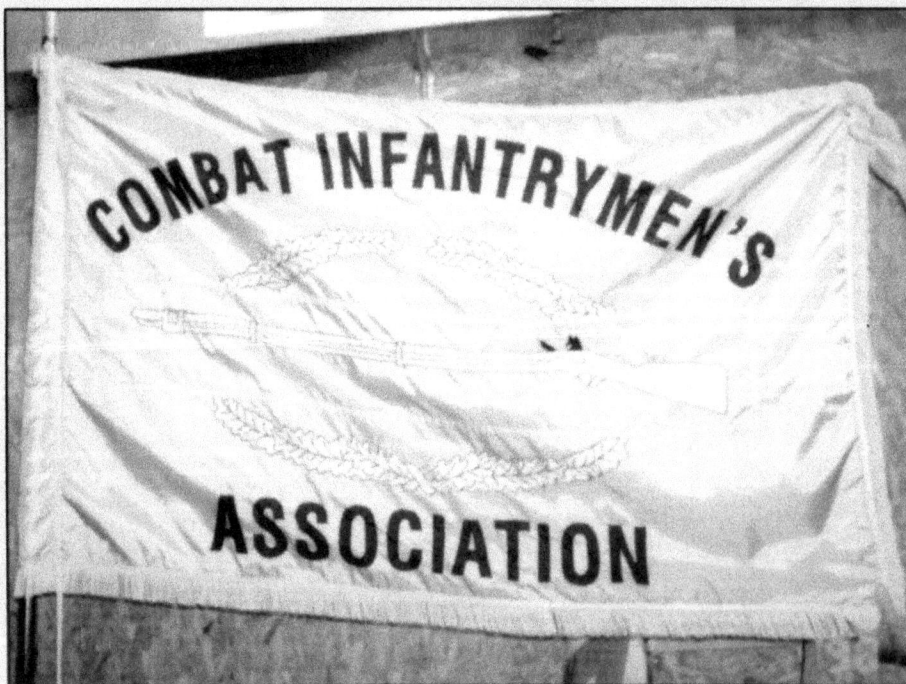

Turner®
PUBLISHING COMPANY

Publishers of Military History
412 Broadway, P.O. Box 3101
Paducah, KY 42002-3101
270-443-0121
www.turnerpublishing.com

Combat Infantrymen Association Staff:
Howard R. Head
Glenn H. Towe

Copyright © 1999, Vol. II 2004
Turner Publishing Company.
All rights reserved.

Turner Publishing Company Staff:
Publishing Consultant: Keith R. Steele

Library of Congress
Catalog Card No.: 99-63739
ISBN: 1-56311-516-6 (VII)
Limited Edition
Printed in the U.S.A.

Additional copies may be purchased directly from Turner Publishing Company.

CONTENTS

DEDICATION

This work, in a very small way, recognizes the contributions of the thousands of individuals who stepped forward and shouldered a weapon in the concept of freedom. Also, we wish to honor the memory or our fallen comrades, and those who have gone on before us. We earnestly thank every American infantryman who has participated in the defense of our nation's causes, and those who continue to serve with pride and honor, and would defend our nation to their last breath. To them this book is dedicated.

Robert L. Towles
National Commander
Combat Infantrymen's Association

Commander Bob Towles and his wife, Kathy.

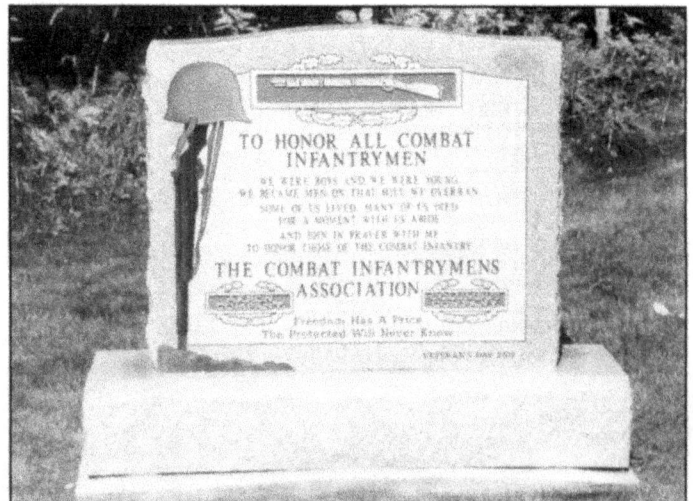

SOLDIER

I was that which others did not want to be.
I went where others feared to go, and did what others failed to do.
I asked nothing from those who gave nothing, and reluctantly
    accepted the thought of eternal loneliness…should I fail.
I have seen the face of terror; felt the stinging cold of fear;
    and enjoyed the sweet taste of a moment's love.
I have cried, pained, and hoped…but most of all,
I have lived times others would say were best forgotten.
At least someday I will be able to say that I was proud of
    what I was…a soldier.

George L. Skypeck

The Combat Infantrymen's Association's First National Memorial Stone dedicated on Veteran's Day, 11 November, 2002 at the Ohio Western Reserve National Veterans Cemetery in Rittman, Ohio.

ACKNOWLEDGMENT

I have watched the Combat Infantrymen's Association, Inc. grow over the past seven years doubling in active membership. Also the most important factor is the growing number of the younger Combat Infantrymen joining the Association. The World War II and Korean War veterans still outnumber all others, yet the younger ones joining today are the most important. They are the ones who will carry our banner in the years ahead, now they are accepting responsibility and stepping into leadership roles. Six years ago the CO and XO were Korean War vets, and the "Blue Badge" editor was Vietnam and the Quartermaster and I were WW II.

Today we have gone to our vast source of expertise for assistance in all areas, instead of doing all the work at National Headquarters. The CO, XO, Finance Officer, and the "Blue Badge" editor are Vietnam veterans. The Adjutant and Membership Officer are from Korea and the Quartermaster and I are WW II. The above officers are spread from Wisconsin to Florida.

These new officers have a great imagination and energy to burn so with them on board I feel that the Association is in good hands and will continue to grow over the coming years.

Be recognized, wear your CIB
Glenn H. Towe
National Chief of Staff
CSM US Army Retired

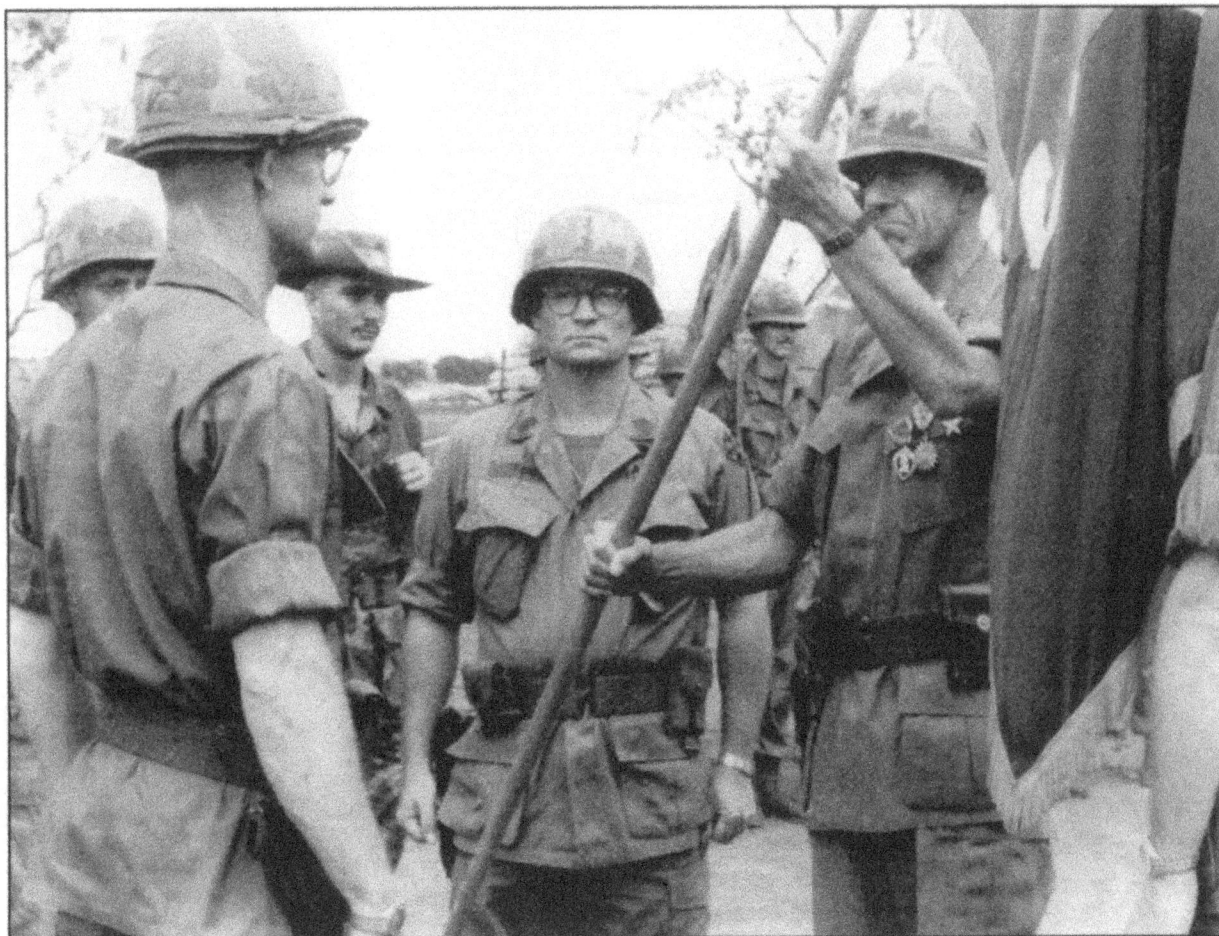

Change of Command 3rd Brigade, 4th Infantry Division. Fire Base, Oasis, west of Pleiku, Vietnam 1969.

FOUNDING FATHERS

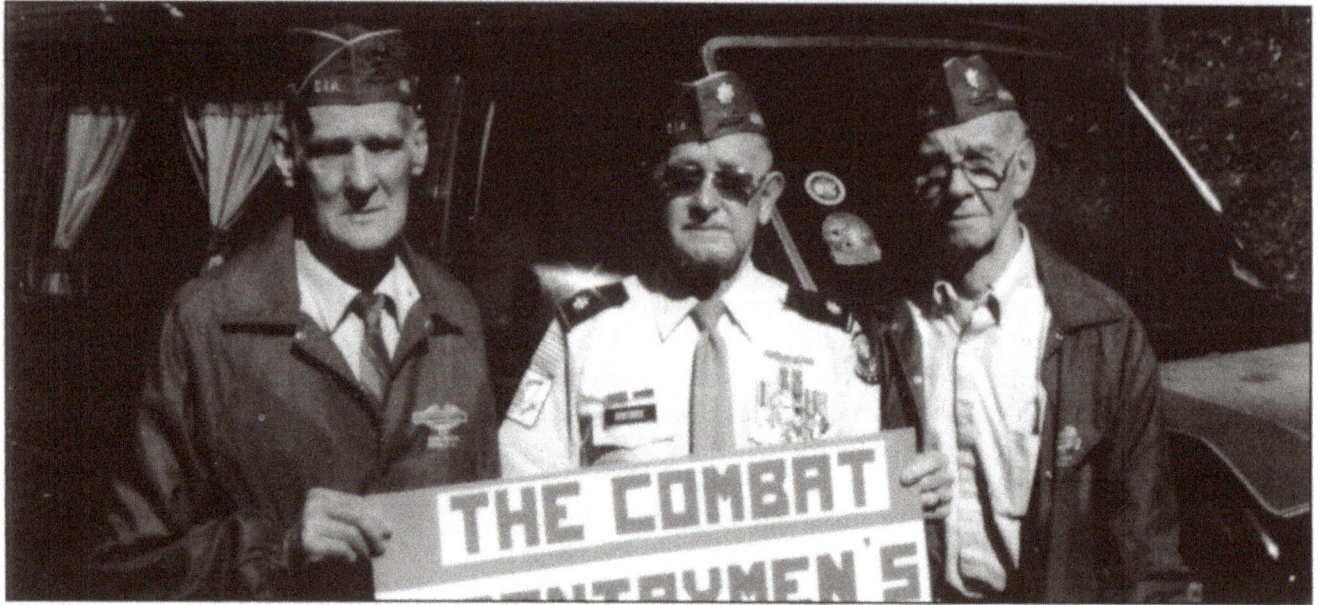

Robert M. Wisecup   *Richard E. Soesbee*   *Paul N. Baker*

☆ THE COMBAT INFANTRYMEN'S ASSOCIATION, INC. ☆

ALL UNIT CHARTER

Know Ye All Men By These Presents:

AN APPROPRIATE number of duly qualified persons having applied for a Charter, establishing a COMPANY of THE COMBAT INFANTRYMEN'S ASSOCIATION and such application having been approved.

Now therefore, in accordance with the Constitution of THE COMBAT INFANTRYMEN'S ASSOCIATION, INC. of THE UNITED STATES OF AMERICA, this Charter is granted and to those applying, together with such others earning THE COMBAT INFANTRYMAN BADGE and as may unite them, are hereby authorized to establish and maintain a CIA COMPANY at

__ASHEVILLE, N.C.__ known as **CIA NATIONAL HQS CO.**

CORPS AREA OF __NORTH CAROLINA__, and this instrument unless revoked or suspended shall be conclusive evidence of the Lawful and legal existence thereof.

By acceptance of this CIA Charter, the said COMPANY, BATTALION, REGIMENT or CORPS AREA acknowledges jurisdiction and declares itself to be subject to the Constitution and By-laws of THE COMBAT INFANTRYMEN'S ASSOCIATION, INC., NATIONAL HEADQUARTERS CO., 1ST BN, 1ST REGIMENT OF the CORPS AREA OF NORTH CARO-LINA, and the rules and regulations and policies promulgated pursuant thereto. And further the said C.I.A. COMPANY pledges itself through its members to uphold, protect and to defend the Constitution of The United States of America and remain loyal to the COMBAT INFANTRYMEN'S ASSOCIATION, keeping membership pure and all blue by the virtue of each member earning the CIB, as the Blue Badge of Courage. . .being the only Membership Qualification.

In Witness Thereof, this Charter, is given under the hand and seal of the NATIONAL COMMANDER of THE COMBAT INFANTRYMEN'S ASSOCIA-TION and duly attested to by said stamp, and signatures of the NATIONAL EXECUTIVE OFFICER and THE NATIONAL ADJUTANT at THE COMBAT INFANTRYMEN'S ASSOCIATION NATIONAL HEADQUARTERS COM-PANY, 1ST BN, 1ST REGIMENT, CORPS AREA OF NORTH CAROLINA on this __6th__ Day of __DECEMBER__, __1986__, both attest and Countersigned at ASHEVILLE, N.C., CIA NATIONAL HEAD-QUARTERS CO.

Robert M. Wisecup, Col.
CIA National Commander

Attest: _Paul N. Baker, LTC._
CIA National Executive Officer

Countersigned: _R.E. Soesbee, Major_
CIA National Adjutant

The Ten National Headquarters Company Charter Members

Richard E. Soesbee

Paul N. Baker

W. Marshall Chaney

Martin L. Daneman

Leroy Schwartz

Robert M. Wisecup

Ralph W. Roberts

Robert L. Walters

John R. DeLay

Robert H. Meuser

COMBAT INFANTRYMEN'S ASSOCIATION HISTORY

The year 1985 marked the beginning of the Combat Infantrymen's Association (CIA). Three men, all World War II veterans and each having earned the Combat Infantry Badge, became disillusioned with the other veteran organizations to which they belonged. Their disappointment arose from the many high paid positions within these organizations, which they felt bred numerous internal and external problems. They met for coffee at a local shop, and began discussing the possibility of having an "elite and volunteer" organization—an association of Combat Infantrymen. The three men, now known as the "Founding Fathers," were Robert W. Wisecup, Paul N. Baker, and Richard E. Soesbee. They began with only their fortitude, drive, and persistence to pave the way to our present Association.

The pioneering Association discovered very little monetary means available. Therefore, much of the money for early expenses came from the pockets of these three men. The Combat Infantrymen's Association formed under Robert Wisecup as National Commander (1985-1993), Paul Baker (deceased) as National Executive Officer (1985-1993), and Richard Soesbee as National Adjutant (1995-1996). Soesbee carved the first National Headquarters office from the cramped quarters of the den in his home located on Dunwell Street in Asheville, North Carolina.

In 1993 the Association made a major move, and rented office space on Haywood Road in West Asheville, North Carolina. With the additional room provided by the new National Headquarters, the Association soon flourished, and began to expand. When Paul Baker (National HQ Company) assumed the duties of National Commander in 1993, he appointed Paul H. Matranga (National HQ Company) National Executive Officer and Earl A. Rubley (National HQ Company) the Association's first National Quartermaster and first National Chaplain. Earl Rubley and Howard R. Head (H-1-1 South Carolina) went into high gear, and dramatically increased the Association's memorabilia sales through expansion of the Quartermaster's department. They located, paid for, and stocked merchandise with money from their own pockets, and accepted refunds only after the Association sold items from the inventory. They worked diligently, and for long hours, purchasing, amassing the inventory, processing sales, and shipping items to buyers, until the Quartermaster became a viable and vital part of the Association. At the present time the Quartermaster is self-supporting, and pays for all expenses of the National Headquarters office.

In 1994 Paul Baker resigned as National Commander and the National Board appointed Robert H. Meuser (deceased) to replace him. September 8-10, 1994 also saw the First Annual Convention of the Combat Infantrymen's Association. The Association held this event at the Radisson Hotel in Asheville, North Carolina. National Quartermaster Earl Rubley and Phillip W. Cochrane (H-2-2 Michigan) hosted the reunion. Although the turnout proved small, the membership, through generous donations, covered all the debts incurred by the Association for the reunion.

During the first ten years of the Association went through many growing pains. The Association grew rapidly from a local organization and "snowballed" going out of state and across the country mostly by word of mouth. The Association's growth soon almost overwhelmed the National, and suspicion and concern developed because of a lack of communications between the officers at National Headquarters, the companies, and the members. National maintained an excessive amount of secrecy, which impeded the normal flow of communications, and complicated matters by not printing very many newsletters during this period. Moreover, the organization did not notify some members to renew their memberships, or when to pay their dues, and this resulted in a large number of members being lost to the organization. Also, during this period Headquarters made a very grievous error in reporting the actual number of members in the Association.

The Holiday Inn in Hickory, North Carolina provided the setting for the Second Annual Convention of the Combat Infantrymen's Association on 7-9 September 1995. Leonard J. Capoziello (H-2-2 Ohio) and Charles W. Slentz, Sr. (H-3-3 Ohio) hosted this reunion. The Radisson Hotel in Columbus, Ohio provided the backdrop for the Third Annual Convention of the Combat Infantrymen's Association on 5-7 September 1996. Leonard Capoziello and Charles Slentz, Sr. again hosted the event.

Neither National Commander Robert Meuser nor National Executive Officer Paul Matranga stood for reelection. The general membership then elected Howard Head National Commander, and Carl E. Lombard (C-1-1 New York) National Executive Officer. Due to declining health National Adjutant Richard Soesbee retired from his office, and on 1 October 1996 the National Commander appointed Glenn H. Towe (H-1-1 South Carolina) National Adjutant. This was the most critical time period in the Association's history.

Therefore, the newly elected and appointed officers immediately tackled the first order of business of the organization, one that would set a course of action for the next two years, and would move the Association into the "present day" world. Their first action informed the membership of the Association's activities. National achieved this through a newsletter, written by the National Adjutant, printed by Office Depot, and hand addressed at National Headquarters. This was mailed on 30 November 1996. In December 1996 the National Commander and National Adjutant met with Larry H. Eckard (National HQ Company) in Hickory, North Carolina, and asked that he become the editor of *The Blue Badge*. He accepted, and the current newsletter was born. He suggested a schedule for the newsletter to follow, and since then the National has published and mailed *The Blue Badge* to all members on a quarterly basis.

National Staff Members moved enough equipment from National Headquarters to Walhalla, South Carolina in order to enable Commander Head and Adjutant Towe to establish a satellite office there, instead of making the five-hour round trip drive from Walhalla to Asheville every day. By January 1997 National Headquarters had computerized all records, and this made it easier to maintain files and communicate with the companies and membership. On 1 July 1997 National Headquarters moved into new quarters at 70 Woodfin Place, Suite 323, Asheville, North Carolina. This relocation provided the organization a step up - less rent, two rooms, one for the office and the other for the quartermaster store.

During 25-28 September 1997 the Radisson Hotel in Columbus, Ohio again provided the stage for the Fourth Annual Convention of the Combat Infantrymen's Association. Leonard Capoziello and William R. McClain (H-2-2 Ohio) hosted the reunion. The general membership determined that the Association's Constitution and By-Laws needed revision, rewritten into an "understandable language," and presented to the members at the next general membership meeting. National Commander Head assigned National Adjutant Towe this huge undertaking.

The Holiday Inn Center City of Columbus, Georgia welcomed members to the Fifth Annual Convention of the Combat

Infantrymen's Association on 27-30 August 1998. Tours included a river ride down the Chattahoochee aboard the *Chattahoochee Princess*, and a visit to the Confederate Naval Museum. Fort Benning also played a key role in the reunion, and the Association presented the Infantry Museum with a gift of two posters, representing all US Army Divisions involved in the Korean War, and a cash donation to benefit the museum. The membership approved the newly revised Constitution and By-Laws during the general membership meeting. *The Blue Badge* printed the entire newly approved text its January 1999 issue, so that all members would be aware of the changes. Also, by vote of acclamation, the general membership endorsed that the current officers remain in office for one more year in order to maintain the continuity of the Association.

During 9-12 September 1999 the Combat Infantrymen's Association held its Sixth Annual Convention at the Holiday Inn in Newburgh, New York where the United States Military Academy, West Point extended a gracious welcome, and figured prominently in the agenda. Attending members elected Carl Lombard National Commander during the general membership meeting. The membership also approved a donation to the Korean War Museum and Library in Tuscola, Illinois, and a change in membership dues to a 50/25/25 percent distribution. The National Board approved the appointment of John M. Nipper as National Executive Officer to fill that vacant position. Also, during 1999 Turner Publishing Company of Paducah, Kentucky printed a history book about the Association entitled *The Combat Infantrymen's Association*, thanks to the hard work of Howard Head and Glenn Towe. This book included general information and brief history of the organization, pictures, personal war stories, and short biographies of some of the members of the Association.

The Combat Infantrymen's Association held its Seventh Annual National Convention at the Holiday Inn & Diamond Casino in downtown Reno, Nevada from 22-25 June 2000. Group activities included a tour of Reno, a trip to Lake Tahoe, and a visit to the "Old West" town of Virginia City. The members present formally elected John Nipper National Executive Officer. Also, during the year Glenn Towe retired from his duties as National Adjutant, and the National Board approved the appointment of Joseph S. Barca (H-1-1 New England) to the position. National Commander Carl Lombard assigned National Historian Robert L. Towles (H-1-2 Ohio) the task of being the official liaison between the Association and the Korea Defense Veterans of America in support of the issuance of a Korea Defense Service Medal for post cease-fire duty.

Throughout 21-24 June 2001 the Ramada Inn Plaza, Pentagon in Alexandria, Virginia hosted the Eighth Annual National Convention of the Combat Infantrymen's Association. The convention included tours of several sites in Washington, D.C. and Arlington National Cemetery. The attending members elected Edward J. Zebrowski (H-1-1 New England) National Commander by acclamation. Also during the convention members selected the CIA's National Flower, the Blue Bell, from several designs submitted by National Finance Officer Robert D. Saxton (H-2-2 Michigan). The National Board approved the appointment of Glenn Towe to the new position of National Chief of Staff, accepted the resignation of National Executive Officer John Nipper, and approved the appointment of Robert Towles to that position.

October 10-13 2002 found the Combat Infantrymen's Association at the Best Western Landmark in Metairie, Louisiana for its Ninth Annual Convention. Points of interest included a swamp boat tour of Bayou Segnette, a visit to Oak Valley Plantation, seeing the D-Day Museum, and spending free time in New Orleans. A representative of Turner Publishing addressed the membership during the general membership meeting regarding the publication of a second addition of the Association's history book. The membership decided to maintain Asheville, North Carolina as its National Headquarters, but not to renew the lease on the present office space. Also, the members voted to allow each established Company to decide whether or not to establish a "Ladies Auxiliary" for their own unit, and resolved that there would be no "Ladies Auxiliary" formed at the National level. National Quartermaster Earl Rubley accepted the position of representative for the Combat Infantrymen's Association to the Veteran's History Project being conducted by the Library of Congress, and began conducting interviews. On Veteran's Day the Association's first monument recognizing all Combat Infantrymen was dedicated at The Ohio Western Reserve National Cemetery. The Association owes a debt of gratitude to the Akron and Columbus, Ohio Companies for the foresight and hard work to accomplish this venture. Before the year ended, President George W. Bush signed the National Defense Authorization Act for the year 2003, and that act authorized the awarding of Korea Defense Service Medal, which the Association had supported.

The Combat Infantrymen's Association held its tenth Annual Convention at the Radisson Penn Harris Hotel in Harrisburg, Pennsylvania from 9-12 October 2003. Lancaster County's Amish country and Gettysburg National Military Park provided a dramatic backdrop for this year's reunion. During the general membership meeting attending members elected Robert Towles National Commander. Additionally, the Association voted to go to Congress and request that the issuance of a Bronze Star Medal, for service, be considered and awarded to post-Second World War holders of the Combat Infantry Badge. National Adjutant Joseph Barca accepted the tasking of making the first contact with Congress. Also approved the appointment of a committee to recommend future sites for reunions, and adopted "The War on Terrorism Recruitment Program" that offers a free two-year membership to all active duty Combat Infantrymen serving in Iraq and Afghanistan who apply for membership. Following the general membership meeting the National Board of officers appointed John R. Wagner (A-1-1 Florida) to the position of National Executive Officer.

The members of the current National Staff of the Combat Infantrymen's Association are: Commander - Robert L. Towles; Executive Officer - John R. Wagner; Chief of Staff - Glenn H. Towe; Adjutant Joseph S. Barca; Finance Officer - Robert D. Saxton; Membership Officer - Daniel R. Sankoff; Quartermaster & Service Officer - Earl A. Rubley; Medical Officer - Doctor J. William Mooney; Staff Judge Advocate - Ray V. Bethel; National Chaplain - Father Leo A. Hetzler; Larry H. Eckard - "Blue Badge" Editor.

Past National Commanders of the Combat Infantrymen's Association are: Robert W. Wisecup, 1985-93; Paul N. Baker (deceased) 1993-94; Robert H. Meuser (deceased) 1994-96, Howard R. Head 1996-99; Carl E. Lombard 1999-2001; Edward J. Zebrowski 2001-03. Past National Adjutants: Richard E. Soesbee; Glenn H. Towe.

These gentlemen have given the Association a great deal of thought, time, and energy. Remember, not one member of the organization receives monetary compensation for services rendered. There are no paid employees—all services are preformed by volunteers—this is another one of the great attributes of our members.

PAST NATIONAL COMMANDERS

Robert W. Wisecup (Founding Father)
1985 - 1993

Paul N. Bake (deceased)
(Founding Father)1994 - 1994

Robert H. Meuser (deceased)
1994 - 1996

Howard R. Head
1996 - 1999

Carl E. Lombard
1999 - 2001

Edward J. Zebrowski
2001-2003

Robert Towles
Commander

John R. Wagner
Executive Officer

Glenn H. Towe
Chief of Staff

Joseph S. Barca
Adjutant

NATIONAL STAFF

Robert D. Saxton
Finance Officer

Daniel R. Sankoff
Membership Officer

Members of the National Staff attending the 2003 Reunion: Front: Earl A. Rubley-Quartermaster/Service Officer; Glenn H. Towe-Chief of Staff; Larry H. Eckard-"Blue Badge" Editor; Jack R. Wagner-XO; Rear: Howard R. Head-Past CO; Joseph S. Barca-Adjutant; Ed Zebrowski-outgoing CO; Dominic Esposito-CO Corps of New York/retiring Service Officer; Daniel R. Sankoff-Membership Officer; Robert L. Towles-CO; Robert D. Saxton-Finance Officer; Ray V. Bethel-Staff Judge Advocate; (not pictured-Father Leo Hetzler-Chaplain).

Earl A. Rubley
Service Officer & Quartermaster

Ray V. Bethel
Staff Judge Advocate

Father Leo Hetzler
Chaplain

J. William Mooney
Medical Officer

Larry H. Eckard
"Blue Badge" Editor

Edward J. Zebrowski
Immediate Past CO

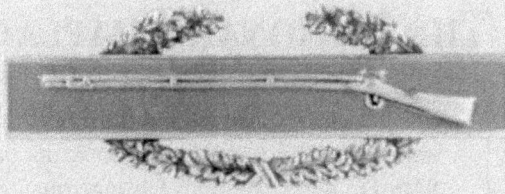

Past National Commander 1996-1999

The year 1985 was the first year of the Combat Infantrymen's Association, Inc. For several years, members consisted mostly of WW II, Korea and a few Vietnam. Today there are younger veterans joining the association that will replace us that are growing older and take the CIA into the future.

In 1996 the CIA was in debt with a bank loan and was about to be dissolved. Today the CIA is financially sound, thanks to you, the members, for your renewal, donations and bringing in new members after a four page newsletter. The bank donated the interest for the loan and you, the members, paid the loan. First, our success is due to the dedication of members. The men who worked many long dedicated hours to bring us Eckard "Blue Badge" Editor.

We now place our trust in our younger men to keep the Combat Infantrymen's Association the elite organization the founding fathers adopted.

Howard (Ray) Head
Korea 4 May 1951 - March 52
I&R Plt. Hq Hq Co 17th Inf Reg 7th Div

Past National Commander 1999-2001

The Combat Infantrymen's Association was conceived in Asheville, North Carolina, by three men who earned the Combat Infantry Badge. The three men were Robert M. Wisecup, Paul N. Baker and Richard Soesbee. In the beginning the CIA struggled to obtain members but they preserved and did what had to be done to make the CIA a viable Veteran's Organization that all members could be proud of.

Through the dedication and determination of the founders and the continued leadership of National Commanders, Robert M. Wisecup, Paul N. Baker, Robert H. Meuser and Howard R. Head, the Combat Infantrymen's Association is recognized around the world.

Today we have members in the USA, Canada, Europe, and beyond, so we have come a long way from our humble beginnings, but we still have a way to go.

At this time I am reminded of a lesson learned, many years ago, that continues to this very day. In the infantry, you must master the greatest challenge of all - yourself. If you can prove yourself in the infantry, you can prove yourself anywhere. Then you can look back over your shoulder and shout, the proud slogan of the infantry that has echoed throughout the years

Carl E. Lombard
A Co., 1st Bn, 14th Inf

NATIONAL ADJUTANTS (Past and Present)

Richard E. Soesbee (deceased)
1985-1990

Glenn H. Towe
1996-1999

Joseph S. Barca
1999 - Present

"It has been a great experience to be associated with the finest group of soldiers known to man." Joe Barca, National Adjutant

THE NATIONAL CHAPLAIN

Father Leo A. Hetzler
National Chaplain

Father Leo A. Hetzler, born in Rochester, New York, on September 7, 1925, enlisted in the Army at 17, took his basic training at Fort Benning, joined the 86th Division at Camp Livingston, Louisiana, where he was trained in jungle fighting and then in amphibious assault on the California Channel Islands. He engaged in three European campaigns: Watch on the Rhine in the Cologne area; the Ruhr Pocket; and the drive into Bavaria and Austria. The 86th Division embarked for the Pacific to subdue the Japanese holdouts in the hills of Mindanao and captured 2500 prisoners.

Back in civilian life, Father Hetzler entered the Basilian Fathers. He received a B.A. and a M.A. in English Literature, and a S.T.D. in Theology from St. Michael's University, and a Ph.D. in English from Cornell University. In 1959 he joined the faculty at St. John Fisher College.

For thirty years he was Assistant Editor for the quarterly *The Chesterton Review* and has published numerous essays, among them a number of articles on the westerns, other novels, and poems of Max Brand (Frederick Schiller Faust).

Father Hetzler considers his service to the Combat Infantrymen's Association a very high honor.

THE NATIONAL EXECUTIVE OFFICER

John R. Wagner
National Executive Officer

As the National Executive Officer of the Combat Infantrymen's Association, I would like to state that one of our goals is to enlist those elite individuals that earned the Combat Infantrymen's Badge into our organization. And, also to educate and perpetuate how the combat infantryman played a major part in all battles and wars.

I was awarded the Combat Infantrymen's Badge in 1965 while serving in "A" Company, 2nd Battalion, 7th Cav of the 1st Cavalry Division in An Khe, Vietnam. I served with that unit in 1965 and 1966.

I was hospitalized for wounds suffered in action from January 1966 to April 1966 in the 106th General Hospital in Yokohama, Japan, and, again from September 1966 to December 1966 in the 249th General Hospital in Asaka, Japan.

I am a graduate of Thomas Moore College with degrees in Business Administration, Sociology and elected studies.

My other duties other than the National Executive Officer in the organization is that of Company Commander of Company "A", 1st Bn, 1st Rgt of southwest Florida. Our company presently has over 250 members. I am also a member of: Military Order of the Purple Heart - Disabled American Veterans - Vietnam Veterans of America - Veterans Of Foreign Wars - 1st Cavalry Division Association - and the 7th Cavalry Association. I take great pride in being a member of the elite Combat Infantrymen's Association.

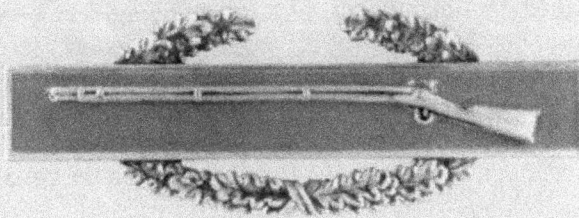

THE BLUE BADGE

"The rifleman fights without promise of either reward or relief. Behind every river there's another hill—and behind that hill, another river. After weeks or months in the line only a wound can offer him the comfort of safety, shelter, and a bed. Those who are left to fight, fight on, evading death but knowing that with each day of evasion they have exhausted one more chance for survival. Sooner or later, unless victory comes this chase must end on the litter or in the grave."
General Omar Bradley, United States Army

This "Blue Badge," the Combat Infantryman Badge, has a strange and compelling mystic about it, and it has become the infantryman's most notable award—next to the Medal of Honor. Unfortunately, many unqualified non-infantry service men and women have attempted to bypass the regulations and acquire one. The current prerequisites clearly prescribe the requirements that an individual must meet in order to be considered for a Combat Infantryman Badge.

I. History:
   (A) The Combat Infantryman Badge (CIB) was established by the War Department on 27 October 1943. Lieutenant General Lesley J. McNair, then the Army Ground Forces commanding general, was instrumental in its creation. He originally recommended that it be called the "Fighter Badge." The CIB was designed to enhance morale and the prestige of the "Queen of Battle." Then Secretary of War, Henry L. Stinson, said, "It is high time we recognize in a personal way the skill and heroism of the American infantry."
   (B) Originally, the regimental commander was the lowest level at which the CIB could be approved, and its award was retroactive to 7 December 1941. There was a separate provision for badge holders to receive a $10 per month pay stipend, which was rescinded in 1948. Several factors led to the creation of the CIB, some of the most prominent factors are as follows:
      (1) The need for large numbers of well-trained infantry to bring about a successful conclusion to the war and the already critical shortage of infantrymen.
      (2) Of all soldiers, it was recognized that the infantryman continuously operated under the worst conditions and performed a mission which was not assigned to any other soldier or unit.
      (3) The infantry, a small portion of the total Armed Forces, was suffering the most casualties while receiving the least public recognition.
      (4) General George C. Marshall's well known affinity for the ground forces soldier and, in particular, the infantryman. All these factors led to the establishment of the CIB, an award which would provide special recognition of the unique role of the Army infantryman, the only soldier whose daily mission is to close with and destroy the enemy and to seize and hold terrain. The badge was intended as an inducement for individuals to join the infantry while serving as a morale booster for infantrymen serving in every theater.
   (C) In developing the CIB, the War Department did not dismiss out of hand or ignore the contributions of other branches. Their vital contributions to the overall war effort were certainly noted, but it was decided that other awards and decorations were sufficient to recognize their contributions. From the beginning, Army leaders have taken care to retain the badge for the unique purpose for which it was established and to prevent the adoption of any other badge which would lower its prestige. At the close of World War II, our largest war in which the armor and artillery played key roles in the ground campaigns, a review was conducted of the CIB criteria with consideration being given to creating either additional badges or authorizing the badge to cavalry and armor units. The review noted that any change in policy would detract from the prestige of the badge.

II. Intent:
   (A) There are basically three requirements for awarding of the CIB. The soldier must be an infantryman satisfactorily performing infantry duties, must be assigned to an infantry unit during such time as the unit is engaged in active ground combat, and must actively participate in such ground combat. Campaign or battle credit alone is not sufficient for the awarding of the CIB.
   (B) The definition or requirement to be "engaged in active ground combat" has generated much dialogue over the years as to the original intent of the CIB.
   (1) The 1943 War Department Circular required infantrymen to demonstrate "satisfactory performance of duty in action against the enemy." The operative words "in action" connoted actual combat.
   (2) A War Department determination in October 1944 specified that: "action against the enemy" for purposes of award of the CIB was to be interpreted as "ground combat against enemy ground forces."
   (3) In 1948, the regulation governing badges stipulated that: "battle participation credit is not sufficient; the unit must have been in contact with the enemy." This clearly indicated that an exchange of hostile fire or equivalent personal exposure was the intent of the Army leadership.
   (4) In 1963 and 1965 HQDA messages to the senior Army commander in the Southeast Asia theater of operations authorized award of the CIB to otherwise qualified personnel "provided they are personally present and under fire." U.S. Army Vietnam regulations went so far as to require documentation of the type and intensity of enemy fire encountered by the soldier. The intended requirement to be "personally present and under fire" has not changed.

III. Specific eligibility requirements:
   (A) A soldier must be an Army infantry or Special Forces

officer (SSI 11 or 18) in the grade of colonel or below, or an Army enlisted soldier or warrant officer with an infantry or special forces MOS, who subsequent to 6 December 1941 has satisfactorily performed duty while assigned or attached as a member of an infantry, ranger or special forces unit of brigade, regimental, or smaller size during any period such unit was engaged in active ground combat. Eligibility for Special Forces personnel (less the Special Forces medical sergeant) accrues from 20 December 1989. Retroactive awards for Special Forces personnel are not authorized.

(B) A recipient must be personally present and under hostile fire while serving in an assigned infantry or Special Forces primary duty, in a unit actively engaged in ground combat with the enemy. The unit in question can be of any size smaller than brigade. For example, personnel possessing an infantry MOS in a rifle squad of a cavalry platoon in a cavalry troop would be eligible for award of the CIB. Battle or campaign participation credit alone is not sufficient; the unit must have been in active ground combat with the enemy during the period.

(C) Personnel with other than an infantry or Special Forces MOS are not eligible, regardless of the circumstances. The infantry or Special Forces SSI or MOS does not necessarily have to be the soldier's primary specialty, as long as the soldier has been properly trained in infantry or Special Forces tactics, possesses the appropriate skill code, and is serving in that specialty when engaged in active ground combat as described above. Commanders are not authorized to make any exceptions to this policy.

(D) Awards will not be made to general officers nor to members of headquarters companies of units larger in size than brigade.

IV. Subsequent awards:

(A) To date, a separate award of the CIB has been authorized for qualified soldiers in any of three conflicts: World War II (7 December 1941 to 3 September 1945), the Korean Conflict (27 June 1950 to 27 July 1953), and the Vietnam Conflict. Service in the Republic of Vietnam conflict (after 1 March 1961) combined with qualifying service in Laos (19 April 1961 to 6 October 1962), the Dominican Republic (28 April 1965 to 1 September 1966), Korea on the DMZ (after 4 January 1969), Grenada (23 October to 21 November 1983) Panama (20 December 1989 to 31 January 1990), and the Persian Gulf War (17 January to 11 April 1991) is recognized by one award only—regardless of whether a soldier has served one or multiple tours in any or all of these areas. If a soldier has been awarded the CIB for service in any of the Vietnam Era areas, that soldier is not eligible to earn the Combat Medical Badge.

(B) Second and third awards of the CIB are indicated by superimposing 1 and 2 stars respectively, centered at the top of the badge between the points of the oak wreath.

V. Special provisions - Republic of Vietnam:

(A) Any officer whose basic branch is other than infantry who, under appropriate orders, has commanded a line infantry (other than a headquarters unit) unit of brigade, regimental, or smaller size for at least 30 consecutive days is deemed to have been detailed in infantry and is eligible for award of the CIB notwithstanding absence of a written directive detailing that soldier in the infantry, provided all other requirements for the award have been met. Orders directing the officer to assume command will be confirmed in writing at the earliest practicable date.

(B) In addition, any officer, warrant officer, or enlisted man whose branch is other than infantry, who under appropriate orders was assigned to advise a unit listed in (D) and (E) below or was assigned as a member of a White Star Mobile Training Team or a member of MAAG-Laos as indicated in VI (A) and (B) below will be eligible for award of the CIB provided all other requirements have been met.

(C) After 1 December 1967 for service in the Republic of Vietnam, noncommissioned officers serving as Command Sergeants Major of infantry battalions and brigades for periods of at least 30 consecutive days in a combat zone are eligible for award of the CIB provided all other requirements have been met.

(D) Subsequent to 1 March 1961, a soldier must have been:

(1) Assigned as advisor to an infantry unit, ranger unit, infantry type unit of the civil guard of regimental or smaller size, and/or infantry-type unit of the self defense corps unit of regimental or smaller size of the Vietnamese government during any period such unit was engaged in actual ground combat.

(2) Assigned as advisor of an irregular force comparable to the above infantry units under similar conditions.

(3) Personally present and under fire while serving in an assigned primary duty as a member of a tactical advisory team while the unit participated in ground combat.

(E) Subsequent to 24 May 1965, to qualify for the CIB, personnel serving in United States units must meet the requirements of III (A) above. Individuals who performed liaison duties with the Royal Thai Army or the Army of the Republic of Korea combat units in Vietnam are eligible for award of the badge provided they meet all other requirements.

VI. Laos - From 19 April 1961 to 6 October 1962 a soldier must have been:

(A) Assigned as member of a White Star Mobile Training Team while the team was attached to, or working with, a unit of regimental (groupment mobile) or smaller size of Forces Armee du Royaume (FAR), or with irregular type forces of regimental or smaller size.

(B) A member of MAAG-Laos assigned as an advisor to a region or zone of FAR, or while serving with irregular type forces of regimental or smaller size.

(C) Personally under hostile fire while assigned as specified in (A) or (B) above.

VII. Dominican Republic - From 28 April 1965 to 21 September 1966, the soldier must have met the criteria prescribed in II and III above. VIII. Korea - Subsequent to 4 January 1969, a soldier must have:

(A) Served in the hostile fire area at least 60 days and been authorized hostile fire pay.

(B) Been assigned to an infantry unit of company or smaller size and must be an infantry officer in the grade of captain or lower. Warrant officers and enlisted men must possess an infantry MOS. In the case of an officer whose basic branch is other than infantry who, under appropriate orders, has commanded an infantry company or smaller size infantry unit for at least 30 days, the award may be made provided all the following requirements are met.

(C) Been engaged with the enemy in the hostile fire area or in active ground combat involving an exchange of small arms fire at least 5 times.

(D) Been recommended personally by each commander in the chain of command and approved at division level. If killed or wounded as a direct result of overt enemy action, he must be recommended personally by each commander in the chain of command and approved at division level. In the case of infantrymen killed by enemy action, the requirement for at least 5 engagements (C) above and the requirement for the incident to have taken place in the hostile fire area, including the 60-day requirement (A) above, will be waived. In the case of individuals wounded, even though outside the hostile fire area, the 5 engagements requirement and the 60 day requirement may be waived when it can be clearly established that the wound was a direct result of overt hostile action.

(E) Been eligible for award of the CIB after 4 January 1969, for service in the Republic of Vietnam, as noncommissioned officers serving as Command Sergeants Major of infantry battalions and brigades for periods of at least 30 consecutive days in a combat zone.

IX. Grenada (Operation Urgent Fury) - From 22 October 1983 to 21 November 1983, the soldier must have met the criteria prescribed in II and III above.

X. Panama (Operation Just Cause) - From 20 December 1989 to 31 January 1990, the soldier must have met the criteria prescribed in II and III above. Special Forces personnel (less the Special Forces medical sergeant) are eligible for the CIB effective 20 December 1989. Retroactive awards are not authorized.

XI. Persian Gulf War (Operation Desert Storm) - From 17 January 1991 to 11 April 1991, the soldier must have met the criteria prescribed in II and III above. Retroactive awards are not authorized.

XII. Who may award:

(A) Current awards. Current awards of the CIB may be awarded by the Commanding General, Eighth U.S. Army, any commander delegated authority by the Secretary of the Army during war time, and the Commanding General, PERSCOM.

(B) Retroactive awards. Retroactive awards of the Combat Infantryman Badge and the Combat Medical Badge may be made to fully qualified individuals. Such awards will not be made except where evidence of injustice is presented. Active duty soldiers will forward their applications through command channels to Commander PERSCOM, ATTN: TAPC-PDA, Alexandria, VA 22332-0471. Reserve Component soldiers, retirees, and veterans should address their application to Commander, ARPERCEN, ATTN; DARP-PAS-EAW, 9700 Page Boulevard, St. Louis, MO 63132-5200.

Changes approved for second and subsequent awards of the Combat Infantryman Badge re:

I. Paragraphs 8-6 and 8-7, AR 600-8-22, 25 February 95.

II. HQ, PERSCOM Message, DTG 051639Z December 01, Subject: Delegation of Wartime approval authority - Operation Enduring Freedom.

III. HQ, PERSCOM Message, DTG 280842Z March 02, Subject: Award of the Combat Infantryman Badge [CIB] - Operation Enduring Freedom.

IV. Chapter 29, AR 670-1, Wear and Appearance of the Army Uniforms and Insignia, 1 July 02.

A. Effective 5 December 01, Operation Enduring Freedom began the 4th conflict qualifying for award of the Combat Infantryman Badge. The Vietnam Era (3rd conflict) to qualify for the CIB) was officially terminated on 10 March 95.

B. World War II and the Korean War were the 1st and 2nd conflicts qualifying for the awarding of the CIB. The Vietnam Era (3rd conflict) include the operations/wars listed below. Soldiers who qualified for award of the CIB for any of these operations are recognized by one award only regardless of whether they served one or multiple tours in any or all of these areas: (1) Vietnam Conflict, 1 March 1961 - 28 March 1973; (2) Laos, 19 April 1961 - 6 October 1962; (3) Dominican Republic, 28 April 1965 - 1 September 1966; (4) Korea on the DMZ, 4 January 1969 - 31 March 1994; (5) El Salvador, 1 January 1981 - 1 February 1992; (6) Grenada, 23 October - 21 November 1983; (7) Panama, 20 December 1989 - 31 January 1990; (8) Persian Gulf War, 17 January 1991 - 11 April 1991; (9) Somalia, 5 June 1992 - 31 March 1994.

C. Second and subsequent awards of the CIB are indicated by superimposing stars, centered at the top of the badge between the points of the oak wreath.

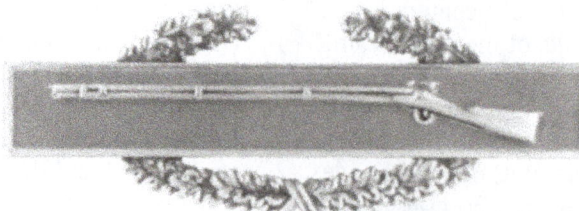

COMBAT INFANTRYMEN'S ASSOCIATION FIRST CONVENTION
September 8-10, 1994
Radisson Hotel, Asheville, North Carolina

Robert H. Meuser
National Commander

Robert E. Soesbee
National Adjutant

Earl A. Rubley
National Quartermaster

Members, wives and guests enjoying the fellowship of the first convention banquet.

SECOND ANNUAL REUNION
September 7-9, 1995
Holiday Inn, Hickory, North Carolina

Leonard Capoziello, Reunion Co-host

Charlie Slentz, Reunion Co-host

Tom Herring speaking at a business meeting.

Left to right: Ray Bethel, Carl Lombard and Tom Herring.

Jessie Childress, National Chaplain

Ray Bethel and wife Janet.

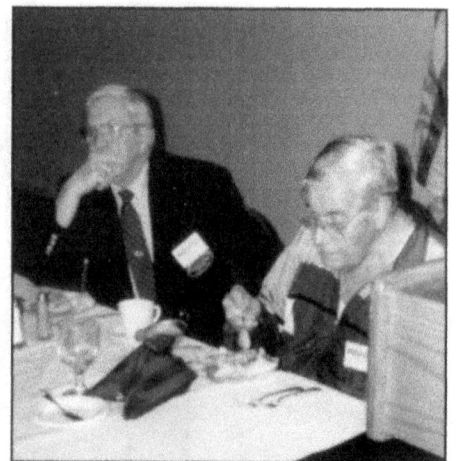

Left to right: Earl Rubley, National Quartermaster and Robert Meuser, National Commander.

THIRD ANNUAL REUNION
September 5-7, 1996
Radisson Hotel, Columbus, Ohio

Members and guests meeting old and new friends at the reunion.

MEETING IN ASHEVILLE, NORTH CAROLINA
December 1998

This was the first time Robert Wisecup had visited the National Headquarters since 1993. Left to right: Bruce Peterson, Asst. Quartermaster; Glenn Towe, National Adjutant; Earl Rubley, Quartermaster; Howard Head, National Commander. Seated: Robert Wisecup, one of the three Founding Fathers and first National Commander.

Earl Rubley presenting Robert Wisecup a recognition award of his contribution to the Association as one of the "Founding Fathers" and the first National Commander for eight years.

Earl Rubley presenting Mrs. Paul Baker a recognition award for Paul N. Baker (deceased) as one of the "Founding Fathers" for his contribution to the Association and second National Commander 1993 to 1994. Mrs. Baker also received a copy of the Combat Infantryman's Association Honor Roll.

FOURTH ANNUAL REUNION
Columbus, Ohio, September 25-28, 1997
Radisson Hotel, Columbus North

William R. McClain
Reunion Co-Host

Leonard J. Capoziello
Reunion Co-Host

4th Annual Reunion
Members, Wives, and Guests

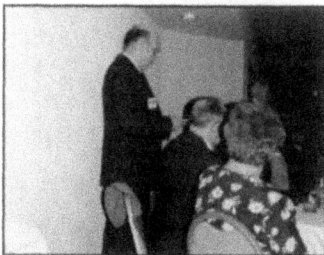

Carl E. Lombard
Reading the Honor Roll of
deceased members

Edward Zebrowski, National Medi-
cal Officer; Glenn Towe, National
Adjutant and Larry Eckard, Na-
tional Editor.

Howard Head, National Com-
mander and Earl Rubley, National
Quartermaster.

Left to right: Ellis Dean, Fred
McGee and Glenn Towe.

Ackels, Harold and Doris
Bethel, Ray and Janet
Bradford, William and Marian
Brown, Carl and Frances
Capoziello, Leonard
Colucci, Rocco and Susan
Danforth, John and Shirley
Dean, Ellis
DiJune, Joseph and Gracy
DiLonardo, Pat and Jean
Eckard, Larry
Feustel, Mae
Franzen, Virgil and Edna
Garceau, Walter
Glenn, Albert
Graves, Gerald
Halperin, Sanford
Head, Howard and Norma
Herman, John
Heston, Thomas and Gale
Holt, Eric and Caroline
Kuligoski, Joseph Sr.
Labrie, Robert and Beverly
Lill, James Max
Lombard, Carl and Joan
McClain, William and Joy

McGee, Fred
Mean, Marilyn
Michaels, August and Fay
Moloney, James
Mooney, John W.
Norman, Gerald
Palmer, Cecil and Necil
Patterson, Leland and Virginia
Phillips, Lewis and Florence
Rolik, Milan
Rubley, Earl
Searcy, James R.
Sharples, Karl
Spears, Ralph
Spence, Thomas C.
Spilker, Oren and Marjorie
Strish, William Sr.
Towe, Glenn
Towles, Robert
Webber, Joseph and Audrey
Whitmore, Shirley
Witt, Clarence J.
Zebrowski, Edward
Zentko, Albert
Zerger, Herman Jr.

Hospitality Room

Members attending business meeting.

Members,
Wives
and
Guests
Enjoying
Old
and
New
Friends
at
the
Banquet.

National Reunion Columbus, Ohio 1997. Left to right: Carl Lombard, National XO; Joe Dijune; Howard Head, National CO; Max Lill, Rochester, New York, Company CO and Jim Moloney.

Father Leo A. Hetzler received the C Company, Rochester, New York Combat Infantryman of the Year award. Left to right: Max Lill, Father Hetzler and Carl Lombard.

FIFTH ANNUAL REUNION
Columbus, Georgia, August 27-30, 1998
Holiday Inn Center City

*Larry Eckard,
Reunion Host*

Nominating Committee Meeting

Members, Wives, and Guests Attending 1998 Reunion

Ackels, Harold and Doris
Arbuckle, Benjamin and Mary
Ayers, John and Mary
Beer, Jan D.
Bethel, Ray and Janet
Childress, Jessie and Lou Ellen
Cook, George
Dilonardo, Pat and Jean
Doar, Henry
Duff, Edward and Marie
Eckard, Larry and Brenda
Edwards, Harold and Etta
Eggle, Robert
Esposito, Dominic
Eve, Louis and Carolyn
Gallo, Peter and Charlotte
Grady, Francis
Harp, Charles
Hauck, Larry
Head, Howard and Norma
Helton, Robert and Wanelle
Herring, Thomas
Hill, Shirley Jean
Hock, Robert and Vivian
Howard, Clenn and Edna
Jackson, Spencer
Johnson, William and Eliz
Jones, Robert and Jacqueline
Justofin, Leonard and Agnes

Kern, William and Florence
Kinsey, Daniel
Knight, Roger and Barbara
Lane, James and Ruby
LoGiudice, Vince
Lombard, Carl and Joan
Madaris, Eddie
Martelli, Daniel
Mathews, Allen and Becky
McClain, William and Joy
McGee, Fred
McKitrick, Edward and Phyllis
Michaels, August and Fay
Nipper, John and Margaret
Pitt, Bill and Bama
Rolik, Milan and Ann
Rubley, Earl
Selmi, Louis Jr. and Marion
Sheipe, Robert
Tarabusi, Raymond
Toscano, John and June
Towe, Glenn
Towles, Robert
Tsungu, Ilir and Janyce
Webber, Joseph Jr. and Audrey
Weeks, Edward
Will, Clarence
Zebrowski, Edward
Zentko, Albert

National Commander, Howard Head and New York State Commander, Dominic Esposito

Members, wives and guests on bus enroute to Fort Benning.

Enjoying lunch with the troops at Fort Benning.

Executive Board Meeting

Attending Airborne graduating class at Fort Benning.

Visit to museum at Fort Benning.

Boarding riverboat for lunch and cruise on the Chattahoochee River.

Enjoying music, dance and fellowship with a Georgia country band.

23

Francis Grady
Hqs. Company Commander,
New Rochelle, NY

Dominic Esposito
New York State Commander

Vincent Logiudice
A Company Commander,
New Rochelle, NY

Fort Benning Honor Guard presenting the colors.

ENJOYING THE BANQUET

Larry Eckard
Blue Badge Editor
Reunion Host

Howard Head
National Commander

Earl Rubley, QM
Speaker

Ed Harp, SJA
Speaker

1998 BANQUET

Left: Glenn Towe presenting certificate of
appreciation to Norma Head.

Right: Glenn Towe, Honor Roll ceremony
IN HONOR OF THOSE GONE BEFORE US.

SIXTH ANNUAL REUNION
Newburgh, New York, September 1999
Holiday Inn, Newburgh

Major General Herbert McChrystal, Cadet John Kendall, Cadet Robert McChrystal, Colonel Scott McChrystal, CSM Glenn Towe.

Cadet Darby Aviles, Cadet Timothy Gries, Cadet Angela Boyle with CWO Larry Eckard.

Waiting in the stands for the Cadet Parade.

The Cadets Pass in Review.

Members, Wives, and Guests Attending 1999 Reunion

Harold & Doris Ackels	Neal & Eleanor Akerlind
John & Susan Bauer	Lawrence Bennett
Ray & Janet Bethel	Wilber & Betty Bishof
Douglas & Teddy Blue	Russell Brami & Tammy Collins
Ivan & Charlotte Busa	Clayton & Anne Bush, Jr.
Brendan & Nora Byrne	William & Gloria Coe
James & Marilyn Colignon	Rocco & Susan Colucci
George & Joan Cook	John Coval
James & Helen Cuddihy	Joseph & Gracy DiJune
Pat & Jean Dilonardo	Robert & Skippy Doak
Larry & Brenda Eckard	Alfonso Eitmant
Dominic Esposito	Richard Evans
Louis & Carolyn Eve	Douglas Fargo
Salvatore & Beverly Gallo	John Garlan
Ted & Jane George	Anthony & Mary Giralico
Francis Grady	Vernon Greene & Linda Swarthout
Philip & Claudia Harbour	Andre & Martha Hartzell
Howard & Edna Head	Leo Hetzler
Glenn & Edna Howard	Larry & Josephine Izzo
Spencer Jackson	Robert Jacobs & William Willis
William & Elizabeth Johnson	Leonard & Agnes Justofin
Marlay & Joan Lacey	Max Lill
Vincent LoGiudice	Carl & Joan Lombard
Robert Magar	Jerome & Marilyn Manley
Daniel Martelli	Marvin Clayton
Allen & Becky Mathews	John May
William & Joy McClain	Fred McGee
Edward & Phyllis McKitrick	August & Fay Michaels
Elwyn Miller	Joseph & Shirley Minto
Rocco & Monica Moretto	Joseph & Jean Munoz
John & Margaret Nipper	James Nolan
Anthony Pellegrino	George & Jo Petcoff
John & Sylvia Pierson	John A. Pierson & Liza Novax
Gerrell Plummer	Milan & Ann Rolik
Earl Rubley	Fred Searles
Alfred & Edna Seebode	Louis & Marion Selmi, Jr.
Karl Sharples	John Skiffington
William Strish	Charles Thomas
Glenn Towe	Robert & Kathleen Towles
John & Eva Vera	Joseph & Arlene Villabol
Joseph & Audrey Webber, Jr.	Edward Weeks
Clarence Will	Edward Zebrowski

Cadet Guard Mount

Cadets Darby Aviles, Angela Boyle, Timothy Gries with CIA Member.

Members,
Wives,
and
Guests
Enjoying
Friendship,
Comradeship,
and the
Program
of the
Banquet

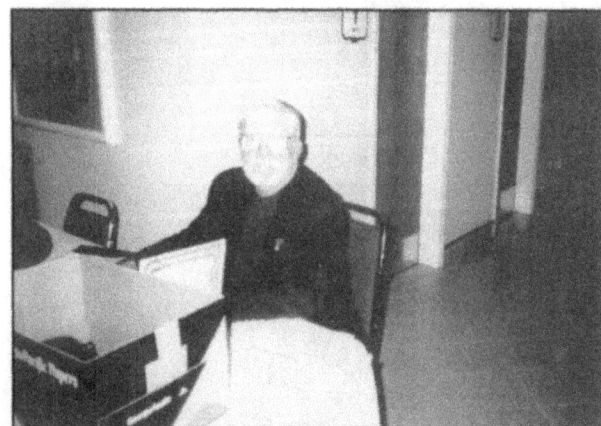

National Quartermaster Earl Rubley is always on duty and conducting CIA business.

Attendees relaxing and enjoying some free time and friends in the Hospitality Room.

SEVENTH ANNUAL REUNION
Reno, Nevada, June 22-25, 2000
Holiday Inn & Diamond Casino

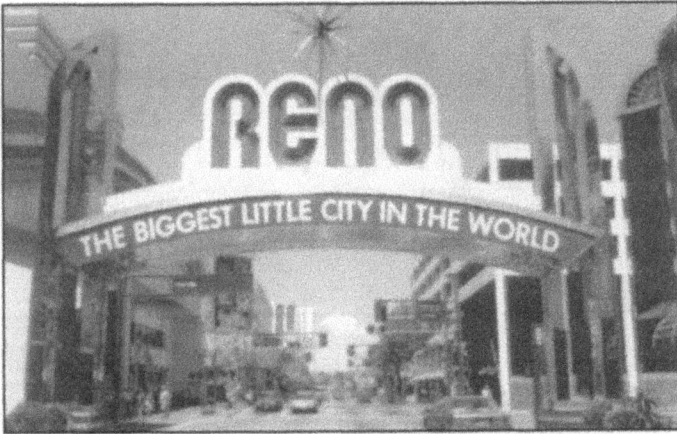

Gateway to the host city.

Members, Wives, and Guests Attending 2000 Reunion

Lawrence & Elaine Beringer
Thomas Cope
James & Jane Dollar
Al Eitmant & Betty Gilbert
Larry Hauck
Glenn & Edna Howard
Milton Lukken
Harold & Jane Malone
August & Fay Michaels
Lloyd & Sally Oler, Sr.
Joseph & Dorothy Pietroforte
Alfred & Edna Seebode
Glenn & Kevin Towe
Joseph & Audrey Webber, Jr.
Richard Woodhouse

Rocco & Susan Colucci
James & Helen Cuddihy
Larry & Brenda Eckard
Jay Gruenfeld
Leo Hetzler
Carl & Joan Lombard
Albert Lumpkin
William & Joy McClain
John & Margaret Nipper
Walter & Donald Pearson
William, Bama & Tosha Pitt
Oren & Marjorie Spilker
Harold & Wilma Vanderwall
Robert & Claire Woodhouse

Bill and Joy McClain prepare to cruise aboard a paddle-wheel steamer on Lake Tahoe.

Sailing into the sunset.

National Commander Carl Lombard and his wife Joan.

Viewing some scenery in the "Old West."

Glenn Howard, August Michaels, Father Leo Hetzler, William McClain and Joseph Webber.

27

Bill and Joy McClain

Harold and Jane Malone and Helen Cuddihy

Father Leo Hetzler, Joe Pietroforte and Larry Beringer

Members,
Wives,
and
Guests
Enjoying
Friendship,
Comradeship,
and the
Program
at the
Saturday
Night
Banquet

Richard Woodhouse and Harold Vanderwall

Larry Hauck and Glenn Howard

Oren Spiler, Al and Betty Gilbert

Glenn Towe and Thomas Cope

EIGHTH ANNUAL REUNION
Alexandria, Virginia, June 21-24, 2001
Ramada Inn Plaza, Pentagon

Our Nation's Capitol

Korean War Memorial

Tomb of the Unknown Soldier

"The Wall"

Guard Mount Inspection

Arlington National Cemetery

Members, Wives, and Guests Attending 2001 Reunion

Joseph Barca
Charles & Elliott Borcom
James & Helen Cuddihy
Robert & Skippy Doak
Dominic Esposito
Howard & Doris Harvier
Leo Hetzler
Lawrence & Josephine Izzo
William & Elizabeth Johnson
Edward Krasovich
James & Jane Lill
Carl & Joan Lombard
William & Joy McClain
August & Fay Michaels
Robert O'Malley
Rudy & Edda Pezzaro
Earl Rubley
Alfred & Edna Seebode
Glenn & Kevin Towe
Joseph & Audrey Webber, Jr.
Clarence Will

Wilbur & Betty Bishof
Lawrence & Miriam Connors
Joseph & Gracy DiJune
Alfonso Eitmant & Betty Gilbert
Francis Grady
Howard Head
Glenn & Edna Howard
Joseph Jimenez
Steve & Laura Korn
James & Ruby Lane
Vincent LoGiudice
Theodore & Mary Luciani
Edward & Phyllis McKitrick
Andrew & Dotty Nix
Carlo & Anne Orlando
Gerrell Plummer
Michael & Ruth Samburg
Oren & Marjorie Spilker
Robert & Kathy Towles
Edward Weeks
Edward Zebrowski

Members,
Wives,
and
Guests
Enjoying
Fellowship
at the
2001
Banquet

Members of the National Staff attending: Front--Bob Towles, XO; Edward Zebrowski, Medical Officer; Glenn Towe, Chief of Staff; Earl Rubley, Quartermaster. Rear--Howard Head, past CO; Joseph Barca, Adjutant; Carl Lombard, CO; Dominic Esposito, Service Officer; (staff not pictured) Father Hetzler, Chaplain and Larry Eckard, "Blue Badge" Editor.

Chaplain Father Leo Hetzler and Commander Carl Lombard, Opening Prayer of the 2001 Banquet.

NINTH ANNUAL REUNION
Best Western Landmark
October 10-13, 2002
Metairie, Louisiana

Standing on the corner of Bourbon Street , Norma and Howard Head, Ed Zebrowski, Kevin and Glenn Towe.

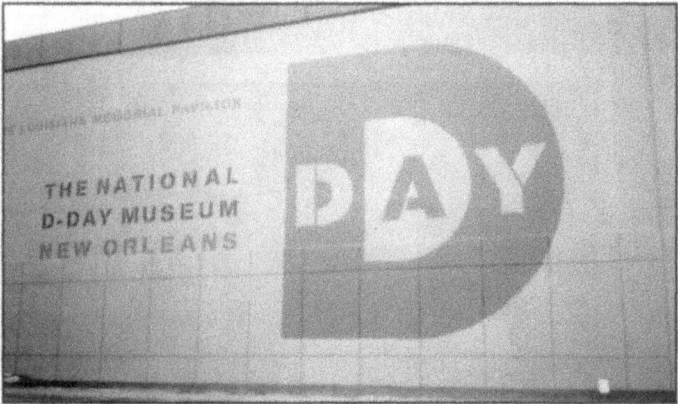

Outside of the D-Day Museum.

Dixieland Band providing entertainment.

Enjoying the Dixieland Music.

Members, Wives, and Guests Attending 2002 Reunion

Conrad Adams	Robert & Louise Alford
Joseph Barca	Ray Bethel
James & Helen Cuddihy	Larry & Brenda Eckard
Alfonso Eitmant	Dominic Esposito
Louis & Carolyn Eve	Al & Betty Gilbert
Ted & Jane George	Francis Grady
Howard & Doris Harvier	Howard & Norma Head
Leo Hetzler	Glenn & Edna Howard
Jack & Elaine Hughes	Robert & Ruth Johnson
Dave Jolly	Vincent LoGiudice
Theodore & Mary Luciani	Milt Lukken
Donald Mayville	William & Joy McClain
Fred McGee	August & Fay Michaels
Joseph & Muriel Minto	Lorenzo Ortega
Paul Lopez	Michael Ottomano
Cecil & Neisel Palmer	William, Bama & Tosha Pitt
Frank Prano	Earl Rubley
Daniel Sankoff	Robert Saxton
Alfred & Edna Seebode	Oren & Marjorie Spilker
Glenn & Kevin Towe	Robert Towles
Joseph & Audrey Webber, Jr.	Harrison & Nancy West
Edward Zebrowski	

The Best Western Landmark, the host hotel.

Carriage rides to enjoy.

Larry Eckard prepares to open the banquet activities.

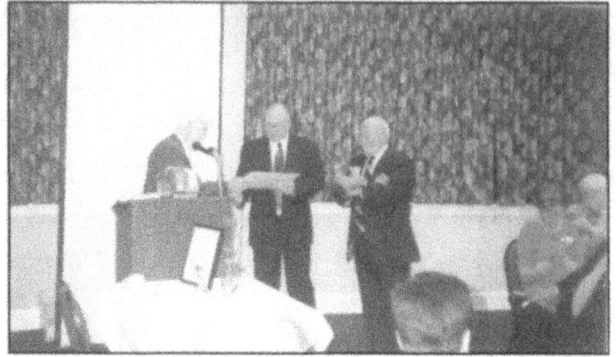
Commander Ed Zebrowski presents an award to Bob Saxton while Dan Sankoff looks on and applauds.

Members, Wives, and Guests Enjoying Themselves in these Scenes from the 2002 Banquet

Louis Eve, Dan Sankoff, and Al Eitmant

Howard Head, Father Leo Hetzler, Alfred Seebode, and Larry Eckard.

TENTH ANNUAL REUNION
Radison Penn Harris Hotel
October 9-12, 2003
Harrisburg, Pennsylvania

The host hotel.

Dan Sankoff viewing an Amish buggy.

Lorenzo Ortega and Paul Lopez, H-1-1-CA.

Members, Wives, and Guests Attending 2003 Reunion

Conrad & Gladys Adams	Richard & Otelia Alvarez
Joseph Barca	Ray Bethel
Wilbur & Betty Bishof	Aram Bobigian
Ernest Busha & Roland Gignac	Harvey & Betty Charbonneau
Sam Cherone	Sylvio & Francis Ciummo
Ralph & June Clark	Lawrence & Miriam Connors
Bill Cowan	Charles & Audry Cripps
James D'Agostino	Larry & Brenda Eckard
Dominic Esposito	William Forbes
James Gallas	Ted & Jane George
Lawrence Gilbert	Jesus & Dora Gonzales
Francis Grady	John Graham
Albert Guarnieri, Jr.	Howard Head
Leo Hetzler	John & Janice Hipson
John & Ruby Hoback	Glenn & Edna Howard
William & Elizabeth Johnson	Mark Labbe
James & Ruby Lane	Vincent LoGiudice
Paul Lopez & Vivian Wood	Theodore & Mary Lucisni
Robert & Eileen Ludwig	David McAllister
William & Joy McClain	Edward & Phyllis McKitrick
Ralph Metivier	August & Fay Michaels
John Mizzoni	John Moore
Lorenzo Ortega	Michael Ottomano
Michael & Barbara Palmeri	Rudy & Edda Pezzaro
Gerrell Plummer	Joseph & Stephanie Poggi
Edward & Mildred Rice	Earl Rubley
Daniel Sankoff	Robert Saxton
Alfred & Shirley Schindler	Alfred & Edna Seebode
Robert Smith	Oren & Marjorie Spilker
James Stokely	Bernard Symczak & Bob Lovering
Glenn Towe	Robert & Kathleen Towles
John & Jean Valerio	Jack Wagner
Joseph & Audrey Webber, Jr.	Edward Zebrowski
Dominic Zinnie	

Gladys and Conrad Adams, Bill McClain, Augie and Fay Michaels in Gettysburg National Military Park.

Open Amish buggy pulls onto dirt lane.

Various views from the banquet in Harrisburg, Pennsylvania

CIA Members wearing their dress blues.

Augie Michaels, Joy McClain, and Fay Michaels prepare to board the tour bus for Gettysburg.

General Officer monument scenes located in Gettysburg National Military Park.

INFANTRY BLUE

By Jim Dollar

There is a spot in Heaven
Reserved for me and you.
God calls this sacred place
A Heaven for Infantry Blue.

To qualify for this honor,
And rest in this paradise due,
Your and your wife together
Will be in Infantry Blue.

For all foot soldiers everywhere,
Past and present too,
Your are the "Queen of Battle,"
And belong in Infantry Blue.

You've served your time in hell,
And paid the price for a viw.
Rest in peace and honor,
We'll see you in Infantry Blue.

EPILOGUE
"A SOLDIER FIRST OF ALL"

CIB

American citizens filling this role, will always bring to the arena, a personal performance of thoughts, words and actions demonstrating the highest forms of citizenship, for the good of the Nation.

The very existence of the soldier supporting the cause will, should and must relfect a sharing and caring aura, for his fellow soldiermen, that have joined him, in this noble and mutual endeavor.

When all have subverted their personal desires for the good order and success of the mission, they will have joined in the communion of

"DUTY-HONOR-COUNTRY"

as this chalice was shared in war, this communion will also be recognized in peace, as a lasting tribute, to one another, for sacrifices, to a fraternity, that marches, to a refrain of long ago,

"A SOLIER FIRST OF ALL"

James V. McNicol

National CIA Memorial Stones and the Florida CIB Monument

Committee Members at the dedication of Ohio's CIA Memorial Stone on Veteran's Day 2002. Shown left to right are members Bill Mooney, Jim Leach, Ted George, Bob Miller, Walt McDonald, Glenn Clegg, and Ray Bethel.

CIA Committee members from the state of New York shown after dedicating their CIA Memorial Stone at Ladson Park's "Trail of Honors" in Somers, New York on Veteran's Day 2003. Left to right: Francis Grady; Frank Yerkes; Sully Yonkers; Frank Valentin; Lt. Col. David Jones, USMA; Vincent LoGiudice; Dominic Esposito (Commander of the Corps of New York).

Kansas' CIA Memorial Stone was dedicated in the National Cemetery at Fort Scott, Kansas on Veteran's Day 2003.

The Florida CIB monument was dedicated on Veteran's Day, 2003 along a walkway beside the SW Florida Museum of History in Fort Meyers, Florida.

Glenn Towe lighting candle on each side of the Honor Roll before the lights were turned off and the names read of those gone before us and ending with Taps. August 29, 1998, Columbus, Georgia, Fifth Annual Reunion.

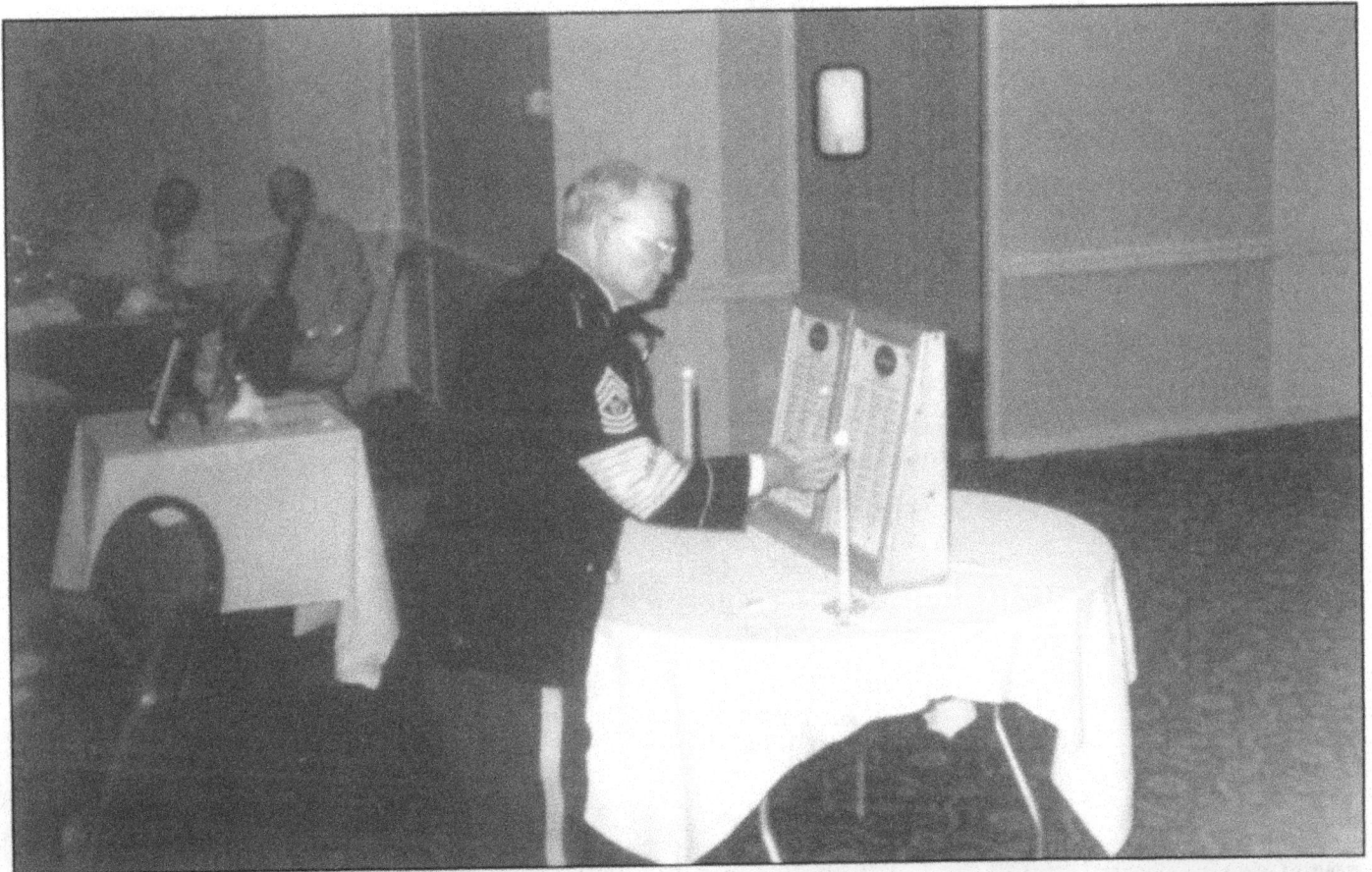

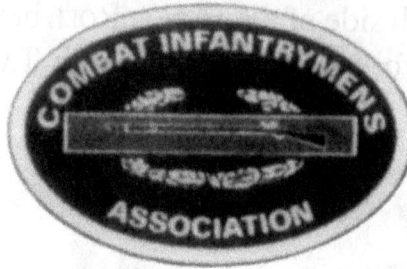

HONOR ROLL
DEDICATED TO THE MEN WHO HAVE GONE BEFORE US

MR. ROBERT A. LABRIE
279TH INF. RCT
45TH INF. DIV.
LOUDON, NH

MR. DOYLE L. GUNN
CO. A, 409TH INF. REGT.
CO. G, 117TH INF.
30TH INF. DIV.
BAYSPRINGS, MS

MR. LEE SNIDOW
CO. B, 320TH INF.
35TH INF. DIV.
BIG RIVER, CA

MR. CARL C. HARMEYER
CO. E, 180TH INF.
45TH INF. DIV.
WEST ALLIS, WI

MR. DARRELL L. FURAN
NO COMPANY LISTED
71ST INF. DIV.
MANKATO, MN

MR. RICHARD C. MAREZ
CO. D, 5TH
SPECIAL FORCES
COLUSA, CA

MR. MALCOLM A. GRANT
461ST INF.
NO DIV. LISTED
BADGER, CA

MR. RONALD A. CHURA
43RD, 11TH INF.
AMERICAL DIV.
SEVEN HILLS, OH

MR. ALFRED STRANGFIELD
NO REGIMENT LISTED
96TH INF. DIV.
LAKEWOOD, CO

MR. JOSEPH H. HRICKO
341ST INF.
86TH INF. DIV.
ALEXANDRIA, VA

MR. JOHN BAGE
CO. H, 259TH INF.
65TH INF. DIV.
AZUSA, CA

LT. THOMAS N. MCLAUCHLIN
CO. M, 30TH INF.
3RD INF. DIV.
HIGH POINT, NC

MR. ROBERT H. JOHNSON
CO. M, 407TH INF.
102ND INF. DIV.
LARCHMONT, NY

MR. WILLIAM PURDY
502ND PCH. INF.
101ST ABN. DIV.
EDWARDSVILLE, PA

MR. ROBERT H. MEUSER
PAST COMMANDER, CIA
36TH INF. DIV.
HICKORY, NC

MR. MARTIN J. NEDUCHAL
CO. H, 391ST INF.
94TH INF. DIV.
CO. D, 32ND INF.
7TH INF. DIV.
SAN FRANCISCO, CA

COL. WILLIAM R. HEMPHILL
3RD BN., 36TH AI REGT.
3RD ARMD. DIV.
ARLINGTON, VA

MR. RUSSELL A. BAKKEN
HQ CO., 87TH INF.
10TH MTN. DIV.
GLENDALE, CA

MR. ROY F. TOREY
CO. A, 184TH INF.
7TH INF. DIV.
POULSBO, WA

MR. WILLIAM BOLTZ JR.
147TH RCT
37TH INF. DIV.
DENVER, CO

MR. JOSEPH ESMOND
NO CO. LISTED
88TH INF. DIV.
MASURY, OH

MR. ROBERT L. KEFFNER
CO. M, 7TH INF.
3RD INF. DIV.
NEW YORK, NY

MR. ARTHUR FERGUSON
17TH RCT
7TH INF. DIV.
ARLINGTON, VA

MR. FRANK J. MILLER
CO. C, 142ND INF.
36TH INF. DIV.
HICKORY, NC

MR. GEORGE W. SEIFERT
3044TH QUARTERMASTER
GRAVE REGT. CO.
COCHISE, AZ

MR. LESLIE R. PARKER
CO. H, 5TH REGT.
COMBAT TEAM
BEACH HAVEN, NJ

MR. STEVEN K. KAPSICK
2ND BN., 30TH INF.
3RD INF. DIV.
LUZERNE, PA

MR. RAYMOND B. RUSSELL
CO. G, 20TH INF.
6TH INF. DIV.
KILLEEN, TX

MR. HENRY F.W. HAAS
CO. G, 264TH INF.
66TH INF. DIV.
NEW ROCHELLE, NY

MR. JOHN R. MCNEESE
CO. H, 137TH INF.
35TH INF. DIV.
HHC, 27TH INF.
25TH INF. DIV.
GLEN BURNIE, MD

CSM ROBERT BATES
CO. I, 187TH ABN., RCT
PITTSBURGH, PA

MR. ELGIN RICHIE
CO. G, 143RD INF.
36TH INF. DIV.
BELLEVILLE, TX

MR. DONALD WHITNER
CO. F, 422ND INF.
106TH INF. DIV.
MILLVILLE, PA

MR. STEPHEN M. ARTNER
CO. K, 330TH INF.
83RD INF. DIV.
OXFORD, OH

MR. WILLIAM WOLF
CO. C, 165TH INF.
27TH INF. DIV.
SCHRUB OAK, NY

MR. EDWIN J. WEBBER
NO REGIMENT LISTED
71ST INF. DIV.
JACKSON HEIGHTS, NY

MR. THEODORE C. LARSON
CO. A, 377TH INF.
95TH INF. DIV.
FRAMINGTON, MA

MSG EUGENE F. SCHILDMAN
CO. F, 14TH INF.
25TH INF. DIV.
DEL CITY, OK

MR. HARVEY D. BRADFORD
SVC. CO., 424TH INF.
106TH INF. DIV.
ASION, PA

MR. CLIFTON S. LUKE
301ST INF.
94TH INF. DIV.
MELROSE, MA

MR. HARRY JOHNSON JR.
CO. I, 12TH INF.
4TH INF. DIV.
CHANUTE, KS

MR. JAMES M. LEWIS
CO. F, 357TH INF.
90TH INF. DIV.
GLEN BURNIE, MD

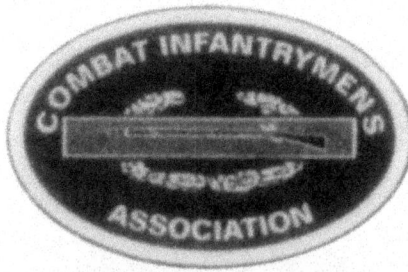

HONOR ROLL
DEDICATED TO THE MEN WHO HAVE GONE BEFORE US

SGM PAUL J. MURMAN
TANK CO., 17TH INF.
77TH INF. DIV.
HOPEWELL, VA

MR. LUCIUS M. BURKETT
GERMAN POW, WWII
28TH INF. DIV.
WALHALLA, SC

MR. WILLARD A. BLOOM
CO. F, 116TH INF.
29TH INF. DIV.
BERWICK, PA

MR. ARNOLD L. BABBIT
CO. B, 18TH INF.
1ST INF. DIV.
FLANDERS, NJ

MR. PAUL D. BLACKMER
CO. K, 143RD INF.
36TH INF. DIV.
CANTON, NY

ROLAND J. GEBO
CO. E, 86TH INF.
10TH MTN. DIV.
WHITEHALL, NY

MR. ROBERT L. O'BRIEN
CO. C, 6TH AIB
1ST ARMD. DIV.
SUN CITY, AZ

MR. ROBERT L. WALKER
CO. L, 386TH INF.
97TH INF. DIV.
CAMP HILL, VA

MR. FRANK T. CICHOCKI
HQ, 394TH INF.
99TH INF. DIV.
HAMMOND, IN

MR. FRANCIS V. GRIFASI
NO REGIMENT LISTED
3RD INF. DIV.
BERWICK, PA

MR. WALTON M. HUDSON
3RD BN., 5TH INF.
71ST INF. DIV.
OCALA, FL

MR. LEO F. LEFEVRE
CO. A, 27TH INF.
25TH INF. DIV.
BUTLER, PA

MR. DEAN T. REDMOND
3RD BN., 442ND INF.
106TH INF. DIV.
STATESVILLE, NC

MR. ROWLAND R. STAGER
CO. E, 310TH INF.
78TH INF. DIV.
LANCASTER, PA

MR. PAUL N. BAKER
FOUNDING FATHER
34TH INF. DIV.
ASHEVILLE, NC

MR. DONALD J. HAMMOND
CO. D, 397TH INF.
100TH INF. DIV.
NORTH SYRACUSE, NY

MR. JAMES N. WHITMAN
NO REGIMENT LISTED
10TH MTN. DIV.
SPRINGFIELD, IL

MR. KARL W. CLEMEN
CO. E, 291ST INF.
75TH INF. DIV.
CHERRY HILL, NJ

MR. HAROLD H. CLARK
CO. K, 5TH INF.
71ST INF. DIV.
VANCOUVER, WA

1LT GUERDON A. HANSON
CO. E, 376TH INF.
94TH INF. DIV.
SAN JOSE, CA

MR. EUGENE L. RUSSELL
HQ CO., 357TH INF.
90TH INF. DIV.
FLORISSANT, MO

MR. WILLIAM F. BROOKS
CO. E, 8TH INF.
4TH INF. DIV.
TWEKSBURY, MA

MR. FRANK A. DEROSA
CO. A, 30TH INF.
3RD INF. DIV.
ARDSLEY, NY

MR. JAMES R. HOWARD
HEAVY MORTAR CO.
224TH REGT. CT
ABILENE, TX

MR. EDWARD J. KELLEY
CO. A, 414TH INF.
104TH INF. DIV.
YAKIMA, WA

MR. GEORGE M. LEINER
417TH INF.
76TH INF. DIV.
LARCHMONT, NY

MR. CALVIN E. SEYMOUR
CO. G, 106TH INF.
27TH INF. DIV.
LADY LAKE, FL

MR. ROBERT W. SUNDERMANN
52ND AIB
9TH ARMD. DIV.
OSSINING, NY

LT JAMES W. HILL
CO. G, 394TH INF.
99TH INF. DIV.
ELLICOTT, MD

MR. PETER P. LINKIEWICZ
CO. C, 132ND INF.
AMERICAL DIV.
WARRIOR RUN, PA

MR. WILLIAM D. MCELFISH
CO. D, 14TH INF.
25TH INF. DIV.
BALTIMORE, MD

MR. MATTHEW B. AITKEN
CO. A, 19TH INF.
24TH INF. DIV.
GROVETOWN, GA

MR. CHARLES J. FUSCO
CO. C, 7TH INF.
3RD INF. DIV.
DREXEL HILL, PA

MR. CHARLES R. KER JR.
N. AFRICA, SICILY, WWII
NO COMBAT UNIT LISTED
VANCOUVER, WA

MR. JOHN J. SANTANGELO
NO REGIMENT LISTED
63RD INF. DIV.
LOS ANGELES, CA

MR. CARL CARLTON
CO. M, 376TH INF.
94TH INF. DIV.
FORT PIERCE, FL

DR. BERNARD L. FRIEDMAN
342ND INF.
86TH INF. DIV.
ROCHESTER, NY

MR. NORMAN L. HOWARD
CO. B, 22ND INF.
4TH INF. DIV.
BLOOMSBURG, PA

CSM ROGER H. KRAMER RETIRED
3RD BN., 7TH INF.
199TH INF. BRIGADE
MOUNT PLEASANT, MI

MR. ROBERT L. MCCANN
HQ, 406TH INF.
102ND INF. DIV.
CAMANO ISLAND, WA

MR. SEYMOUR SIMON
7TH INF. 3RD INF. DIV.
JESSUP, MO

MR. EDWARD TEIXIERA
168TH INF.
34TH INF. DIV.
PEABODY, MA

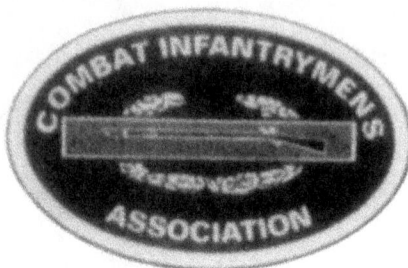

HONOR ROLL
DEDICATED TO THE MEN WHO HAVE GONE BEFORE US

SSG JACK V. BLACKWELL RET.
199TH INF. BRIGADE
KOREA AND VIETNAM
WALHALLA, SC

MR. GEORGE J. LAI
CO. E, 301ST INF.
94TH INF. DIV., WWII
NORTHGLEEN, CO

MR. JAMES C. HAWKINS
CO. C, 351ST INF.
88TH INF. DIV., WWII
TAYLORS, SC

MR. STEFANO SALEMO
CO. A, 5TH REGIMENTAL
COMBAT TEAM, KOREA
ROCHESTER, NY

LTC ALBERT T. WILLIS RETIRED
MERRILL'S MARAUDERS
Z FORCE CHINA, WWII
NEW BREN, NC

MR. JOSE S. GARCIA
CO. C, 362ND INF.
91ST INF. DIV., WWII
EL PASO, TX

COL. THOMAS B. BISHOP RETIRED
223RD INF.
40TH INF. DIV., KOREA
SPRINGFIELD, IL

MR. WILLIAM H. SACHAU
59TH ARMORED INF. BN.
3RD INF. DIV., WWII
TULSA, OK

MR. ROGER H. NITCHMAN
CO. G, 160TH INF.
40TH INF. DIV., KOREA
TUCSON, AZ

MR. RALPH R. ALLEN
HQ CO., 25TH INF.
25TH INF. DIV., WWII
ROSELLE, IL

MR. SHELDON BITNER
CO. B, 378TH INF.
95TH INF. DIV., WWII
MILL HALL, PA

MR. GEORGE A. MANIZZA
DETACHMENT B, 39TH INF.
9TH INF. DIV., WWII
NEW MILFORD, CT

MR. NICK T. SAVKO SR.
359TH INF.
90TH INF. DIV., WWII
BALTIMORE, MD

MR. HENRY E. CRANDALL
1ST BN., 301ST INF.
94TH INF. DIV., WWII
SENECA, SC

MR. RICHARD D. BRADBURY
CO. I, 320TH INF.
35TH INF. DIV., WWII
MILBRIDGE, ME

MR. JULIAN L. CRONCE
CO. L, 10TH INF.
5TH INF. DIV., WWII
SOUTHGATE, MI

MR. JOHN J. CYLKOWSKI JR.
CO. I, 101ST INF.
26TH INF. DIV., WWII
CLINTON TOWNSHIP, MI

LTC FRED A. GROHGAN JR., RET.
CO. A, 2ND INF.
5TH INF. DIV., WWII
WARRENTON, VA

MR. JOHN J. GUSS
CO. L, 330TH INF.
83RD INF. DIV., WWII
PLAINS, PA

MR. JOSEPH HANKO
NO COMBAT UNIT LISTED WWII
EAST BRUNSWICK, NJ

MR. G.A. LEVASSER
328TH RCT
26TH INF. DIV., WWII
MIAMI, FL

MR. WILLIAM LOSITO
CO. B, 23RD INF.
2ND INF. DIV., KOREA
BORDENTOWN, NJ

MR. LEE E. MCDONALD
CO. E, 136TH INF.
23RD INF. DIV., WWII
PELLSTON, MI

MR. DONALD J. MONTEROSSO
CO.'S A & I, 31ST INF.
7TH INF. DIV., KOREA
SAINT CLAIR SHORES, MI

MR. JOHN A. NICHOLSON
333RD INF.
84TH INF. DIV., WWII
WEYMOUTH, MA

MR. JAMES H. HUNTSMAN
ANTI-TANK CO.
184TH INF.
7TH INF. DIV., WWII
LITTLE ROCK, AR

MR. J.B. HOLDEN
CO. D, 302ND INF.
WWII
WALHALLA, SC

MR. JOSEPH A. PISACK
NO COMBAT UNIT LISTED WWII
WILKES BARRE, PA

MR. FRED J. POPE
CO. L, 26TH INF.
1ST INF. DIV., WWII
WILKES BARRE, PA

MR. ALBERT LUMPKIN
CO. I, 15TH INF.
3RD INF. DIV., KOREA
SAN BERNARDINO, CA

MR. HAROLD H. SCHUSTER
CO. L, 393RD INF.
99TH INF. DIV., WWII
PRESCOTT, MI

MR. JOHN M. VERA
CO. A, 315TH INF.
79TH INF. DIV., WWII
MONTERERY PARK, CA

MR. CLIFFORD J. SPENCER
CO. D, 23RD INF.
2ND INF. DIV., KOREA
INDIAN RIVER, MI

MR. RAYMOND B. RUSSELL
CO. G, 20TH INF.
6TH INF. DIV., WWII
KILEEN, TX

MR. JOHN (JACK) P. RYAN
CO. L, 395TH INF.
90TH INF. DIV., WWII
SUAMICO, WI

MR. DANIEL M. ABBOTT
EUROPEAN THEATER, WWII
MARTINSBURG, WV

MR. TRUMAN G. CRABBE
60TH INF.
9TH INF. DIV., WWII
CLINTON, PARK, NJ

MR. ANTHONY J. COLELLO
173RD ABN. BRIGADE, VN
TUEKONOE, NY

MR. WILLIAM "BILL" J. KLINK
CO. A, 328TH INF.
26TH INF. DIV., WWII
MIDDLETOWN, NY

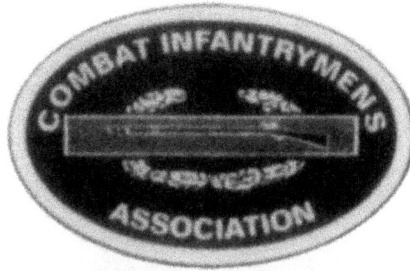

HONOR ROLL
DEDICATED TO THE MEN WHO HAVE GONE BEFORE US

COL. CLINTON W. SNYDER (RET.)
US ARMY
REPUBLIC OF VN, VN
NAPLES, FL

MR. BOBBY G. TAYLOR
CO. C, 1/12TH CAV.
1ST CAV. DIV., VN
LANCASTER, PA

DR. JOHN R. JACKSON EDD
358TH INF.
90TH INF. DIV., WWII
FREDERICKSBURG, TX

MR. ERIC M. HOLT
95TH INF. DIV., WWII
SOUTH WHALES, NY

MR. JOHN F. SWEENEY
CO. I, 129TH INF.
37TH INF. DIV., WWII
GREEN VALLEY

MR. STEWARD H. MCFADDEN
CO. F, 23RD INF.
24TH INF. DIV., WWII
LYNDHURST, NJ

MR. HOWARD W. SPILLMAN
CO. L, 346TH INF.
24TH INF. DIV., WWII
KENTON, OH

MR. RAYMOND L. BIRSEN
CO. G, 276TH INF.
70TH INF. DIV., WWII
TOLEDO, OH

MR. KENNETH L. KEAN
35TH INF.
225TH INF. DIV., KOREA
BRIDGEVILLE, PA

MR. RICHARD O. BIERING JR.
19TH INF.
24TH INF. DIV., WWII
RIO FRIO, TX

MR. BERNARD W. LADUE
CO. B, 272ND INF.
69TH INF. DIV., WWII
HILTON, NY

MR. ALFRED W. PORTERFIELD
I & R PLT., 31ST INF.
7TH INF. DIV., KOREA
ROCKVILLE CENTER, NY

MR. COY D. BURTON
104TH INF. DIV., WWII
CINCINNATI, OH

COL. CHESTER B. MCCORD (RET.)
CO. B, 507TH INF., WWII
2ND BN., 23RD INF. KOREA
1ST BDE., 101ST ABN. DIV., VN
MIDDLETON, CT (Three time winner of the CIB)

MR. FRANK R. KASEE
CO. L, 187TH ABN.
RCT, KOREA
TOLEDO, OH

MR. STEVE SALERNO
CO. A, 5TH RCT, KOREA
ROCHESTER, NY

MR. FRED S. TORTELLO
CO. K, 119TH INF.
30TH INF. DIV., WWII
HARRISON, NY

MR. ROBERT W. GRAVES
CO. K, 179TH INF.
45TH INF. DIV., KOREA
GREENFIELD, IN

MR. ROBERT C. KESS
CO. B, 168TH INF., WWII
BROOKLINE, MA

MR. CARL M. YODERS
CO. M, 12TH INF.
4TH INF. DIV., WWII
FLEMINGTON, NJ

MR. JOHN M. MITCHELL
CO. F, 346TH INF.
87TH INF. DIV., WWII
CUYAHOGA FALLS, OH

MR. RAYMOND DIMAS
CO. L, 9TH INF.
2ND INF. DIV.
CAMERON, LA, WWII

MR. PAUL H. MURDOCK
HQ CO., 273RD INF.
69TH INF. DIV., WWII
ANAHEIM, CA

MR. EVERETT P. WHITEHOUSE
CO. D., 17TH INF.
7TH INF. DIV., WWII
LEBANON, KY

MR. EVERETT E. GOULD
CO. C., 279TH INF., KOREA
DENVER, CO

BG RICHARD M. BURRAGE (RET.)
143RD INF.
36TH INF. DIV., WWII
BELLAIRE, TX

MR. CHARLES L. STEWART
KILLED IN ACTION, VN
OCT. 31, 1972
GLADSTONE, MI

MR. STEPHEN BARNICK
106TH INF. DIV., WWII
KINGSTON, PA

MR. WILLIAM G. SMITH
CO. F, 253RD INF.
63RD INF. DIV., WWII
MADISON, OH

MR. ROSARIO J. PALERMO
CO. I, 254TH INF.
63RD INF. DIV., WWII
WEBSTER, NY

MR. WAYNE CLOVE SR.
CO. L, 19TH INF.
24TH INF. DIV., KOREA
MILROY, IN

MR. JOHN H. ANDERSEN
99TH INF. BN., WWII
TOCOMA, WA

MR. THOMAS F. ROSA
CO. L., 315TH INF.
79TH INF. DIV. WWII
MIDDLETON, RI

MR. FRANK E. ABELL
CO. G, 23RD INF.
8TH INF. DIV., WWII
BALTIMORE, MD

MR. CHARLES G. BOELKINS
CO. G, 379TH INF.
95TH INF. DIV., WWII
MIDLAND, MI

MR. JOHN I. HOGAN
CO. E, 342ND INF., WWII
CHICAGO, IL

MR. SIDNEY G. ADAMS
CO. B, 363RD INF.
91ST INF. DIV., WWII
WARNER, GA

MR. CHARLES L. STREETMAN
CO. B, 3/21ST INF.
196TH LIGHT INF. BDE., VN
SIMPSONVILLE, SC

MR. JOHN STREICHER
29TH INF.
25TH INF. DIV., KOREA
AKRON, OH

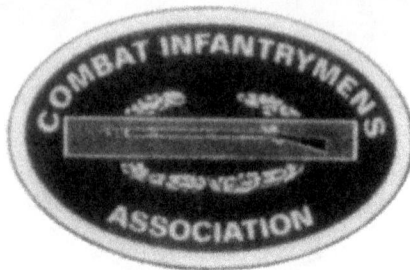

HONOR ROLL
DEDICATED TO THE MEN WHO HAVE GONE BEFORE US

SSG JOHN J. HOLLAND
15 JAN 1945, BELGIUM
CO. K, 330TH INF.
83RD INF. DIV., WWII
NORTH HAVEN, CT

MR. LIONEL F. PINN SR.
6TH RANGER, 58TH INF. SF
CIB, WWII, KOREA, VN
GUNTERSVILLE, AL

MR. ELMER F. BRIGHT
56TH ARMD. INF. BN.
12TH ARMD. DIV, WWII
LUTHERVILLE, MD

MR. ANDRES RAMIREZ
CO. C, 337TH INF.
85TH INF. DIV., WWII
WHITTIER, CA

MR. JOSEPH B. SIMPSON JR.
CO. A, 337TH INF.
85TH INF. DIV., WWII
ELKIN, NC

MR. DALE E. SEMSABOUGH
CO. K, 31ST INF.
7TH INF. DIV., KOREA
FREELAND, MI

MR. JOHN J. BRANDT
CO. B, 11TH INF.
5TH INF. DIV., WWII
WALHALLA, SC

MR. GEORGE L. MOORE
CO. B, 422ND INF.
106TH INF. DIV., WWII
SALEM, MA

MR. WILLIAM C. MAY
CO. 1120TH INF.
30TH INF. DIV., WWII
CARLSBAD, NM

MR. STANLEY STYPULKOWSKI
ANTI-TANK CO.
16TH INF.
1ST INF. DIV., WWII
YONKERS, NY

MR. ROBERT J. RUSSELL
CO. G, 9TH INF.
2ND INF. DIV., KOREA
KILLEEN, TX

MR. ARTHUR R. ALLENDER
CO. E, 9TH INF. , KOREA
2ND INF. DIV.

MR. THOMAS E. WILLIAMS
CO. A, 5TH RCT, KOREA
FRANKLIN, MA

MR. HERMAN J. EBERLE
SVC. CO.
273RD INF.
69TH INF. DIV., WWII
SUN LAKES, AZ

MR. ANTHONY L. MALEK
CO. E, 117TH INF.
30TH INF. DIV.
ROCHESTER, NY

MR. ALLEN R. SMITH
30TH INF.
3RD INF. DIV., WWII
SPRINGFIELD, IL

MR. HARVEY W. WORRELL
CO. C, 32ND INF.
7TH INF. DIV., KOREA
CROSSVILLE, TN

MR. WILLIAM H. TOWNSEND
CO. K, 38TH INF.
2ND INF. DIV., KOREA
GULFPORT, FL

MR. FRANK J. DORKO
CO. F., 143RD INF.
36TH INF. DIV., WWII
LAKEWOOD, OH

COL. GEORGE H. RANKIN
HQ CO. 301ST INF., WWII
WALHALLA, SC

MR. WILLIAM C. DIERKER
CO. F., 415TH INF.
104TH INF. DIV., WWII
ST. LOUIS, MO

MR. HENRY T. DAVIS
CO. K, 47TH INF.
9TH INF. DIV., WWII
WILKS-BARRE, PA

MR. MARTIN A. MCCOY
CANNOR CO. 14TH INF.
71ST INF. DIV., WWII
HAMPTON, IA

MR. CHARLES E. ANTHONY JR.
5TH RCT,
KOREA
CENTERVILLE, MD

MR. DENNIS E. CHRISTIAN
CO. B, 339TH INF.
85TH IND. DIV., WWII
CHURCH HILL, TN

MR. EDWIN W. BEERS
ANTI-TANK CO. 271ST INF.
69TH INF. DIV.
HARWICK, MA

MR. CHARLES E. HARP
ANTI-TANK CO. 65TH INF.
65TH INF. DIV., WWII
LAS VEGAS, NV

MR. GRAHAM K. TEFFT
CO. F., 346TH INF.
87TH INF. DIV., WWII
HUDSON FALLS, NY

MR. DENNIS E. CHRISTIAN
CO. B 339TH INF.
85TH INF. DIV., WWII
CHURCH HILL, TN

MR. RALPH J. LEBLANK
CO. A, 23RD INF.
2ND INF. DIV., WWII
MANISTIQUE, MI

MR. PETER J. FUINO
CO. G, 331ST INF.
83RD INF. DIV., WWII
ROCHESTER, NY

MR. LEWIS G. PHILLIPS
CO. G, 7TH INF.
3RD INF. DIV.
GLENNWILLARD, PA, WWII

MR. NORMAN J. RIEGLER
CO. C, 19TH INF.
24TH INF. DIV., KOREA
CANTON, OH

MR. EDWIN W. STANTON
CO. L, 395TH INF.
99TH INF. DIV., WWII
OLIVEHURST, CA

MR. ROBERT A. SHIEPE
CO. I, 160TH INF.
40TH INF. DIV., WWII
TEMPLE, PA

MR. WILLIAM G. ALBRIGHT
HQ TROOP RECON. SQDN.
6TH CAV.
SIOUX CITY, IA

MR. HAROLD N. MARTLING
CO. F, 133RD INF.
34TH INF. DIV., WWII
GLOVERSVILLE, NY

MR. EARL D. FAUST
CO. F, 272ND INF.
69TH INF. DIV.
HUDDLESTON, VA

MR. DONALD E. JEWELL
HQ CO., 3RD BN.
60TH INF.
9TH INF. DIV., WWII
COLUMBUS, OH

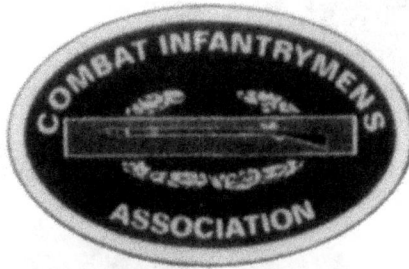

HONOR ROLL
DEDICATED TO THE MEN WHO HAVE GONE BEFORE US

1SG ROBERT G. CRAIG (RET.)
187TH ABN. RCT, KOREA
1ST CAV. DIV., VN
SAN DIEGO, CA

MR. JACK W. RALLS
328TH INF., WWII
KENSINGTON, CA

MR. ERVIN E. PRATT
2ND BN., 27TH INF.
25TH INF. DIV.
BOSWELL IN KOREA

MR. ROLAND J. DANDURAND
CO. G, 255TH INF.
63RD INF. DIV., WWII
BOYTON BEACH, FL

MR. JURL D. CAMP
CO. G., 261ST INF., WWII
65TH INF. DIV.
SANTA PAULA, CA

MR. VAN B. CUNNINGHAM
MILITARY ADVISORY TEAM
1X50 TEAM 71, VN
FAIRFAX STATION, VA

MR. THOMAS G. CAMPANELLA
CO. K, 334TH INF.
86TH INF. DIV., WWII
NORTH BERGEN, NJ

MR. PAUL M. COX
HQ 2ND BN., 399TH INF. DIV.
100TH INF., WWII
NEW BREN, NC

MR. JOSEPH A. WYDRA
317TH INF.
80TH INF. DIV., WWII
MOUNT CARMEL, PA

MR. WALTER I. ROBINSON
HEAVY MORTAR CO.
5TH CAV., 1ST CAV. DIV.
KOREA
COPPERAS COVE, TX

MR. BERNARD J. KRZYWULAK
23RD INF.
69TH INF. DIV., WWII
TRENTON, NJ

MR. ROBERT L. JACOBS
HEAVY TANK CO.
32ND INF. REGT., KOREA
LEE'S SUMMIT, MO

MR. GEORGE R. BROUSE
CO. E, 39TH INF., 9TH INF. DIV., CO. A
87TH INF. DIV., 10TH INF. DIV., WWII
PHILADELPHIA, PA

MR. DONALD W. BEHNKE
CO. B, 262ND INF.
66TH INF. DIV., WWII
WEBSTER, NY

MR. WILLIAM HANNAN
95TH INF. DIV., WWII
MADISON, CT

MR. ELMER STAMP
ANTI-TANK CO., 273RD INF.
69TH INF. DIV., WWII
CRANBERRY TWP., PA

MR. WILLARD E. WOOD
CO. C, 7TH INF.
3RD INF. DIV., KOREA
LITCHFIELD, MN

MR. JOHN E. WESTBROOK
HQ CO. 359TH INF.
90TH INF. DIV., WWII
ALBUQUERQUE, NM

MR. ARTHUR H. YOUNG
CO. B, 23RD INF.
2ND INF. DIV., WWII
NEW ROCHELLE, NY

MR. BURTON PIERCE
HQ CO., 23RD AIB
7TH ARMD. DIV., WWII
NORTH FORT MYERS, FL

MR. WILLIAM MACH
HEAVY TANK CO., 278TH INF.
45TH INF. DIV., KOREA
MEDFORD, NY

MR. STEPHEN E. KMUSH
CO. C, 422ND INF.
106TH INF. DIV., WWII
PLYMOUTH, PA

MR. GEORGE F. KLINE
ANTI-TANK CO., 302ND INF.
94TH INF. DIV., WWII
YORK, PA

MR. ORVILLE D. STOLLAR
CO. I, 104TH INF.
26TH INF. DIV., WWII
HENRIETTA, NY

MR. MICHAEL DIBELLA SR.
CO. I, 397TH INF.
100TH INF. DIV., WWII
HENRIETTA, NY

MR. BRENDAN M. BYRNE
HQ CO., 3RD BN.
223RD INF.
40TH INF. DIV., KOREA
CHEPACHET, RI

CWO STEPHEN S. HARPER (RET.)
5TH SPEC. FORCES GP.
TEAM A, VN
KINGWOOD, WV

MR. ROBERT G. SCHEPPAN JR.
NO COMBAT UNIT ON RECORD
WWII
NORTH CANTON, OH

MR. ROBERT W. WAGNER
5TH RCT, KOREA
TONKHANNOCK, PA

MR. NICHOLAS J. NOSACH
CO. B, 179TH INF
45TH INF. DIV., WWII
NORTH FORT MYERS, FL

MR. DONALD W. SMITH
3RD BN., 311TH INF.
78TH INF. DIV., WWII
WESTERVILLE, OH

MR. WILLIAM A. MCGRATH SR.
3RD BN., 342ND INF.
86TH INF. DIV., WWII
ROCHESTER, NY

MR. JOSEPH J. LIVINGSTON
ANTI-TANK CO.
339TH INF.
85TH INF. DIV., WWII
ERIE, PA

MR. RICHARD E. KEMP
179TH INF.
45TH INF. DIV., KOREA
NEWARK, NY

MR. DONALD A. DIEFENBACH
CO. 114TH INF.
25TH INF. DIV., KOREA
TOLEDO, OH

MR. WILLIAM F. MCHUGH
CO. C, 162TH INF.
41ST INF. DIV., WWII
ROCHESTER, NY

MR. JAMES H. SWEENEY
CO. I, 379TH INF.
95TH INF. DIV., WWII
FARMINGTON, MI

MR. JOSEPH CARBONE
CO. L, 180TH INF.
45TH INF. DIV.
ROCHESTER, NY

MR. HAROLD CHAIET
CO. F, 11TH INF.
5TH INF. DIV.
BROOKLYN, NY

Earl Rubley, Quartermaster in the
National Headquarters Office.

Bruce Peterson
Past Assistant Quartermaster

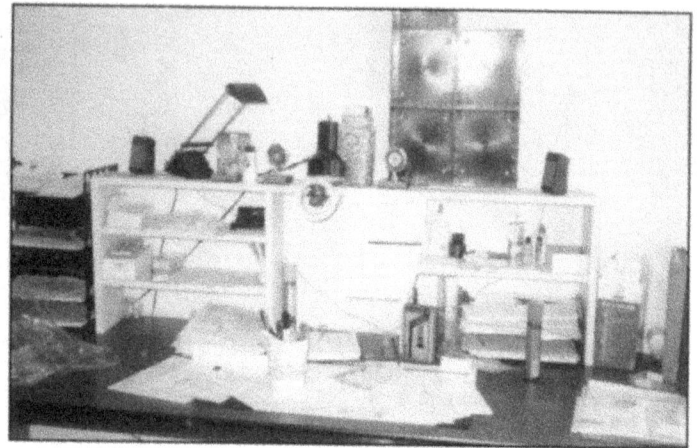

Quartermaster work area in National Headquarters Office

January 1997 meeting of the Headquarters Company 1st Battalion, 1st Regiment, Walhalla, SC. Left to right: Earl A. Rubley, WW II; 1SG George White, Retired-Vietnam; LTC Dillard E. Medford, Retired-Vietnam; John W. Danforth, Vietnam; COL George H. Rankin, Retired-WW II, Korea & Vietnam; Howard R. Head, Korea; SFC Dock W. Stephens, Retired-Korea & Vietnam; Clifton Kelley, WW II; David Turner, WW II; CSM Glenn H. Towe, Retired-WW II, Korea & Vietnam; James E. Singleton, Vietnam; SSG Jack V. Blackwell, Retired-Korea & Vietnam; Clay D. Oliver, WW II; Jessie Childress, Korea.

October 30, 1998 thirty members met to organize their chartered Headquarters Company, 1st Battalion, 1st Regiment, Trenton, NJ. Thomas B. Gorse was elected Company Commander and Frank Miller Executive Officer.

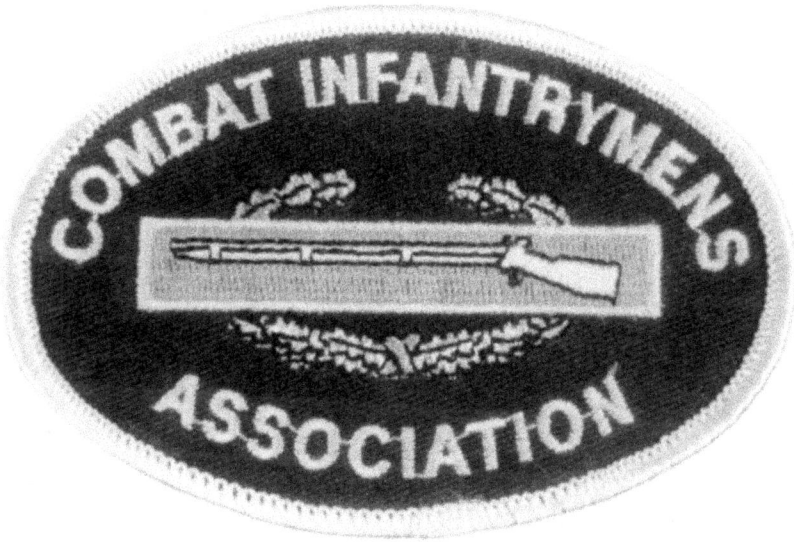

SPECIAL STORIES

Editor's Note: All members of the Combat Infantrymen's Association were invited to write and submit biographies for inclusion in this publication. The following are from those who chose to participate. The biographies were typeset exactly as received, with a minimum of editing. As such, the publisher is not responsible for errors or omissions.

3rd Battalion Command Post, 255th Regt., 63rd Infantry Division near Sarreguemines, France in early 1945. Note Army vehicles parked around the traditional manure pile in the foreground. (Herb Carlson Photograph, courtesy of Pfc. Donald G. Cronan)

OPERATION GRENADE

Written by Kivein M. Hymel and submitted by Joseph T. Capone

As the British pushed through the Reichswald, Lt. Gen. William Simpson's Ninth U.S. Army, supported by Lt. Gen. "Lighting Joe" Collins' VII Corps attacked across the Roer River to the south, launching Operation Grenade. The VII Corps included the 104th "Timberwolves" Infantry Division, a unit both feared and respected by the enemy because of its proclivity for night attacks. The Germans referred to the 104th as "night fighting wolves."

The 104th's commander, Maj. Gen. Terry de la Mesa Allen, had led the famed 1st Infantry Division, "the Big Red One," through combat in North Africa and Sicily. When he took over the 104th, Allen insisted his men be able to find each other in the dark and trained the whole division for night fighting. The training paid off on the battlefields of Europe.

On Feb. 23, 1945, after the Roer dams had been blown and the flooding subsided, the division crossed the river. The plan called for two regiments, the 415th and the 413th, to assault the river at 3.30 a.m. while the third regiment, the 414th, crossed the next day and advanced to the ancient city of Cologne on the Rhine River.

After a half-hour artillery barrage, the 415th and the 413th hurled themselves across the Roer. The current was strong and the river as deep as 12 feet in some spots. The 415th managed to cross with little trouble, although German gunfire caused some men to panic as their boats were swept downstream. The 413th met stiffer resistance. After enemy fire knocked out eight assault boats, one of the regiment's battalions followed the 415's path.

As the boat carrying Joseph Capone of the 415th grounded on the east bank, he jumped out and his helmet fell into the water. "A feeling of nakedness crept over me as the constant enemy fire grew fiercer," he later remembered. "A look back showed the confusion and turmoil on our western bank." Later, while searching upstream for the rest of his company, Capone was knocked out when a shell landed behind him. Upon regaining consciousness, he realized he could not move his limbs. "I was paralyzed from head to foot," he recalled. He lay in the freezing waters of the Roer for 11 hours before medics retrieved him.

With the assault a success and three bridges erected across the Roer by midnight, the 414th crossed via a Bailey bridge and prepared for the assault on its first objective, the town of Golzheim. The plan called for a three-pronged night attack along the three roads converging on the town from the west. The infantry transported to Golzheim on tanks, dismounted at the edge of town and charged under covering tank fire. It was the U.S. Army's first nighttime combined tank-infantry assault.

Things started badly. A tanker in the center column spotted a Sherman in the northern column and, thinking it was German, fired his .50 caliber machine gun at the tank, wounding two men. On the edge of town the infantrymen dismounted and waited for the tanks to open up. The ground was moist and tank tracks left deep grooves in the road, which the infantrymen rolled into for protection—until they realized that the Shermans still ahead were backing up to get better fields of fire. Fortunately, the men were able to scramble out of these improvised trenches without injuries.

The tanks began firing on the town as the infantry rushed in. "When you go into a town," remembered Sgt. John H. Light of C Company, "you don't go into the first house. That's where the Germans were waiting for you." Instead, the men bypassed the first house and attacked the others. They entered some homes and instinctively ran into the basements, where they knew from experience they would find knocked out walls that led to adjacent houses. "We got into town so fast that we captured 400 Germans," Light recalled. "I don't remember seeing any American casualties, although I'm sure there were some." Despite its shaky beginning, the attack was a complete success. The well coordinated tank fire and infantry attack literally caught the Germans with their pants down. "We disrupted a party," added Light. "Some Germans surrendered wearing nothing but a coat. Most of the women with the Germans were completely undressed."

The 414th cleared the town and advanced. Soon the 413th and 415th joined them, and the Timberwolves rolled forward. Operation Grenade had succeeded. Low casualty rates, the relative ease of the river crossing, a large number of enemy prisoners and the amount of ground taken revealed a deteriorating German army. But after the men of the 104th reached their objective Cologne, they were called to a new location—the Ludendorff Bridge at Remagen.

THE SOLDIERS HAD ANGELS

A true story from WWII as told to Valerie Morra by her father, Jack Doyle

After only a few short weeks as a replacement infantryman on the front lines, his unit was pinned down in a small German town known as Oggersheim. Other units had already reached their target, the Rhine River. The troops were being accompanied by heavy artillery to ensure the progress of the mission. It is only about a month before the end of the war, and the allies knew they were close to victory. That victory would come at a very high price for some.

There was a lot of rifle fire, shells and mortars were exploding on this spring day, March 22, 1945. The tanks were firing from behind the American lines, but for some reason, they were not reaching the intended target, the German lines. Behind his location, a radio man was frantically calling for the tank command to raise their elevation, screaming frantically that the American GIs were taking the fire, the shells are short of their mark. Suddenly the radio operator is silent, the young replacement is blown into the air and is laying on the thawing ground, his wounded body bleeding.

The firing continued, and he realized that the radio operator was no longer broadcasting his message, and that he had been critically injured by his own army's shrapnel. Knowing that he needed help to survive, he began trying to raise his head so that someone might notice that he was in fact alive. The bullets were everywhere, the fire was too heavy, so he decided it would be safer to lift only his foot. He was having a hard time breathing and was losing a lot of blood. He began bargaining with God, he would do anything if God would just get him out of that place alive.

Time passed and he started to wonder if anyone would find him, the pain was horrific and the situation frightening and seemingly hopeless. When he had been blown up into the air, his rifle had landed a few feet in front of him; he thought if he could just get to it, he could shoot himself and end the pain and fear. Nothing would move, he could not even crawl or drag himself the few short feet to salvation.

A medic did finally find him, it seemed an endless wait, although it probably wasn't. If that much time had passed, he probably would have bled to death. The medic bandaged the gaping hole where the 11th and 12th ribs had been blown away, which closed the sucking wound and made it a little easier to breathe. More bandaging wouldn't have helped since the bleeding was internal and would require surgery; so the medic humorously told him, "don't go away, I'll be right back." He returned a short time later with a litter and another soldier. The soldier asked him, what about the other guy. The medic said, "that one's dead;" he was the radio operator. As they carried him toward that zone of relative safety away from the front line, the firing picked up and the other guy said, let's drop him and get out of here. The medic just said, "no, keep going."

After a triage period, he reached the train depot in town where the field doctor's had set up their equipment to perform the emergency surgeries hoping to get the wounded out alive. By this time, he was drifting in and out of consciousness. Another GI walked past the wounded young replacement and coldly said, "this one's not gonna make it." The bleeding infantryman was sent a Chaplain who would give him the last rites. When the Chaplain came along and asked him could he do anything for him, the brave soldier just told him, "no sir, I'm going to be all right."

On his 19th birthday, June 16, 1945, he was airlifted home to the United States. He was discharged from the army on Dec. 3, 1945, after spending almost nine months in various hospitals and receiving too many blood transfusions to count. He was awarded a Purple Heart for his injuries, a Combat Infantry Badge given for front-line riflemen who have engaged in combat (one of the most coveted awards in the army), a Bronze Star for meritorious achievement against the enemy, and two Battle Stars for participating in two separate battle campaigns of the war. He forgot about his bargain with God, and was sure that he had survived because he was tough.

So for many years, he lived like the tough guy he knew he was, but always wanted to know about the medic who had risked his life to save him. One day years later he tried to find him, to thank him for his selfless courage and honor on the battlefield, soldier to soldier. The problem was, the army had little or no records about the battle, not even the history books seemed to notice the battle at Oggersheim. Even after writing an open letter to the 94th Division, that his unit was a part of, asking for any information that anyone might have, nothing was ever found.

Who was it that had saved him on the field of battle, what force wouldn't let him move to reach his rifle a few feet away, what spirit gave him the knowledge that he was going to be okay? What ever force it was, those of us who are part of this soldier's life are grateful for his presence, his wit and wisdom, his love of God and Country, and his stubborn will to survive.

We earthly mortals often try to bargain with God, and sometimes we feel that we have won the bargain. The true bargain, however, is God's prevenient grace, and his infinite mercy and love for his creations (Eph2:4-10). While we have our short time on earth, he provides us with his ministering angels (Heb1: 14) to guard and protect us (Isa63:9) until we are prepared to receive his gifts (Ac2:38). So, to the angels on the battlefields, thanks.

THE DEUCE FOUR
by Col. Thomas D. Gillis

Much has been written about the 24th Infantry Regiment, and the vast bulk of it has been biased, warped, slanted, and untrue. I can speak up for the regiment in Korea for I commanded it in combat. In fact, I was the last CO of the regiment which, for the first time in history, was withdrawn from combat and inactivated. I saw the very ultimate in bravery and dedication to duty. I saw strength of character overcome cowardice. I saw esprit de corps hold the line when many other units would have evaporated in thin air. I saw individuals point with pride to their foxholes and, eyes gleaming, vow that they would never be pushed out. I saw a comradeship and a sense of belonging lacking in a great many other units.

I saw the ultimate in hand-to-hand fighting… the last bayonet and hand grenade charge in the history of the US Army. And, time and time again, I was on the receiving end of the ultimate in loyalty, gratefulness, and appreciation.

Why has the "Deuce Four" been so illy treated by the press, the bulk of our commanders, and even the historians ensconced in luxury and easy living deep within the bowels of the Pentagon? For one reason, and one reason alone its enlisted men were black! The best definition I have heard of racism is the one published by "Dear Abby: Racism is a belief in an innate inequality among races, and conduct in accordance with that belief." And rabid racism, rampant throughout the South, is also spreading its hate and damage within our military establishment. The 24th really never had a chance. Our Army corps of officers is made up of its due proportion of Southerners, with their inborn dislike of and antipathy towards the black race. And a great majority of Northerners have been inbred with these same debasing attributes. Take, for example, just the GIs of Eighth Army who, when fresh cannon fodder from the States arrived for assignment, carefully scraped the bottom of the barrel and screened out all the undesirable officers - those with little or no command experience and with black marks on their efficiency reports - and shipped them off to the Deuce Four.

Leadership stems from the top. And the 24th ever since it was introduced into Korea, was sadly deficient in leadership at the top. Lt. Col. B., a regimental executive officer feigned a heart attack. A regimental commander, Col. C., foolishly exposed himself to sniper fire and was seriously wounded. Col. B. was grossly inebriated while on duty. Lt. Col. C., a battalion commander, absented himself from duty for three days. Another battalion commander, Lt. Col. B., failed at a critical juncture to

report his battalion's (CP) command post in Kunuri to the regimental commander and went back to sleep as the enemy was beginning to assault his combat companies on the MLR (Main Line of Resistance)

The regiment did have a few outstanding commanders the most notable being my close friend Col. Corley (early September 1950 to late February 1951) and another Lt. Col. Roberts (late February to mid-March 1951).

But to get on with my story about this black-listed regiment. On June 29, 1951, I was promoted out of my job as executive officer of the 7th Cavalry Regiment. Shortly thereafter I was accorded the important sounding but completely innocuous title of deputy assistant division commander of the 25th Infantry Division. On Aug. 18, 1951, Maj. Gen. Swift, the division C.G., called me in, told me that the 24th Infantry Regiment was to be inactivated about October 1st, and asked if I would be willing to command the regiment for its last 43 days. I was completely familiar with the 24th, its record, and its reputation, having had the unique opportunity since the very earliest days of the war in my job as armor officer and G-3 Air for Lt. Gen. "Shrimp" Milburn's I Corps, to follow closely the victories and set-backs of the regiment. In addition, that great fighting commander, Col. John Corley, was a long-time friend of mine and we had had many conversations together.

Two thoughts raced through my mind: (1) I would have a chance to see that the Regiment went out in a blaze of glory, and (2) My career would undoubtedly be enhanced by the fact that I, an Armor colonel, had commanded an infantry regiment in combat. My first goal was realized. Unfortunately, due to the non-submission of efficiency reports during combat, my second was not.

And so, I grabbed at the opportunity and took command on Aug. 19, 1951. My first official act was to call my regimental chaplain, a fine black officer whose name I deeply regret has escaped me, to my C.P. van that evening. As we each polished off a bourbon and water, I informed him that he was now the most important man in the Regiment since he was to be my eyes and ears. I asked him to keep both open and to report back to me in a week.

I soon found that my worst fears were realized. Morale was the pits, and no wonder! The men had no confidence in either themselves or their leaders. And their situation was hopeless. Instead of being awarded a star, my immediate predecessor in command should have been court-martialed (a) for his criminal error in placing his regiment in untenable positions, half way up a mountainside, with no fields of fire and no MSR (Main Supply Route), and

(b) for permitting this condition to continue month after month in one of the most critical spots in Eighth Army, the Chorwan - Kumhwa portion of the Iron Triangle. Had an all-out attack by the North Koreans (NOKs) occurred, I would not have blamed the GIs one bit had they turned tail and bugged out.

Doubtless the worst feature of this predicament was the fact that, had a man been wounded, he could not have received timely medical attention. Access to the MSR and hence the Regimental aid station was only by time consuming hiking over the mountain or round-about by vehicle through the positions of the Turkish Brigade on our left, or around the right toward Kumhwa on a small, circuitous dirt road under direct observation from the heights to our front. Driving that road was a game of Russian roulette, with mortar shells bracketing anything that tried to move. But the immediate effect of no MSR meant that the men never received hot meals. Everything, rations, ammunition, mines, barbed wire, mail, etc. had to be back packed on A-frames up and over the mountain by Korean civilian porters. They required about four hours one way, or one trip per man per day. And by the time marmite cans reached the troops, all the food was cold.

To compound my problems, I had no regimental reserve! The low esteem in which the 24th was held by all the Army brass was evidenced by the fact that my blue (3rd) battalion was 35 miles to the rear guarding a tungsten mine at SANDOK! And so, with two battalions on the line, my reserve was a rifle company that I had dug in on a high hill to our front, with the mission of denying the position to the enemy so that they couldn't look down our throats. In the event of an all-out enemy attack, the company was to conduct an orderly withdrawal and reconstitute itself behind our Main Line of Resistance (MLR) as the regimental reserve.

Added to no hot meals, no adequate means of resupply, and no assurance of immediate medical care, my men were constantly harassed (and many frightened) by the Chinese constantly blowing bugles day and night, and having no way to retaliate. And, of course, they could only dream of the luxury of a hot shower, a change of underwear, the ethereal experience of seeing a movie, or even the bliss of a full night's sleep.

One day after assuming command, and after having walked the line in this critical Iron Triangle portion of the front, I told Gen. Swift about the intolerable situation, and said that I was going to move the line forward down onto the flats, generally along the Chorwon-Kumhwa railroad line,

where the men could get grazing fire. He approved the move.

And so, what was done to bring the men of the Regiment back to their rightful destiny as proud, determined, self-confident fighting men, anxious to do their very best? As I mentioned, their MLR was moved down onto the flats where pairs of GIs dug into the railroad embankment and made firing port holes to the front, while gaining additional protection by piling extra railroad ties and dirt on top of their positions.

On the second morning after the move was made and, as I was walking the line inspecting the work being done, one of my men invited me into his bunker and, with great pride, pointed out to me his firing slits to the front, his firing stakes left and right I had suggested, marking the limits of his supporting cross fires to cover the men on both of his flanks, and the shelf he had dug for his ammunition supply and rations. His sleeping bag, like that of his buddy, was carefully laid out to one side. He remarked about the excellent fields of grazing fire he now had and said, "Colonel, this is my home. I feel safe and if the Chinks come at us, I'm ready to give it to them!" I have never been prouder of a man.

I finally wheedled an engineer platoon from Eighth Army and, leading the platoon c.o., walked the trace of the new road I wanted up the mountainside and down the other side, thus giving us a centrally located and urgently needed MSR. The platoon started carving the road and completed it in short order. The Regiment was soon back in business again. The men were receiving three hot meals a day. Rolls of barbed wire, pickets, concertina, mines, booby traps, and hundreds of sand bags for the revetments were soon pouring into the MLR to strengthen our defensive positions, 4,000 sandbags were delivered to Red Battalion, and 16,000 to White. Mail was delivered every day. Re-supply of ammunition was no longer a problem.

As mentioned previously, we were being blasted at all hours of the day and night by the Chinese blowing their bugles. Upon inquiring around, I found that one of my men had been a trumpeter in Tommy Dorsey's band. With a little scrounging, I managed to glom onto an old, beat up bugle and we were all set to match the enemy, blow for blow. My bugler was transferred to Regimental Headquarters and in addition to his blasting back at the Chinese every time they blew a bugle, he played all the usual bugle calls, from reveille to taps, at headquarters.

Now, when the CCF (Chinese Communist Forces) blew bugles at us, we blew right back at them and the men loved it.

I was delighted when four men in Regi-

mental headquarters volunteered to act as color guard. They dolled themselves up in clean, pressed fatigues; laced their shining boots with stark white laces; and concocted the darndest quick step ritual for posting the colors. At reveille each morning they would post the colors on either side of my van, and retire them each evening with a flourish preparatory to furling the colors.

The men did not need an invitation to get into the chow line three times a day, but they loved being summoned by soupy, soupy, soupy. And mail call was an even sweeter melody for all. The 24th Infantry Regiment was the only unit in all of Korea that had bugle calls all day long!

As I covered briefly before, the intolerable situation of the Deuce Four since its arrival in Korea was due to the long standing practice up the entire chain of command, through, division, corps, army, the upper reaches of the Pentagon, and even into the inner office of the White House of short-changing black units at every turn. And particularly with regard to personnel replacements.

It was unvarying Standing Operating Procedure to foist off the very dregs from the bottom of the personnel pipeline onto the 24th Regiment.

A case in point: On August 21, just two days after I had assumed command, I was in dire need of a replacement battalion commander. My plea to the Division G-1 was met with the assignment of a Lt. Col. D. who reported to me for duty. He was an obese, over- age-in-grade, completely out of condition, poorest excuse for an officer who could not possibly have climbed the hills in Korea. I was so incensed that I made a special trip to Division to complain to the C.G. and ask to have him relieved immediately. Gen. Swift's reaction was, "Now, Tom, you could not possibly evaluate a man in one day, you'll have to give him a fair chance." And so I returned to my regiment and started a notebook on the omissions, failures, incompetence, and downright dereliction of duty of one L/C. It wasn't until September 2, twelve days later, that Gen. Swift finally agreed that the man would not work out, and I relieved him. I gave command of the 2nd battalion to Maj. Baranousky, an officer who had impressed me greatly and who soon justified all the confidence I had in him.

The battalion commander I had relieved was not an isolated instance, by any means. I was constantly engaged in a fight with our G-1 when I should have been fighting the NOKs and CCF. On the same September 2 that L/C. D. was relieved, our G-1 sent me a captain as a company commander replacement. His sole experience was as a battalion headquarter company commander and he admitted that he couldn't hack it as a line company commander. Fortunately, when, I sent him back to G-1, I never saw the man again. Five days later I had to relieve a lieutenant from G Co. because he had failed miserably and couldn't produce. On September 11 I was forced to relieve a completely inefficient and ineffectual major who was the S-3 of my 2nd battalion. A couple of lieutenants also received their walking papers. And the list went on.

I had seen neither hide nor hair of my regimental chaplain all this time, but on August 25, exactly one week since I assumed command he reported to me in my trailer one evening. Fortified by a shot of bourbon, he began his report. "Colonel, the men hate your guts! You are working them too hard. They are tired and worn out. And just as soon as they complete one job, you have another one for them. But they say that they know you are right!" Those words were sweet music to my ears. I couldn't have been more pleased. In just one week my men and I had come to an understanding. An affinity, no matter how rough, had grown up between us. And, what counted the most, we both had the utmost confidence in each other! I shook my chaplain's hand; we were friends.

In consonance with my "Triple R (rest, relaxation & recuperation) the men construct benches and log seats in a natural depression in the regimental headquarters area, and we dedicated the Captain Kenneth E. Brown Memorial Amphitheater in memory of one of our most respected KIAs. That night the 25th Inf. Div. band put on a show for us. I than made arrangements for division to send us movies as frequently as possible and for Army to send a mobile bath unit once a week. Then I asked my battalion commanders to take turns sending a deserving platoon back to the Regimental C.P. each Friday afternoon for showers, a change of underwear, a good meal or two, entertainment, and a good night's sleep.

On August 25 I ordered "G" Company out to burn Mando and Kumgong-Ni, develop enemy positions in the area, encircle Objective Gillis entrapping the Reds, capture POWs, and inflict maximum damage. I arrived at the "G" Co. OP (observation post) at 0945. The 1st (left) platoon was on its first objective and the 2nd (middle) platoon on the outskirts of Mando. But all I saw of the 3rd (right) platoon was three men at CT631415, about 500 meters south of Kumgong-Ni and about 200 yards past the LD (line of departure) on the RR tracks. The 0840 radio report from the platoon had located it at CT632418, "receiving 15 rounds of estimated 120mm mortar fire," or about 300 meters north of the three men

I had seen. The ground was open and no one was in sight even though we searched every inch of the ground with binoculars and a 20-power scope. I called this discrepancy to the attention of the company commander and a lieutenant who were with me.

At 0950 a report came in that this platoon was at the south end of Kumgong-Ni (vicinity CT633421), that an enemy mortar was located at CT633429 (Hill 454), "it received 14 rounds of 105mm friendly artillery and was silenced," and that our elements are moving forward. All this time there was no evidence of any troops, enemy or friendly, and there was no firing. It was quite evident that the platoon lieutenant, confident that his regimental commander was miles to the rear, was sending him false radio reports. He would have had apoplexy had he known that I was right on the front line, looking down on his position from the company CP!

During the next hour we watched the progress of the other two platoons but couldn't pick up any activity whatsoever in the 3rd platoon zone. I prodded the battalion c.o. to get the 3rd platoon to move and several messages were sent relative to its position and the fact that no huts had been set on fire. At 1050 the platoon reported it was in Kumgong-Ni receiving some small arms fire and that it had observed an estimated enemy platoon vicinity of CT634427 (a ridge just north of the village) at 1030 hours. The report further stated that 81mm fire was being placed on the enemy. But during this time there was no movement of any sort, no enemy platoon on the ridge, and no firing.

By now there was no doubt whatsoever that false reports were being received from the 3rd platoon. I ordered it to move out at once on its objective and, at 1155, a squad broke cover from CT631415, where I had first seen the three men and, in the intervening 2 hours and 10 minutes, about four or five more men. Explanations were being given me that this squad was the covering force for one squad in the middle of the village and one in the north edge. The platoon consisted of 33 men. A few minutes later another squad broke cover from the same spot and started moving north toward the village. By 1205 the third squad was moving out and I counted 30 men visible at this time.

The platoon had crossed the LD at 0730 and had advanced about 200 to 300 meters where it dispersed in the foliage and rested for 4 hours and 25 minutes, disregarding its orders and sending in false official reports! By 1210 one squad was in the middle of Kumgong-Ni, one on its southern edge, and one just leaving the "rest" area. At this time two enemy mortar

shells landed in the general vicinity of the village and I couldn't believe my eyes as the entire platoon turned tail and raced pell-mell for its rest area! The well-dispersed formation swarmed into a solid line, straight down the middle of the trail, whereupon the enemy opened up with about six rounds of scattered mortar fire on both sides of the trail.

The platoon had begged off setting the shacks on fire (when they were no where near the village) because they didn't want to disclose their positions, and "would burn the village on their return trip"!

I wrote a long, detailed letter to the 25th Division JAG (Judge Advocate General) regarding the charges I was placing against Lieut. B. and I was later informed that the investigating officer, Capt. M., had found that the evidence did not substantiate any charges against him! The charges were dropped! So much for a lack of leadership.

All during this time, while the peace talks were in progress at Pamunjon, sporadic fighting was going on. For instance, shortly before midnight on September 6, White Bn. was hit on the OPLR (Outpost Line of Resistance) by a probing attack estimated to be about a hundred. "G" Co. was surrounded and received casualties of 4 KIA and 4 WIA. The MLR opened up and poured fire on both sides of the "G" Co. outpost and toward the "E" Co. outpost also attacked. Our artillery and mortars proved very effective. No enemy were able to approach our MLR.

The following evening at 2233 hours, the "G" Co. outpost was hit by approximately 200 enemy and the "E" Co. outpost was also attacked. Two bunkers of the former were overrun by the enemy with SA fire and grenades and our outposts were withdrawn. Our artillery and mortar fires were right on the button and the enemy was badly disorganized with many casualties. The effects were seen by flares. Everything was fairly quiet by midnight although our artillery was still firing. No enemy mortar or artillery fire was received.

On September 8, a division operation was initiated to relieve two companies of the 35th Regiment, surrounded on a patrol base north of the TAFC (Turkish) sector. The 35th, 1st Bn. TAFC, and one company 89th Tank Bn. attacked north. The 24th Regiment pushed out "B" Co. onto Hill 351 to secure the right shoulder.

I arrived at the "B" Co. MLR positions at 0830 on September 9 to find three batteries of artillery and a battalion of infantry (White/19) milling around in the 24th sector with no prior notice, no coordination, no organization, and nothing but confusion. This was the worst, most horrible maneuver I have ever seen in my entire career. I arrived just in time to stop the lead elements of White/19 from walking through my minefield in a line of skirmishers, preparatory to attacking objectives occupied by my B/24. The battalion commander, a Lt. Col. M., had no idea what he was doing. My liaison officer, sent to him the night before, had been ignored and not told anything. In fact, his presence was immediately forgotten after he reported.

A few rounds of artillery came in on my "B" outpost and White/19 cowered in a draw behind my MLR. Then the lead company proceeded to dig in all over the front slopes of my "C" Co. positions, ruining all natural camouflage. I tried to find Lt. Col. M. but none of his officers knew where he had disappeared to and he had no Tac. C.P. set up. The regimental commander was equally unavailable.

All of my ground wires had been chewed up by track vehicles plowing unannounced through the fields. I finally got through to our division Chief of Staff on an artillery phone and raised holy hell. He knew nothing about the battalion streaming through the center of my line; it wasn't in the plan and they weren't supposed to take my objectives. Although ordered to jump off at 0730, the battalion was still behind my MLR at 1030! By late afternoon, they did succeed in reaching my "B" Co.

That afternoon I toured White/24 front with P., the CO/14, showing him my positions. "G" Co. was still sitting on its duff and many men were sleeping. There was no supervision at all, and I was forced to relieve the company commander, Lt. C, on the spot.

On September 10, I "celebrated" my first year in Korea. I dropped in at the TAC CP of the 19th Regiment and then visited our Division TAC where I talked with Gen. Hoge, IX Corps Commander Gen. Hodes and Gen. Swift. Future plans and the deactivation of the 24th were discussed. Returning home, I initiated plans for shortening our frontage and backing up our MLR with more positions in depth.

The following day I toured all of the 2nd Bn. front with Gen. Mitchell. He had lunch with me, and Gen. Swift dropped in afterward to explain Operation SLOAN for tomorrow. I visited the 2nd Bn. CP and marveled at the transformation Maj. Baronouski had wrought…positions dug in, a large operations dugout, officers and men comfortable, officers' mess running, superb sanitation and police, and excellent communications.

On the 12th, the 27th pushed out on our right to come abreast of us and to straighten its lines. We made a diversionary attack with "C" Co. and B/89 Tk. Bn. I watched the progress of the attack from the "E" Co. OP, and then went out and joined

the tanks near the cross roads, firing at scattered enemy on objectives #1 and #2. I then inspected all of our outposts.

The next day, September 13, as I was checking the progress White Bn. was making on its MLR, F Co. received some m.g. fire, effectively breaking up the wire laying. I saw the urgency of establishing strong points on Objectives #1 and #2 to prevent this in the future. I approved Plan Impregnable, the shortening of our MLR and effecting positions in depth, and directed it to be put into action tomorrow. The 2nd Bn., 14th Regt. was directed to take over part of our Red sector, commencing at 0600 tomorrow. In the afternoon, I issued Commander's Guidance Memo #1, "Command Supervision."

On Sept. 14th, the 3rd Bn., 14th Inf., came in on our left, taking over part of the TAFC (Turkish) sector east of the river, our "B" Co. area, and half of "C" Co., plus our outposts for "B" and "C" and our patrol base on Hill 251. The relief was completed by 1150 hours. I took Lt. Col. W. up the 2nd Bn. MSR to the pass and showed him where to put his new forward CP.

September 15th proved to be heartening and a stunning example of what coordination and good leadership can accomplish: the 24th Infantry Regiment showed that it CAN fight when properly led!

In mounting the attack on Objective #1, "F" Co. was slow at first and uncoordinated, committing squads and platoons piecemeal and being overly cautious. Maj. Baranouski and I went up to the base of Objective #O and started influencing the action. Finally, at 1330 we got things really rolling. A superb mortar concentration was followed up right away by the lead platoon and, in no time, a squad was near the top of the hill. Then there followed the damndest hand-to-hand grenade and bayonet fight I've ever seen. I told "The Baron" to be certain to get the names of the four individuals, especially the lead one who dueled with a CCF on a bunker on the top of the crest. The platoon took Objective #1 and stayed on this time, instead of being pushed off as they had been in the morning.

In the words of newspaper correspondent James Gilbert who witnessed the fight, "Heroic 24th Regiment infantrymen added another chapter to the unit's history book recently when they took a hill north of Kumhwa in a ten hour battle that ended with bayonet charges and fierce hand to hand combat. 'The Regiment's most famous battle, San Juan hill, will be only another paragraph in the history books' one 25th Division officer said."

Continuing Gilbert's account, "First Lieut. James E. Hale told how the Eagle infantrymen charged up the steep slopes,

time after time, in an attempt to dislodge the enemy from their bunker fortresses. 'We fought the steep hill with one hand and the Communists with the other,' he said. Hale told of the heroic deeds performed by Pvt. Marion Clark, a Fox Company recruit of six months Army service. 'Clark', he said, 'led five charges through mortar, small arms, machinegun fire and grenade barrages.'"

Gilbert continues, "During one of the assaults, Clark spotted a wounded comrade. He charged through fire from four machineguns to rescue the soldier and bring him to safety. Clark's actions could be seen from the battalion command post, as he was wearing a faded field jacket.

"Second Lt. Wilfred Bittale, a platoon leader who had just returned from the hospital, led his platoon in one of the bayonet charges. When wounded, he refused evacuation and continued to direct the bayonet assaults until forcibly carried from the hill.

"One platoon tried to advance under covering tank fire. They were pinned down for hours by four machineguns. The platoon leader, disregarding personal safety, walked into the deadly wall of fire and killed four Reds in a bunker, and wounded three more before he was cut down by small arms fire."

As Gilbert concludes, "Shortly after noon, an Eagle infantryman asked Hale, 'When am I going to get Communist blood on my bayonet?' Hale then ordered the "fix bayonets" command and the company charged up the hill for the final assault. 'We had to use steel,' the shy lieutenant said, we were almost out of ammunition.'"

Mortars and artillery were shifted to Objective #2, but fire from there, Objective #3 (Hill 275) and long range machine guns from the base of Hill 600 prevented taking Objective #2 that afternoon. We were also hampered by a shortage of hand grenades. When Objective #1 was secured at 1430, I started carrying parties up from Red Bn. with barbed wire, trip flares, AP mines, sandbags, and concertina. A Red raider platoon and a reinforced platoon from "A" Co. took over for the night and started digging in.

My guardian angel certainly worked overtime on September 16. I've never had a closer call! I had emphasized that "C" Co. must take Hill #2 early so as to have all day to prepare positions with adequate overhead cover and so be able to withstand attacks that night without excessive casualties. The hill was secured at 0930 and for two hours I watched the digging in progress from our Red OP. Two platoons of "B" Co. had been diverted to carry logs onto the position and civilian labor was carrying wire, pickets, sandbags, trip flares, and mines. About 1500, my S-3 reported that he thought progress was unsatisfactory, so I went out on Objectives #1 and #2 to get first hand information, help organize, and speed things up. I arrived to find many of the men unoccupied, many emplacements just begun, and overhead cover insufficient.

I rounded up Capt. Parker and his lieutenants, explained the seriousness of the situation, and read the riot act to them. Then I went from group to group, explaining to the men that the next four hours were the most critical period in their lives, that they had to get good positions and adequate overhead cover before darkness in order to withstand the attack expected at nightfall without becoming a casualty.

My faithful shot-gun driver, Sgt. Paul E. Smith, was with me as we neared the crest of Hill 2 (CT613428), due west of Mando, when the CCF laid on a mortar concentration at 1635. Smith and I were no more than two yards apart. I shoved him into the nearest slit trench and I took cover behind an embankment when the fifth or sixth mortar round landed between us. It must have hit the edge of the embankment for the direct force just missed me. I was bruised and nicked on the left side and dazed for about a minute. Then I heard Smith calling my name and saw him with a chunk taken out of his left hand and a portion of his left leg shot away. We administered first aid, gave him a shot of morphine, and got him on a stretcher, but it took two hours before we got him down off the mountain, onto a litter jeep, and back to the 1st Bn. aid station. I stayed with him while the docs fixed him up, gave him some blood and put and put a splint on his leg. The medics weren't satisfied with his protestations that I was O.K. except for not being able to hear out of my left ear, and insisted that I take down my trousers so they could check my leg. It was then that they found the skin broken and put me in for the one medal I didn't want – the CCF Marksmanship Medal. Ever since, when I have been asked where I was wounded, I have always given the geographical location, not the anatomical!

Very fortunately there was no attack that night; everything was quiet. On September 17, Red Bn. got to work at daylight and, in spite of mortar fire throughout the day that hampered defensive preparations somewhat, had a strong position by nightfall. The new road through the pass and down to the valley floor had just been completed and we were able for the first time to supply directly to the MLR without any hand carrying.

On the 19th, I traversed the new MSR road for the first time, all the way around the loop, and found it passable but badly in need of improvement in places. We were now able to construct a forward aid station

for both battalions and evacuate the wounded by vehicle directly to the rear. The day marked my first month in command of the Regiment.

On the 22nd, a "B" Co. patrol and the Red rangers advanced to Hill 419 without contact, but were then pinned down by crossfire from snipers and hand grenades. "B" Co. mounted a counter attack, laid down fire and extricated its men and all casualties (6 KIA and 7 WIA) except two. The following morning, from the Red OP, I saw a superb show of force by "B" Co., marked by a superlative job by the 4.2 mortars walking the ridge along Hill 419. Their patrols recovered the two bodies from yesterday's action without receiving any casualties. I wrote another memo on leadership and command to insure that no inadequate leaders were left in responsible positions, thus avoiding needless casualties.

LAST CP OF THE REGIMENT

Maj. Stevens, the regimental adjutant, was placed in charge of setting up our last command post in the Division Assembly Area. Our personnel sections were brought up from the rear at SUWON. In spite of the fact that we still had received nothing in writing from Division, I drafted the Regimental Order for our relief and inactivation.

On September 30th, I made my final inspection of then MLR and found that many emplacements had caved in due to the heavy rains. Instructions were issued to correct everything and build the emplacements back into A-1 shape preparatory to turning them over tomorrow. Rain continued to fall. I sent my XO down to organize a CID area that would be a credit to the Regiment. I checked in at the Division JAG (Judge Advocate General) section to discuss pending court-martial cases and the witnesses to be retained. Then to G-1 regarding rotation and reassignment, and the IG concerning morale. I requested of Gen. Swift that, since the men had been in the line for 72 days without relief, those scheduled to remain in the theater be transferred to their new units, and the C.O's thereof be instructed to leave the men in rear areas temporarily and not shoved right back into the front line.

I also requested that the criteria set for rotation of troops back to the Zone of the Interior be dropped to "six months in combat" period. This meant that we could rotate about 1,200, instead of only the 5 to 600 previously planned. The criteria for officers remained at 55 "points."

Lynx (the 14th Infantry Regiment) started the relief of the 24th at 0620 hours on October 1st, and it was completed with the CO of the 14th assuming responsibili-

ties for the sector at 0925. Our Eagle tactical CP closed at 1015 and our administrative CP opened the same hour in the vicinity of Chipori (CT529240). By 1330 the entire Regiment had closed in the assembly area, and by 1600 hours 726 men were en route to our Replacement Company for rotation or to division units for reassignment. The 24th Infantry Regiment had become non-existant on paper, and the 25th Infantry Division had lost its best fighting regiment!

The following morning, October 2, Gen. Swift came down to give out some Silver Star and Bronze Star medals. He was impressed with the ceremony we put on and, particularly, with the spit and polish of the men participating. The day was spent in processing and shipping enlisted men to the Replacement Company for rotation or to other units, and in cleaning and turning in supplies and equipment. A total of 601 men were processed and shipped, bringing the total for the two days to 1,327 men.

On the afternoon of October 3, cameramen from Metro-Goldwyn Mayer showed up as scheduled to record for posterity the first time in the history of our country that a regiment was withdrawn from combat and deactivated. The Color Guard put on its final performance with its usual snap and precision as the Honor Platoon and Regimental Staff witnessed the casing of the colors for the last time by the NCO who had been in the regiment the longest. By nightfall, another 656 men had been processed, bringing the total to 2085.

Processing continued on October 4 and the turn-in of supplies and equipment was about 98% completed. Property books were zeroed out. All individual and organizational property was turned in and old records destroyed. A total of 2,354 individuals had been processed (matching the soldier to his record jacket) and shipped, of which 827 had been sent home on rotation. Also rotated were 38 officers I had recommended with 42 points or more.

As I loaded a few men and my regimental adjutant on the last truck and pointed it southward toward Pusan, the inactivation had been completed in the five days as planned. Wearily, I returned to the Division Headquarters at 1800.

A NIGHT RECONNAISSANCE PATROL
by Jesus Gonzales

This is my recollection of what happen on the night of Sept. 2, 1951. I was in the 2nd Platoon, George Company, 2nd Battalion, 8th Cavalry. Our platoon sergeant was Sgt. White. As we used to say when telling a war story put your steel pot or high boots on (just kidding) it's hard to remember all that goes on while engaged in combat fierce fighting or a small scrimmage. You do what you have been trained to do, and later you might recall parts of what happened. I, as many others like me, came home forgot, kept quiet and did not talk about what had happened back in Korea, the forgotten war as it was called. We blocked it in our mind for a long time, so after 50 years I can only recall part of what happened.

We were sent on a night reconnaissance patrol; it was dark and hard to see. Sometimes we would put a small piece of wood that had been hit by white phosphorus bombs on the back of our helmets, holding it with the strap on our helmet, it would glow at night and you could see the person in front of you better.

We started out up and down over hills, and about one and half hours later, our south Korean interpreter said we are being followed. I asked how he knew and he said he could smell them if the wind was blowing in our direction. He said they ate a lot of garlic. Sgt. White stopped the patrol for about five minutes. We did not see or hear anything so we continued up and down the ridgeline 30 or so minutes. Later, we stopped again and the sergeant said to be on guard. He called the artillery for flares so we could see if we were being followed. As the flares lit the sky above they were short of the objective area. Hell broke loose. They had us surrounded. We exchanged fire with them for about 10 minutes or so. Bill, our BAR man, had been hit bad. He was guarding our rear radioman who was also wounded. I don't remember who else. I, and others, went down a ravine to our right until we came to a small creek that we followed for a few hundred yards, then found a clearing and a road which lead us back to our lines. We got to the bottom of the hill where George Company was positioned on line Wyoming. Going up the hill we were getting fire from top of the hill and we hollered. They asked for the pass word and we told them who we were and up we went. To my surprise others had made it back before us, Sgt. White included. It was late at night or early morning (I don't recall) and we took a short nap. At daylight next morning, we started back to where we had been attacked to pick up the rest of the platoon that had not made it back. On the way back we came across Ralph, my buddy. We had both taken basic training in Hawaii and came together to Korea. He had been hit by a grenade in his forehead but stayed with Bill all night. They hid in the underbrush until morning then he started back to our lines for help and met us. He told us where Bill was hiding and medics were sent to pick him up. By the way, after 50 years I

found Bill three or four months ago and he's not in good shape. I plan to continue talking with him and who knows maybe I'll go and visit.

This is my recollection of what happen that night of Sept. 1 or 2, 1951. Others might recall different. I would love to hear from any one that was there.

COMPANY L'S BRIDGEHEAD ACROSS THE NAKTONG RIVER
September 20, 1950
by Larry L. Hauck

After three years of prior service, and at the age of 20, I ended up at Fort Lewis, Washington, as the runner in the 3rd Platoon of L Company, 23rd Infantry Regiment, in the 2nd Infantry Division. The Korean War broke out on June 25, 1950. The 2nd Infantry Division was alerted for shipment to Korea. On July 17, the leading elements of the division steamed west out of Seattle on the USNS *M.M. Patrick,* bound for Korea. (In September of 1947 I sailed on the same ship from San Francisco to Sapporo, Japan and was assigned to the 11th Airborne Division.) By August 20th the entire division had arrived.

The only part of Korea not occupied by the North Koreans was a small patch in the south east portion, referred to as, "The Pusan Perimeter." The battle in that perimeter raged back and forth for a month. Much of the fighting was near the Naktong River where I was wounded the first time on a night patrol out to the river. Finally, on the 20th of September, the 23rd Infantry Regiment, in the center of the line, placed three companies across the river. One of them was L Company, Commanded by highly respected, Capt. Robert F. Aline. He had received a Battle Field Commission in North Africa with the 3rd Infantry Division in WWII.

This story is about my part in that river crossing, and in the successful defense of L Company's bridgehead. Our regular platoon radioman didn't cross the river with us. I took over his job of taking care of the 3rd platoon's radio and telephone communications. I had been a field wire lineman in my first enlistment. The platoon leader was Lt. Stephen Gray. He had been recommended for the Distinguished Service Cross three days earlier. "You will be my eyes and ears, corporal, stick to me like glue. Do you understand that?" Those were the lieutenant's instructions. I assured him I understood.

On the night of the 19th we were briefed on the company's mission by a man from Division Intelligence and Reconnaissance (MR). His briefing for the mission was, "Your company has been given the

task of making the initial assault across the Naktong. This will be a commando style operation to gain a foothold on the north bank. Collapsible assault boats will be placed on the south bank by the engineers. They will guide you to the boats and show you how to put them together. The element of surprise is essential. You will fire only if you are fired upon. Use your bayonet and stealth to take them out. The hill you will take has three principal peaks. The right hand peak is the 3rd Platoon's objective."

We received camouflaged nets for our helmets, and black and olive cream for our faces and hands. We wrapped our dog tags in tape to prevent them from rattling. We all joked about how good we would look in a movie. Sgt. Baggley, our platoon sergeant, a veteran of WWII, checked us out and gave us a pep-talk about doing exactly as we were told. We all admired him. His value in the coming fight would soon be proven. Even though Lt. Gray was the platoon leader, Sgt. Baggley ran the platoon.

The assault boats were designed to carry a squad of 12 men. They were equipped with canoe type paddles. The boats were locked into an open position when the seats were wedged in place. None of the men had ever seen one before, much less knew how to put one together in the dark. In spite of the engineer's help, we really had a problem trying to get it ready. Lt. Gray was to ride in our boat.

Sgt. Baggley was in another boat. He planned to get together with Lt. Gray after the crossing. One by one, each boat was put together and the company started across. We were not able to get our seats jammed into place until well after the others were out of sight. We no longer heard the others paddling across the river. We were all alone on the south side.

The boat was finally put together and everyone crawled in. The men started to row, quite nosily, as they banged and bumped their paddles together. I started to chant, "row, row, row" to make a paddling cadence. The men began to paddle together quietly. After several minutes Lt. Gray told the squad leader that it seemed a long way across the river. I looked back in the dark, and discovered that the boat hadn't moved any, as it was stuck in the sand. It hadn't been pushed out far enough into the river before we all climbed aboard. I passed the word to Lt. Gray that we were stuck in the sand. Everyone got out of the boat pushed it further out in the river and climbed back in. Nearly everyone tried to get back in on the same side and nearly swamped the boat. Once again, I did the "row, row, row" thing, and the rowers bent to their task. We reached the north bank of the Naktong River in short time, and discovered another problem—no one was there. No boats, no anything. Lt. Gray had not allowed for the current and we were down stream from the landing site.

We turned upstream and paddled until we saw the other boats. We pulled in and we quietly made our way up the hill. The first thing we saw was a large group of North Korean prisoners. They had been taken by complete surprise without a shot being fired. No casualties occurred. We reported in to Capt. Aline. He asked Lt. Gray where he had been all this time? Capt. Aline was not happy when Lt. Gray finished his explanation. "Well lieutenant," he said sternly, "while you were down the river singing, row, row, row your boat, Sgt. Baggley did an outstanding job of leading your platoon. I suggest you pay attention to what he has to say. You might just learn something from him."

Our company had caught the North Koreans asleep. Their guards were killed or captured without firing a shot. Many prisoners were taken. Among them was a North Korean colonel and several other officers. Our South Korean interpreters said that we had taken a North Korean battalion headquarters and a communications section. I saw a Russian switchboard they had been using. It was smaller and lighter than ours and could handle more lines. We started using it rather than ours.

When we made our way to the third platoon position we found Sgt. Baggley and our medic, Corporal James Bear. He was a full-blooded Indian from Montana. He was digging the platoon command post foxhole. Sgt. Baggley told me to get the EE-8 battery powered telephone hooked up to the L Company Command Post (CP). Sgt. Baggley told Lt. Gray we could expect a counter-attack any time, and we must get ready for it. Lt. Grey told him that he had talked to Capt. Aline, who suggested that Sgt. Baggley should take charge of the platoon, which he had already done.

I brought up a SCR-536 walkie talkie, the EE-8 telephone, and a reel of assault wire. I set up the phone and hooked up the wire in the dark. I then took off down the rear slope, stringing the wire behind me. I cut to the right until I got to the Company CP. I hooked the wire onto the switchboard. The operator talked to Sgt. Baggley and got a ring-back. I told the communication sergeant that the line was okay. I still had plenty of wire left on the reel. He told me to keep the reel with me, and to carry some bandoleers of ammunition back when I returned. I re-traced my route back up. When I looked at my watch, it was 0300 hours. I was a little tired, but don't remember being sleepy.

Sgt. Baggley told me to get some sleep, while he went out and checked the platoon positions. He said he and Cpl. Bear would stand guard. I sat down beside Lt. Gray, who was sound asleep. I finally dozed off. It seemed like I had just closed my eyes when Cpl. Bear woke me up and handed me a box of "C" rations. It was the morning of September 20, our first day across the Naktong River.

We heard the sound of trucks behind us on the other side of the river. We also heard lots of rifle fire, a long ways off to our left. I looked down below us to the right and saw six North Korean solders half a mile away. They were casually walking along a rice paddy. We saw them go into a farmhouse. No one fired at them. We just sat and watched. It was obvious they had no idea we were there. We saw no other activity

All I knew about the locations of other units came from our Platoon CP. Most of it was sketchy. I though the other two rifle companies of our 3rd Battalion had made it across the river after we did. I felt they must be on line with us, enlarging the bridgehead. I didn't know that for certain though. I did know that there was a lot of activity behind us. Our instructions were to hold our positions at "all costs." That's what we intended to do.

We spent our first day across the Naktong River improving the North Korea's positions we had taken. Sgt. Baggley told the squad leaders to have us dig secondary positions to the rear of the forward foxholes. The forward observation team, protected by a squad was positioned out on the end of a finger of lower ground that jutted out from our ridge'.

It took the North Koreans some time to bring up the artillery and mortars and organize a counter attack. The attack came just after daylight the second morning. That delay gave us time to get plenty of ammunition to each man on the line.

Lt. Gray was in our C.P. foxhole on the phone when the first rounds hit behind us. "My God!" he yelled "The line went dead!" I grabbed the reel of wire, jumped out of the hole and ran, holding the wire in my hand and followed it down the ridge. I had gone only a short distance when an artillery round hit to my left. I hit the dirt, got back up and ran about one hundred yards to where the wire was broken. I laid on my stomach and made a staggered line splice to the wire on the reel.

Another round hit to my right while I lay there. I though I would be hit if I remained there. I got up and ran, stringing out the new wire a little to the right of where the old wire had been laid. I kept running all the way to the company C.P. When I got there I saw that they were using the captured Russian switchboard. I removed the old wire and hooked up the new one. The switchboard operator checked for talk and ring-back to the third platoon. I got another reel of wire and another load of ammunition.

Capt. Aline stopped me as I was leaving. He asked how it was going. I told him Lt. Gray was on the battery phone in the platoon C.P. and Sgt. Baggley was busy with the squad leaders. Capt. Aline asked me where the wires had been cut. I told him. He said; "You're doing a fine job Corporal. Keep your head down."

"Thank you sir," I replied, "I'll try."

When I got back up the hill, Sgt. Baggley told me the Walkie-Talkie, wasn't working. "I hate to send you right back there, Hauck, but the battery phone is all we have, and Lt. Gray says it's not working either. The lieutenant was hunkered down in his foxhole with his carbine at the ready, sticking straight up in the air. I took his phone and checked it. It was okay, the wire must be broken again. I told Sgt. Baggley I would go out and fix it.

The enemy artillery fire let up and heavy small arms fire broke out to our front, as the North Koreans infantry began their attack. I took the wire in my hand, and jumped out of the foxhole running. I found the break, quickly spliced the wire onto the reel, and ran all the way back to the company C.P. I picked up more ammunition. As I was leaving, the communications sergeant said, "Isn't this the second time that wire has been hit?" I told him it was, and this time I hoped it would be the last. I looked back up the hill and saw several explosions. I told him I thought it was mortar fire. He agreed. "Take care of yourself," was his parting remark. I replied that I would sure try.

When I got back to the 3rd Platoon C.P. I heard a man down the hill, forward of us on that finger of lower ground calling for a medic. He continued to cry for help. I asked Sgt. Baggley why the medic didn't help him. He said the squad that had been down there had to withdraw to their secondary position, as they were too exposed there. "Nobody can get to him," Sgt. Beggley said.

I thought about it for a minute. It seemed to me that if I was down there, I would want someone to help me. Well, I thought if I'm going to do it, I will have to strip down light and run fast. I removed all my equipment, stripped bare to the waist, and handed my rifle to Sgt. Baggley. I started to run towards the sound of his voice before Sgt. Baggley could say anything. As I ran past the forward squad I hollered, "cover me!" I ran down the slope on that finger, zig-zagging as I went. Intense fire was directed towards me by the North Koreans with an equal amount of fire coming from the squad behind me. In a cloud of dirt, I slide feet first into the wounded soldier's foxhole.

"God," he said, "I was praying someone would come." He was in real bad shape. He had a lot of blood in and around his eyes. He had been hit in his left cheek. Part of his lip and nose was gone. His gums and teeth were red and exposed.

"Don't worry buddy," I told him, "I'm going to get you out of here." He had tried to put a bandage around his mouth and nose. It was hanging down like a bandanna. I took the bandage from my first aid pouch and covered his eyes and nose as best I could. He also had blood on his hand and lower arm. I though his right arm might he broken, so I unbuttoned his fatigue jacket and put his wrist inside and buttoned it up, to make a temporary sling. Our squad was still firing. There didn't seem to be much incoming fire.

I asked him how his legs were. "My legs are okay, but I can't see," was his reply. I told him, "when we leave here, we have to run as fast as we can." I turned him around to face uphill towards the squad. My final instructions to him was, "take hold of my hand, and for God's sake, don't let go," and "when I count to three, let's go." I took his left hand in my right hand and counted to three. "Lets go!" he yelled.

We jumped up and took off running towards the top of the hill. In his weakened condition he was holding me back. He was doing the best he could. Incoming fire was popping up the dirt around us. When we neared the squad I saw some North Korean communications wire strung two feet off the ground. I was afraid he would trip on it. He was quite a bit taller than me, and was stepping high as we ran. In the middle of that life and death run, I had to laugh at the sight of him, and his "high stepping." As we passed back through the squad I heard someone yell above the noise of the firing, "God, he made it."

When we got down the back side of the hill, out of the line of fire, we stopped to rest. "Do you know the Lord's Prayer"? I asked. "Yes he said." We prayed together. I knew that only God could have kept that hail of fire from hitting us, and I wanted to thank Him.

We went on down the hill to the L Company C.P. I took him to the medics, who put him on a litter. "What can I do to thank you for saving my life?" he asked. I took out a piece of paper and pencil and wrote down my mother's name and address. I put it under the bandage over his eyes, and asked him to do this: "When you get back to the states, write my mother and tell her I love her." He did just that and also told her what I had done for him.

That was Sept. 21, 1950. He was Private First Class, Ray E. Watford, age 17,

from the division's 37th Field Artillery. Our paths crossed once again - many years later.

I gathered up another load of ammunition to take back up the hill. Before I headed back the communications sergeant came over and said, "I hate to tell you this, but your wire is out again." I grabbed another reel of wire and hooked it up to the Russian switchboard.

"I'll run this new wire straight up the back side of the hill to the P Platoon this time. It will be a shorter run and I hope it's better protected there." I told him.

Capt. Aline came over to me and said, "how many times have you repaired that wire to the 3rd Platoon corporal?

"This will be three times sir," I said, and "I'm going to run the new line all the way by a different route. I will go directly up the back side. A few more mortars shells have hit there, but that's all. I hope it stays in this time, sir. "

"I talked with Sgt. Baggley just before the line went out," he said, and "he told me what you did to get that artilleryman back here. That was a brave thing you did corporal. Baggley said you went out there unarmed, and stripped to the waist. I see you still don't have a jacket and no M-1."

"Well, sir," I answered "I figured that if I was down there, I'd want someone to help me. I knew I would have to run fast to keep from being hit. I had to be light, and my M-1 would have held me back. It just seemed the best thing to do, so I did it sir."

"I'm going to make sure you get a medal for what you did, and I'm not forgetting the work you did to keep your communications in, and repairing the wire three times under fire," the Captain said with a smile. He added, "I don't want to see you back down here, corporal. Keep your head down, I don't want to lose you."

Capt. Aline was true to his word. I was later awarded the Silver Star Medal for saving Ray Watford. I was also awarded the Bronze Star Medal with a "V" Device, for Valor, for repairing the wire three times under fire.

I went back to the 3rd Platoon and hooked up the new wire and checked the ring-back. I gave the telephone back to Lt. Gray and explained to Sgt. Baggley that I had run the new line straight up the back side of the hill, all the way from the Company C.P., which would made it harder to hit, knocking it out again.

"I'm sure glad to see you Hauck," Sgt. Baggley said," and "I haven't heard from the 1st Squad. I didn't know if you made it back with the artillery forward observer or not. The firing was very heavy when you went down there." I told him it was bad alright, and described the man's injuries. It was a miracle he could even talk. When we ran back up that finger, we went through a

hail of bullets. I still don't know how we made it. "It had to be God," I said. Sgt. Baggley replied, "Well Hauck, you must be in good with the 'Man Upstairs.'"

While we were talking heavy fire began coming in from our left front. The North Korean's mortar rounds continued to land in the area where our left flank merged with that of the 1st Platoon. Sgt. Baggley said he was worried about our 3rd Squad, over there. They also had a walkie-talkie, but it only worked on line of sight. Our Company C.P. had to relay messages from them by telephone to us. We weren't having much luck receiving their messages, as our lines had been cut three times.

I was putting my jacket on and checking my rifle when two South Korean replacements reported in to Sgt. Baggley. He told me to take them and the ammunition up, to the 1st Squad. "Oh Hauck, after you get these guys settled down, I would appreciate it if you could work your way around to the 3rd Squad and let me know what's going on over there," Sgt. Baggley said with a grin. I pointed the replacements in the direction of the 1st Squad and fell in behind the last man.

We had only gone 50 feet when I saw a North Korean hand grenade flying through the air coming our way. It fell to the right of the man in front of me. I dived to the ground and felt the grenade go off while I was still falling. The South Korean soldier I was following, fell on top of me. I heard the other soldier scream and knew he had been hit. I was wounded in the right upper part of my arm, and in the calf of my right leg. It felt like a hot poker had been jammed into my leg.

"Medic, medic, I hollered!" Sgt. Baggley and the medic both got to me at the same time. They pulled the Korean off me. "This guy is dead!" was Cpl. Bear's observation. I replied, "You know, if this guy had been following me, that would be me there instead of him."

Sgt. Baggley's comment to our medic was, "They don't make the one with Hauck's name on it. He's in too good with the Man Upstairs." I told Cpl. Bear where I was hit. He cut off my fight sleeve and my right pants leg.

He gave me a shot of morphine, and told me to leave the fragments where they were, until the doctor at the battalion aid station could take care of it. Cpl. Bear said it didn't look too bad, and that I would be back within a week or two. I looked at the inside of my arm, and saw a piece of jagged metal sticking out of it. He put a loose bandage around my arm and did the same for my leg. Cpl. Bear left me with Sgt. Baggley and went over to the other Korean that was wounded and was moaning loud enough to be heard over the rifle fire. Four Korean litter bearers came up and took the wounded man and me down to the medics at the Company C.P.

Sgt. Baggley took the load of ammunition I was carrying, and delivered it to the 1st Squad. The medic sergeant said, "Hey Captain, look who's back!"

Capt. Aline came over to me and looked down at me with a stern expression and said, "Corporal, didn't I tell you I didn't want to see you back here?" I pointed to the South Korean on the other fitter and explained what happened. The medic looked me over and told Capt. Aline that my wounds were not bad, and that he believed I would be back in no time at all.

The doctor at the 3rd Battalion aid station pulled the grenade fragments out, put some stitches in my leg, and cleaned me up. He also removed some stitches from my forehead from a previous wound and sent me back to "L" Company the next day. At least I did get a good hot meal from their mess truck, and a good nights sleep on a litter, which, I really needed.

First Sgt. Bellomy told the communications sergeant to put me on the switchboard and send the regular operator to take over my job as the 3rd Platoon runner, until I was able to get around again. Two days later, the North Korean defenses crumbled and we really started taking ground. We went all the way, far into North Korea the following weeks. But that's another story.

TWIN TUNNELS - MY LAST DAY

By Larry L Hauck, 23rd Inf., L Co

It has been 46 years since the Battle of Twin Tunnels. I have decided to make the trip back to the place where it all happened.

I have mixed feelings about this journey. I feel excitement and even some fear of how I am going to feel when I again stand where I was hit, on Feb. 1, 1951, the first day of the battle.

During January L Company, 23rd Infantry had been in and around the city of Wonju and had very little contact with the Chinese.

We had heard that B Company, 38th Infantry had gone up the Wonju Chipyong-ni road where it was ambushed by the Chinese and had suffered heavy casualties.

The next day we left our positions and trucked up past Wonju and went on foot to Chipyong-ni. We made no contact and that evening my company, along with the rest of the 3rd Battalion, had taken positions along a line of hills that paralleled the Wonju-Chipyong-ni Railroad tracks, which ran through two tunnels. I Company was on the left, "L" was in the center, and "K" was on the right flank, with the French Battalion in reserve.

Our 3rd Platoon was on the right flank,

and my squad was on the right flank of the platoon. As the other men started to dig their fox holes, my squad leader, Elesio Garcia, told me to take my assistant and one man, and make our way over to the right and make contact with the men on the left flank of "K" Company. He told me to dig in and send a man back to tell him that we had made contact. We went down the saddle of the hill a hundred yards or so before we saw the "K" Company men; we waved to them, and I sent the new man back to report and come back with some bandoleers of ammunition. That was the last time that I saw the man! (Just two months ago, I was able to locate my squad leader, and he told me that he never saw the man that I had sent back to him, and when the three of us never showed up after a day had gone by, he reported all of us as MIA.) Within 24 hours, this man would be MIA, my ammo-bearer would be KIA, and I would be WIA.

It got dark and very cold, and as my ammo-bearer stood guard, I got under my poncho, lit a can of Sterno and tried to get warm, but the fumes got so bad that I could not breathe. So I put the Sterno out, and resigned myself to the cold.

As time went by, I began to fret about the man who failed to return. Also, we were on rocky ground, and it was impossible to dig a foxhole. We had to use the trees as cover, and I didn't like where we were. We were too exposed, and we had no contact with our squad. Garcia had said that we would move out as soon as it got daylight, so we just had to sweat out the night.

At 2200 hours I took guard and let my assistant try to get some sleep. It got colder, it was very quiet, I couldn't see a thing, and I was feeling apprehensive. At midnight, I

woke my assistant, and tried to get to get some rest. It seemed like I just got to sleep when my man woke me, saying that he heard strange voices. I could hear Chinese directly between us and where our squad was. I was afraid to fire my BAR, because I would be firing into my own men. The Chinese had apparently found the gap between me and my squad, and we stood a very good chance of being captured if we stayed where we were.

I decided to try to make it over to "K" Company. We could fight from there. I told my man the situation, that I would cover him and he was to be as quiet as he could getting over there. He left, and I waited about five minutes and made my way down the saddle, over to the "K" Company men. My man had made it there without being detected by the Chinese.

These guys wanted to know what was happening to my company I told them that the Chinese had gotten through, and we had nearly been captured. By this time there was a very heavy volume of fire coming from "L" Company and artillery shells were landing on the hills across from us and in the valley below. And because nobody could see anything to shoot at, nobody was firing.

We had learned a valuable lesson in the five months that we had been fighting: It is foolish to fire into the darkness with nothing to shoot at; all you do is waste ammunition that could save your life. So we waited for the artillery to send up star-bursts, so that we could see our target. To our misfortune this didn't happen, so we had to wait for daylight to come. All this time "L" Company kept firing and there was also heavy firing coming from our left rear. I figured

L to R: Ralph Hockley, Lucy Hauck, Larry Hauck, Ray Watford and his wife, Judy. It was Ralph who got Ray and Larry together after 48 years.

that the French in reserve were fighting with the Chinese who infiltrated through the gap between our two units.

Finally it started to get light. I saw a bush move down the hill in front of us a hundred yards away. I put the selector on "slow fire" and fired three rounds into the bush. Two Chinese fell, one to the left and one to the right of the bush. I was the first man to fire from "K" Company since the fighting began.

A sergeant came down to see his men, and I told him who my assistant and I were, and what had happened to us. I told him that I figured that when the Chinese were done with my company that his company would be next. He agreed with me, and told his men to get up the hill. He departed with two of his men, and left the other two with us, telling us to cover them, and then come up behind them.

I looked at the two Chinese that I had hit, and they were not moving. I looked carefully for anything to shoot at, and there was nothing I could see. (The two Chinese I had killed had to be scouts.) I looked at the hill across the valley in front of us, and I saw a line of maybe 20 Chinese coming in single file from the left side of the hill. It was a long way over there, maybe a half mile or more. They looked like tiny ants. I ran my rear sight up to the maximum elevation, 1,500 yards. I steadied my BAR on the mound of dirt on the edge of our fox hole, and flipped the selector to "fast fire" and holding my BAR to steady it, I took a bead on the center of the line of Chinese and fired the 17 rounds that were left in the clip. One Chinese fell and went over the side of a bank. All the rest ran back around the hill where they had come from. The guys asked me what I had shot at, I pointed to the hill, and told them that there had been at least 20 Chinese over there, and if they looked close, they would see the one that I had just killed. They said they had not seen anything, and I said, "Man, you just have to look." My assistant asked me for the empty clip, as I loaded a full clip in my BAR. He immediately reloaded the empty clip. As he was loading he said, "I want you to know that I am glad that I am with you, because you really know what to do. You killed three Chinese when none of us saw anything. If I get through this, it will be because of you." Within the next two hours, he would be dead. I remember saying, "You have been with me only three days, and this is your first fight. I know you are scared, but you are doing a real good job, and I am proud to have you with me." "Just keep your eyes open, carry plenty of ammo, and fire only when you have a target, and keep those clips full" I slapped his shoulder, and said, "One day you will be the BAR man if God is good enough to let me rotate out of here."

There was no more activity in front of us, and I figured that it was safe to move, so I told the two "K" Company men to make it up the hill, and that we would cover them. We watched them disappear over the crest above us, and I told my assistant to give me his M-1, and I gave him my BAR. I told him to take it up the hill, and I would cover him. (I reasoned that since he was a big-man well over six feet, he could get it up the hill faster and easier than I could). I waited five minutes, and sprinted up the hill until I got into some deep snow that had drifted into a small ravine. I got bogged down, and had a very hard time moving. I had stepped off a ledge that was hidden under the snow, and fallen forward. I could not get up, because the ground was not level, and I couldn't get my feet under me. I ended up tunneling through the snow, which was over my head. At first I tried to get through by going up the slope, but I kept slipping backwards. Finally I got turned around, and got out by going down the way I came into it. I was frustrated and angry with myself for not going straight up the hill the way the others had gone. I had heard heavy firing up the hill to the left, and I was afraid of being exposed on the crown of the slope. It had taken me maybe 15 minutes to get myself out of that mess. I was so cold that I was numb all over, and my face was frozen. I got my scarf over as much of my face as I could, which saved me from frost bite.

When I finally started towards the top, I began to get that feeling of fear as the hair stood up on the back of my neck. I was exposed and afraid of getting hit by the Chinese that I knew had to be watching me. I could still hear firing coming from "L" and figured they were keeping the Chinese busy. When I got to the top of the hill, I found that the Chinese had made their way around to the right of "K" and the men on that side were in heavy fighting, but on my side, there still had been nothing to shoot.

I reported to the sergeant, and told him where I was from and what happened to my assistant, and that we would give them support until we had a chance to get back to our own outfit. I told him that I had sent my ammo bearer ahead of me with the BAR and as I was talking to him, my buddy came up to us and showed me my new BAR where a bullet had gone through the gas chamber. He said he had been over on the right where the Chinese were, and it got hit over there. I asked him how he did, and he said, "Well, I did like you told me to do, I put it on slow fire and waited till I had a target. There are three Chinese that I know I got." I said, "Good job, I am proud of you." The "K" sergeant told us he was happy we were with them and that he would make sure that we got back to our company when this fight was over and that he would make sure

that our CO knew how much we had done for them. I said that we would do what we could. My assistant said, "What do you want me to do now?" I told him to find another M-1, and go back where he had been and do what he could to help out there. "Keep your head down." I reached over and shook his hand. He looked at me and smiled. I waved as he turned around to go. He took one step, I was looking right at him, he was not five feet away when a bullet hit his head. The sergeant and I both hit the dirt. I looked over at my man, and his face was towards me, he was looking right at me with his mouth open - hit exactly between his eyes. I said, "Oh my God." Tears welled in my eyes. I felt the Sergeant wiping my cheek with his glove, removing what spatter had hit me.

This man had come to me as a replacement just three days earlier, he was very tall and skinny, and wore glasses. I remember my squad leader, Elesio Garcia had said, "This guy is just the man for you, Hauck, You two will make a good pair." They called us "Mutt and Jeff." He was over six feet tall and I am only five foot two. The first thing he said to me was, "Just tell me what to do Cpl. Hauck, and I will do it, no matter how scared I am. I only knew him three days. I did not even know his name. He was a very brave man, and he lived up to his word. Right to the end. This man deserved a Bronze Star for his bravery under fire, but he was only one man out of thousands, who deserved a medal.

In combat, death was all around me and I became hardened to it. To me, it was like anesthesia that deadened me to emotion. You just go on and do your job and try not to make friends with anybody. With my assistant it was different, and I really can't put my finger on why.

The sergeant said, "Good man?" and I said, "Yes, he was a very good man. I had him only three days, but I liked him." We got up, and walked away from the body without looking back. "Where do you want me?" I asked. He told me to fill in the gap on the left side near the Command Post. So I moved over to that side. There was no fox-hole there and the only cover I could find was a small tree, so I took up a prone position beside it. I was about 10 feet to the left of a red headed guy who was bare-headed.

I looked at this little tree, and I was thinking, "Boy, wouldn't that look pretty all dressed up with Christmas decorations?" I saw it shake, and some snow fell from the branches. Then it shook again, and puffs of snow popped up just in front of my face. I realized that a Chinese had me zeroed in and I would have to get off my exposed position.

I raised up on my left knee to crawl backwards, and was in this position when a bullet hit me directly through my left femur. The shot came from my right front, at an angle of 45 degrees. The force of the hit knocked me over on my left side, and I lost my rifle. When the bone shattered, I had the sensation of flexing my left leg back and forward, as I lost the traction of the leg. It felt like I had been hit by a hammer, but there was no pain.

The man who was on my right called over and said, "You are exposed. Try to roll back out of the line of fire, I will cover you" I said, "OK, I'll try." In that second or two this man stood up, exposed to the Chinese that had hit me, and started firing to his front. I saw his M-1 go up and to the left, his right hand went towards his face, and he fell towards me. He had taken a round through the right side of his head. His last thought was to help me and it cost him his life.

I thought, God help me. I gritted my teeth, and rolled to my left and went over a bank, and was stopped by another small fir tree at the bottom. I came to rest face up. I cried out, "Medic, Medic" A lieutenant, I think was an artillery forward observer came up and said, "Don't holler for the Medic, he's dead." "I will try to get another Medic for you on my way back. Let me have those bandoleers; you won't be needing them anymore. You have it made, corporal you are headed for the States." He took my ammo and left.

I found my First Aid Pack, got out the ace bandage, and tried to get it around my leg. The numbness had gone and the pain was so bad I couldn't get it under my leg, so I lay it against the hole in the side of my leg. When I looked past my foot, I saw four men lying close together, 50 yards forward from me. I figured they were dead.

I heard continuous firing from "L" and "K" Companies. The thought came to me that we might fail to hold, and if that happened, the Chinese would take the hill. I thought, "if I only had a grenade, I could take one of them with me." The firing got louder, and I heard the Chinese yelling. Then I saw them, there was an officer and maybe 20 men. They had fixed bayonets. They came up to the four other men, and they kicked and bayoneted them all.

I closed my eyes, and rolled my head to the left. I prayed, "Oh, God," I said "I don't want to die. Please God, make me like dead."

When they got to me, one kicked me in the side, just below my armpit. Then one of them picked up my left hand, and took my watch. Next he went through my parka, and took the money out of my wallet, and put the wallet back in my chest pocket and left me for dead.

I don't have any idea how long that it was. I did not try to move my head, or even open my eyes. It seemed like the firing was a long way off, back in the direction the Chinese had gone. (Years later I read about what had happened that day in the 2nd Infantry Division History: The Chinese had found the weak spot between K and L Companies where my assistant and I had been, and had broken through, trying to encircle "L", which they came close to doing, but were stopped by the 3rd Battalion Headquarters people, along with the French, and a few tanks. The hill I was on, changed hands six times that day. The Artillery Forward Observer that had taken my ammo, fought with "K", each time they went up that hill, directing the men that day, and was awarded the DSC for his heroism.)

I don't think I passed out, but the history book said that "K" lost the hill the first time at 10 am and it took them an hour to get it back. This tells me that I had to have been lying there a little over an hour before the Medics found me. I felt warm, and very much at peace, and there was contentment. The pain had gone away.

I heard the firing getting very close. Next, I heard the Chinese all around me, hollering. There was intense firing, and the Chinese went by me in retreat. I wanted to open my eyes after they left, but somehow it did not seem important to me and the thought of what was happening was beyond me. I had lost the ability to think. The next month, I would be at Letterman Army Hospital in San Francisco. An Army psychiatrist talked to me, and asked me if I could talk about what had happened to me. I told him that I had written everything to my mother. He said that this was the best thing I could do to get it off my chest. He said I was very lucky the medics had gotten to me when they did. I had come very close to dying. Then I heard two guys talking close to me. One said, "You go and check those men over there, and I will check this one." "Thank you, God" I thought, "The medics finally came." The other medic had gone over to check the four men and I heard him say. "This one is dead, I'm going to look at these others."

The other medic came over to me and said, "I don't think there's a man left alive up here, I'll just check this last one." I wanted to yell at this guy, "Hey, I'm alive." But I found that I couldn't talk. Couldn't even open my eyes. The only sense that I still had was my ability to hear. The doctors told me later, that when the blood stops going to the brain, that your ability to function ceases, and that you are close to death. Your hearing is the last thing you have before you die.

The medic said, "This guy has lost a lot of blood and there doesn't seem to be any pulse." The other medic said, "See if your mirror will fog under his nose." The medic that was by me did that test, and he said, "By God! This guy is alive - quick give me that plasma that you have in your bag. We're going to save this guy." He found the vein in my arm, stuck the needle in, and taped the tube down. In a matter of seconds, the plasma was replenishing the blood that I had lost, my blood pressure went up, and into my brain. My senses returned in those few seconds, and I was able to open my eyes and my vision returned. The medic had turned my head forward to do the mirror test, and the first thing I saw was him bending over, his face close to mine, and his buddy next to him, holding the plasma. I said in a whisper, "God, I thought I was lost! Thank you for saving me."

"Well, buddy," the medic said, "We've got to get a tourniquet on that leg of yours. The blood has frozen, and that is the only reason you were still alive. But when we try to move you, it will break open and start bleeding again. This plasma is all that we got to give you, we can't afford to let any of it leak out of that wound." "Another thing, we don't have a litter to carry you on, so we are going to have to get you onto a blanket, and drag you. Buddy —it's really going to hurt." I told them that I didn't care how bad it hurt, "Just get me out of here" I said. Along with my sight and my voice, I got back feeling and with it pain. I let out a scream when they raised my leg to get the tourniquet around it and I gritted my teeth when he tightened it up. It hurt even worse when they rolled me onto my blanket, but the torture was just starting. When they got ready to drag me, they told me to hold my right arm, which had the needle and plasma tube in it, with my left hand and try not to let it move. They reminded me that my life depended on that plasma needle staying where it was, and while they were moving me, it would be my responsibility. The medic asked me if I understood what I was to do, and I said "Yes, just get me out of here."

The two medics started up the draw we were in, figuring that was the best way to stay out of the line of fire. Even so, we started taking fire. The medics would "hit the dirt" as the rounds hit close to us. I was worried that all the screaming I was doing was giving our position away, and it was really up to me to stop it. So I told the Medics I would try and keep quiet. It is impossible for me to put into words how bad the pain was. As they dragged me, my foot would bounce along the ground, and snag on anything in the way. I swear! If they had cut my leg off, it couldn't have been worse. I prayed that I would pass out, but I didn't. This had to come to an end, and after dragging me for a hundred yards back to the CP on the rear slope, the two medics left me with a medic sergeant. There was a stretcher there, and two litter bearers. All together, four men got around me and lifted me in my blanket, onto the litter. They loosened the tourniquet, and re-set it. I was given my first morphine. I was still faithfully holding my right arm with my left hand.

The two men who had saved my life, turned around and started back to the forward slope, where there was the sound of heavy fire. I opened my mouth and all that came out was, "Thank you." One of them just smiled at me as he turned around. They both broke into a trot, and went over the top of the hill and out of sight. Neither one had said a word to me.

The morphine was starting to take effect, by the time the litter bearers picked me up and started down the hill, I was feeling better. These were both Americans, and I had confidence that they would get me to the Aid Station in one piece. If they had been South Koreans, it would have been different.

We had not gone 300 yards when we started getting fire from the rear side of the hill that L Co. was on. These guys dropped me and hit the dirt! I let out a scream as pain shot through my leg. I cussed at them, and they picked me up and started running, with me bouncing up and down and back and forth on the litter. I let go of my arm with my left hand, and tried to hold onto the litter, but that didn't help. Finally they stopped behind a ledge, and set me down. They were both completely out of breath. The pain was really bad when they ran with me, and they were both ashamed because they were so rough with me, and they both apologized to me. One of them looked at my leg to see if it had started bleeding. He said it looked like it was OK, and they picked me up and this time they did not stop until they got me back to Battalion Aid.

The guy in back with the plasma hollered over to one of the medics who came over to look at me. He took the note from the sergeant at the K Co. CP, and the guys that had carried me down, wished me luck, and left. The medic got a new pack of plasma, and clamped a rod to hold the plasma on my litter. Next he loosened the tourniquet, and gave me a shot of morphine, without saying a word to me.

After what seemed like an hour, a doctor came out of the Aid Station, and cut my pant leg off, looked at my wound and told me that the blood had clotted, and frozen, which had stopped the flow of blood. They did not want to bother it, because I had lost so much blood when I was hit. He would get me to the MASH, where they were equipped to work on me.

Soon a jeep pulled up that was rigged to carry two litters. They loaded me and another wounded soldier on it, and we headed out for 23rd Regiment Collecting point.

LASTING MEMORIES

by Richard L. "Glen" Propes, 82nd AAA, B Btry.

During the month of April 1951, the 2nd Infantry Division prepared for "Operation Rugged" in a push toward the area of the Hwachon Reservoir. For some reason, the weather was somewhat pleasant compared to other times in Korea.

It wasn't anything like the blistering, dry, record-breaking drought and heat wave during the July-August-September of 1950 in the Pusan Perimeter. Nor was it like the sub-zero temperature of KuJangDong and Kunu-Ri, North Korea where temperatures fell to 30 and 60 below zero in November 1950. All this without most of the winter gear.

In February 1951, the Battles of Twin Tunnels and Chipyong-Ni were fought in deep snow and frigid, freezing temperatures. At Chipyong-Ni, the gallant men of the 23rd Regimental Combat Team (RCT), including the great soldiers of the French Battalion, fought and defeated four Chinese divisions while completely surrounded for several days. All men were decorated for this historic battle. This surely was an example of the American spirit.

After Chipyong-Ni, the North Koreans and Chinese, as they fled they began laying mines that became a problem as mine casualties mounted rapidly. In early April 1951, we lost several tanks and a couple of M-19 (Twin Forties) tanks to mines as we moved forward.

One day a young soldier whom we did not know, a runner for the 23rd Infantry, perhaps 18 or 19 years of age, pulled up beside us on the road. He was very excited and tremendously happy. He just had to talk to somebody. Because he found out that as soon as he ran a message to battalion, he was to leave on R&R. As we laughed and joked with him, he waved and left in his jeep.

As we moved forward to other positions, just five minutes later, we were jolted by a tremendous blast that stung and burned into our skin. Soon we recovered and saw a jeep had run over a tank mine in the road where we crossed.

As several soldiers gathered to help, we quickly saw there was nothing we could do in this hopeless situation. Here was a man mauled and mangled by a tank mine, lying face down, quivering and dying. As we cleared the road a corporal reached down to clean and turn his face out of the dirt and gravel. Oh, No! Such a heartbreak! It was the young runner from the 23rd Infantry. A fine looking young soldier. A man that was somebody's son, maybe a brother, surely loved by family and friends. Someone who gave his life for his Country.

As we grow older it seems we have a tendency to stop memories in a time frame. As I look back to the years of my life in 1950-51, it is still locked in a time frame, probably never to be erased and never to get out.

As a veteran, we know that freedom isn't free. After more than 45 years, we know this soldier, and thousands of others, paid the ultimate price for ours.

Did I say the weather was pleasant in April? I take that back, not a day in Korea was worth a damn! And, I still have memories, lasting frozen memories.

Note: No soldier in this story ever got R&R. In the next few days, one was wounded, one was killed on April 9th, and one rotated home in July 1951.

HEROISM OF 600 GIs IN KOREA

by Roy Maccartney, Dallas Times Herald and submitted by Larry L. Hauck

This is the story of a Korean Custer's last stand. It is the story of how 600 exhausted GIs fought for three days, stumbling over their own dead and wounded, against overwhelming Communist numbers flooding in a tight circle around them.

They are the men of the 1st Battalion, 23rd Regiment of the United States 2nd Division. Their heroic stand virtually turned the tide of the battle in the Naktong Bulge, and stopped the Communist drive across the river into the heart of American-held Korea.

Again and again they hurled back incessant North Korean attacks while 61 helpless, wounded Americans lay in their midst.

Without rations for 36 hours, without water for 18, the desperate defenders were practically down to "throwing rocks" before a supply air-drop by Air Force C-47s saved them.

Tanks and infantry which tried to battle through to the beleaguered defenders were repulsed, with heavy losses.

It is a story of unrivaled heroism—of American officers, mangled in their front-line trenches by North Korean grenades, left with extra clips of ammunition besides them, to take as many Communists as possible with them. In three days the battalion lost 300 men.

Once the enemy penetrated their perimeter to take a high knoll with wounded GIs lying in an aid station directly beneath them. A day and night counterattack, with bloody hand-to-hand fighting, hurled them off.

Late on September 3, the North Koreans with a hundred bodies littering the perimeter, had had enough. A relief column got through to the battalion and the main line of American resistance was established on the lines held by the 600. Tanks immediately escorted out truck loads of wounded.

"It was like Custer's stand only most of them came out." commented an officer. Their heroic stand was made on a V-shaped finger of land on the northern face of Upo Lake, four miles west of Changnyong.

Clair E. Hutchins Jr., 34, a lieutenant colonel from St. Petersburg, Florida. Unfolded the story of the battalions stand to this reporter.

It was a 72-hour nightmare of yelling, attacking North Koreans; but supplied from the air, we held and could have gone on holding down to the last man and last round," he declared.

On our side, Hutchins said, we had the defensibility of a tightly-knit perimeter supplied from the air and the ground.

"The men were so tired they were falling asleep at their posts, with officers constantly on the move to awaken them—without food for 36 hours and water for 18. But they were nevertheless able to lift themselves and counterattack when the desperate situation warranted it.

1995—A YEAR OF MANY MEMORIES
by Carl W. Jeffers

Half a century after the most crucial time in America's World War II history, a number of major commemorations are under way.

During 1994 and again this year, thousands of American veterans have been recalling momentous events in the Pacific and European Mediterranean theatres of war.

One such veteran is Carl W. Jeffers of Millville, a 69-year-old World War II combat veteran who served in the European Theater of Operations under Gen. George S. Patton. An anti-tank gunner in the 1st Battalion's 355th Regimental Combat Team, of the 89th Division (the "Rolling W) his outfit served as 3rd Army shock troops.

After rigorous and thorough training in the States, they were sent overseas and landed at Camp Lucky Strike near Le Havre in France. During the brief period in which the 89th was in combat, from March 9, 1945 until the war ended in May, they displayed aggressiveness and know-how that was a tribute to the 3rd Army.

"I was a member of a 57mm anti-tank gun crew," Jeffers recalls, "Our mission was to destroy or immobilize enemy tanks. Shortly after arriving in Europe, the 89th Division was assigned to Gen. Patton's 3rd Army and entered combat in Germany near Trier on the Siegfried Line. In our first three days under fire we advanced some 50 miles to the west bank of the Moselle River, and stormed across to establish a bridgehead

through which the 11th Armored Division passed."

The end of the German offensive in the Ardennes, after the "Battle of the Bulge," left the Germans greatly weakened. And by the end of February 1945 the Allies had advanced to the west bank of the Rhine. The Germans, desperate to prevent a crossing, methodically destroyed the Rhine's bridges. But, on March 7 elements of the American 9th Armored Division found the Remagen Bridge across the Rhine had not been destroyed and seized a bridgehead on the other side. A second bridge was seized near Oppenheim on March 22 by Patton's 3rd Army. The next day a massive amphibious assault over the Rhine to the north also succeeded.

On the night of March 25-26 PFC Carl Jeffers' outfit made an assault crossing of the Rhine River at St. Goar in the face of heavy fire and in spite of the most difficult conditions of terrain. "We lost a lot of men fording the Rhine at St. Goar," Carl Jeffers points out. "The Germans had anchored a barge in mid-stream loaded with explosives and inflammables. As our infantrymen crossed the Rhine in rubber rafts, they were shot into the river from enemy gun emplacements high on the opposite shore. At this point the Rhine is 90-feet deep and the current is swift. Laden down with rifles and heavy equipment, many men drowned. We encountered heavy resistance at both the Moselle and Rhine river crossings. But in helping to achieve victory, the 89th Division's capture of 40,000 German prisoners and advance 350 miles deep into the German heartland stands out as a distinct accomplishment."

"By early April, British and Canadian armies were also moving well into Germany in the north, while the U.S. Armies to the south had encircled Germany's industrial heartland, the Ruhr. Further south, Patton's 3rd Army was advancing toward Austria and Czechoslovakia. On April 25 Soviet troops advancing from the east finally met Americans moving from the west at Torgau on the Elbe River, and linked up with our outfit at Zwickau near Dresden!

"On the way there our Division came upon and liberated the Nazi concentration camp at Ohrdruf near Gotha and Eisenach. As we entered the compound there were bodies strewn on the ground that had just recently been shot because they were unable to flee with their captors and Hitler's SS troops wanted no inmates left alive to tell their gruesome tale to Allied troops. In a storage building nearby bodies were stacked like cord wood. The stench was overwhelming and caused your stomach to retch. This place was just one of the many Nazi "death camps" where by war's end almost six million Jews, as well as millions

of others, had been killed by systematic mass murder as part of Hitler's final solution.

"Apart from seeing some of my fallen comrades die during combat, my most vivid memory of the war was the day our unit liberated the Nazi concentration camp. It was literally a slaughter house. As the camp was cleaned out after the Nazi's systematic, scientific mass murder, the living and the dead were intermingled indiscriminately. Those that were living were in such advanced stages of starvation, and frequently tuberculosis, that there was little hope for them."

"On V-E Day, 50 years ago, our outfit was in Zwickau the last city captured by the 89th Division, in the center of Western Saxony, not far from Dresden and Leipzig. The Division was awarded high honors including two Battle Stars for its campaigns in Germany. The war was finally over for them but, after all they had been through as 'Patton's Shock Troops,' the memories lingered on, and still do for the surviving members of the outfit half a century later."

To commemorate the 50th anniversary of their part in World War II, Carl Jeffers, and a number of other members of "the Rolling W" 89th went back to Europe last September for a nostalgic remembrance tour and retraced the places they had fought battles in, step-by-step, from start-to-finish.

THE VILLAGE OF BEN CHUA
by David McAllister

It was mid-September 1969, the monsoons were loosing some of their punch and we felt fortunate to be on a village security mission other than positioned in the thick jungle sites we normally ambushed in. We were to secure a section just outside the village of Ben Chua, north of Highway 14 near the Michelin Rubber Plantation. We had moved into ambush position with a rome plowed area directly to our front and flanks with an old abandoned cellar hole and the village to our rear. Around 0130 hrs. the first AK rounds started to tear up the position directly to my right, as the enemy retreated back into the rome plowed area we returned fire and cared for our dead and wounded. It wasn't long until the 82mm mortars started to rain down, walking in a straight line toward our CP group and fortunately right over us. As we all know the theory of bracketing incoming works very well and if they hadn't run out of mortars while walking them back I wouldn't be writing this. Gunships unfortunately were off station at the time so our flank machine gunners really got a work out providing cover for the "Dust Off" to come in. Dark, fog, incoming, and small arms fire couldn't stop those brave pilots that night as they hovered down through tree tops with their rotor blade chipping wood and blowing debris everywhere. They were there to complete their mission and support us through thick and thin, we deeply appreciate their heroism and wish they could be recognized in a similar way as we were with the Combat Infantrymen's Badge.

AN EXCITING DAY IN VIETNAM
by David McAllister

The air was full of the typical late morning oppressive humidity we'd grown used to as our platoon moved through the jungle swatting bugs and wiping our brows. Our mission was to recon an area of reported activity with a possible base camp situation. Just as the wind shifted our right hand squad alerted and dropped to a crouch, the rest of the platoon followed suit as the call came in from the alerting squad. The scent of an enemy latrine was picked up; Intelligence really was intelligent on this one.

The first fire, of course, were the AKs, soon followed by an RPG exploding about 5 meters high, dead center of the platoon. As many of you know the heat and concussion from that type of blast has you looking back to see if your legs are still there. It took what seemed like a very long time for the shrapnel to come down to body temperature and before long the hearing partially returned. With covering fire we were able to get our point man back and assess the condition of the wounded, it was time to call battalion for a sit-rep. The hearing loss got a little scary until I realized the RPG blast had severed the handset cord as clean as a pair of scissors would cut; SOP dictated an extra handset be carried and soon we raised battalion for Dust-Off. We thought we had done a good job of keeping their heads down but all medivacs took fire as they hovered like ducks while the penetrator pulled most of our wounded up, up and away and the gunships worked the area. FAC was bringing in the Aussies with the 500 1b. Bunker Busters to work the base camp so we could get another medivac in for the last one wounded. What an air show and how great to have them on our side. I was half way up the penetrator when guess what, Sir Charles started to pepper the area with AK fire again, knocking out the hydraulics of the Huey and suddenly the penetrator stopped its ascent also. The pilot had to move with or without me and I will never forget the job he did winding through the tree tops with me dangling below. Finally inside the chopper I was told "hang on, it isn't over yet" and again what an experience to see the sparks flying of the skids as we landed in Dau Tieng, coming to a stop like an airplane. The Infantry is full of heroes and many brave men who wear the Combat Infantrymen's Badge and because of that all of us know and respect the pilots and crew who flew close support overhead. We the Combat Infantrymen will always hold you in high esteem. Thank You!

A NIGHT IN VIETNAM
by David McAllister

It was October 1969, southwest of the Michelin Rubber Plantation, we had set up night ambush in the tree line. To our front was a rome plowed area outside the village of Ben Chua, a known Vietcong stronghold. We were well settled into our ambush site, the moon was full and my thoughts drifted back to more pleasant nights stateside. I marveled at how the moon in this war torn environment could be the very same as "ours" back in hometown, USA.

Around 2200 hrs. the monsoon clouds started to skirt across the face of the moon and the wind began to pickup. We as in many times before, prepared our bedsites (poncho liners) for a good drenching from Mother Nature. As the rains and winds started to make our visit to Vietnam even more uncomfortable, a report came in from a guard that one enemy had been sighted running away from the tree line toward the village. Was he running to get across the rome plow area or had he spotted our position?

Now the heavy winds and rain were mixed with thunder and lightning, giving our ambush site an almost eerie horror movie appearance. As the lightning flashed we just wanted to settle back down to keep warm and get as close to the ground, away from the lightning strikes, as possible. Even though we knew we should change our position we all grumbled and complained as we moved 200 meters further east along the tree line and set bush" again during the downpour.

Soon the lightning stopped, the winds died and the rains abated, once again I lay gazing at the RVN/USA moon as I drifted off to sleep. The sickening noise from the launch of the first RPG started my heart racing as I wondered, as many times before, would this be "the time"? Once the platoon realized what was happening to our old ambush site, it was like watching a movie of your own demise, similar to what an "out of body" experience must be like. Enemy RPGs, AK-47s and grenades threw heavy fire into our old position for a good 2-3 minutes. We called in the "Night Hawks" for support and tried to catch them in the rome plow but we all know how good Mr. C was at disappearing into the night. A morning sweep of the area was very sobering as we surveyed the damage and realized what could have been.

I will never forget the sights and sounds of that night and credit our "first infantry" training, experience and leadership (Alpha 2/28, 2nd Platoon) for helping me see "moon USA" again, my sincere thanks and best wishes to all the guys.

MEMORIES OF VIETNAM
by David McAllister

It was August 1969, our area of operation was northwest of the Michelin Rubber Plantation in War Zone C, III Corps. Generally our platoon strength ran about 20 strong and our method of operation was search and ambush during 5-7 day runs. We had been inserted into a supposedly hot LZ, and none of us complained when we found it cold. Our mission was to investigate an old bunker/base-camp area and stir things up if there was further building or occupation. Our objective was approximately 1-2 klicks further north and as we moved across the LZ in two columns our senses were in "high gear."

It was one of those hot and steamy, still days that make you appreciate the jungle cover, unfortunately we had to "make time" and meet another platoon at the objective. Our quickest route took us directly through the long, shadeless landing zone.

The first shouts of surprise came from the rear of the left hand column and we could see two men down. As we turned, clicked off safeties, and lowered into the waist high grass there was confusion in the ranks as something was moving among us. The "mystery" movement brought shouts and fear with it as it moved forward through our file until it moved into a clearing and we realized who our "enemy" was.

We had flushed a pygmy deer from his hiding spot in the tall grass and his initial jump had knocked men down as he ran forward through our platoon, bumping into our legs and equipment as he escaped.

I credit the training and experience we received while serving with the Big Red One (Alpha 2/28 2nd Platoon) with preventing a potentially trigger happy, tragic situation from occurring, God knows we had some awesome firepower "off" safety and ready to rock and roll.

LED INTO A TRAP
by John F. McBurney

The following is an account of an incident that is on file at the United States Army Military History Institute in Carlisle, Pennsylvania.

At daybreak, Dec. 10, 1944, after an all night patrol of Company E, 411th Regiment of the 103rd Division a fire fight erupted with the enemy outpost one-mile southwest of Woerth-Alsace, France.

Suddenly and surprisingly the enemy

bolted from his fortifications and retreated into the town.

BAR man, William Chick, Private Harold Spinner and Private John McBurney gave chase.

As it turned out they were being led into a trap as the town was still enemy occupied.

When McBurney reached the main street he was met with a demand to surrender by several of the enemy. Without responding, McBurney ducked back into the courtyard and bolted the door of a high wooded fence. McBurney then hid in the house of the mayor where he joined up with Chick and Spinner. The trio took up positions on the second floor giving them an unlimited field of fire.

Although surrounded, Chick killed the enemy commander with a burst of the BAR. His body lay in the street for the remainder of the day, but was removed under cover of darkness.

That night no one slept in the small room. The sounds of enemy activity could be heard through most of the night.

Before dawn, loud hob nail boots could be heard coming up the stairs and believing this to be the enemy, firing positions were assumed. However, it only turned out to be the mayor himself. He came with the news that the "Boche" had moved out during the night.

SOME OF MY MEMORIES
by James V. McNicol

As the antics of the Japanese continued for a period of time a Forward Observation Post (FOP) was established by the Anti-Tank Company about 200-300 yards to the front of our main line of troops. The movement of the Japanese was difficult to understand, they were very bold. It was possible that we were seeing a testing or feeling out of the American position, as bold movements continued on the face of the hill, to our front.

After a period of time the forward observer was called back and a volunteer was requested to man the FOP. I took up that position under a sapling and there was a very minimum of cover. It was less than I desired, but it had to do—this was not the time to be picky.

In this period of time, an "artillery observation plane, L-4, arrived on the scene, and this was a distinct advantage for us. The pilot directed his attention to the terrain to our front and called for artillery. The results seemed to make the Japanese to pull in there horns, but Japanese casualties were unknown to the pilot or the Americans on the ground.

In this period of time, as the artillery rounds arrived, my position was prone, hugging Mother Earth like a rug, wishing I was a gopher. Shrapnel could be heard and felt as we were now feeling the cutting of the air over and around this position. The pilot being directly over me made it possible for me to monitor conversation between the plane and his unit doing the firing. The pilot gave a commentary as to what was happening. A short fire of death continued to my front, as artillery rounds landed on target. This was indeed, "a ring side atmosphere", like an event that a commentator might be describing to an audience at least from my position.

The pilot described the fire as falling on the heads of the Japanese troops, they in turn were attempting to diffuse the situation on the hill, discarding possible dead victims at varying locations, making it difficult for us to make an accurate body count.

At various intervals, Japanese were seen on the terrain to our front and we would attempt to thwart their movements as we fired into these Japanese forces. It was still difficult to understand why the Japanese exposed themselves prior to the arrival of the artillery observation aircraft, L-4, unless they were attempting to possibly estimate the American force, it didn't make sense. We were using walkie-talkies and SER 300's. The former were questionable at times.

My position as the forward observer for our company, this position was at best 200-300 yards forward of the main line of troops, might make one believe the pilot did not see me, his view and interest was the Japanese. With all considered he did a good job, the taunting of the Japanese came to a stop, but later in the night there was another artillery barrage.

We were ordered to pull back down the hill. Arriving at our designated location, we proceeded to dig in and this was done at the time of approaching darkness and under the cover of small arms fire. Ample security was in place for the night. We set up our perimeter for the night.

On March 7, 1945, an early morning scouting mission was in order. Our patrol covered several miles in several directions, attempting to pick up any Japanese that may still be in the area. We did find Japanese equipment such as helmets, ammunition, belts, and foul weather gear. There were the "Thousand Stitches," a belt of the individual Japanese soldier that was worn around the waist. It carried the history of the soldier. Other items were found, but being cautious and wishing to retain my physical parts, it was wise to refrain from any fool hardy souvenir gathering as these possibly could be booby-trapped. If you were wise, you lived another day. We did find articles that were blood stained as we moved about the area.

After a few hours of this action our only reward was finding that our Japanese adversaries had cut and run, at least vacated this particular Philippine real estate for more friendly surroundings. We finally returned to the "Tubao Pass."

Our unit remained in the Tubao area for approximately two weeks and while here, we scouted in and around the locale of Tubao for a closer and more personal look at this barrio. One such visit was an opportunity to visit the Catholic Church.

I was able to converse with the nuns and the priests. They were out of a Belgian Order.

The Japanese had used the Catholic School at Tubao a command post (CP). American aircraft hit this Command Post (CP) with a surgical strike or strikes, it was very impressive, so accurate that only minor damage was done to the church, but the school was demolished. As I entered the church, looking around, inspecting the church, I noticed minimal damage. There was a little cracked plaster in the ceiling overhead to my right. I thought this was some kind of a miracle. The command post school had been destroyed, but the "House Of God" was intact. The priests and the nuns had concealed most of the vestments, chalices and other church accessories in caves in the surrounding hills of the barrio, thus putting crimps into a possible Japanese looting activity. As the Americans appeared in 1945, accessories came into view

Many years later in the city of East Liverpool, Ohio (USA) I had the opportunity to exchange thoughts of this experience with nuns of this Belgian Order, as they were in the United States attempting to raise funds for their missions in the Philippine Islands. We compared experiences of those days of liberation in 1945 and shared what was life, death and everything in between for the freedom scene for this island chain that the United States had the responsibility for. Recollections of this meeting was for "Tubao-Baguio-Bontoc" and surrounding areas. A walk back in time indeed.

After the barrio of Tubao was liberated, an escape route from the northern provinces came into being. This trail was known as Refugee Trail. There were probably an excess of 12,000 refugees that traveled this trail of freedom. Many a notable escaped, there were also many that died on this arduous journey, attempting to flee the "Japanese Boot." A sect of Philippine tribesmen, known to all in "freedom experience," were the "IGOROTS", a tribe of natives that were primitive to say the least, out of the stone ages. They were very instrumental in the rescue of those traveling this trail, assisting the Americans in the flight for freedom.

About 1500 hours (3:00 p.m.) on April 20, 1945, I was standing on the crest of prime Philippine real estate, Hill Charley and looking into the valley below when 3rd Battalion Commander, Maj. Sanford I. "Bud" Wolfe, approached. He informed all of us on the crest that his experience led him to believe that the Japanese might be working a "sucker play," a ruse permitting us access to Hill Charley, as all this had been certainly less than expected and he was feeling apprehensive about the situation.

He suggested the "Native Carrying Party" be off-loaded PDQ, and that we get the native personnel out of the area soon and the quicker the better, as he expected trouble. Standing at this vantage point and observing the foot patrols along the valley floor below us, we were aware of the anxiety as the patrols scouted the next line of hills and the approaches to "Hill 4980." When the "Carrying Party" was off-loaded, we moved the natives as the "Major" had suggested.

The trip back down the mountain with the "Igorots" was with dispatch. We wasted no time in clearing the area, and maybe fortunate for us as the events of the day transpired. As we settled in our foxholes for the night, word was passed by field phone, that, as the major had suspected, the Japanese had made a "prophet" out of the American officer. Havoc had been created on "Hill Charley," it was in a vice, Japanese actions had it zeroed in, and we would witness this as the next few hours would bear this out.

We were alerted that field ambulances and other traffic, in due time, would be moving down the mountain road during the hours of darkness, carrying causalities from this Japanese ruse on Hill Charley.

We observed this traffic from the safety of our foxholes for the better part of the night. Our thoughts returned to the "Major," and how right he was. We truly had what one might call our own "Moses" and his tablets of stone at our mount, the "Major" was truly a prophet.

American Flag

The American Flag that had flown over Baguio prior to the Japanese invasion of Luzon in December 1941 was lowered before the Japanese entry into Baguio. This "Caretaker" of the Colors," Juan Arellano, surmised the Japanese military in all probability would deface the American Flag as they would later do at Bataan and at the island of Corregidor. The caretaker in a moment of inspirational thinking had his wife sew the "colors" in a pillow, and here the colors remained until the American military arrived again in 1945. His home was raided by the Japanese military, he braved beatings and threats of death, but the secret remained secure.

During a bombardment, as the Americans worked their way toward Baguio, this native caretaker, Juan Arellano, took his family through Japanese lines, with great personal risk, over the mountains to Rosario, LaUnion Province. He requested a meeting with the commander of the 33rd Infantry Division, Maj. Gen. Percy J. Clarkson. At the meeting he requested a favor on behalf of the Philippine people, that this flag he had preserved in a family pillow be the first "colors" to be flown over the city of Baguio on the liberation of the summer capitol.

Official ceremonies for the Liberation of Baguio was held on April 29, 1945, and as Juan Arellano had requested, the American Flag that he cherished in a family pillow in the years of Japanese occupation, was raised proudly over Baguio. Later this flag was presented to Maj. Gen. Percy J. Clarkson by the citizens of Baguio as an expression of their gratitude for the liberation—this city was once again in Philippine hands. Gen. Douglas MacArthur was rumored as a possible participant in the official ceremonies, but it did not happen. Only a bare representation was on hand, the rest of us were searching for Japanese, about the city. During our short stay at Baguio I would find myself in three different locations, but visits were taken to the Roman Catholic Cathedral.

Arriving at the Naguilian site after our departure from Baguio, we set up our camp—our living accommodations were squad tents. There was also a newly activated Philippine Army unit in our immediate area. Our purpose in this area was to run patrols against the Japanese in the areas of concern.

The sergeant requested two American volunteers from the Anti-Tank Company and I told, him "look no further." I answered the call. He told me, "you do not have to go, if you do not want to, it was strictly on a volunteer basis." I insisted, and he was informed that I was going. He then told me to get another volunteer for this mission. I made my rounds of the company personnel and came across Maurice Protsman. I put the offer to him and he thought I was crazy. During the verbal exchange I added spice to a possible mix when I explained that this would give us something to do, "it will in all likelihood, juice up our adventure." Finally our search for a second volunteer was finalized, and he agreed to go on this patrol.

This patrol was something that we would look back on. Sometimes there was anxiety and anticipation. We might even question our reasoning about this patrol, but in all campaigns, fate beckons. We were off into the mountains—a challenge for mutual satisfaction, Bayabas Valley lay ahead of us.

Living in the field with the newly organized unit of the Philippine Army in this particular military operation in the Bayabas Valley was very educational. This patrol, an operation of several days, required the Americans to partake the eating of native foods, eating off of the land. The rations we had brought with us had been meager and it wasn't good policy to refuse food at the table of the native.

In one such meal that the native military prepared, they dug around the roots of a tree and removed this root. In a short while they had peeled the root like a potato and slicing the root, it was ready for the pan. This was then boiled and while this was left to cook, the native went to another type of tree and cut leaves from it and placed them in the boiling water with the root that had been in preparation for this mystery potion. In a fashion, this in the eyes of the American, resembled American Potato Soup but here it ended.

This soup seemed to have a familiar taste as your taste buds came into play until you bit into one of the leaves and then it was another world. The sensation of fire and heat was immediate; your tongue, mouth and everything you owned seemed to be on fire; it was for sure your senses were active. The more water you drank the worse the sensation. The natives, of course, appreciated the scene with much gusto, they were killing themselves laughing. If you refrained from biting into the leaves the soup was bearable, otherwise it was HOT-HOT. The members of this Philippine Army company prepared this native dish a few more times while we were out on this patrol. With all future native offerings of this military detachment, we took our cue from the natives, watching what they did at the table and this was our safety valve. It seemed this soup cooked for an hour to an hour and a half.

While in the Bayabas Valley with this Philippine Army detachment we came upon a large native hut built of bamboo, and this was built on stilts as most of these native huts were in the Philippine archipelago. The reason for this native hut being vacant was that the local native valued his life. Japanese were in the area and the local native was not returning until the area was secure.

The command of this Philippine detachment insisted on certain courtesies and that was the hut was for the living quarters of the Americans, and the Yanks were excused from any guard duty during the hours of darkness. We accepted this courtesy with one eye open as the Americans recalled the actions of a similar Philippine Army Detachment on "Hill 3000" and that unit displayed little discipline with their firearms after darkness. This time around we experienced no trigger happy natives.

Oct. 13, 1945: Kenneth Brauner, Maurice Protsman and myself took a trip to Kobe, and as our train was pulling into the train station, an amusing yet strange sight was before us.

Our train was moving into the station and another train, passing us in the opposite direction, was moving out of the station, and just a few feet away was a woman holding her child out of the train window with buttocks bared, and strange to behold, the child was answering the call of Mother Nature. Incidents such as this were witnessed in the "Land of Nippon" at intervals, and it continued for the remainder of my tour.

MY TIME IN KOREA
by Samuel Harvey Merritt

One day when I was back in the rear at the battalion aid station being treated for my frost bite and trench foot, we noticed there was an American fighter buzzing the aid station and the artillery area like he was going to make a strafing pass, when two more American planes appeared and escorted him out of the area The troops manning the anti-aircraft weapons were getting ready to fire at him when they saw the other planes. Apparently he was lost and thought we were the enemy.

Another time during the day, the company to our right sent a man out onto the valley floor that was the main line of resistance (MLR) to check out an old box car for an enemy gun emplacement, he worked his way out there creeping and crawling when all of a sudden a machine gun in the box car opened up on him. Well I have never seen any body run so fast as this man did, he had his rifle in one hand swinging it fore and aft but staying just ahead of the enemy fire and made it back to concealment without a scratch. I know it was very scary, but standing where I was, it looked like something out of a cartoon, and I was glad he wasn't hurt.

At that same position one night while on guard duty, I was talking on the "sound powered phone" (no batteries) to the gun emplacement to our right, when all of a sudden the phone went dead, well I didn't hear any noise, like some one walking around, assuming that an enemy troop was sneaking over the line to "sabotage" our rear area and cut our phone line on the way. The next day we repaired the wire. That night we could hear explosions in the rear and figured it was the enemy troop that cut the wire between our two phones. The wire was repaired again. The next night the phones went dead again which was a sign that the enemy troop had gone back to his side. Now knowing that the enemy was that good at sneaking over the line, caused us to double up on our guard posts.

Another thing that was disheartening was when our artillery fired shells over our heads toward the enemy, occasionally some of the shells inadvertently exploded, causing shrapnel to drop around us. We were told that these shells had proximity fuses that were supposed explode a certain distance from the ground. Well some times if the cloud cover was dense enough with moisture, it would cause them to explode and if that happened above us, look out.

I was thinking about all of the artillery and mortar barrages that I was caught in and wondered why I was not injured or killed, the only thing that comes to mind is that I did pray a lot.

I had dirt piled on top of me from one, and another one knocked my helmet off, two of the shells were "duds" (they did not explode) one was not real close but I saw it after the dust settled and the other one landed right next to my right leg, that one I had to ease away from. Talk about being scared, I was one scared soldier waiting for the shell to go off but luckily it did not.

An article in the newspaper caught my eye the other day. There was a picture of two British peacekeepers in Kabul drinking "tea." Well this brought to mind when I was in Korea, rumors had it that the British would always take their afternoon "tea" time. Of course the enemy would have to stop the war until tea time was over.

MY RIFLE
by Philip J. Morana

In Korea in my first week in Company E, 7th Infantry Regiment, 3rd Division. We were in Reserve behind the line. When I went for chow I left my rifle on the ground leaning against a log (remember the rule never separate yourself from your rifle). When I returned with my chow my rifle was bent and the stock broken, having been run over by the jeep that brought the chow up.

The company commander was a 1st lieutenant, probably 19 years old, I was 20 years old. He really chewed me out saying "I'm of no use now without a weapon if we were to be attacked.

I returned to my squad with new respect for my rifle. One month later, I talked my way into the kitchen to get away from training and the boredom of behind the lines.

I was a cook for several weeks when our company was moved up to the front lines. Our company was split up so the food had to be sent up to the company in three and four different locations.

My portion of food looked very small for the number of men I was serving, so not to reduce each portion, I served until I ran out of food with three or four men not fed yet. One of these men was our new company commander, a captain who asked

"What were they going to eat and why did I run out of food." I said "I couldn't cut each portion down any more so I ran out." He said "We'll see about this."

The next day I was back with my squad. We were ordered to the front line to move up and reinforce the company Lip there. The word spread that we were into a counterattack. We were single file going up with mortars falling on us and all hell broke out.

Later that night in the trench. I volunteered to carry a man on a stretcher back to first aid. In the Army you never volunteer but I wanted to do something rather than wait for that mortar with my name on it to get me.

I left my rifle against the trench wall and helped carry the wounded soldier back to first aid. A task very difficult because this guy was over six foot tall and his legs extended well beyond the end of the stretcher.

It was here that the mortar with my name on it hit just over the trench outside wall blowing my helmet off and me over with all the dust and dirt accompanying. Fortunately, I survived without a scratch. (I think today you call it friendly fire because of the explosive force it had.) My thoughts went to the sergeant who carried the front of the stretcher. "Sarge are you okay." He said, "It'll take more than that to get me." (A little guy with all them stripes.)

It was here I saw the waste of war; dead GIs were on stretchers (20 or more).

The sergeant and I split up and I went forward to find my squad when I came to the spot where my squad was before. All I saw was a pile of dirt and helmets and not my rifle.

No rifle to defend myself I went forward where I saw the captain who was hollering orders and I asked him where my squad was. He pointed and said "that way." He also said, "Come with me, we're going after them bastards." I said, "I must get to my squad they have my rifle."

I was amazed to see him climb the trench wall saying "Follow me men." Two GIs went with him and disappeared into the night. This amazed me because of all the mortars that were falling on us.

In the morning I heard that the captain was killed that night and probably the two GIs that went with him. I found my squad safe in a bunker, but not my rifle.

I must have taken a different trench back to the face of the hill because all my squad was alive. I thought they were all buried with my rifle at that mound of dirt and helmets I saw earlier.

So would I have followed the captain if I had my rifle? I'll never know.

P.S.: Can someone in the CIA find out the captain's name for me? He was with us for such a short time – and its so long ago.

Probably KIA between June 10-18, 1953? I was in Company E, 3rd Division, 7th Infantry Regiment, Korea.

AFTER THE BULGE

by Rocco J. Moretto, Co. C, 26th Inf. Regt., First Div. WWII

After straightening out the so-called "Bulge" and retaking the territories occupied by the Germans since the start of their winter offensive of Dec. 16, 1944, the 26th Infantry Regiment was sent to the Roer River in the vicinity of Obermanbach and Biltstein, considered to be the gateway to the Cologne Plain and the Rhine River.

At the Roer River the regiment relieved the U.S. Second Infantry Division which had been at that location since before the Bulge started and remained there in place until we relieved them.

The reason for the move being that the First Division had been designated by the powers to be to make the river crossing.

The Germans occupied defensive positions on the high ground on one side of the Roer and we sat on the other side. observation on both sides couldn't be better and we traded artillery and mortar fire constantly.

Additionally, we also maintained outposts along the banks of the river. This was to warn our main body of any enemy patrols attempting to cross over to our side. During the day our outposts observed and never left their foxholes. Because we were under constant observation, the outposts were supplied at night only by our patrols. Also, the broken telephone lines were repaired at night only. The constant artillery and mortar barrages played havoc with the wiring and at those times when the wiring was damaged we used #536 walkie-talkie radios for communication.

For the first few days on the Roer things were really jumping with plenty of mortar and artillery fire going back and forth and the men making themselves familiar with the company's positions and improving upon them.

Company "C" relieved our counterparts of the 2nd Infantry Division in place and they briefed us on the situation. They further advised us to be extra careful of mines as they had mined the whole area at the time of the German breakthrough, fearing the attackers would be soon arriving at this location.

As events developed the breakthrough was stopped in its tracks after a number of days and the Germans never got to this location, but they remained on the alert as the general situation had remained very fluid.

In any case they told us that they had hurriedly placed mines all over the area but were unable to give us any details as to their exact placement.

In addition, the minefields were not marked and overlays on the area maps were not made.

Our company commander, Capt. Donald Lister, wasn't too pleased with the above info and voiced his dissatisfaction in no uncertain terms.

Never one to sit on his hands, he personally inspected every inch of Company C's positions and further ordered the company's leadership to do the same.

Capt. Lister was always such a stickler for detail and it certainly paid off as the company sustained zero casualties to mines while we were at this location.

On the second or third day after arriving there I was observing the German side of the river looking for any sign of enemy movement.

From my vantage point in the early A.M. and just as dawn was breaking I spotted a German soldier easily identifiable wearing the distinctive German helmet. He was almost sitting on his haunches seemingly relieving himself. I said to myself "What the hell is going on! Is this guy nuts?"

Anyway, my heart skipped a few beats as I lifted my M-1 and took careful aim at the target, even remembering to hold my breath before squeezing the trigger just as we were taught in training. As I fired, the soldier rolled over and then I lost complete sight of him.

To this day I sometimes think of the incident and I wonder if indeed he was hit and simply crawled to his foxhole. Now these many years later the mindset changes and I sort of wish it was only the often talked about "million dollar wound" for him, and frankly I wouldn't be too displeased now if I had missed him all together.

On Feb. 25, 1945, approximately 10 days to two weeks after we arrived at the Roer, we received our orders to make the crossing and under the cover of darkness an engineering unit erected a flimsy footbridge at the Roer's shortest point. As dawn broke we made the crossing with the help of the bridge and got over with dry feet.

Much to our surprise, the crossing was made without incident - a major mistake on the part of the Germans. If they had chosen to make a stand there I would hate to think about the casualties we would have taken. So thanks to the Germans for small favors.

With the crossing, the race across the Cologne Plain was on and we began to think and talk about the dreaded crossing of the Rhine River. What an obstacle that would be! We thought of it as close to being another invasion and our fears at the time were that it would be a repeat of Omaha Beach.

Fortunately, we got lucky for a change as the 9th Armored Division captured the Remagen Bridge before the Germans could blow it up, and the Allies were able to pour troops and materiel across the Rhine before the bridge became unusable.

Most of Company C got across the Rhine in LCVPs, although some of us got over in a large rubber raft. But that's another story!

The Cologne Plain was extremely flat terrain and you could observe for miles. The area didn't offer much in cover and/or concealment for the infantry soldier so therefore all our attacks in that area were made at night only.

The 26th Infantry attacked on a battalion front and each battalion passed through each other's front, one battalion at a time. Similar tactics were used as we attacked our way out of the "Bulge." This strategy worked very well for us and gave the enemy little time to reorganize and launch counterattacks against us. However, the Germans did impede the speed of our advance at times by pushing their own civilian population, which included women and children, right into our path. While this did succeed in slowing us down, it was a pretty shoddy way to use their own people!

At approximately midnight the morning of March 1, 1945, Company C was assigned the mission of taking the town of Erp. As we advanced in the moonlight and got within a few hundred yards of Erp, we were fired upon. As per usual Capt. Lister was right up there with the scouts and point squad along with Platoon Leader Lt. Leon P. Kowalski and his platoon, who had been assigned the point that night.

We were stopped principally by rifle and machine gunfire. Because of the flat terrain, we could easily see the defensive setup. The riflemen and machine guns sat right out there in the open. Also out there on the line was a section of mortars, which were not dug in, that the enemy made no effort to conceal. This was one of the strange sights of WWII as far as I'm concerned and certainly not indicative of German army know-how. In my opinion these troops were no doubt not top of the line. In addition to this forward set-up there was a tank which was perhaps a hundred yards or more behind the forward group to our left front, who also joined in the firing.

Further, we did not have any tank support with us because we were attacking cross-country and avoiding the roads. In that area the Germans had set up numerous roadblocks along the roads so that our tanks were unable to negotiate. After the objective was taken they would be brought up to help in the defense, etc. Anyway, when we were fired upon, we scrambled for whatever cover we could find. In that area which consisted of turnip patches, the turnips were piled up to resemble a small pyramid, approximately four feet high. The turnips afforded some degree of cover and concealment. As we ducked behind the turnips, Capt. Lister wondered aloud on how best to handle the situation. He said we could call for artillery fire or we could fix bayonets and charge the enemy. I certainly thought his decision would be easy and voiced my opinion for an artillery barrage. As usual, the old man made his own decision. He said to pass it back to the company, fix bayonets and on his command to start shooting and charge the enemy. I could not believe my eyes when the Germans turned tail and took off in the direction of Erp as the company charged at them. Capt. Lister never failed to amaze me with his know-how and intuition and most times he was right on the money.

When we started out that night we were short of officers. Lt. Charles Whiting and our XO, Lt. Marlin Brockette, were both wounded that night, further reducing our corps of officers. Lt. Charles Haskell, who commanded the Company D 81mm Mortar Section and acted as the Mortar Section F.O., was loaned to Company C in November 1944. At that time, he joined the First Battalion as a replacement while we were fighting the Battle of the Hurtgen Forest. Capt. Lister subsequently pulled strings to keep him with us and we were fortunate to have him aboard. Lt. Haskell filled in whenever the need arose, which was almost always, and during one stretch he even acted as Company C's XO.

During the engagement that night we took numerous casualties in the open ground and again as we fought our way into Erp. There is no doubt in my mind that our ca-sualties would have been considerably higher if Capt. Lister hadn't acted so swiftly and with such daring.

Incidents such as I have just outlined were very common in the life of The Big Red One infantryman as he fought his way across Europe during WWII.

I have a Nazi flag and armband at home which I liberated on March 1, 1945 from a house in Erp, Germany which I sometimes take to our reunions.

It makes a great conversation piece and especially for the men who took part in the attack of Erp.

PUSHING BACK THE ENEMY
The battle for Stolberg-Diepenlinchin
by Rocco J. Moretto

On Sept. 16, 1944 the First Battalion, 26th Infantry Regiment, First Division attacked and captured the complex of pill boxes and the high ground in the vicinity of Busbach, Germany, while Company C captured the town of Busbach itself. Besides inflicting casualties on the enemy, they also took three prisoners.

While C Company was consolidating their positions, they sustained 10 casualties including one killed from German mortar and artillery fire. The expected German counter attack never developed.

By September 17 the 1st Battalion had assumed defensive positions and reinforced them. By that morning, we took an additional five prisoners.

At 1700 hours on September 17, Company C was sent out on an independent mission to the vicinity of Diepenlinchin, Germany. There a battalion of armored infantry of the 36th Regiment of the 3rd Armored Division was being mauled by a numerically superior German force.

Now back on July 25, 1944 at St. Lo, France, the 1st Battalion, 26th Infantry teamed up with the 33rd Regiment of the famed 3rd Armored (Spearhead) Division. Supported with 3,000 American planes and artillery firing at specific targets, the Allies broke out of the stalemate in France and the race through Normandy was on its way.

It was here that the two units joined forces. This joint unit was commanded by Lt. Col. Samuel M. Hogan and aptly named Task Force Hogan.

The 1st Battalion remained under Col. Hogan's command from July 25 to September 21.

However, during this entire period each of the two units occasionally went off on independent missions as the situation warranted and upon completion of their respective missions, both units would again join up together.

On September 12/13 together we breached the West Wall more commonly referred to as the Siegfried Line.

During the joint venture, the 1st Battalion's infantry rode on the 3rd Armored Division's tanks across France and into Belgium.

Now returning to September 17, Company C's mission was to establish contact with the 36th Armored in the vicinity of Diepenlinchin. There the 36th had suffered great losses from a much larger force who were solidly in place and had pre-registered the whole area with mortar and artillery fire.

Company C traveled approximately five miles from Busbach to the vicinity of Diepenlinchin in 6 by 6s (trucks) and arrived at 1800 hours.

At that time Capt. Allan B. Ferry was briefed on the mission which was to attack and secure enough ground so that the 36th might get their dead and wounded out of the area.

At 2000 hours Company C kicked off with six tanks attached. The visibility was extremely poor with a very heavy mist prevailing.

In retrospect, taking the tanks along at night during such bad weather conditions and such poor visibility turned out to be a bad decision.

We attacked straight down the road to Diepenlinchin. The lead tank lagged behind the point and the rest of the company followed closely behind. We were forced to keep a tight interval so that the men wouldn't lose contact with each other because of the poor visibility. Therefore, the troops were bunched close together.

From left: PFC Gerald F. Cook, killed Sept 17, 1944 Diepenlinehen, Germany; Sgt. Emmit Ferretti, wounded Sept. 1944; PFC Rocky Moretto; PFC Ray Grooms, wounded Sept. 18, 1944. Photo taken April 1944, Blandford, England before D-Day Invasion of France.

A brick wall ran parallel to the road. For a time the attack was uneventful then suddenly someone yelled "Medics!" An infantryman had been squeezed between the tank and the brick wall.

With that cry for medics, all hell broke loose.

The Germans were laying in wait, and we walked right into a trap. The enemy tossed hand grenades and fired straight down the road with rifles and machine guns. It was like shooting fish in a barrel with nowhere to go.

Our 2nd platoon was the point and was led by Lt. Forest E. Wilson who was almost immediately captured. Fortunately he was able to escape his captors after approximately an hour during a subsequent fire fight which added confusion, and the cover of darkness.

Quickly following the initial assault, Capt. Ferry set the company in defensive positions.

After finding his way to our positions, Lt. Wilson walked into the Company CP and asked, Do we have anything to eat? Lt. Wilson was quite a man and looked none the worse for wear and tear.

Early the following morning, September 18, Company C led by Capt. Ferry went into the attack. This time they took a different route and bypassed Diepenlinchin and traveled cross country.

Again, we were sucked in and walked into a trap.

Badly outnumbered, we were no match for the numerically superior force.

Out in the open we were receiving intense artillery and mortar fire from pre-registered concentrations.

The German infantry familiar with the area was easily able to outflank and encircle the smaller force and proceeded to close in.

Quickly assessing the situation, Capt. Ferry gave me the order to withdraw followed with instructions to pass it back to the rest of the company.

Shortly thereafter with Germans all around us, Capt. Ferry gave the second order. This time it was pass it back "get out the best way you can." The rout was on. The enemy was closing in, but, undaunted, Capt. Ferry stood fast in an attempt to get most of the company out safely

Finally he said to me, "Take off," which I did. That was the last time I saw the Captain until 40 years later. He was captured with 12 others.

It seemed to me that Capt. Ferry was destined to go down with the ship in his attempt to get the company out safely, and he actually sacrificed himself.

In the meantime, about 40 others came through Diepenlinchin in an attempt to get out and these men were captured by the Germans.

Some others in small isolated groups took refuge wherever they could. Some were to find their way back to the company around Sept. 21 and beyond.

Early that same afternoon of Sept. 18, the rest of the 1st Battalion was ordered to vacate their positions around Busbach and were rushed by truck to the Diepenlinchin area.

On arrival, Company B quickly went into the attack with Company A in support. They were also supported by our artillery and mortars and captured Diepenlinchin.

Besides inflicting many casualties on the enemy, Company B also liberated the 40 or so men of Company C who had been captured by the Germans that morning. In addition they also took 49 prisoners.

Again that same evening we were ordered to attack. This time the attack would be in battalion force and at approximately 1900 hours Company C led out as the battalion's point.

We started out under cover of heavy smoke screen and went about 300 yards. There the smoke screen was lifted.

It was then that we realized the rest of the battalion did not join the attack for whatever reason.

Again, we had walked into a trap. We were being hit from three sides with direct tank fire and heavy concentrations of artillery and mortars.

The battalion commander gave us the order by radio to withdraw.

On our left flank, which was on our right on the way back, was an extremely high slag pile. From the top of the slag pile we were being fired on with small arms.

Hand grenades were also being rolled down the hill on us as we tried to get out of there. Again we sustained heavy casualties, and some casualties were left behind.

By now our forces were so depleted that we had lost most of our fighting effectiveness. But again on the following afternoon, Sept. 19, Company C was ordered to attack.

This time the orders were to attack and occupy the high ground S.E. of Stolberg. Finally after a very tough fight, we were successful. After occupying the high ground, we were taking heavy mortar and artillery fire, and we repulsed an enemy counter attack.

I doubt whether we could have held off another try, but by this time the Germans were also badly bent.

Late that night we were relieved one or two men at a time. When we got to a safe area a few hundred yards away, the battalion commander (who I believe was Col. Rippert) shook hands with and thanked each and every man. A head count of Company C was taken at that time, and we were down to 36 men.

After Capt. Ferry was captured, Lt. Emory P Jones had assumed command, and Lt. Wilson was the only other remaining officer.

Platoon sergeants Bill Costello and Jack Gray had assumed the roll of officers.

We were not finished yet. On the morning of Sept. 21, we were ordered to come off the high ground S.E. of Stolberg and attack the city of Stolberg.

We had numerous tanks attached and coming off the high ground going to Stolberg which was set in a valley, we were being heavily shelled. most of the attached tanks were knocked out.

As we proceeded into the city, we were receiving small arms fire. After approximately an hour of cleaning out houses on the outskirts, we got the word to stop the advance as the 9th Infantry Division was about to relieve us.

Upon being relieved we went to an area outside of Aachen.

There we got some rest and hot chow, received replacements, were supplied with non coms from the 2nd and 3rd Battalions of the 26th with some remaining members of Company C receiving promotions.

In addition, we were resupplied and given new clothing while we received repairs to equipment.

The new replacements received some training as we prepared to take Aachen (which was destined to be the first large city in Germany to fall.)

Subsequent to the capture of Aachen, we would go into the treacherous Huertgen Forest, but that's another story.

For the action in and around Diepenlinchin, the First Battalion, 26th Infantry was awarded the Presidential Citation. During WWII the 1st Battalion was the only battalion in the regiment to receive that honor.

In part the citation read: Vigorous hostile resistance was counterbalanced by an insuperable urge to close with and destroy the enemy. This unit grimly pushed into the town, engaged in intense street fighting, captured or killed the enemy, and took its objective.

The men fought bravely and valiantly...the enemy fought savagely, tenaciously refusing to yield ground, but sheer dint of courage and magnificent fighting spirit of this infantry unit achieved another glorious victory.

Despite enormous losses incurred in this offensive, the 1st Battalion, allowing the enemy no respite, assaulted Stolberg at 0700 hours on Sept. 21, 1944.

Withering artillery fire from enemy batteries split the attacking forces; the infantry gained the outer reaches of the town, while the tanks suffered heavy losses.

During the period Sept. 13-22, 1944, the 1st Battalion demonstrated unwavering courage and matchless aggressiveness in the face of tremendous odds…fighting gallantly and bravely and displaying conspicuous combat skill and devotion to duty, despite casualties which greatly depleted its ranks.

The 1st Battalion's losses in this sustained drive included 27 killed, 157 wounded, and 41 missing.

Over 300 prisoners were taken and twice as many enemy soldiers were killed or seriously wounded.

The unconquerable spirit and extraordinary heroism displayed by the 1st Battalion, 26th Infantry, in accomplishing all attack missions…paved the way for more deadly blows against the Germans and rendered an invaluable contribution to the Allied cause.

RECOVERING A BODY
by Carl Siegel

About six AM in "the land of the morning calm," on a date long forgotten I was sacked out on the dirt floor of a dugout that served as the company CP. I was unconsciously listening to kitchen noises as our cooks prepared a morning meal for a couple squads scheduled to reclaim an OP (observation post) on a hill called Nori located on the other side of the Imjim River in Korea. The squad hoped to secure the OP peacefully from the Chinese through a pre-arranged schedule that gave them the hill from dusk-to-dawn while we did likewise from daybreak to dusk. Normally the change was peaceful but the Chinks had the bad habit of frequently over staying their visit and it was necessary to shag them off with a sometimes-heavy firefight.

This particular morning was one of those times. Unknown to us the Chinese had moved a strong contingent of men on the OP during the night along with a few mortars and, we were told, a machine gun. After our detail ate its morning chow the two squads waded across the Imjim River with rifles overhead and began ascending the hill along a frequently used path. More than halfway up the hill the squads drew enemy rifle and mortar fire causing our undermanned detail to exchange fire as they backed down from the hill. The enemy was equipped to go beyond a routine firefight so our detail radioed back they were holding ground but needed help to remove two wounded and a KIA (killed in action). We knew if we didn't regain the body of the deceased he would be declared a MIA (missing in action) and his folks would forever be living in hope he would someday walk through their front door.

Back at the CP we rounded up all available help including cooks, supply people, and orderly room personnel. We loaded ourselves down with bandoleers of ammo, grenades, and two BARs (Browning Automatic Rifles), as we waded across the Imjim we drew mortar fire but luckily the Chinese firing squad was having an off day. Once on the other side of the river we were hit with small arms fire but progressed up Nori far enough to join the original squads. The exchange of fire increased as we neared the crest of the hill to the spot the body. Under heavy cover fire our rescue team secured the body, rolled it on a poncho and began sliding it down hill. While doing this a member of the rescue party took a fatal hit. His body, too, was placed on the poncho and slid downhill. Once we returned to the CP we discovered the second body was that of a soldier who had just joined the company the night before. At the moment we didn't know his name or anything about him. It indicates the way the war was going at the time causing replacements to often be only temporary acquaintance.

LOST APPETITE
by Rayman C. Spalsbury

On Feb. 25, 1945, my unit was in Intramuros (Spanish Walled City) Manila. We had cleared out the Japanese, but there were many left in the government buildings nearby. The artillery was shelling these buildings prior to an assault. Our company kitchen had brought up hot food, the first in quite a long time. After getting my food and drink, I sat down on a pile of rubble. As I started to place my spoon in the food, my mess kit exploded, falling to the ground along with the canteen cup of coffee. After catching my breath, I saw that a piece of shrapnel from our artillery the size of my hand had landed in my mess kit. Needless to say, I not only lost my food, but my appetite as well.

ACTION ON THE PEAK OF "DAGMAR"
Submitted by Burton Steinburg

When Lt. Weyand was just down from the peak he could see Lt. Ellis, Lt. Richter, and three or four of their men coming up the other side of the hill. Lt. Richter backed up from a trench and put his foot near an aperture where an enemy machine gun was firing. Lt. Weyand saw this and hollered to him to "Watch out" but there was to much noise and Lt. Richter couldn't hear him. Lt. Weyand moved closer, hollered again and as Lt. Richter moved away he hollered, "Hell they've been firing at me for 30 minutes now and haven't hit me yet!" Cpl. Fleming was hit by a concussion grenade and hollered. I can't move my shoulder." However, he was just shaken up as the grenade had landed nearby and knocked the wind out of him. He was all right when Powers (the Aid man), got to him. Lt. Weyand was hit in the head by grenade fragments which knocked his helmet off and made a gash in his scalp but didn't penetrate the skull bone. Powers put a bandage on his head and told him, "You better go on down the hill," but though he couldn't wear his helmet, Lt. Weyand went forward again. The group was now 25 yards down from the peak and the enemy were throwing grenades but were staying below the top of their trenches. The enemy was having to throw their hand grenades pretty high to get them out of the trenches and over the crest so the men were not receiving too many right on their positions and were actually dodging those they saw. These hand grenades were mostly concussion type. Lt. Weyand told Sgt. McCoy, "Don't go up any further but stay out of the grenade range until it slows up." Sgt. McCoy with two other men moved to their left and started to swing in behind because the men had seen some of the enemy in bunkers and they were going to keep them from coming in on the squad. Pvt. Escobido was back where the group had originally moved forward on the finger and he kept the enemy pinned down in their bunkers and trenches by maintaining a constant rate of BAR fire. This enabled the men to move on up the hill with no more casualties than were suffered. Escobido was hit in the face and leg by a fragmentary grenade landing near him but he kept right on firing. Lt. Steinberg and Sgt. Gruver were both hit by grenade fragments; Steinberg in his right knee and Gruver in the left leg, though both wounds were only slight.

Cpl. Shortt was hit under his left eye by a fragmentary grenade so Powers finished bandaging Lt. Weyand and then went over to Shortt. He couldn't see out of his left eye because it was beginning to swell badly as the fragment had penetrated his cheek bone. Lt. Weyand was knocked down by another concussion grenade and rolled down the hill by Shortt and Powers. Powers finished with Shortt and went to Lt. Weyand. When he got to him he saw he had also been hit by small arms fire under the left shoulder. The flesh hadn't been badly torn but there was a hole in him. Powers bandaged him and Lt. Weyand again went up the hill. Shortt was evacuated down to the bottom of the hill and another man took his radio on forward to insure communications. As the group moved forward they saw two enemy outside a bunker door and these were killed by small arms fire.

The majority of the assault elements of Company G and the group from Company E were now (0638 hours) on the peak of "Dagmar" and into the enemy trenches. When the two mortar FO parties met on the hill, Lt. Steinberg asked Sgt. Schomaker, "What the hell are you doing up here?" and he promptly replied, "Same damn thing you're doing." The enemy who got out of their positions and trenches never did get back but were killed, so those remaining in the positions were confused because they didn't know for sure what was going on or what size the friendly force was. The enemy here had clean fatigues which were thinner than U.S. type and of brown color. Some were wearing cotton caps, tennis shoes and their pants were bloused above their shoes. Some had on steel helmets but none were wearing boots. There was no trash in or around the area but everything was completely policed. Most of the equipment seen seemed to be in fair condition but there was no oil at all on any of the weapons so some of them were rusty. A stuffed dummy was evidently propped up behind a machine gun because when the troops got into this trench the dummy was lying across the weapon and it had to be moved to get at the machine gun to take it off the hill. This dummy was stuffed with a straw type material and was full of holes and shrapnel.

To fulfill the mission of capturing a Prisoner of War, the men on reaching the peak, began to look for wounded enemy. Lt. Ellis with the assistance of Sgt. Kostick pulled one that had been wounded out of a firing position and threw him down the hill. Sgt. Greathouse and Sgt. Parker helped him take the Prisoner of War down. However, before they could move to the draw, other enemy threw a fragmentary grenade, killing the Prisoner of War and wounding Lt. Ellis in the right hand. The enemy also threw concussion grenades and one knocked Sgt. Greathouse down the hill. Lt. Ellis asked if he was all right and then they

moved back up to the crest. As they moved to the right three - four enemy came out of bunkers to their left front and those were shot as soon as they came through the entrance. One enemy was dragged to the side of this position but he was already dead so was left laying there where Sgt. Greathouse had jumped into the trench and started throwing enemy concussion grenades. Lt. Richter saw one of the enemy was only wounded so he jumped into the trench and pulled him out and took him to Powers so he could try and save him from dying. He had a chest wound approximately four inches in diameter which went into his lung. They cut off his clothes and took everything out of his pockets. He had shoe laces and some kind of a pack of tobacco with the name "Sun Valley" on it in English. He seemed to feel no pain at all but his eyes would follow any movement that anyone would make. He watched Powers all the time he was dressing his wounds but he never did flinch or grimace from the pain. His clothes were covered with blood and he was coughing, however it was not a "sucking type" wound. For lack of other material, Powers put the prisoner's clothes over the wound and tied the shoe laces around to keep them in place. At this time, Pvt. Howard Priester, 2nd platoon, Company G radio operator, who had helped carry this PW down, was hit in his back and he was lying on his stomach with his radio still strapped to him. Powers told a man by him to apply pressure on the PW's wound and immediately ran over to Priester. He was lying approximately 10 feet below the crest and as Powers was bandaging him, a concussion grenade exploded nearby and knocked Powers down. He received a concussion of the head but crawled back and finished working on Priester.

When he finished he had him evacuated down the hill but only got halfway and then had to wait because artillery was coming in steadily now. When Powers got back to the PW he was still alive but within two minutes he coughed, choked and died. Powers was surprised he had lived that long because he was so badly shot up. He estimated that he had actually died from internal bleeding.

Cpl. James Combs and PFC Earnest Jackson, riflemen, 3rd Platoon, Company G, on the peak of the hill were hit by fragments from the same hand grenade. Combs was hit in the left posterior chest and shoulder and Jackson in the left leg. PFC Siegert bandaged them and had them taken to the 1st platoon's position. When the group of Company E got to the peak of the objective there was a number of Company G men around an open bunker position which contained five - six wounded enemy. Everyone was looking down into the position and someone said "If we only had some concussion grenades." Lt. Weyand remembered his PW team had some so he hollered for them to come forward. Pvt. Henry Jackson tossed the grenades up and those were all used while the men tried to grab prisoners. You could lie down and almost reach the enemy's feet. Lt. Weyand threw a grenade and Lt. Steinberg, Mortar Company jumped in, grabbed one of them and threw him out of the position. He was immediately searched and a cigarette light, diary, pictures of himself and letters were taken from his pockets. Lt. Steinberg and Sgt. Gruver, his radio operator, took the PW down the hill and gave him to Powers. Lt. Weyand told Powers to help bandage him and keep him alive and to "Treat him just as good as you would one of our own men."

The Combat Infantryman"s Badge is the most respected award the U.S. Army can bestow on ground troops, with the Military Occupational Speciality Number 0745, with the rank of Colonel or below who have proven themselves in "Armed Combat." This Badge was the highest recognition that was bestowed upon Dogfaces only; it paid the recipient $10.00 per month for the duration of the Doggie's Service in WW II; as long as his MOS was 0745. The CIB was designed in 1943, by Trygve A. Rovelstad, who was the first Heraldic Artist and Medalist Sculpter of the U.S. War Department, when in WW II the fight was being carried to the enemy, and the GI Infantrymen were doing over 70% of the fighting and dying.

BIOGRAPHIES

April 1951, after Sunday Mass offered by Father Frank L. Wood, a missionary Priest who joined the 2nd Division, 23rd Reg. After mission being destroyed in 1950. Became 2nd Battalion Chaplain. Men from 2nd and 3rd HV Mortar Platoons.

BILLY R. ADAMS, born Dec. 27, 1923, Albany, MO. He graduated from Albany High School and attended South Dakota State College at Brookings, SD. He enlisted in the U.S. Army Feb. 18, 1943 and served with the Co. A and HQ Co., 1st Bn., 397th Inf. Regt., 100th Inf. Div.

He was stationed at Fort Lewis, WA; Fort Benning, GA and participated in battles during WWII in Rhineland and Central Europe. Wounded in Germany on March 20, 1945, he received the Purple Heart, Combat Infantryman Badge and Bronze Star. He was discharged April 16, 1946 with the rank private first class and retired March 10, 1968 with the rank of captain.

Billy and his wife Patricia have two children and five grandchildren. He worked for the U.S. Postal Service and retired as postmaster Oct. 2, 1992.

CONRAD A. "FRENCHIE" ADAMS of Gulfport, MS, was born July 5, 1925, Lockport, Lafourche Parish, LA. On Oct. 20, 1943, Conrad was sent to Camp Wolters, TX. At Christmas time he experienced his first snow while standing at Reveille and his fingers, numbed by cold, dropped his rifle. The corporal ordered him to sleep with his rifle for the next two days. After training and a 65-march in Camp Shelby, MS, he was sent to New York.

On June 6, 1944 Conrad and 10,000 other GIs were on a ship departing New York. He was sent to E Co., 8th Regt., 4th Inf. Div. and assigned to a 60mm mortar. On his 19th birthday they were in the Battle of St. Lo. Shortly after, he was captured by the Germans but managed to escape a few days later. Picked up by 2nd Armd. Tank Div. and interrogated at G-2. The information he gave about the Germans helped Generals Patton and Montgomery close in on that pocket much quicker than they could have done without his input.

His next assignment was to help liberate Paris. They were were sent into Paris on patrol then brought back out so Gen. DeGaulle could be the first to walk beneath the Arch de Triumph. History may credit the General as being the first, but Conrad can say proudly that he at least was one of the first to enter the city.

They fought at various locations in Germany, liberated Luxembourg and participated in the Battle of the Bulge. Finally it was all over and he returned to the States and was discharged Nov. 14, 1945.

Conrad is the recipient of the European Theater Ribbon, PUC, five Battle Stars (Campaign Stars), Ex-POW Medal, Purple Heart, Bronze Star, Good Conduct Medal, Utah Beach Landing Medal, Omaha Beach Landing Medal, Battle of Bulge Medal, American Campaign Ribbon and WWII Victory Medal.

Conrad and his five brothers all served in WWII: Manny in Fiji and Philippines, Dave in India, Earl stayed at Camp Bowie in Texas, Ferdinand fought with the 8th Air Corps in England and Francis in Germany. All returned to home safely.

GROVER ADKINS, born July 29, 1918, Lawrence County, KY. Joined the Army, Oct. 30, 1943 at Huntington, WV and served as private first class with Co. A, 10th Armd. Inf. Bn., 4th Armd. Div.

He was in the battle of Ardennes-Rhineland, and served with an armored division in the European Theatre for 13 months. He was wounded twice and received two Purple Hearts. Other decorations and citations include American Theater Ribbon, EAME Theater Ribbon w/2 Bronze Stars, Good Conduct Medal, Distinguished Unit Badge, WWII Victory Medal and Combat Infantryman's Badge.

After he was discharged Jan. 25, 1946 he married his wife Ruth and moved to Fort Gay, WV. He and Ruth had five children. He retired from the construction business in 1980 to fox hunt and raise foxhounds. He is a member of the VFW, American Legion, Order of the Purple Heart, Battle of Bulge Association, and the Combat Infantrymen's Association.

DENNIS A. ALBA, born July 27, 1931. Kapaa-Kauai, Hawaii. Enlisted in the US Army in October 1950 and was at the following locations: Republic of Korea; Schofield Barracks, HI; Wildflecken, Germany; Fort Carson, CO; Fort Benning, GA; Republic of Vietnam, Aberdeen Proving Grounds, MD; Fort Riley, KS.

Missions and battles include 1966-Vietnam, Binh Dinh Prov., Operations White Wing, Paul Revere, Irving, Thayer II, Pleiku Province.

On Sept. 12, 1953 he married Loretta in Hawaii. They have six wonderful children, 14 beautiful grandchildren and six lovely great-grandchildren. They celebrated their 50th anniversary at Fort Shafter, HI in 2003. Two sons are still serving in our military forces: Lt/Cmdr, Bathseda Naval Hospital, MD and CSM Signal Command, Springfield, IL.

Discharged in November 1970, he received the Bronze Star, Air Medal, Army Commendation, National Defense w/OLC, Korean Service, Expeditionary Medal, Vietnam Service, Vietnamese Cross of Gallantry, UN Service, Vietnam Campaign and the Korean War Service Medal. He achieved the rank (E-7) weapons platoon sergeant (81mm-4.2 in mortars).

Civilian employment as US Army Ammunition Inspector. 1970-95. He is an active member with VFW Post 10276, DAV Post 1, NRA, Korean War Vet Assn., Vietnam War Vet Assn. and is a recent member of Combat Infantrymens Assn.

FRANK F. APLAN, 69th Inf. Div., WWII, a native of Fort Pierre, SD, he enlisted in the Army in November 1942. After basic infantry training, he was assigned to the 60mm Mortar Section, I Co., 272 Inf., 69th Div. at Camp Shelby, MS and went overseas in

November 1944. His division first saw action on the Siegfried Line.

Memorable experiences were carrying that 42 lb. mortar across Germany to the Elbe and when he almost "bought the farm" several times in the attack east from Kassel to Leipzig. In early August 1945 he was one of the "lucky" ones en route to fight yet another war in the Pacific. The atom bomb undoubtedly saved his life.

Discharged in June 1946 as a tech sergeant holding the Combat Infantryman's Badge, the Bronze Star Medal and two Battle Stars.

Then re-entered the South Dakota School of Mines and Technology, receiving a BS degree in metallurgical engineering and later an MS degree from Montana Tech and a doctorate from MIT. He has had professional experience in the mining, metallurgical and chemical industries and as a university professor, recently retiring from Penn State. He holds many professional awards and is a member of the National Academy of Engineering.

He lives with his wife, Clare, in State College, PA. They have three children and five grandchildren.

EDWARD ARTHUR, born in Columbus, OH. At age 13 in 1949 he joined Ohio National Guard, 174th Field Artillery, Fort Hayes, Columbus. Entered US Army, Paratroopers, 508th Abn. Inf., Fort Benning, GA at 15. Entered US Army, 1st Sqdn., 9th Cav., 1st Air Cav. Div. in 1966. His helicopter was shot down in Vietnam by enemy gunfire near Duc Pho.

Honorably discharged in 1969, he re-enlisted in 1970 and returned to Vietnam as a Recon-Rat Patrol Scout. Medivaced home, he was NCO instructor, Reconnaissance Commando School (RECONDO) Fort Carson, CO, training Army Airborne Rangers.

Honorably discharged in 1971, due to wounds received in combat. Some of his military awards include Bronze Star, Purple Heart w/ OLC, five Air Medals w/Combat V, Army Good Conduct Medal, Combat Infantry Badge, Recondo Badge and Flight Crewman Wings, Vietnam Service Medal w/4 Campaign Stars and Vietnam Cross of Gallantry Medal w/ Gold Palm. Attained the rank of major with Ohio Military Reserve.

Following his military career, he entered law enforcement as Undersheriff of Teller County, CO and worked undercover narcotics in the Southwest. He received the Silver Star while in law enforcement and was later awarded Lifetime Achievement Award from the Police Hall of Fame. Retired as police captain.

Edward is founder and a director of the Ohio Military Hall of Fame, recognizing those veterans decorated for valor on the battlefield; life member of AMVETS, DAV, Underage Veterans Association, Bullwhip Squadron - 1/9, First Cavalry Association and MOPH. He currently serves on the Fairfield County Veterans Commission as vice president, was featured in the Mott's Military Museum, Grove City, OH, with a large military display spanning 1949 to present. He is the father of three girls and one boy.

JOSEPH S. BARCA, born Oct. 12, 1929, South Boston, MA. He served in the U.S. Army, U.S. Constabulary and Military Police in German occupation, 1946-49. Assigned to 7th Cav. Regt., 1st Cav. Div., Korean War, July 1950 to June 1951.

Memorable experiences include the Battle of Naktong River; advance to and retreat from Yalu River;

the terrible winter of 1950-51 when they were without adequate winter clothing and suffered with frozen feet etc.

Discharged July 27, 1952. His awards include Combat Infantry Badge, five Battle Stars etc.

One of eight children, he is a life member of 1st Cav. Div. Assn., Korean War Vet Assn. and is national adjutant of Combat Infantrymen's Assn. Self-employed, he is now retired.

CHARLES BERNAT, born Oct. 22, 1928, Niobrara, NE. He enlisted Nov. 8, 1950, Portland, OR and served with Co. L, Service Co. APO6 Clerk 160th RCT 40th Div. Stationed at Fort Lewis, WA; Camp Cooke, CA; Camp Haugen; Camp McNair; Japan and Korea.

Spent 12 months in **Japan on occupation duty** then sent to Korea for six months as infantryman and later assigned to Regimental Post Office APO 6 RCT as a mail truck guard.

Discharged Aug. 7, 1952 with the rank PFC, his awards include the Occupation Medal (Japan), Korean Service Medal w/3 Bronze Stars, Combat Infantry Badge and UN Service Medal.

Returned to Nebraska after discharge, met and married his wife Charlene in 1955. He was an insurance agent with American Family Ins. Co. and retired in 1990. He was also a volunteer police reserve officer with the Norfolk Police Dept. for 22 years. He is a member of Board of Directors of annual Nebraska Korean Veterans Reunion, Inc. and a member of American Legion, VFW and Combat Infantrymen Assn.

JOSEPH G. BISHOP, born in Detroit, MI on Dec. 1, 1931 and enlisted in the US Army on Dec. 22, 1947 at 16. He served with the 6th and 7th Inf. Divs. in pre-war Korea and the 5th Regimental Combat Team in Hawaii and Korea.

Stationed at Schofield Barracks in Hawaii when the Korean War broke out and returned to Korea with the 5th RCT as a corporal with Fox Co. arriving at Pusan on July 30, 1950. He was assigned on TDY to Service Co. 5th RCT where he performed duty as Regimental Signal Supply NCO.

He returned to the States in July 1951, stationed at Camp McCoy, WI where he was honorably discharged on Aug. 10, 1952. His decorations include Army of Occupation Medal, Combat Infantryman's Badge, UN Medal, Korean Campaign Medal w/5 Battle Stars, Good Conduct Medal and the Cold War Medal.

Finishing his education under the GI bill, his career covered 48 years in automotive engineering with retirement in 1999.

Most memorable events in his Army career were

being visited by Vice President Alban Barkley at Tripler General Hospital in Hawaii where the Veep made a caricature drawing of him; occupation duty in pre-war Korea; Garrison duty at Schofield Barracks; returning to Korea for combat operations; and his honorable discharge to civilian life.

HOWARD E. BJERKE, born June 11, 1925 on a farm in Slope County, New England, ND, the fifth of eight children in a Scandinavian family. All four brothers served in the Armed Forces during WWII. In 1942 the family moved to Vancouver, WA where he worked in the defense industry before being drafted into the Army on Aug. 24, 1943. Inducted at Fort Lewis, WA, assigned to the 70th Inf. Div. and underwent basic training at Camp Adair, OR.

In 1944 he was sent to Europe as a replacement and stationed near Bath, England. Because he could speak Norwegian he was assigned to HQ of the American School Center for special training in combat intelligence, completing in June 1944.

On Dec. 16, 1944, Hitler launched one desperate counteroffensive called the Battle of the Bulge. Howard was assigned as a replacement rifleman to the 99th Inf. Div., 395th Regt., Co. B. His time on the front ended March 1, 1945 while the 395th Regt. was attached to the 3rd Armd. Div. The 395th was given the mission to clear a wooded area near Elsdorf, Germany. They were in a deep trench and sighted the enemy advancing toward them, Howard had been shot but managed to throw a grenade into the mist of Germans.

He still vividly recalls seeing his first buzz-bomb, digging and occupying foxholes, the anti-personnel mines that were covered by the snow and hard to detect, and encountering booby-trapped bodies - both our own and the enemy's.

Wounded on March 1, 1945, he received a medical discharge on August 31 of the same year from McCaw General Hospital in Walla Walla, WA. His awards include the Sharpshooter Badge w/Rifle Bar, Marksman Badge w/Automatic Rifle Bar, Bronze Star, Good Conduct Medal, American Campaign Medal, EAME Campaign Medal w/2 Bronze Stars, WWII Victory Medal, Army of Occupation Medal w/Germany Clasp, Combat Infantryman Badge, Purple Heart, Belgian Fourragere and Honorable Service Lapel Button.

Received his BA degree and was employed by the Santa Clara County Probation Department for 28 years. Retired in 1982 and currently lives in San Jose, CA with his wife Arlene (Zipp). They have three daughters: Sharon Lee, Michele and Laurie, and two grandchildren, Jason and Daniel.

PATRICK F. BLACK JR., born May 25, 1925, Providence, RI. Units served with include Co. B, 1st

Bn., 337th Regt., 1208th Engrs. Fire Department, 248th Cbt. Engrs., 85th Inf. Div. and trained at Camp Blanding, FL (IRTC).

Participated in battles at Casino, Rome-Arno and Northern Apennines Mountains. He was wounded in action Oct. 5, 1944.

Everyday was an experience that he will never forget. One of his fondest memories was when he finally anchored on Dec. 22, 1945 in New York Harbor and there was the Statue of Liberty. Another wonderful memory was arriving home on Dec. 25, 1945, Christmas Day.

Discharged Jan. 9, 1946 with the rank private first class. His awards include the Bronze Star, Purple Heart, Combat Infantry Badge, Victory Medal, Freedom Medal, German Occupation Medal, EAME Theater Campaigns, Good Conduct Medal as well as a certificate from the French Government awarded on the deck of the USS *Massachusetts.*

Civilian employment was with the U.S. Post Office for 39 years of service. Now retired, his hobbies include spending time with his family, gardening, photography and refinishing furniture.

His family includes wife Sheryl (Vizvary); children: Gregg, Kristin, Elena and Lindsey Vizvary; Andrea (Vizvary) Larson; son-in-law Daniel Larson; and grandson Syler Larson.

CHARLES B. "BEN" BOWEN, born Sept. 15, 1927, Piedmont, SC. Joined the U.S. Army, Dec. 28, 1951 with basic training and Leadership School at Scofield Barracks, HI.

Assigned to 40th Inf. Div., 160th Inf. Regt., Fox Co. in Korea where he served at Heartbreak Ridge, Bloody Ridge, Kum Wah Valley and Koje Do Island.

Memorable experience include struggling to survive the subfreezing weather and nearly freezing to death on combat patrols in the winter time; the excruciating heat in the summertime on the top of the mountains where all the trees were blown off with no shade; his company being overrun and company commander blown out of his bunker and Chinese and North Koreans all over their positions in the ensuing fight driving them back; also remembers observing the cruelty of the prisoners to each other on Koje Do Island.

Discharged Nov. 17, 1953 with the rank of staff sergeant, his awards include the Combat Infantry Badge, Korean Service Medal, three Bronze Service Stars, UN Service Medal, National Defense Service Medal, three Overseas Bars, Korean Government Medal, Expert Rifleman's Award and Good Conduct Medal.

He married Vera Trammell and they have two sons, Charles "Chuck" Jr. and Brian Bowen. Chuck has three children and Brian has one child. Chuck practices law with his father and Brian is a Federal Probation Officer in Greenville, SC.

After completing military service he attended Furman University and the University of South Carolina and received his BS in 1957 and LLB degrees in 1959 from University of South Carolina. Since then he has practiced law in Greenville, SC, is a member of the American Legion and active in numerous professional and community organizations.

WILLIAM CARPENTER BRIDGES, born May 13, 1925, Palestine Anderson County, TX. While a sophomore at University of TX he was drafted and inducted at Fort Sam Houston in July 1943. He had almost completed basic infantry training at Camp McClellan, AL when he was ordered to Keesler Field, MS for testing to qualify for Air Corps Cadet Program, which he did. Waiting for assignment as an Air Cadet he took basic training again.

He was in pre-flight training at Oklahoma A&M when his class of cadets was notified that they were being transferred to the Infantry as rifleman replacements were needed more than air crew replacements.

At Camp Howze, TX, he took basic training for the third time with Co. L, 411th Inf., 103rd Inf. Div. and was awarded the Expert Infantryman's Badge before shipping overseas to Marseilles, France in October 1944. In November after assembling much of the Division's motorized equipment on the Marseilles docks, the 103rd moved north in 40 & 8 boxcars, and relieved 36th Inf. Div. at St. Die. On Nov. 11, 1944, the 103rd went into action with the mission of clearing the Germans out of the Vosges Mountains, then deep in snow in one of the worst winters on record in Europe. On Jan. 19, 1945 he was captured at Sessenheim, Germany during the "Little Bulge," which the Germans called "Operation Nordwind." His feet were frozen during one of the many train movements before winding up at Stalag XIII-C at Hammelburg, Germany. He was then sent on "Arbeit Kommando" to Marktsteft am Main, near Wurzburg where he worked in a brewery. When American POWs began to be withdrawn to keep them from being liberated by advancing American and Russian forces, the Marktsteft group suddenly was told to be ready to March the next day (April 1945). He and four other POWs decided to hide out and wait for the American Third Army's arrival, which seemed imminent. The others in the group elected to walk. Afterwards he learned that the group walked all the way to Czechoslovakia before the Americans finally caught up with them. In that bitter cold, without proper food or clothing, not all of them made it, he was told.

When the Americans did not liberate Marktsteft as anticipated, the five at-large POWs managed to get across the Main River, and reached Third Army lines April 21, 1945. After a stay at the 59th Evac Hospital near Worms, he was flown via hospital plane to England, where he was hospitalized with acute infectious hepatitis, blood poisoning, dysentery, malnutrition, and frozen feet residuals. When he could travel, he was sent by hospital ship to Camp Miles Standish, near Boston, then by hospital train to Brook Army Hospital at Fort Sam Houston, TX, where he had started his Army career in 1943. While there, he was promoted to corporal by Act of Congress.

After some months of recuperation, he was discharged at Camp Chaffee, AR in January 1946.

Had the Japanese not surrendered, he had been told he was to be shipped to the Pacific as a rifleman replacement for the Battle of Japan. When the Korean War started, he was a member of an Army Reserve MI (CIC) unit in Houston, TX, where he lived at that time.

In 1955 he moved to California, and spent the next 25 years there working as a magazine photographer. After retiring he authored *The Great American Chili Book,* published in 1981 and still in print.

His wife, Anne Barbour Bridges, died of cancer in 1985, after 38 years of marriage and two children, Ward Burnett and Kate Barbour Bridges. In 1989 he returned to his family home in Texas and married Charmane Lee Halsey of Charlotte, MI. He has two stepdaughters, Kelly Jo Williams and Beth Green, both of whom live in Michigan.

His awards and medals include CIB, Bronze Star, Purple Heart w/OLC, POW, and EAME w/2 stars.

RAYMOND H. BROWN, born in Harrisburg, PA in 1947. He graduated from Steelton-Highspire High School in 1966. He met his wife Peg while in high school and they have been married since 1966.

He was drafted into the Army in 1966 and re-

ceived his basic and advanced training at Fort Knox, KY. In April 1967 he went to Vietnam and served a one year tour with the First Cav. Div. Airmoble Inf. He achieved the rank of sergeant E-5 and was awarded the CIB, Silver Star, Bronze Star, Air Medal, and others.

After his active duty discharge, he went back to work as a millwright for Bethlehem Steel in his home town of Steelton, PA. He is now retired after 32 years of service.

Ray is a member of the Combat Infantrymen's Association, V.Vn.W, VVA, VFW, American Legion, Vietnam Veterans of Mechanicsburg Area and PA Concerned Citizens for POW/MIAs.

MILLER BRYANT, born Dec. 27, 1920, Wellsburg, WV. Enlisted in the Army June 25, 1942, served with 75th Inf. Div. and was stationed in Germany, Holland, France, Belgium, England, Scotland, Fort Dix, Fort Benning, Fort Hood, Camp Wilmer, Camp Bowie, Camp Maxey, Fort Bragg and Fort Leonard Wood.

Participated in action in Normandy, Northern France, Rhineland, Central Europe and Korea. His medals include the Good Conduct Medal, American Campaign Medal, ETO w/4 stars and Bronze Arrowhead, Combat Infantry Badge, WWII Victory Medal and Army of Occupation Medal. Retired March 1, 1964 after 21 years service with the rank of sergeant first class (E-6).

Married Sarah Norwood Feb. 24, 1950 and had three children: Robert, Cathy and Laura. Miller Bryant passed away Nov. 3, 1988.

RICHARD S. BUCCA, born April 24, 1911, Sicily, Italy. He enlisted in the Army April 15, 1940, served with the 36th Inf. Div., Co. A and was stationed at Fort Dix, NJ; Camp Forrest, TN; Las Cruces, NM; Fort Ontario, NY and Trenton, NJ.

Participated in action in France, Germany and Austria. The day after war's end in Kufstein, Austria, the captain directed Richard to take his platoon up a hill to eliminate a group of SS Troops who were firing at them. They hated to be shot up especially after the war ended. To their surprise, the SS troops were firing their ammunition, drinking, and enjoying the company of the opposite sex. They too were elated of war's end.

Discharged Jan. 28, 1946 with the rank of tech sergeant. His awards include the Combat Infantry Badge, Bronze Star, WWII Victory Medal, European Medal and Good Conduct Medal.

He married Agnes Antypas Jan. 3, 1943 and they are still enjoying life together.

HAROLD A. BUCHLER, born in Westwego, LA and volunteered for Navy, Coast Guard, Air Force but was rejected due to color blindness. He joined the ASTP Program while in law school. He entered active service in 1943. He was assigned to Co. M, 341st Inf. Div. at Camp Howze, TX. He was sent to Europe in 1945 and wounded in the Battle of the Ruhr.

Decorations include Purple Heart, Bronze Star, Good Conduct Medal, Combat Infantry Badge, WWII Victory Medal, American Campaign Medal, Asiatic-Pacific Campaign Medal and EAME Campaign Medal. Returned to States, then sent to the Philippines and was stationed at Lipa, Luzon until February 1946.

After the service he finished law school and married Margaret Maloney. He became first assistant district attorney for the Parish of Jefferson and later helped organize the National Bank of Commerce in Jefferson Parish and became chairman of the Board. He now has five children and 10 grandchildren.

He is a member and past commander of VWF 7732, member of American Legion Post 175, 86 Blackhawk Division and Combat Infantry Association. He is a volunteer at the National D-Day Museum. He was one of the original boat builders of the LCVP Higgins Boat presently on display.

CLAYTON F. "PETE" BUSH JR., born Feb. 12, 1928 in Rochester, NY. Enlisted in U.S. Army on Aug. 20, 1951, trained at Fort Dix, NJ for 24 weeks. Served in Infantry as squad leader, 5th RCT, 53rd C/F Plt. and was stationed at Korea (May 1952-February 1953), Inje, Punch Bowl and Yangu.

Memorable experiences include locating enemy weapons using muzzle blast to record data to obtain fixes and send to FDC for fire missions and being pinned down by enemy fire in open areas while repairing phone lines.

Awards include Korean Service Medal w/2 Battle Stars, UN Medal and CIB. Discharged to Reserves May 19, 1953 as sergeant. Discharged from Reserves in 1960.

He and wife Anne (Dillon) have nine children: Eric, USMC, staff sergeant (deceased); Hans, 13 years U.S. Army, CIB, Sp. Forces; Aaron (major); daughters are Cynthia, Heidi, Colleen, Kathleen, Pollyanna and Gretchen. They also have 12 grandchildren.

Bush is a retired teacher and now does volunteer work and enjoys gardening and relaxing.

GEORGE M. BUSSEY, born Jan. 10, 1928. He enlisted in the Army Dec. 24, 1947 and took basic training at Fort Dix, NJ.

In June 1948 he was sent to Japan, assigned to the 24th Inf. Regt., Love Co. and conducted Occupation Duty in Japan until the Korean War started June 25, 1950. The next month he was sent to Korea with the 24th Regt. to the Pusan Perimeter. In November

1950 he was at the Yalu River. Wounded in April 1951 and sent to a Japan hospital for three months.

Returned to the States in August 1951 and was sent to the hospital in Fort Gordon, GA for three months. In February 1952 he returned for a second tour of duty in Japan with the 24th, followed by duty in Korea, June 1953. Returned to the States in December 1953. Spent three years, 1961-64, in Germany and in August 1965, he was sent to Vietnam, back to the States, then after 21 years of dedicated service he retired in August 1968 with the rank of first sergeant. Among his awards was the Silver Star and Purple Heart medals.

From 1968-90 he was employed by the Burlington County Bridge Commission and retired as superintendent of toll. George is presently residing in Willingboro, NJ with his wife Jean. He remains active in his community and is a member of DAV, MOPH, JVA, CIB, NCOA, Silver Star Assn., NE Infantry Regiment Assn., Willingboro, NJ, and the Buffalo Soldiers. He is also the Willingboro Township photographer. He is the father of two daughters and two sons.

STEPHEN J. BUTKO, born May 25, 1925 in Glassmere, PA, now known as East Deer Township. Entered U.S. Army Aug. 28, 1943 and took training with the 42nd (Rainbow) Inf. Div. at Camp Gruber, OK from September 1943 to May 1944 where he was trained as a light machine gunner.

He was sent overseas the latter part of June 1944 to the European Theater of Operations as a replacement and assigned to the 8th Inf. Div. Although his first assignment was part of a detachment of troops to guard a colonel who was the 28th Regimental Commander. Subsequently he was assigned to Co. E as a machine gunner and saw action in the campaigns of Normandy, Northern France and the Rhineland. He recalls the areas of Brest, Crozon Peninsula, Rennes all in France and into Luxembourg. After a short stay in Luxembourg, he was sent to Germany into the Hürtgen Forest (The Bloody Forest) which was described as one of the bloodiest and for the U.S. Army most disastrous campaigns of WWII.

After the Hürtgen Campaign, his unit was relocated to the city of Duren, Germany on the Roer River. On Feb. 23, 1945 he crossed the Roer River at Niederau (an outskirt of Duren) where his best buddy was killed. A series of leap frogging battles took him to the outskirts of Cologne on the Rhine River. It was here that he was evacuated to several hospitals in Paris and England. Ultimately he was returned to the zone of the interior (United States) and subsequently received a medical discharge with disability.

Memorable Experience: While awaiting the Roer River crossing in the Duren, Germany area, his machine gun section sergeant was evacuated to a hospital. Both his platoon leader and company commander told him he was going to be the new machine gun section sergeant. He declined the promotion giving his reasons to the two officers. He suggested they give the promotion to his assistant gunner who was with him since July 1944. Two days later his buddy was killed during the river crossing. He has not forgotten this incident and to this day he blames himself for him getting killed, because he did not accept the promotion. This has been bothering him for 58 years and will continue so.

AWARDS include CIB, Bronze Star, Good Conduct Medal, American Campaign EAME Campaign w/3 campaign stars and WWII Victory Medal. He was discharged July 21, 1945 from Fort Story Convalescent Hospital in Fort Story, VA with the rank private first class.

Married his Marie on June 26, 1948 on her 19th Birthday. She died Jan. 21, 1981 after 32 years of a happy marriage. Their first child Stephen died May 29, 1950 at the age of 2 days; daughter Andrea is married and she and her husband have a son named James; son David is married and he and his wife have two daughters and one grandson, Sherie, Laura and Kaleb.

As a civilian he worked for PPG Industries for over 45 years before retiring in 1991. He was a production supervisor responsible for 150 hourly employees and five salaried foremen. Presently, he is involved with the Veterans of Foreign Wars and family interests.

LLOYD W. BUTLER, born in Gibson County, TN and reared there in the Brazil Community. In 1958 at age 12, his family moved to El Monte, CA. After graduation from Arryo High School, he was drafted in the U.S. Army. Basic training and AIT were completed at Fort Ord, CA in 1966 and Fort Hood, TX was his first duty station.

In late 1966 orders arrived to go to Vietnam. Butler served with the 2nd Bn. of the 7th U.S. Cav. Regt. "Garry Owen." He was a part of the 1st Cav. Div. Air Mobile during his year long tour.

In January 1968, Butler returned to Fort Lewis, WA, where he was discharged with the rank of sergeant E-5. Many friendships were made while serving his country. Butler enjoys talking with old buddies and meeting them at the 1st Cavalry reunions.

He lived many years in California, until he returned to Tennessee in 1990. Butler is a retired farmer/truck driver. Presently, Lloyd and his wife, Charlotte, live on a farm in rural west Tennessee where they raise horses and mules. They are active in the Brazil United Methodist Church and Butler is a member of the Trenton, TN Masonic Lodge. Much of their time is spent in California visiting their two sons and grandchildren.

FRANK L. CAMPANARO, born June 20, 1923 in Yonkers, NY. Inducted in the service Jan. 15, 1943 and served with the 38th Inf. Div., 152nd Inf., Co. E. After 13 weeks basic training at Camp Croft, SC, he was shipped to Camp Livingston, LA and participated in action in New Guinea, Leyte and Luzon.

His memorable experience was having the mission of cracking this impregnable fortress zig-zag pass that led to Bataan. He played possum while being fired at in a fox hole. He had red clay on his helmet and his comrade said they got Campanaro and the other comrade killed the Japanese soldier who was shooting at him from the tree with his Bar. After 19 days of bloody fighting, Bataan was liberated.

Discharged Nov. 16, 1945, his awards include the Combat Infantry Badge, Asiatic-Pacific Campaign Medal w/3 Bronze Stars, Philippine Liberation Ribbon and the Republic of the Philippines Presidential Unit Citation Badge.

Married May 20, 1950 and has a daughter, son and five grandchildren. He's a member of Combat Infantry Assn. HQ Co., Shrub Oak, NY. He's a member of American Legion and life member of VFW. Retired, he joined Cortlandt Senior Citizens Club.

JOHN T. CAMPBELL, born in Providence, RI. He re-enlisted in the Army March 17, 1943 and left Fort Devens and went to Fort Jackson, where he joined the 106th Inf. Div., 1st Bn., Co. C, 424th Regt. After basic training at Fort Jackson, he went to Tennessee for advanced training, then to Camp Atterbury, IN.

Overseas he participated in the Battle of the Bulge where he was wounded and taken prisoner by the Germans.

Discharged with the rank of staff sergeant on Nov. 1, 1945. His awards include the Purple Heart, Combat Infantryman's Badge, Bronze Star, POW Medal, Good Conduct Medal, WWII Victory Medal, American Campaign Medal, EAME Campaign Medal w/2 stars and the Belgium Fourragere.

John and Rita were married July 19, 1947. They have six sons, three daughters, 21 grandchildren and three great-grandchildren.

After 30 years, he retired from the U.S. Postal Department.

JOSEPH T. CAPONE, born April 21, 1923. Enlisted in the U.S. Army Feb. 15, 1943 and assigned to Co. E, 415th Inf. Regt., 104th "Timberwolf" Div.

Military locations were at Fort George Meade, MD; Fort Jackson, SC; Camp Gordon, GA; The Citadel, Charleston, SC; University of Illinois, Champaign, IL; Fort Sheridan, IL; Camp Granite, Indio, CA; Camp Carson, CO; Camp Kilmer, NJ; ETO; Stark General Hospital, Charleston, SC and Butner General Hospital, Durham, NC. He participated in battles in Northern France, Ardennes, Rhineland and Central Europe.

Memorable Experiences: being rifleman and scout in combat in France, Belgium, Holland and Germany. His most traumatic experience was the Roer River crossing "Operation Grenade."

Discharged Nov. 5, 1945, Butner General Hospital, Durham, NC. His awards include the Combat Infantry Badge, ETO w/4 Battle Stars, Bronze Star for Valor, Purple Heart, Presidential Distinguished Unit Citation, Good Conduct Medal, American Theater of Operation Medal, WWII Victory Medal and eight division foreign awards.

Joseph and Rosemarie have been married since 1951 and they have four sons, four daughters, 23 grandchildren and three great-grandchildren. For 35 years he was a high school business teacher, Pittsburgh Board of Public Education. He is member of VFW, DAV,

American Legion, Order of Purple Heart, Combat Infantryman Assn. and was inducted in 1980 to World Drum Corps Hall of Fame.

ANGELO L. CARBONE, born Jan. 1, 1926 in Italy. Enlisted in the service Feb. 23, 1944 and served in the Army Infantry as a machine gunner in the 65th Div. Stationed at Camp Upton, NY; Camp Blanding, FL, Camp Shelby, MS and Camp Shanks, NY.

With the 65th Inf. Div., Patton's Third Army, he participated in missions in France, Belgium, Germany, Austria, Rhineland and Central Europe.

Memorable experience was when E Co., 260th Regt., 65th Inf. Div. started crossing the Danube River to Austria in rubber rafts when all hell broke loose and they were hit by machine gun fire and mortar shells, and losing a few men.

Awards include the CIB, Bronze Star Medal, two Battle Stars for Rhineland and Central Europe, WWII Victory Medal, Good Conduct Medal, Occupation of Germany Medal, Expert Infantrymen's Badge. He was discharged May 9, 1946 with the rank private first class.

On July 18, 1948 he married Julia Gulino and they have three sons, one daughter and 10 grandchildren. Retired with the rank of lieutenant from New York City Fire Department. He is commander of VFW Post 1688.

LARRY J. CARBONE, born June 26, 1923, Worcester, MA. Joined the U.S. Army March 15, 1942, trained at Camp Polk, LA and fought in action at Rhineland, Ardennes and Central Europe. He was assigned to the 8th Armd. Div., A Co. 7th Inf. Bn. and was wounded at Nening, Germany in February 1945.

His memorable experience was knocking out a German "Tiger Tank" with a bazooka.

Discharged Jan. 9, 1946 with the rank of staff sergeant. His awards include the Bronze, Star, Purple Heart, Presidential Unit Citation, American Campaign, EAME Campaign Medal, WWII Victory Medal, Army of Occupation Medal w/German Clasp, Combat Infantry Badge, Good Conduct Medal and was recommended for the Silver Star.

He was married 52 years when his wife passed away in 1993. The owner of a import, export and antique business until he retired in 2001. He now travels with his son, grandkids and great-grandkids.

CIRO E. "GENE" CERRA, born Aug. 16, 1924 in Allston, MA. Enlisted in the Army in April 1943 and started in 571st AAA as a gunner, then transferred to the 97th Inf. HQ Btry. 303rd, May 30, 1944, and trained in communications to be a radio operator.

His military locations were Fort Devens, MA; Fort Eustis, VA; Camp Edwards, MA; Camp Campbell, KY; Fort Leonard Wood, MO; Camp San Luis Obispo, CA; Camp Callan, CA; Camp Pendleton, CA; and Camp Cooke, CA.

Memorable Experiences: landing in Le Havre, France and his first sight of war was going through Aachen (there wasn't any town left); Dusseldorf where he first saw death - there were still Germans lying along the roadside when he entered the city after the battle; the Rhur Pocket; crossing the Sieg River; being in Pisen when the war ended.

Discharged in March 1946 with the rank of Tech 4. His awards include the Good Conduct Medal, WWII Victory Medal, American Campaign Medal, EAME Campaign Medal, Combat Infantry Medal and three Battle Stars.

Spent most of his life in the construction field and owned Gene's Construction Co., G.R.7 Realty and was a notary public. He moved to Florida in 1991 and worked until May 2003. His wife of 49 years still works five days a week. They had eight children (1 deceased), 25 grandchildren and three great-grandchildren.

WILLIAM F. CHARBONEAU, born Oct. 12, 1925, Johnston, RI. He served in the 89th Inf. Div. as a rifleman. His military locations were at Fort Eustis, VA; Camp Robinson, AR; Camp Butner, NC and saw action in Rhineland and Central Europe.

Memorable experiences include Rhine crossing and the liberation of Nazi Concentration at Ohrdruf, Germany (it was then they knew why we were fighting the war).

Discharged April 20, 1946 as tech 5. His awards include the Combat Infantry Badge, Bronze Star Medal and Purple Heart.

Married to Nancy for 50 plus years, they have three children, seven grandchildren and five great-grandchildren. William taught high school and was an accountant. He is now retired with both legs amputated.

SYLVIO P. CIUMMO, born Oct. 14, 1924 in West Warwick, RI. He enlisted in the service on May 26, 1943. He was a member of the U.S. Army's 81st Mortar, D Co., 169th Inf., 43rd Div. He was stationed at New Caledonia, Guadalcanal, New Zealand, Aitape, New Guinea, Luzon, Philippine Islands, Camp Wheeler, GA and Fort Ord, CA. He fought in battles at Driniumor River, Aitape, New Guinea, Lingayan Gulf, Luzon and the Philippine Islands.

He received the Asiatic-Pacific Campaign Medal

w/Arrowhead and two Battle Stars, Good Conduct, WWII Victory Medal, Presidential Unit Emblem, CIB, Bronze Star and the Philippine Liberation Ribbon. He was discharged on Dec. 8, 1945 with the rank of private first class.

Memorable Experiences: in January 1944, going to Guadalcanal from New Caledonia on the *Antique* merchant ship with 200 replacements for the 43rd Div. and they were hit by a typhoon. He also remembers the beachhead at Lingayan Gulf on Jan. 9, 1945 and the night of Jan. 17, 1945, when the Japanese attacked D Co., 169th Inf. at the road block at Hwy. 3, Palacpalac.

SHELBY T. CLARK SR., born Feb. 25, 1921 in Washington, PA. He graduated Madonna Catholic High School, Cincinnati, OH in 1938, enlisted in the Army Sept. 22, 1939 at Fort Dix, NJ with basic training at Fort Benning, GA.

Served in WWII in North Africa, Sicily, Italy and Southwest Pacific, 1942-47 with 10th Horse Cav. Regt., 366th Inf. Regt., 370th Inf. Regt. of 92nd Inf. Buffalo Div.; 555th Abn. Inf. Bn., Fort Bragg, 1947-48; 505th AIR, 1948-50; in Korea 1950-53 with 24th Inf. Regt. and 35th Inf. Regt. of 25th Inf. Div.; and in Vietnam 1962-64 as Army military advisor for Vietnam army airborne rangers.

Awards include the Good Conduct Medal (6th awd.), Unit Citation, American Theater, American Defense, WWII Victory Medal, Army Occupation WWII, Berlin Airlift, Meritorious Unit Commendation, ROK Presidential Citation, UN National Defense Service, Philippine Liberation, Independence and Philippine Presidential Citation Ribbons, Purple Heart, Combat Infantry Badge (3rd awd.), EAME Ribbon w/ 4 BBS, Asiatic-Pacific Ribbon w/2 BBS, Army Master Parachutist Badge, Korean Service Ribbon w/3 BBS, Vietnam Service Ribbon w/2 BBS, Vietnam Presidential Unit Citation and RVN Civil Actions Unit Citations.

Retired after 25 years at rank of SGM, but still active in community. He is national president of 92nd Inf. Buffalo Div. WWI and WWII Assns. He, wife Deborah, and son Shelby Jr., reside in Riverhead, Long Island, NY.

WILLIAM EDWARD CLARK, born Dec. 24, 1917. Enlisted in the Army in September 1942, served first in Army Air Corps and later assigned to railway battalion.

Arrived European Theater of Operations May 15, 1944. During Battle of Bulge transferred to Corp of Engineers. Served with Construction Battalion and Engineer Combat Battalion.

Returned to States Dec. 30, 1945 and released to Enlisted Reserve Corps Jan. 6, 1946 with the rank of sergeant. Recalled to active duty Oct. 30, 1950 and arrived in Korea where he was assigned to 24th Inf. Div. 19th Regt., L Co. as squad leader 1st Squad 3rd Plt.

Decorations include CIB, Korean service Medal, 3 Bronze Stars, American Defense Medal, UN Service Medal, ROK War Service Medal and Appreciation Certificate for Service - Cold War.

Returned to States in September 1951, assigned ERC Inactive, and discharged Aug. 31, 1952.

William married Berenice on March 6, 1939. Their son John was born on their anniversary, March 6, 1942. William had a career as insurance sales executive from 1952 until retirement Jan. 2, 1982.

JAMES R. CLAYPOTE, born Oct. 20, 1924. Enlisted in Army in March 1943, assigned to 8th Armd. Div. then on to 79th Inf. Div., Co. L, 313th Regt. as light machine gunner.

He participated in Normandy invasion, Utah Beach, Northern France, Rhineland and Central Europe. He will never forget the Normandy invasion and hedge row fighting.

Discharged Dec. 18, 1945 with the rank of corporal. His awards include the Combat Infantry Badge, Purple Heart, and Bronze Star.

James and his wife have two married daughters, four grandchildren and one great-grandson. A locomotive engineer, he worked 40 years for AT&SF Railroad. He's active in church, does some travel and fishing.

CLARENCE A. "BUD" COLLETTE, born Nov. 25, 1929, Los Angeles, CA. Drafted into the Army in January 1951 with basic training at Fort Ord, CA. He served 11 months in Korea, 1951-52 with the 5th RCT, 24th Inf. Div. Wounded and taken to a MASH unit, then air evacuated to another field hospital for surgery. After two weeks there he was taken by hospital train to Pusan, where he stayed for over a month in the Swedish Hospital.

With a wobbly knee he volunteered to go back to the infantry. His regiment was in a reserve position and he knew he would go home soon after he got back. He arrived back in California in May 1952, had his leave and was assigned to Camp Irwin, near Death Valley, CA. He was there from July to his discharge in October 1952, then served in the National Guard as the first sergeant of an infantry battalion headquarters company for three years.

Married Jean M. McDonald in January 1953 and they have two grown children and two grandsons. He retired after 33 years with Pacific Telephone Co. He's a member of MOPH, DAV and VFW. Most honored military decoration is the Combat Infantry Badge.

ARNON W. COOL, born in Webster Springs, WV. Left school to join the Army, enlisting in November 1950. Basic training was at Fort Knox, KY, Infantry and Airborne School at Fort Benning, GA. He joined the 187th Abn. Regimental Combat Team (ARCT) in Korea and was wounded during combat operations at Munsan-ni, South Korea, March 23, 1951. Volunteered for Special Forces.

Retired April 1, 1973, with the rank of master sergeant (E-8). Worked in law enforcement in Kansas

and Ohio. Arnon is a direct descendant of Walter Cool, first Sheriff of Webster County, VA (WV) 1860-64. Currently resides with wife Ann, in Akron, OH. He is a life member of the Military Order of Purple Heart, VFW, American Legion, DAV, Korean War Veterans Association, Special Forces Association, Combat Infantryman Association, The Retired Enlisted Association and the 187th Rakkasans (Buckeye Chapter) Association, where he is the president and an active member.

HARVEY COOPER, born in Miami, FL and attended Mays High School and Florida A&M University. He enlisted in the Army in October 1963, and was assigned to the 2nd Div. in Fort Benning, GA.

He went to Vietnam with the First Cav. Div. and participated in the Battle of Ia Drang, Bong Son, Happy Valley and many more. The Purple Heart, Air Medal and Army Commendation Medal were awarded to him.

In August 1966, he went back to live in Miami. There, he married Geneva and had one daughter name Karen, and she had a son name Joshua.

He played minor league baseball with the San Diego Padres, and later he graduated from Florida International University and Nova University. He is a teacher and a coach at Miami's Public Schools.

The First Cavalry Association, Combat Infantry Association and Vietnam Veteran Association are his military organization.

AUSTIN H COX SR., born Dec. 15, 1919, Crisfield, MD. Enlisted in MDNG Aug. 10, 1938. Served in Army 115th Inf. Regt. Co. L, 29th Div., Weapons Platoon. Stationed at Fort Meade, MD. Fort Dix, NJ, Tidworth and Bodmin, <u>England</u>.

Federalized U.S. Army 1940 and division sent to England in 1941 where they trained for D-Day until 1944. They were only NG division to land on Omaha Beach on June 6, 1944.

Memorable experiences include from the beach to the Elbe where they met the Russian troops; Battle of St. Lo; Battle of Normandy; Submarine Pens and U-boats; Wursburg, Germany; being wounded; Holland; Hürtgen Forest; Leige, Belgium; 50th anniversary of D-day; beach and cemetery at St. Lo.

Awards include the CIB, Purple Heart, Bronze Star, Presidential Citation, medals from France, four

Battle Stars and Spearhead. Discharged Aug. 28. 1945 and re-enlisted in the National Guard. Serving a total of 30 years, he retired as master sergeant.

Married his lovely wife Jeanne in 1943, London, England. They have six children and 12 grandchildren. They recently celebrated their 55th wedding anniversary. A self-employed mechanical contractor, he is now retired and his son is in charge. He enjoys playing golf, traveling, fishing and his family.

RUSSELL CUMMINS, born in Dodge City, KS. He joined the USAAFR in high school and upon graduation he entered service in 1944 with cadet training. In October 1945 came an early discharge, followed by University of Nebraska and Army ROTC.

Entered service in June 1951 and served in Korea in 1952 for five months as rifle platoon leader, K Co., 223rd Inf. in the Punch Bowl area and five months as Defense Platoon leader, 40th Div., HQ Co. He was discharged in April 1954 as first lieutenant.

Married Jacqueline Schmitz in 1956 in Omaha and they reared two daughters and a son. He is now retired in Fort Myers, FL.

GENE E. DANIELS, born July 20, 1949 in Maryville, MO. He entered the U.S. Army Oct. 26, 1967 and served as squad leader instructor with the 1st Inf. Div., 6th Army, 3rd Inf. Div. Military locations/stations included basic training at Fort Ord, CA; advanced infantry training, Fort Gordon, GA; 1st Inf. Div. Vietnam infantry training, NCO Fort Lewis, WA; and 3rd Infantry Div., Germany. He was discharged July 27, 1970 with the rank of staff sergeant.

Gene participated in the TET Offensive, TET Counter Offensive, Battle of An Loc, Operation Toan Thang, Battle of FSB Julie and Battle of Trapezoid IV.

Memorable experiences: FSB Victor exploding; Song Be Mountain where he was wounded the first time; KIA MG Keith L. Ware, 1st Div. commander, near Loc Ninh on Sept. 13, 1968; and battles in Iron Triangle, Black Virgin Mountain and Parrots Beak (where he was wounded the second time).

He was awarded the Combat Infantry Badge, Purple, Heart, American Campaign Medal, Air Medal, Vietnamese Cross of Gallantry and Vietnam Service Medal.

Gene is married to Rita and has one daughter, Michelle; one son, Scott; and five grandchildren. Civilian employment was as a telephone technician. He is currently retired and resides in Bedford, IA.

CHARLES H. DELLANGELO, born July 4, 1920 in Diorite, MI. He entered the U.S. Army Aug. 12, 1943 and served with the 90th Div. Military locations/stations included Normandy, Northern France, Ardennes and Rhineland. He was discharged Dec. 20, 1945 with rank of corporal.

He participated in battles at Normandy, Ardennes,

Paris and some in Germany. Memorable experiences: Landing on Normandy, Utah Beach; being on Top Hill 122, surrounded by Germans.

Awarded the EAME Theater Ribbon w/4 Bronze Stars, Purple Heart, WWII Victory Medal and Bronze Arrowhead.

Charles is married to Lucille (56 years) and has two children, Amy Marie and Gregory, three grandchildren and six great-grandchildren. He spent 38 years with Inland Steel Co. He is now retired and enjoying life and his family (as well as his camp) and reading. He resides in Iron River, MI.

JOSEPH DE LUCA JR., born Sept. 16, 1925 in Wooster, OH. Enlisted in the Army Inf. October 1943. Stationed at Fort Hayes, OH; Fort McClellan, AL; Fort Meade, MD; Camp Howze, TX where he joined Co. C, 411th Regt., 103rd Div.; and the ETO.

Memorable experiences include "walking and fighting the entire way through France, Germany and Austria." He remembers Thanksgiving Day, 1944, when meals didn't catch up to company and he shared a frozen head of cabbage from a Frenchman's garden with another fella.

Awards include the Combat Infantryman Badge, Bronze Star, ETO Medal, Good Conduct Medal, Victory Medal and Army of Occupation Medal. He achieved rank of corporal.

Following the war, he stayed in Germany (Heidelberg) with Co. C, 504th Bn. as street sergeant, MPs. During this time he was selected to serve on Gen. George Patton's Honor Guard.

Returned home to Wooster, OH in June 1946. Married 45 years to Janis De Luca; no children.

Two memorable experiences since the war: Taking a tour of their ETO battle sites, military cemeteries, etc. with 60 of his 103rd comrades in July 1992. Also memorable was attending 103rd, Co. C reunion in Branson, MO, June 1, 1994 where he met 17 men from his company that he hadn't seen for 50 years (one of them, Weber Young, was the fella he had shared the frozen head of cabbage with).

LEONARD DELUCA, born July 27, 1924 in Chicago, IL. He entered the CCC July 5, 1939 and entered the Army in 1942 and served with the 10th Mtn. Div.. Military locations/stations include Camp Robinson, Fort Jackson, SC; Camp Hale, CO; Rome; Arno; and Northern Apennines. He was wounded in the Mt. Belveder action. He was discharged Nov. 26, 1945 with rank of technical sergeant, platoon sergeant.

Memorable experiences: The Battle of Mt. Belveder was one of the toughest, coldest battles ever. The mountain was dubbed "Nite Climb" because it was mostly climbed at night, never during the day. If the moon came out while climbing, we hid in the cracks and crevices until the clouds covered the moon. From that battle on to Mt. Castel Dianno, then on to Cannoli.

he was wounded in March 1945. After some months in the hospital, he was transferred into a non-combat unit!

Shipped out to Livorno, Italy he was assigned to CO 2691, T/S/R Regt. (Technical Supervisional Regt.) This was a stopping point to ship the POWs back to their homes. Most of them were Italians, French, Germans and a few Russians. The compound was on a bombed out air field. They built the camp with the aid of all the POWs. There was a mess hall, barber shop, dental clinic and a first aid station. They had gotten the dental chair and the barber chair out of a shot-down bomber.

Besides himself, there was a sergeant from Ohio and a second lieutenant from the Italian infantry. The lieutenant's name was Nando Bondioli. There was no barbed wire while they were in command, but later on, the Russians took over and the first thing they did was to put up barbed wire and had guards patrolling the area.

This camp had a capacity of 350 POWs, but more and more prisoners came in. Soon, they could not handle all of them. The POWs had no place to return to, no home, not knowing if their families were alive. But, in CO 2691, they had three meals a day, clean clothing and almost all of their needs were met. In talking to Lt. Bondioli and Sgt. Nick, a decision was made to make them leave. In the morning, Lt. Bondioli reported for roll call dressed in full parade uniform–saber, plumes—he looked like a movie star! The lieutenant read 35 names and asked each of them to step forward and to pack up whatever they owned and to report to Sgt. DeLuca. These POWs were all Italian men. He told them that tomorrow at 7:00 a.m., they were to board trucks and would be sent to a new camp and P.O.E. to help fight the Japanese. By God, on the next roll call we had, the called POW roll call was short 35 men. The Japan war was not their war. We followed this procedure every time the camp was overpopulated. Being captured by the Americans was a good deal. A few weeks later at reveille, Sgt. Nick from Ohio came up to me and said, "Sgt. DeLuca, do you know a Sgt. DeLuca?" he answered, "Yes, I have a brother, Fred DeLuca, who was captured and wounded in Bastogne. But the last time I saw him was three years ago in Camp Robinson, AR. He was in the 101st Abn. Why?" Sgt. Nick handed me a new sheet with the names of new Italian and German prisoners, and on the first list was Sgt. DeLuca, Fred, my brother. Fred was on his way home. Well, he can't tell you the feelings we had, crying, hugging and kissing. Our dad always said never be ashamed to kiss your brother or your dad.

On Christmas Eve, 1945, my brother, Fred, picked me up at TC R.R. Station in Chicago. He did not tell our mom or dad that he was going to pick up. They thought he was still in Europe. Well, again he can't describe the crying, hugging and kissing among all of my family members. It was the best Christmas he had to this day.

He was awarded the Purple Heart, Bronze Star, Good Conduct Medal and Combat Infantryman Badge.

Leonard's wife, Joyce Marie, is deceased. He has three children: Pete, Toni and Dino; eight grandchildren; and two great-grandchildren. Civilian employment as a steeple Jack, barber, hair dresser and teacher. He currently resides in Matteson, IL and is a barber.

DANTE C. "DAN" DE MIO, born Oct. 1, 1928, in Italy of U.S. parents. The family returned to the U.S. in 1938 and settled in New Haven, CT. He graduated from Hillhouse High School. He received a BSE in civil engineering from the University of Connecticut and an MSE in civil engineering from the University of Michigan. After a short period of working for the Navy on submarine design and construction, he was ordered to active duty from the Army Reserve in October 1953. He completed basic training at Fort Dix,

NJ and was assigned to the 86th Engr. Constr. Bn. In June 1955, he was commissioned a 2nd lieutenant from OCS. Subsequent assignments included Fort Bliss, TX; USAEUR and 7th Army, Germany; Fort Sill, OK; WSMR, NM. He served in Vietnam as an infantry adviser to ARVN infantry units in Binh Dinh Province for 13 months, 1965-66. During this time he participated with the 1st Air Cav. Div. in Operations Masher/White Wing, Crazy Horse, Washington Irving, Thayer I, II. He also participated in several helicopter assaults and survived several ambushes. Further assignments included NORAD, CO; Army Command and General Staff College (Gen. Colin Powell was his classmate); 3rd Corps, Fort Hood, TX; Hq. 8th Army and 2nd Div., Korea, 1972-73. He retired at Fort Carson, CO, as a lieutenant colonel in July 1976.

Following retirement, he taught engineering at Colorado Tech for two years. Then, employed as a civil engineer by the Air Force, he managed the design and construction of satellite tracking stations worldwide. He retired from the Air Force in July 1997.

He married Edie De Mio in August 1969. They have three sons: Brooks, Brian and Andrew. Brooks and Brian served a hitch in the Marines. Brian switched to the Coast Guard and is a physician assistant (PA) and is stationed on Kodiak Island, AK. Dan plays golf, travels, visits with his grandchildren. He belongs to the VFW, DAV, CIA and is a registered professional engineer (PE). He and Edie currently reside in Colorado Springs, CO.

His awards/medals include Legion of Merit, Meritorious Service Medal w/1 OLC, Air Medal, Joint Service Commendation Medal, Army Commendation Medal w/1 OLC, Air Force Outstanding Unit Ribbon, Good Conduct Medal, National Defense Medal w/1 OLC, Armed Forces Expeditionary Medal, Vietnam Service Medal w/3 Bronze Stars, Armed Forces Reserve Medal, Vietnam Campaign Medal w/60 device, Vietnam Cross of Gallantry w/Silver Star, Vietnam Gallantry Cross Unit w/palm, two Overseas Bars, Combat Infantryman Badge and Parachutist Badge.

CARL DESENDORF, born Feb. 29, 1920 in Sterling, CO. Attended schools in Sterling, a musician and farming. In 1940 moved to Woodland, CA. In 1942 was drafted into the U.S. Army. Fourteen weeks of training at Sheppard Field, TX. Shipped to Moody Field in 1943. Was at Moody for two years then was shipped to Germany by way of France. In Germany with the 71st Div., 14th Inf., 3rd Plt. made sergeant. Was a scout all the way to Linz Austria. Then sent to Günzburg Germany for occupation. Transferred to the Transportation Corps for six months then back to Günzburg. He is now a commander in the Legion plus working as maintenance.

Memorable experiences: Daily battles taking in prisoners. Being a scout. Getting shot at every day. A walking target.

He was awarded the American Campaign Medal, WWII Victory Medal, Good Conduct Medal and EAME Campaign Medal. Discharged in March 1946.

In Georgia he married his wife who was a WAC. He has one daughter. He is currently retired and resides in Woodland, CA.

BILL DILLON, born June 3, 1930 in Brooklyn, NY. Drafted into the service in 1951 and served with 3rd Inf. Div. and 1st Cav. Div. Military locations/stations included Korea and Koje Island. They had to round up 40,000 North Korean POWs at Koje and put them back into their compound. He participated in battles at Hill 355, Iron Triangle, Big Nori and Little Nori. Discharged in 1953 with rank of corporal.

Memorable experiences: Bill standing in picture, Joe O'Conner behind an 81mm mortar. Picture taken three days before Joe was KIA by a North Korean tank. They knew each other as kids in Brooklyn 1940s. They never got along as kids but became good friends in the Army.

He was awarded the Korean Service Medal w/4 Bronze Stars, Purple Heart, Combat Infantryman Badge, New York Conspicuous Service Cross, National Defense Medal and United Nations Medal.

He and his wife, June, married two weeks before he shipped out to Korea in January 1952. They had four children: Deborah, Patricia, Thomas and Michael (died at birth). Civilian employment as a fire safety inspector in a nuclear power plant. He is now retired and volunteers at six libraries teaching children chess (690 kids in four years). Bill currently resides in Lancaster, PA.

JOHN A. DOBBINS, born Nov. 16, 1924 in Akron, OH. Inducted July 6, 1944 at Fort McClellan, AL trained in heavy weapons and began active duty Jan. 1, 1945.

Departed Port of New York on the *HMS Queen Mary* landed Glasgow, Scotland Jan. 5, 1945. Entered the Battle of the Bulge in Belgium with the 84th Inf. Div., 333rd Inf. Regt., 1st Bn., Co. A, 4th Wpns. Plt. Received battlefield promotion from private first class to sergeant.

Earned three Battle Stars for Ardennes, Central Europe and Rhineland campaigns. Discharged while in Germany: re-enlisted in the Regular Army and was assigned to the 115th AAA Gun Bn., Btry. B as Railway Security Police. Discharged at Fort Dix, NJ.

Retired from the Bricklayers Union in 1985 and resides in North Canton, OH. His wife is now deceased. He has two sons and three grandchildren.

STEVEN F. DONARSKI, Colonel, born in Green Bay, WI, graduated from St. Norbert College in 1951 and was awarded a regular Army commission as a second lieutenant of infantry. He was the first graduate so honored. He served for 36 years in the regular and re-

serve forces of the U.S. Army. He retired in 1987 with the rank of colonel.

He earned his Combat Infantryman Badge in the Korean War serving as a company commander with the 17th Inf. Regt. He participated in action on Pork Chop Hill, Old Baldy, White Horse Mountain and T-Bone Hill. He has served overseas in Japan, Korea and Germany. Among his awards and decorations are the Combat Infantryman Badge, Legion of Merit, Bronze Star w/V, Purple Heart, Meritorious Service w/3 OLCs, Army Commendation, Army Achievement, Republic of Korea Presidential Citation and the U.S. Presidential Unit Citation.

He earned an advanced degree in education from University of Wisconsin-Green Bay. He also is a graduate of the U.S. Army's Advanced Schools in infantry, chemical, transportation and civil affairs. He has graduated from the U.S. Command and General Staff College and the Industrial College of the Armed Forces.

Married to the former Jacqueline M. Erdmann with five grown children. He was president of Indian Springs Land Company and the vice president/secretary of Fedon and Don, Inc. He is now retired.

JAMES E. DORETY, born in Philadelphia, PA April 24, 1925. Enlisted in Army April 22, 1943 and sent to Camp Shelby, MS to 69th Inf. Div., 271st Inf. Regt., Co. G in May 1943.

Sent overseas in May 1944 as infantry replacement and arrived in England May 24, 1944. Sent to Normandy, France June 10, 1944 and joined 79th Inf. Div., 313th Inf. Regt., Co. F as ammunition bearer, 30 cal. light machine gun. He was in combat until Oct. 21, 1944 when wounded and sent to 46th General Hospital. Recovered from wounds and spent remainder of war with 99th General Hospital.

Discharged Dec. 9, 1945, Indiantown Gap, PA. Awards and decorations include Combat Infantry Badge and Bronze Star Medal. Highest rank was private first class.

Married 42 years to Alice; they have a daughter, Maureen. Employed 39 years with Honeywell, Inc., Fort Washington, PA as electronic assembler.

CHARLES W. DOUGHERTY, born June 30, 1945 in Joliet, IL. Enlisted in the U.S. Army Sept. 26, 1966 and served with the 1st Air Cav. Div., 7th Cav. Regt. He served in Vietnam with B Co., 1st Bn., 7th Cav., 1st Air Cav. Military locations, stations included I Corp., II Corp. to Demilitarized Zone. Participated in battles at Bong Son, An Lun, Frag Hill, Tamry, Hue, Tet 68 and lots more.

He was awarded three Vietnam Medals and Presidential certificates, three Purple Hearts, Army Commendation, Bronze Star, Combat Infantry Badge, Good Conduct, Air Medal, VCB, Presidential Unit Citation, VG and MUA medals.

He and his wife, Sandra currently reside in Port-

land, OR. He has two daughters, Lariss and Janna. Civilian employment in finance. He is 100% disabled (service related).

JOHN F. "JACK" DOYLE, born in Baltimore, MD on June 16, 1926. He reached his 18th birthday in 1944 and was drafted into the Army in October of that year. Shortly thereafter he reached Camp Croft, SC where he had 15 weeks of intensive infantry training. He then went to Camp Shanks, NY and shipped out on the HMS *Aquatania*. They were told this rusty old bucket was the third largest ship in the British Navy. Landed in Glasgow, Scotland and then by train to Southampton and ferryboat to Le Havre, France. Trucked up to the front line somewhere past Metz and was assigned to Co. C, 376th Inf. Regt., 94th Inf. Div. on or about March 1, 1945. On March 22, while making a frontal assault on entrenched Krauts, Jack was seriously wounded by shrapnel from friendly fire. The attack was out of Oggersheim making their way to Ludwigshafen. Never got to see the Rhine River. Spent the next nine months in various Army hospitals.

Awards include the ETO Medal w/2 Battle Stars and the WWII Victory Medal. Also a Purple Heart, a Bronze Star Medal and the coveted Combat Infantry Badge. He was discharged on Dec. 3, 1945 with the rank of private first class.

Jack was married in 1950 to Patricia and has two children, Tim and Val. As of this writing he has been happily married for 53 years. He worked for the Baltimore County Government as a construction inspector until his early retirement in 1976, with a heart condition. This ailment combined with his 100% service connected disability prevented him from continuing work. He is a life member of the DAV and the 94th Inf. Div. Assn. and also a member of the Combat Infantry Assn. Under another heading you may want to read *The Soldiers Had Angels*, a story told to Valerie about Jack's last day in combat.

GILBERT R. ESQUER, right after high school graduation in June 1941, he entered the Army in January 1942 and was sent to Camp Robinson, AR for basic training. Then he was shipped to Fort Mead, MD and assigned to the 76th Mtn. Inf. Then trucked to A.P. Hill, VA, where he underwent "Jungle Warfare" training along the Mississippi swamps and bayous between May and September in temperatures of 100 and 130 degrees Fahrenheit.

Completing the training they were shipped to Sparta, WI, joining the 2nd Ranger Bn. for sub-zero weather training, mountain climbing, ski training living in sub-zero weather conditions and parachute training, etc.

Beginning in September to April 1942, the division began maneuvers from Ironwood City to Sault Ste. Marie, in upper Michigan where the Great Lakes, Superior, Michigan and Huron join. The weather averages 60 to 70 degrees below freezing with a chill factor blowing off the Great Lakes.

After completion of this training he boarded a train to Fort Shanks, NJ to ship out in one of the largest convoys to ever sail out of the USA prior to the Normandy Invasion, according to the *Stars and Strips* Army newspaper. Their destination was Anzio, but about 1,000 miles out they called on the bullhorn that the people who were going to Anzio to go topside in the vicinity of the bow of the ship. Whereupon an Army colonel called them to attention, then told them that the original mission to jump behind Mt. Cassino was cancelled. At this point they all shouted a big cheer. Then he said that their regiment was to be divided between the 504th Parachute Inf. Regt. which he was assigned to originally, and the other half to the 325th Glider Inf. Regt. Pursuant to Normandy he was reassigned to Co. B, 1st Bn., 325th GIF, 82nd Abn. Div. They were loaded onto trucks then trucked to the outskirts of the village of Scroptoft England were he stayed with the 325th for the duration of the war. Prior to the invasion of Holland (Market Garden) he was assigned to Pathfinder training at a village called Oady, England, then began training for "Operation Market-Garden" that began on September 17 to Nov. 13, 1944.

His "Odyssey" carried him from Normandy (Operation Overload), Holland (Market Garden), to Epinal, France, for some R&R, which was cancelled December 17, he had just finished guard duty at 1000 and was getting ready to hit the hay when this young new lieutenant (a replacement) entered the guard room shouting "hit the deck, we're moving out." They were scheduled for R&R in Paris the following day and some of the old timers yelled back "bull shit" we just got back from Holland. The officer once again shouted, "I am not kidding hit the deck troopers." Someone shouted "blow it out your stacking swivel" where upon the lieutenant lost his composure and withdrew his side arm and fired three rounds into the room ceiling, which got their attention. He yelled "do you hear those trucks outside milling around, that's our ride. There has been a breakthrough in the Ardennes Forrest near Bastogne". Then he said "report to the supply room and draw K&C rations (rats), ammunition, grenades, etc., then meet in front of the regimental headquarters and start loading on to the trucks". The weather was cold and it was beginning to snow. After two or three hours of driving at high speeds in a northeast direction they stopped at a "Y" in the road. A few minutes later another convoy stopped behind them, it was the "Screaming Turkey Heads" of the 101st Abn. After some discussion with Gen. Gavin and his staff of the 82nd that were in command of all airborne units in Europe, it was decided that the 82nd continue up north 125 miles to Liege, Luxembourg. The 325th GIR Inf. Regt. was to start the offensive southerly, clearing all the towns and villages and link up with the 101st Abn. In "Bastogne", and of course the 101st took the right leg of the 'Y' to "Bastogne."

The 325th drove approximately 25 miles south of Liege to a town called Werbomont, Belgium and liberated a concentration camp that had bodies stacked six-eight feet high along side of the buildings that housed the prisoners and also six huge brick ovens where they burned the emancipated bodies. At 0800 they started their offensive south toward Bastogne. The 325th began attacking the Germans and driving them north and east, they had them on the run. Their objective was the high ground of the town of Hierlot, a good military vantage point which the Germans held, because from Hierlot they controlled all the surrounding countryside for miles around. They were able to pinpoint artillery shells on all the valleys and roads as they pleased, so it was important that we take that high ground and hold it at all costs.

To reach Hierlot the 325th had to clear the woods at the foot of the town of Hierlot. Wading through waist deep drifts of snow, on January 2, within the Ardennes Forrest (Bastogne) at 1000 hours they launched their attack and had the Germans on the run. At about 1400

hours he was severely wounded on Jan. 3, 1945 and his platoon leader, an excellent officer, Lt. Elwood Brey also was seriously wounded and died the following day. An SS Tiger Tank had pulled up at their two o'clock alongside a German MG 42 machine gun and decimated their platoon. Esquer was hospitalized from January 4 to April 30.

Lt. Brey, Co. B commanding officer, began his war in North Africa, Sicily, Italy, Normandy, Holland and Belgium. Chasing Hitler's "Super Men" back to Berlin through Africa, France and Holland and tragically ending his life in a four-foot waist-high snow covered field at the foot of the town of Hierlot so close to the end of the war. He paid the supreme sacrifice, and to his brother "Troopers," he died wearing the highest and most prestigious medal an infantry soldier can earn, the "Combat Infantry Badge" barring none, superceding all other combat awards and badges. The "Combat Infantry Badge" is awarded to the men who fought down and dirty in the rain, mud and snow and in the bushes, day after day and face to face with the enemy. The "Combat Infantry Badge" is earned and not issued. Lt. Elwood Brey will always live in our memories as a "True American Hero."

Esquer was discharged to join his unit before he was completely healed because they needed the hospital beds for a big influx of wounded soldiers. They loaded all 82nd Abn. troopers on 20x20 stake bed cattle trucks, driving day and night, stopping only for "pee call" at different intervals, until they intercepted their unit at Cologne, Germany on the Rhine River. From there they did not stop until they reached Ludwigslust, Germany on the Elbe River where they linked up with the Russian army.

On May 2 the 21st German army, under Lt. Gen. Von Tippelskirch, surrendered to the 82nd Abn. Div. at the 325th Co. B, 1st Bn. outpost on a bridge leading out from Berlin over the Elbe River, then on May 3 Germany signed the official unconditional surrender papers. Officially the war was over for Esquer and James Ennis, his "fox hole" buddy for approximately 42 months, and they survived to see the end of the war. "Thank God!" they made it.

After the war the 82nd Abn. Div. was chosen to serve as Honor Guard in Berlin. They served with the occupation of Berlin from July 1945 until their discharge on Dec. 24, 1945. James Ennis and he both were "single" so they had a ball those nine months that they served with the 82nd Abn. "Honor Guard."

Decorations and awards: Combat Infantry Badge, Bronze Star, Purple Heart w/OLC (2), Glider Wing Badge, Parachute Novice Wing Badge, Pathfinder Badge, Good Conduct Medal w/2 Knot Bronze Clasp, EAME Campaign Medal w/4 Bronze Stars (representing four campaigns) and two Bronze Arrowheads (representing Normandy and Holland invasions), WWII Victory Medal, Army of Occupation Medal w/Germany Clasp, Presidential Unit Citation-Army, Meritorious Unit Citation-Army, French Fourragere, Belgium Fourragere, Holland, Royal Netherlands House of Orange Lanyard and American Campaign Medal.

He received his BS, MS degree in civil and structural engineering from California State University in Los Angeles 1971, and retired from the Los Angeles Department of Public Works, Flood Control Division, after 36 years of service. He and his wife, Donna, reside in Whittier, CA. They have two sons, a civil and a structural engineer; a daughter, a college teacher; and nine grandchildren. He was wounded twice in Holland on Oct. 2, 1944 and in Belgium on Jan. 4, 1945 and discharged on Dec. 25, 1945 at midnight. "Merry Christmas."

Veteran Organizations (life memberships): 82nd Abn. Div. Southern California Chapter, Lakewood, CA; 325th Glider Inf. Assn., 82nd Abn. Div. WWII, Champaign, IL; 504t PIR Inf. Regt. Assn., Inc., Fayetteville, NC; The Combat Infantrymen's Assn., Asheville, NC; Military Order of the Purple Heart, Audie Murphy Chapter, Beverly Hills, CA; Veterans of the Bulge, Southern California, Chapter XVI,

Westlake Village, CA; Veterans of Foreign Wars, Post No. 9148, La Mirada, CA; American Legion Post No. 295, Cypress, CA; and DAV, National, Legislative Headquarters, Washington, DC.

DOUGLAS C. "DOUG" FARGO, First Lieutenant, born Oct. 3, 1925 in Lincoln Park, MI. Entered the service April 1944. Received basic training, jungle and some ranger training at Camp Hood, TX. Joined Co. I, 14th Inf., 71st Inf. Div. at Fort Benning, GA October 1944. Sent overseas January 1945 to Europe. The unit was assigned to Patton's 3rd Army in March 1945. Other military locations/stations included Camp Lucky Strike; Fort Dix, NJ; Fort Lewis, WA; Camp Forcer, Japan; Fort Custer, MI; and Camp Atterbury, IN. Private first class to technical sergeant, platoon sergeant/platoon leader with field commission pending.

Memorable experiences: Combat infantryman – France, Germany and Austria (February 1945-March 1946); Korea; Heartbreak Ridge; Punch Bowl (November 1951-March 1952); assistant to war crimes chief and commanding officer of company. Also solitary confinement Commandant Dachan (October 1945-March 1946).

Discharged June 1946. Received commission second lieutenant. Recalled to active duty January 1951. Reassigned to Co. L, 32nd Inf., 7th Inf. Div., Korea November 1951 as infantry platoon leader and commanding officer executive. Returned to the States April 1952. Discharged June 1952.

Awards include two Combat Infantry Badges, two Bronze Stars for combat operations in WWII and Korea, Good Conduct Medal, National Defense Service Medal, ETO w/2 stars, Victory Medal, Occupation ETO, American Defense Service Medal, Korean Service Medal, United Nations Medal, Korean Defense and French Liberty.

He was employed as an industrial engineer in the automotive industry and supervisor management analyst in the Dept. of the Army. Retired November 1988 and currently is a management representative for Business Co-op of America.

He married Marie L.M. Anderson June 1948 and has one son, Maj. Douglas A. Fargo (Ret.) and three grandchildren. Resides in Tuscawilla Hills, Charles Town, WV. He has a home-based business, Indoor Air Purification and Sanitation Systems.

Life member of American Legion, VFW, ROA, MOAA, KWFA, National Infantry Assn., National Assn. of Retired Federal Employees, 32nd Inf. Regt. Assn., 71st Inf. Div. Assn., Harper's Ferry/Boliver Veterans, Chapter 142 KWFA and Combat Inf. Assn.

MALCOLM E. FARRIS SR., born April 26, 1921 in Columbus, OH. Drafted into the service Oct. 13, 1943 and served with the 9th Inf. Div., 47th Co. G as mortarman. Military locations/stations were Fort Ben Harrison, ETO, Indiantown Gap, PA and Camp Wheeler, GA for basic. He participated in battles at Normandy, Northern France, Rhineland, Ardennes and Central Europe. Discharged Sept. 17, 1945 with rank of private first class.

Memorable experiences: Bombing of St. Lo (Cobra) Mortain, Falaise Gap, bypassed Paris to Belgium (Philippine), Dieant, Liege, September 15 Siegfried line to Huertgen Forrest (hospital). December 12 Battle of the Bulge, headed to Rhine (hospital), back to meet Russians at Dessau.

Awarded the Victory Medal, Occupation Medal, Good Conduct Medal, Combat Infantry Badge, Presidential Citation, Bronze Star Medal, Purple Heart w/ cluster, ETO and five Battle Stars.

Farris has one son, Malcolm Jr. (Navy); one daughter, Margie Ball; and plenty of grandchildren. He was employed by Westinghouse for 22 years doing machine repairs. He is currently retired and resides in Columbus, OH. Life member of VFW 8736, life member of Amvets 1922, life member Purple Heart, life member American Legion, CIB and DAV-3.

FRANK FIDLER, born Aug. 5, 1925 in Tottenville, NY. Entered active duty in October 1943 and trained at Fort Eustis, VA; Fort Benning, GA; Camp McCain, MS; and Fort Jackson, SC.

Arrived in Elsenborn, Germany Dec. 29, 1944. Assigned to HQ Co., 1st Bn., 39th Inf., 9th Div. as a scout and observer. Participated in the Ardennes Campaign, the Rhineland Campaign, Central Europe Campaign and the Army of Occupation.

Discharged as technician fifth grade from Fort Dix, NJ May 23, 1946. Awards include Bronze Star Medal, Combat Infantry Badge, Presidential Unit Citation, Belgian Fourragere, European Campaign Medal and Army of Occupation Medal.

An architectural draftsman in civilian life, he retired in 1991. He presently lives in Snellville, GA with his wife, Constance. They have four sons: Frank A., Paul, George and James; and six grandchildren.

CLAYTON F. FINK, born in Rochester, NY. Entered active duty in February 1943. Arrived in Camp Howze, TX with 86th Inf. Div. Moved to Fort Sam Houston. TX with 88th Div.

Landed in Casablanca, Morocco in North Africa, December 1943 and moved east to south of Oran, Algeria. Moved into Italy, went into combat duty and was wounded in September 1944. Entered reconditioning camp in October 1944; arrived in Western Pacific in June 1945; served in Philippines in Manila area and northern Luzon and in Japan.

Arrived in the States in November 1945. Received Battle Stars for Rome-Arno, Northern Apennines and Po Valley campaigns; Purple Heart; Combat Infantry Badge; EAME Service Medal; Philippines Liberation Ribbon; Good Conduct Medal; and WWII Victory Medal. Separated from the service in December 1945.

Married September 1950 and lives in Penfield, NY with wife, Florence. They have two children, Karen and Jim, and three grandchildren. Currently a member of VFW, DAV and Co. C (New York) Combat Infantrymen's Assn. Retired in 1988 as a rural mail carrier in Webster, NY.

JOSEPH GABORSKY JR., born May 30, 1929 in Manhattan, NY. Moved to Rittman, OH in the 30s. Drafted into the U.S. Army Infantry Jan. 16, 1951 and served as first machine gunner, squad leader. Basic training at Fort Knox, KY. Sent directly to front line duty in Korea with 1st Cav. Div., 7th Regt., Co. "B." "B" Co. lost 131 men (KIA) during the war. Front line duty full time in Korea, no R&R, Operation Commando Oct. 3, 1951. Seriously wounded Oct. 6, 1951. Discharged July 31, 1953 with rank of corporal.

Memorable experiences: Old Baldy, Bloody Ridge and Heartbreak Ridge.

Awarded the Purple Heart (wounded twice), Bronze Star w/V, Presidential Unit Citation-Republic of Korea, Combat Infantry Badge, Korean Service Medal, United Nations Medal and Good Conduct Medal.

Gaborsky was married in August 1950 and called to military service in January 1951. Daughter born 1955, deceased 1997 and buried at Western Reserve National Cemetery in Rittman, OH. Civilian employment as design engineer and Real Estate broker. Currently retired and resides in Wadsworth, OH.

ARMAND L. GALDI, born April 15, 1920 in Somerville, MA. Entered the Army Feb. 26, 1942. Basic training at Camp Croft, SC. Joined 4th Inf. Div., 8th Inf. Regt. June 6, 1942.

Awarded the Purple Heart, Bronze Star w/cluster, Presidential Unit Emblem, American Campaign Medal, EAME Theater Ribbon, three Bronze Stars, Bronze Arrowhead, WWII Victory Medal, Combat Infantry Badge, Good Conduct Medal and Belgium Fourragere.

Participated in battles at Normandy, Northern France and Rhineland.

The 8th Inf. Regt., 4th Div. was one of the first Allied units to land on Utah Beach on June 6, 1944. Relieving the 82nd Abn. At St. Mere Eglise, the 4th cleaned the Cotentin Peninsula and took part in the capture of Cherbourg. The division broke through the left flank of the German Seventh army. By the end of August had assisted the French in the liberation of Paris. The division moved into Belgium to attack the Siegfried Line. By November the division reached the Heurtgen Forest, where on Nov. 23, 1944 he was wounded and sent back to the States. Discharged from the Army Hospital at Fort Devens, MA Dec. 6, 1945.

Married to Frances Frazer, has one son, three daughters, 12 grandchildren and three great-grandchildren. Retired after 33 years from New Tel. & Tel. Co.

THEODORE E. "TED" GEORGE, born March 23, 1932, Wadsworth, OH. Enlisted Dec. 29, 1951 with basic training at Schofield Barracks, HI.

Arrived in Japan in late August or early September of 1952. Stationed near Sapporo with 1st Cav. Div. Arrived in Inchon, Korea in November 1952 and assigned to Co. K, 3rd Bn., 224th Inf. Regt., 40th Div. occupying MLR between Sandbag Castle and the Punch Bowl.

In early February 1953 was relieved of front line duty and moved to reserve area. While in reserve transferred to Regt. 1 and R Plt. Returned to line position in late March or early April 1953 in the Punch Bowl. Remained in front line position until rotation.

Sailed for the States the morning the armistice was signed. Completed enlistment as instructor in the Light Weapons School, Fort Riley, KS.

Separated from active duty as corporal on Dec. 15, 1953. Received discharge from Army Reserve as sergeant first class in late 1959 or early 1960. Awards include the National Defense Service Medal, Korean Service Medal w/2 BCS, United Nations Service Medal, Army Commendation Medal, Bronze Star w/ V and Combat Infantry Badge.

He spent 37 years as a self-employed dairy farmer. At the same time he spent 27 years as a high school football and basketball official (referee). He retired in 1997 from Rexroth Corp. (formerly Borg Warner) after almost 40 years of service. He and his wife, Jane, presently live in Westfield Center, OH near their three grown children and five grandchildren. They are enjoying retirement with gardening, golfing, hunting and touring on their motorcycles.

THOMAS D. GILLIS, Colonel. (Ret.), born Oct. 29, 1912 in Presidio, San Francisco. Served in the U.S. Army with 4th Armd. Div. during WWII and G-3 Air, J Corps in Korea. Participated in five battles in WWII and five battles in Korea. Discharged with the rank of colonel.

Memorable experiences: First commander, 1st USA Missile Command (Italy) and last commander 24th Inf. Regt.

Col. Gillis is a distinguished retired career Army officer who won two Silver Stars for his bravery, the Legion of Merit, Purple Heart, Bronze Star, Air Medal and the Combat Infantryman's Badge (unusual for an officer of the Armored Branch). In 1958 he was in command of a Missile Command in Italy equipped with the Honest John and Corporal missiles.

He is in the process of writing a remarkable book entitled *Sabers and Spur-Vignettes In The Life Of A Cavalryman*, which he has been working on for the past two years. He is a national leader within the Sons of the American Revolution. His family has a remarkable history of military service to the country dating from the Revolutionary War. He is currently retired and resides in California.

JESUS GONZALES, born Dec. 25, 1932 in Rockdale, TX. At age 18 enlisted in U.S. Army. On March 21, 1951 was sent to Hawaii for 14 weeks basic training at Hawaiian Infantry Center, Schofield Barracks on Oahu. Shipped to Korea after training, arrived Korea Aug. 13, 1951 and assigned to 8th Cav. Regt., 1st Cav. Div. Left Korea Dec. 31, 1951 and went to Camp Chitose II in Hokkaido Japan. Returned to Korea in October 1952. Rotated back to the U.S. on Dec. 6, 1952 and assigned to Hq. Btry., 513th AAA

and his wife, Lucy, moved from San Antonio, TX to San Diego, CA where they now reside at Santee, CA. Larry's e-mail is E7HAUCK@AOL.COM.

Larry's most memorable experience was his last day of combat when he was badly wounded and saw the Chinese bayoneting the other men after they took the hill at Twin Tunnels in Korea. Larry played dead and the Chinks took his watch and money and left him for dead. The medics found him when the hill was retaken.

Larry is an amateur musician with a good voice. He plays his keyboard and entertains the senior community.

ROBERT HETTIGER, born April 15, 1948 in Southampton, NY, entered the service Jan. 20, 1969, serving with the U.S. Army, 1st Inf. Div. (1/26 Inf. Regt.), 170th Assault Heli. Co., 52nd CAB.

His military locations and stations include Lai Khe III Corps, Kontum II Corps, Toan Thang II June 1-Jan. 31, 1969. He started a combat art section (1st Inf. Div. 1969). From 1969 to 1970 he was a combat artist for the 1st Inf. Div. in Vietnam. The paintings were exhibited in Saigon, the Pentagon in Washington, DC and will remain the permanent collection of the First Division Historical Museum.

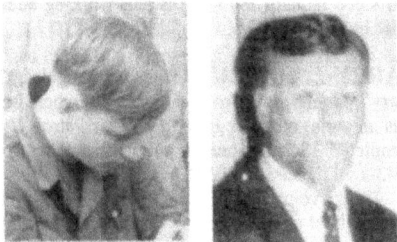

Awards include the New York State Conspicuous Service Cross, Vietnam Service Ribbon, Combat Infantry Badge, Army Commendation, National Defense Service and Vietnam Campaign Medal. He was discharged Jan. 20, 1971 as specialist 4.

In January 1976 he went on a photographic safari in Kenya and Tanzania, East Africa. He was able to obtain much valuable subject matter for new series of paintings. In July 1976 he received a partial grant from the Florida Audubon Society to attend a bird painting seminar in Trinidad. The seminar was under the instruction of Don R. Eckelberry. The Nature Conservancy picked his work to be used on their greeting cards and calendars. In February 1977 he went to the Florida Everglades to paint and photograph. In March 1978 his design was selected for the Long Island Wetlands and Waterfowl League Duck Stamp. It was also selected in 1980. The money raised from the stamp will be used to buy wetlands for waterfowl on Long Island. From 1980-83 he worked on local paintings and East African Wildlife. In 1983 he went to New Mexico to photograph native cliff dwellings. From the mid-1980s to present he has been working on wildlife paintings and his experiences in Vietnam. Also at this time he is doing a series of tropical saltwater fish carvings. He is presently working on a show for the New York State Vietnam Memorial Gallery in Albany, NY.

His parents are deceased. He has one brother in the service, 82nd Abn. Div., U.S. Army. Hettiger is employed with D. Griffiths Inc. and enjoys carpentry, painting landscapes and wildlife.

WILLIAM J. HORAN, born Feb. 24, 1933 in Boston, MA. Entered the U.S. Army July 12, 1950. Military locations and stations include Fort Devens, Fort Sam Houston, Korea and later, Boston and Rehobeth, MA. Participated in many battles while retreating and then advancing Hill 355. They never quite knew there they were or had support. Discharged in 1953 with rank of second lieutenant, U.S. Army retired.

Memorable experiences: All north of Seoul, he was an old veteran when he turned 18. (He later was

with Northern England's Bomb Disposal at Fort Devens, MA.) In Korea he was a machine gunner but had trained as a medic at Fort Sam Houston and could save many wounded.

He was awarded 19 decorations, Combat Infantry Badge, two Korean Medals and one Greek Medal.

Again served with 18th Inf. Reserve Boston as a second lieutenant and on active duty with missile unit in Massachusetts and retired at age 60.

He has one son, William, who attends the University of Massachusetts-Amherst and one daughter, Mary, who attends the University of Massachusetts-Amherst. Civilian employment as chief accountant and is currently retired. He travels throughout the world with Peace Corps and other charitable Catholic charities. He stopped the beating of children in Fiji Schools and made the International News and received a 3rd Div. award nationwide a few years ago. He now resides in Brookline, MA.

WILLIAM C. HOSLER, born Dec. 31, 1931 in Newville, PA. Army enlistment on Jan. 6, 1949. Basic training at Camp Pickett, VA. Permanent duty station unit, Kyushu Japan. Served with Co. F, 19th Inf. Regt., 24th Inf. Div. Served in Korea from July, 4 1950 to Jan. 3, 1951. Participated in battles at Kum River, north of Taejon, July 16, 1950; Taejon, July 19 and 20; and Chinju, July 29 and 30. All three battles rate highly memorable. The month of August at Pusan Perimeter. September 1950-December 1950 went on offensive north to near Yalu River. Chinese intervention then back south to Uijongbu near Seoul. Wounded on Jan. 3, 1951. Hospitalized at Swedish Hospital, Pusan Korea; Tokyo Army Hospital, Japan; and Yokohama Army Hospital, Japan. Returned to the States to Fort Devens, MA Army Hospital. Returned to duty in September 1951 at Fort Benning, GA. Discharged in May 1952 as sergeant.

Awards and medals: Combat Infantry Badge, Bronze Star, Purple Heart, Good Conduct, Army Occupation-Japan, Korean Service Medal, United National Medal, National Defense, U.S. Presidential Unit Citation, Republic of Korea Presidential Citation and Korean War Service Medal.

He is married to Pat and has two sons, Jeffery and Gregory. Civilian employment with the Department of Defense, Defense Logistics Agency. He is currently retired and resides in Mechanicsburg, PA. Volunteers at VA once a week.

JACK E. HUGHES, born June 18, 1929 in Dallas, TX. Enlisted into the U.S. Army Oct. 21, 1947. Military locations/stations included Japan, 11th Abn. Div.,

7th Inf. Div., Korea, 24th Inf. Div., Germany, 26th Avn. Co., 11th Avn. Co., Fort Benning, Post HQ Co. Participated in battle at Kum River/Tajon in July 1950. Discharged in June 1978 with rank of staff sergeant E6.

Memorable experiences: Had a lot of good ones and some bad ones. Main one was he made it through the Army after being wounded and being in the hospital for almost two years. Retired after 21 years, four months.

Awarded the Combat Infantry Badge, Purple Heart, Army Commendation, OJ, National Defense, Korean Service Medal, Good Conduct Medal, United Nations Medal, KWM, Presidential Unit Citation, MUC, Korean Presidential Unit Citation, PB and ACB.

He and his wife, Elaine, were married Nov. 21, 1997. He has five stepchildren, six grandchildren and four great-grandchildren. Civilian employment as warehouse foreman Hinde Co./Eyeglasses for 25 years. He now spends time volunteering. Hughes resides in Plano, TX.

JAMES A. HUSING, born Aug. 14, 1944 in Ohsand, GA. Drafted into the U.S. Army Infantry July 26, 1965 and served with the 1st Inf. Div. Military locations/stations: Training at Fort Ord, CA; Lai Khe, South Vietnam January 1966-January 1967; 1st Inf. Div.; 2nd Bn.; 2nd Inf. Discharged July 25, 1967 with rank of sergeant E-5.

Major operations: Buckskin, Mastiff, Birmingham, El Paso II, Pacification Program Phu Loi area.

Memorable experiences: At one time being the only surviving member of his fire team. All others killed or wounded.

Awarded the Combat Infantry Badge, National Defense Service Medal, Good Conduct Medal, Republic of Vietnam Campaign Medal, Vietnam Service Medal, Sharpshooter (Rifle), Expert (Bayonet).

Married to Gwen and has one son, Chris. Retired police officer, Mountain View, CA. Currently working for Dept. of Defense as a background investigator and resides in Santa Clara, CA.

WARREN W. INGLESE, born July 13, 1925 in Mt. Vernon, NY. Enlisted March 1, 1943. After training at Fort Benning and Camp Campbell, he was sent to the European Theater of Operations, arriving in France on Omaha Beach after D Day. Later he flew to Italy joining the 361st Inf., 91st Div. As a first scout in G Co., which raised the American flag on Mt. Adone, he single-handedly captured 11 prisoners after a bitter 60 hour battle. Many winter months had been spent on the Apennine Mountains in difficult defense positions. Among the awards he received are the Presidential Unit Citation, the Bronze Star and the Combat Infantrymen's Badge.

After discharge in 1946, he became a private pilot. He spent 43 years as a photojournalist with Gannett

Newspapers, receiving two Pulitzer Prize nominations and over 100 awards. He continues to work in creative photography with his artist wife, Patricia, in Congers, NY.

CARL W. JEFFERS, born Oct. 27, 1925 in Cumberland, MD left school and was drafted into the Army at 18. He served with HQ 1st Bn., 355th Inf., 89th Div. Military locations/stations were Fort McClellan, AL; Camp Butner, NC; and Camp Lucky Strike, France. He served in the European Theater of Operations in the 89th Inf. Div. of Gen. Patton's 3rd Army during WWII. Discharged in May 1946 with rank of technician fourth grade, sergeant first class.

Memorable experiences: Rhine River crossing, liberation of the Nazi Death Camp at Ohrdruf, Germany.

His awards include the Combat Infantry Badge and Bronze Star.

Returning home in 1946 Carl attended school to get his high school diploma. In 1947 he met and married a student nurse and he and Evelyn will soon celebrate their 55th anniversary.

In August 1950 Carl was recalled to active duty with the Army Reserve Corps, and served on Okinawa. After returning to civilian life he attended the University of Baltimore at night while working days, earning a degree in business management.

After 25 years of service with Maryland State Government Carl retired. He purchased a motor home and traveled extensively in the USA, Canada and Mexico. He is a member of the VFW, American Legion, 89th Inf. Assn. and Combat Infantrymen's Assn.

JOSEPH W. JIMENEZ, born in Magnolia, MD and entered the service in Baltimore, MD on April 11, 1946. He enlisted in the Army Air Corps with the hope that he might become a radio operator/mechanic. He was 16 years old but told everyone he was 17; he had his father's permission. While in basic training, he was ordered to report to the squadron commander, and was told that they knew he was not 17 years old. He asked the commander to let him stay in the Army, and the commander said he could stay because he was a good soldier.

After basic training at Amarillo AAFB, TX, Joe was assigned to the Air Training command at Scott Army Air Force Base, Illinois where he discovered that he would not be trained in the field he had chosen. He was then trained as a telephone and teletype installer/repairman.

When he graduated from the telephone and teletype school, he was sent to Hamilton AFB, CA, for shipment overseas. He was promoted to private first class on Dec. 5, 1946, less than three months after his 17th birthday. He was assigned to Far East Air Force headquarters in Tokyo, Japan and further assigned to the 16th Communications Sqdn. He received

the WWII Victory Medal and qualified for the Army Occupation Medal with Japan Bar.

He worked as a telephone and switchboard repairman in the Meiji building about three blocks from Gen. MacArthur's headquarters. This assignment lasted from January 1947 to December 1948. When he returned to the USA he was assigned to Bolling AFB in Washington, DC.

Having been transferred to the USAF when it was established on Sept. 18, 1947, he was discharged from the USAF in April 1949 and re-enlisted in the U.S. Army Signal Corps. He was reassigned to Japan initially in the First Cav. Div. in Tokyo then later to Ninth Corps headquarters in Sendai. When he arrived in Sendai he found the Ninth Corps had orders to deactivate and he was fortunate to be sent to the Eighth Army Signal School in Yokohama to attend the Telephone Central Office Supervisor Course. This was a four month course with a very important Military Occupational Specialty (MOS), which when someone has this MOS he is usually not assigned to any other duty. This duty was also called "wire chief".

During the second month of the course, the school was moved from Yokohama to Eta Jima Island in the Hiroshima Prefecture. Eta Jima was the Japanese Naval Academy until the end of WWII. He graduated on June 24, 1950 and was ordered back to Sendai to an assignment in the Seventh Inf. Div. He caught the midnight train from Hiroshima to Yokohama where he was to change trains for Sendai. He met a friend in the Yokohama train station who asked him what he thought about the war. Having not heard any news he did not know that North Korea had invaded South Korea while he was on the train. When he learned that U.S. troops had been ordered to South Korea, he felt very bad because he knew he could not get out of the infantry.

He was assigned to the 7th Signal Co. as a telephone wireman and made the Inchon invasion on Sept. 18, 1950. While his unit was in convoy going to Pusan to board ships for the invasion of North Korea, the convoy was ambushed twice by North Korean troops. During the second ambush, Joe captured three enemy soldiers.

After his unit boarded ships, they were returned to the pier in Pusan to see a USO show with Bob Hope. Soon as the show ended his unit reboarded the ships and they proceeded to Iwon on the east coast of North Korea where they made an amphibious landing on Oct. 26, 1950. While waiting for the order to proceed to the debarkation station where they were to climb down cargo nets into landing craft, Joe heard his name called over the ship's intercom. He was ordered to the Promenade deck where he received orders to go on a special mission separate from the main landing. He was told to go down the other side of the ship and get in a Higgins boat, also known as a LCVP (landing craft, vehicles and personnel). He was the only troop in the boat and the coxswain took him to a place where tree logs were floating beside the beach. The coxswain said Joe had to crawl over the logs to get to the beach because the Higgins boat could not get closer. This was scary because the logs could come apart and Joe could fall into the water with his pack, weapon, steel helmet, ammunition and water; but he made it and reported to the Navy commander as instructed. The commander said Joe was NCO in charge of installing a phone connection from the tent on the beach to the nearest railroad station. Joe had four men assigned to him so he had two carrying wire while the other two carried their weapons. Joe carried a 6-volt lantern, his weapon and a field phone. Soon as it became dark, Joe turned on the lantern so they could see the tracks clearly. Within minutes of turning on the light, they were fired upon by small arms fire.

Joe ordered the men to take cover beside the rails and wait. One of the men asked if they should return fire and Joe told them not to because they were receiving friendly fire. Soon as the firing let up, after about 30 rounds had hit near them, mostly in the reel

of telephone wire, Joe called out to the troops that they were American and to please stop shooting. The anti-aircraft artillerymen who were assigned to guard the supply dumps asked if anyone was hurt and Joe said it was lucky that none of them were shot. The task took much longer because they had to stop frequently to tape or splice where a bullet had damaged the wire.

They returned to the beach after establishing the required communications and had to sleep there on the beach because their unit had moved inland and there was no transportation available. The next day Joe's team got a ride North to catch up with the rest of the Signal Co. in a town named Pukchong, just south of Haesanjin on the border of Manchuria.

After spending the month of November 1950 beside the Yalu River, the 7th Div. had to withdraw to Hamhung and Hungnam to leave North Korea because the Chinese Army had crossed the Yalu with an overwhelmingly large force.

They boarded ships after midnight and returned to Pusan two days later where they were loaded on trains and moved to a town named Chechon just south of the 38th parallel.

He was transferred to the 17th Inf. Regt. in February 1951 to participate in the first United Nations Offensive Battle. He was sent to the Second Bn. to help make it a Battalion Combat Team, and they went behind enemy lines that very night. After five days behind the lines the Battalion Combat Team was surrounded by the enemy and had to fight 36 hours to get back into their lines. They suffered heavy losses and he was injured while saving three wounded soldiers. He got them to the medical aid station as soon as they were back in their lines. He went on sick call for his back injury after he returned to regimental headquarters and was medically air evacuated to Japan. He was placed in traction for six weeks because of the injury but his back did not improve. He was sent back to his regiment and continued to perform the duties of an infantry field wireman. While in action on a hill called Old Baldy, he was wounded by enemy mortar fire on the first of September 1951. Joe was awarded the Combat Infantryman's Badge and the Purple Heart Medal. He also received the Korea Campaign Medal w/6 Battle Stars and the United Nations Service Medal among many other awards. He earned the Army Good Conduct Medal w/2 loops for three awards.

He returned to the USA in November 1951 and was assigned to teach switchboard installation in the U.S. Army Signal School at Fort Gordon, Augusta, GA.

He was later assigned to the Alaska Communications System (ACS) in the Federal Building in Seattle, WA where he was responsible for the maintenance and operation of all radiotelephone links between the continental USA and the Territory of Alaska for 40 hours each week. In December 1952 he was assigned to the ACS station in Big Delta also known as Delta Triangle and Delta Junction at the end of the Alaska Highway where it joins the Richardson Highway for Fairbanks 100 miles away. At this small station he was responsible for electronic equipment maintenance, overseas telephone operation and overseas teletype operation during his eight-hour shift each day.

As one of three sergeants on the station, he was assigned additional duties as site repair and utilities NCO (non commissioned officer) until his return to Seattle in June 1953. Back in the ACS headquarters, he became the electronic parts supply sergeant until his discharge in September 1953.

He re-enlisted and was sent to Japan for the third time. This time he finally got the chance to supervise telephone exchanges after a short assignment as an advisor to the Japanese Self Defense Forces Communications School in Kurihama, just south of Yokosuka where Adm. Perry landed when he first went to Japan. He worked three years in many of the U.S. Army telephone exchanges in and around Tokyo.

During the time he was supervising telephone exchanges in Tokyo, he was offered a direct commission and advised to submit the necessary paperwork.

The appointment did not materialize before his tour of duty ended in Japan but he was able to get an assignment to Clark AFB in the Philippines direct from Tokyo. He worked in the Army Command and Administrative Network (ACAN) station on Clark Field until his commission as a second lieutenant in the Army Reserves was approved.

He went on active duty as an officer in April 1957 and was assigned to the Fourth Inf. Div. in Fort Lewis, WA. He became a platoon leader in the 124th Signal Bn.'s Co. B, until July 1959 when he was ordered to Germany. He was promoted to first lieutenant in October 1958. In Germany he was assigned to the 17th Signal Bn. where he became platoon leader of the Radio Relay Plt. until he was transferred to the job of assistant S-4, battalion supply officer in 1960. Later in 1961 he was transferred to HQ 516th Signal Gp. where he served as headquarters detachment commander and was promoted to captain in November 1961.

He was ordered back to the U.S. in September 1962 and assigned to the 2nd Amphibious Gp. in Fort Lewis, WA. Within the group he was assigned as Signal Company commander in the 592nd Engr. Bn. He was reassigned to the U.S. Army Signal Communications Agency, Taiwan (USARSCAT) in July 1964.

In USARSCAT, he was responsible for half of the island's military telecommunications until July 1966 when he was reassigned to the White Sands Missile Range, New Mexico. He served as communications security officer at White Sands until his retirement from active duty on June 1, 1967, as a captain in the Signal Corps.

After retirement Joe first worked for C&P Telephone Co. that is now known as Verizon. He then worked for Lockheed Electronics Co. on a project to build an earth station at Greenbelt, MD. Here he had his first experience at being laid off because NASA had a budget cut. He then went to work in Georgetown (part of Washington, DC) as a logistics management specialist until the Trust Territory of the Pacific Islands (TTPI) hired him as a telephone systems engineer.

The TTPI headquarters was on Saipan Island, in the Marianna's north of Guam. Joe was responsible for telephone systems in six islands. Besides Saipan in the Marianna's, there was Yap and Palau in the western Caroline Islands; Trak and Ponape in the eastern Carolines and Majuro in the Marshall Islands. He worked there over four years and built seven telephone systems.

Upon his return home he attended Computer School under the GI bill and became an honor graduate as a programmer of the IBM 360. He worked on government programs as a logistics consultant on electronic warfare devices and flight simulators.

Continuing to work on his college degree, he graduated with a BA in management and applied behavioral sciences in 1988. His last place of employment was with the Bureau of the Census in 1999 and 2000.

Joe currently resides with his wife, Helena, at 1723 Pebble Beach Drive, Vienna, VA. He is fully retired and is commander of the VFW Post 8469 in Fairfax.

OTIS KLEAVER SR., born Dec. 13, 1918, at Guyandotte, WV. Went to school in Michigan. Entered the Army in May 1944 at Port Sheridan, IL. Took basic training at Camp Fannin, TX. Was in Co. D, 59th Bn., 12th Regt. Inf. Was transferred to Fort George G. Meade, MD in September 1944.

First engagement, Guemar, France with Co. E, 30th Inf. Regt., 3rd Div. CO Capt. Ralph Carpenter. R&R Nancy, France, Siegfried Line in March 1945.

Decorations include the Silver Star, Bronze Star, Purple Heart, French

Fourragere, Combat Infantry Badge, Presidential Unit Citation and eight other decorations.

Returned to U.S. in December 1945. Later joined the MING. He was activated into the Regular Army in 1968 for riot control in Detroit, MI.

Retired after 22 years of service in 1974 as sergeant first class E-07. Married 65 years to Dorothy Lewis Kleaver with three children: Otis F., John and David.

ARTHUR KNUTE KNUDSEN JR., born in Chicago, IL March 26, 1926. Inducted into Army Aug. 27, 1944 at Camp Wheeler, GA. Due to go to Officer's Candidate School, but due to Battle of the Bulge was on board ship with 10,000 men on Dec. 31, 1944.

Assigned to 273rd Regt., Co. H of the 69th Inf. Div. Member of a heavy weapon company, a machine gun squad.

Feb. 8, 1945 replaced the men of 393rd Regt. at Siegfried Line. Crossed the Rhine River at Remagen on his 19th birthday. Battle at Leipzig Germany on April 17. His division was the first to meet the Russians on the Elbe River at Torgau. German soldiers surrender to them on April 24. After fighting stopped he was stationed at Kasel, Germany in charge of the PX. Returned home as a sergeant in June 1946.

Received bachelor of laws from Duke University in June 1950. Practiced law in Fort Myers, FL from December 1950 until he retired in December 2001. Married Christie Kerth in Paducah, KY Dec. 21, 1947. Has one daughter and two grandchildren. Lives at 7706 Bay Lake Dr., Fort Myers, FL 33907, phone 239-334-0069.

WILLIAM M. KOCZWARA, born Nov. 14, 1921 in Dunkirk, NY. Enlisted in the U.S. Army Sept. 8, 1943 and served with L Co., 359th Inf., 90th Div. Trained at Camp Blanding, FL. M-1 rifle marksman Nov. 20, 1943. Battles participated in were D-Day, second wave Utah Beach, Battle of the Bulge, Normandy, Northern France, Central Europe and Rhineland. Discharged Dec. 2, 1945 with rank of private first class.

Memorable experiences: Nearly getting killed 29 times. Captured two German soldiers behind Allied lines.

Koczwara was awarded three Purple Hearts, Bronze Star, ETO Medal w/5 Battle Stars and two Presidential Unit Citations.

He came from a family of seven, four girls and three boys. Married twice, divorced. Has one beautiful daughter, Susan Debra. Civilian employment with Becton, Dickinson & Co. for 45 years. He retired at the end of 1985. Currently retired after a long and hectic life. Resides in Lakeworth, FL.

C. RAY KUES JR., born May 14, 1925, Baltimore, MD and was drafted in August 1943, age 18, upon graduation from high school. After basic he departed

for New Caledonia where he served two years with the renowned 17th "Wolfhound" Inf. Regt. of the 25th Tropic Lightning Div. He was a sergeant with the 2nd Sqdn., 2nd Plt., G Co., 27th Regt., 25th Div., February 1944-January 1946.

Combat highlight: Luzon, January-June 1945, served as combat scout along with J.T. Jones (of Louisville) and Filipino Fernando Lazo (KIA) in G Co.'s bold and secret penetration behind enemy lines and up horrendous terrain to the surprise and demise of the Japanese defenders on Lone Tree Hill. This was the key strategic and dominating point overlooking Balete Pass and the Cagayen Valley.

BGen. Brown commemorated this outstanding performance by G Co. and the 1st Plt. of H Co. against the fanatical resistance of the Japanese in "Battle Honors" citation published in General Orders No. 494 on Dec. 5, 1945 in Nagoya, Japan. Of the infamous "165" days, he was off-line the first part of May as a combat casualty when hit by an 8-inch shell canister dropped by their Cessna L-5 plane delivering supplies on Lone Tree Hill.

He departed Luzon for the occupation of Japan, October 1945-January 1946, and was discharged in February 1946. Awards include the Combat Infantry Badge, Bronze Star, Expert Rifleman M-1, Good Conduct, American Theater, Asiatic-Pacific, WWII Victory, Army Occupation-Japan, Army Service, Army Service Overseas, Philippine Liberation, Philippine Independence and Philippine Presidential Unit Citation.

In the January 1998 issue of *WII Magazine*, in an article entitled *Battle for Balete Pass*, Tracy Derks, the author, relates the action in the taking of Lone Tree Hill, Luzon, Philippine Islands where he and J.T. Jones were lead scouts and caught the defenders totally unawares.

Kues resides in Hereford, MD.

JOHN E. LAMLE, born July 14, 1931 in Aline, OK. Served with HV Mort., 224th Regt., 40th Div. Military locations/stations were Camp Roberts, CA; Sandbag; Punchbowl from Triangle; Pork Chop Hill; Bloody Ridge; and Satere Valley. Discharged in October 1954 with rank of sergeant E-5.

Memorable experiences: His first night on Sand Bag Castle O.P. he was in a tent alone behind the outpost, fixing some assault rations and he heard two Koreans talking. He thought they were Katusas so he gave them some food. They ate it and left. They walked a few feet and were challenged by a guard. They turned out to be North Koreans wanting to give themselves up. The GI who was on guard got 10 days R and R in Japan for this action.

Civilian employment two years with Air Force crash rescue and 40 years with the postal service. He is a life member of VFW and American Legion serving as service officer and commander. Currently farming and ranching in Aline, OK.

TILL LECIAN, Staff Sergeant, born Feb. 14, 1929 in Louisville, KY. Graduate of Central High School and attended University of Louisville – Southern Police Institute. Worked for Ford Motor Co., Dearborn, MI plant. Drafted in February 1952 and assigned to 8th Cav. in Japan and trained for invasion. Reassigned to 25th Div., 27th Wolfhound Regt., E Co., MOS 1812 heavy weapons specialist. Commanded E Co., Heavy Wpn. Plt. Graduated from NCO School with diploma signed by Gen. Sam Williams. Assigned to E Co. command after finishing NCO School. Promoted to staff sergeant. Fought at Sandbag Castle, Kumhwa Valley, Iron Triangle Pamun John. After separation joined Louisville Police Dept. and served 38 years. Became commander of KWVA-KY C.H. Dodd-E.E. West Chapter in 1996. Inducted into the Metro Parks Hall of Fame, Southwick Community Center (1992).

Organizations: 25th Div. Assn.; 27th Inf. Historical Society; Korean Society; Project 2000 Foundation, Gen. Westmoreland, president; Grand Lodge Fraternal Order of Police; American Legion; Disabled Veterans; life member, 1st Cav. Assn.; chairman of Board of Directors – Louisville Police Officers Credit Union; Douglas MacArthur Foundation; and Combat Infantryman's Assn.

Discharged Nov. 20, 1953 with rank of staff sergeant. Lecian earned the Combat Infantryman Badge, Green Combat Leadership Stripes, Korean Service Medal w/3 Combat Battlefield Stars and Arrow, United Nations Service Medal, National Defense Service Medal, Sygman Rhee Citation, Korean 50th Commemorative Medal, U.S. Dept. of Defense 50th Commemorative Medal, U.S. Dept. of Defense Cold War Citation (Donald Rumsfeld), Kentucky Dept. of Veterans Affairs 50th Anniversary Citation and Derek Anderson Foundation – Veteran Award (Medallion).

Memorable experiences: Relieving 7th Div. Bn. off of Sandbag Castle where they had held for 28 days.

His father, Till, was a brakeman for the Illinois Central Railroad for 33 years; his mother, Hallie, was a self-employed cosmetologist. Lecian is retired from the Louisville Police Dept.

EDWARD W. LEEMING, born North Kingstown, RI. Enlisted in the Army in October 1949. Basic training Fort Dix, NJ, then sent to the 2nd Div., Fort Lewis, WA. In July 1950 division was alerted and shipped to Korea. Saw action from Pusan Perimeter to Kunuki where he was seriously wounded and medivaced out.

Awarded Purple Heart w/cluster, Korean Service Medal w/3 Battle Stars, National Defense, United Nations Medal, Good Conduct Medal and Combat Infantry Badge.

Retired from active duty because of wounds in September 1951. Married Hilda Conly on Dec. 12, 1953. They are the proud parents of three boys, four girls: Edward Jr., John, Roger, Patricia, Carol, Mary and Karen.

Worked for Rhode Island DOT as a supervisor of highways. Retired in 1988 with 30 years service. Active with VFW and the 2nd Div. Assn.

ROBERT L. LESLIE, born Jan. 6, 1924 in New Castle, PA. Inducted into the Army March 22, 1943. Was member of the 8th Armd. Div. in Camp Polk, LA until November 1943. Then went to ASTP program at the University of Oklahoma.

Joined G Co., 409th Inf., 103rd Div. at Camp Howze in March 1944. From October 1944 to August 1945 served overseas with the 103rd Div. as a sergeant. From August 1945 until November 1945 was with the 9th Inf. Div. Came home with the 94th Div. in January 1945. Spent 10 years in 79th Div. Reserve as sergeant first class.

Particularly remembers the fighting at St. Die, Selestat, Siegfried Line (Grassburg Hill) in December, Kindwiller raid in February and the Siegfried Line and Task Force in March.

Received the Bronze Star Medal and Oak Leaf Cluster, Purple Heart, EAME w/3 Battle Stars, Army of Occupation (Germany) and Combat Infantry Badge.

Married to Betty Coryea with three children and five grandchildren. Retired as president of Spencer Paint & Glass Co.

GEORGE A. LEVASSER (changed from Levasseur), Master Sergeant, was drafted in Salem, MA on March 18, 1941. Stationed at Camp Edwards, MA for training. Married March 7, 1942. Transferred to Florida for coastal duty. Was on maneuvers in North Carolina, Kentucky and Tennessee. Trained in Fort Jackson, SC and at Fort Gordon, GA. Shipped on SS *Floyd T. Gibbons* to Utah Beach, Normandy, France.

Fought with Gen. Patton in the Battle of the Bulge, and several campaigns through to Vlachovo Breeze, Czechoslovakia. Injured in Germany and awarded the Bronze Star. At war's end, transferred to school at Prestwick, Scotland. Arrived home Sept. 21, 1945.

Received honorable discharge at Fort Devens, MA in October 1945. Moved with family to Miami, FL Oct. 18, 1945. Worked as an accountant, then founded Tropic Oil Co. in February 1952. Retired in 1973 when two sons took over. Tropic Oil is still family operated. Member of Combat Infantry Association. Died Dec. 4, 1999. Survived by his wife, two sons, one daughter, five grandchildren and two great-grandchildren.

JOSEPH L. LILES, born Jan. 4, 1940 in Lima, OH. Enlisted in the U.S. Army in January 1957. Served with HHC, 2nd Bn., 7th Cav., 1st Cav. Div. Military locations/stations were Fort Knox, KY; Fort Stewart, GA; Kaiserslautern, Germany; Fort Belvoir, VA; Fort Benning, GA; and Vietnam. Participated in battles at Plei Me, Ia Drang, Bong Son, Happy Valley, Hwy. 19, all operations in II Corps 1965-66 and Advisory Team 72-28-69. Discharged Dec. 15, 1969 with rank of specialist 5.

Memorable experiences: He had the distinct pleasure of helping clear the green line on base Camp An Khe, got to blow a huge tree out of the ground; I Drang Valley; and Bong Son.

Awarded the National Defense Medal, Army Commendation, Good Conduct Medal, Combat Infantry Badge, Presidential Unit Citation, etc.

Wife #1, Sandra J.; wife #2, Patricia J.; wife #3, Mary K.; current wife, Beverly J. (for past years). Sons: George, Kevin, James, Kevin Wittenberg and Robert Wittenberg; daughter, Joan Daniels; five grandchildren. Civilian employment includes home improvement and truck driver. He is a 100% disabled veteran. Liles currently resides in Lehigh Acres, FL.

LLOYD M. LIPPMAN, born Jan. 7, 1926 at Granville, ND. Graduated from high school in June 1944; inducted June 23, 1944 at Fort Snelling, MN and took AA (40mm) basic training at Camp Stewart, GA. He completed training just in time for Thanksgiving and was reassigned in December 1994 to Camp Howze, TX.

He received AIT, then was shipped to Europe and assigned to Co. K, 273rd Inf. in February 1945, as a rifleman and then as a BAR automatic rifleman in the 3rd Sqdn., 1st Plt. In late June or early July 1945 he transferred to the 107th Lt. Ord. Co. and a week later to the 910th HAM Ord. Co. because of low rotation points. He was then discharged June 12, 1946 at Camp McCoy, WI.

Lippman is divorced and has three sons and five grandchildren. He worked for the Montana Army NG for 30 years of civil service in the personnel and finance fields. He retired as CW4 (AUS-Res).

VINCENT J. LOGIUDICE, born April 9, 1923 in Harrison, NY. Enlisted in the U.S. Army Feb. 10, 1943 and served with the 84th Inf. Div., 333rd Regt., "L" Co. Military locations/stations were Fort Sheridan, IL; Michigan State University; Lehigh University; Johns Hopkins University; Camp Claiborne, LA; ETO; Siegfried Line; Rhineland and Central Europe. Discharged Nov. 13, 1945 at Fort Sill, OK with rank of corporal.

Memorable experiences: Was captured Thanksgiving eve in 1944 and prisoner of war until May 3, 1945; Army Specialized Training Program; Anti-aircraft Basic Infantry Training at Camp Claiborne.

Vincent earned the Combat Infantry Badge, Bronze Star, Purple Heart and Prisoner of War Medal.

Married Sylvia Feb. 19, 1949 and has two sons, Kenneth and Vincent Jr.; and two grandchildren, Tiffany and Christopher. He owns a landscaping firm and retired from the U.S. postal service in 1985. He has been a volunteer at the veterans hospital for 17 years volunteering 13,500 hours in 1985. Adjutant, New York Corps Combat Infantry Men's Assn. Vincent is a member of the DAV, VFW, Ex-POW, American Legion and MOPH-CIA.

RODERICK ALEXANDER MACKENZIE III, born Dec. 22, 1934 in Lowell, MA. Joined the Army March 3, 1952. Saw combat with the 21st Inf., 24th Div. at Song Wan, Korea and elsewhere. Saw three battles and time at Kojedo, Korea POW Camp. TDY to UNPFIK and saw combat with one infiltration and extraction of Republic of Korea partisan forces. Stationed in Camp Schimmelpenning, Sendai, Japan, Camp Wood, Japan (187th ARCT), 278th RCT and 74th RRCT at Fort Devens, MA. Discharged there March 4, 1955.

Re-enlisted in 1956. Stationed with 508th RCT at Fort Bragg, NC. Volunteered for Vietnam in 1957. Saw action with Advisory Forces there. Ranger trained and airborne trained. Discharged second time at Fort Bragg, NC in 1960.

Earned EOD Badge, all Vietnam Expeditionary Medals, United Nations Service Medal-Korea, all Korean medals, Senior Parachute Badge, Combat Infantry Badge (x2), Korean Service Medal, Bronze Star w/V and Purple Heart.

Now owns Circus Acts and Carnival games at his winter quarters in Newberry, FL. Expects a long full life. Healthy as the proverbial horse. Married six times, looking for "Miss Good" at present. He provides aerial acts to circuses worldwide. Builds circus and carnival equipment at Florida winter quarters and property in Washington state.

RAYMOND A. MANZ, born Dec. 11, 1929 in Pittsburgh, PA. Enlisted in the U.S. Army Feb. 13, 1948 and served with the 23rd Inf., 2nd Div. Military locations/stations were Fort Dix; Fort Lewis, WA; and Fort Indiantown Gap, PA. Battles in which he participated include Pusan Perimeter, Kunuri Twin Tunnels and Chipyong-ni. Discharged Feb. 15, 1952 with rank of sergeant.

Memorable experiences: The ride out of Kunuri on tanks in 40 below zero and being wounded.

Manz earned the Combat Infantry Badge, Bronze Star and Purple Heart.

He is married to Ann and has four children. Civilian employment with Sears Roebuck. Raymond is currently retired and resides in North Versailles, PA.

JOHN MARSHALEK, born June 8, 1921 to Polish immigrants in Russellton, PA, a coal mining town, all farms and coal mines – no better place on earth for a young boy to grow up. Things were tough, coal miners on strike for 18 months in 1927 and then the depression in 1932.

He started working in the mines in 1939. The work was hard but he liked it.

In 1942 he was drafted and served with Cannon Co., 148th Inf., 37th Div. Military locations/stations include Camp Roberts, CA. Basic training was like a picnic. Every move after that was worse than your present location. He was initiated into combat on Bougainville-Solomon Islands. Then the invasion of Luzon, Philippine Islands, Manila, Baguio, Balete Pass and the Cagayen Valley where the war ended. Discharged Dec. 27, 1945 with rank of sergeant.

John earned the USA Presidential Unit Citation, two Bronze Stars, Philippine Presidential Unit Infantry Combat badges.

He wrote his girlfriend to plan on getting married soon after the got home. He had enough of the military life. He came home Dec. 28, 1945. They were married May 11, 1946 and had three children. She died of diabetes March 7, 1985. Started playing golf at 76 years of age. Currently retired. Swims for one-half hour five days a week. Shoots pool in the evenings.

ALBERT MASSO, born July 11, 1917 in Providence, RI. Enlisted in the service Feb. 2, 1942 and served with the 104th Inf., 26th Div., Co. I. Basic training at Camp Blanding, AL; 26th Div., Massachusetts, Florida coast patrol, Georgia, Tennessee, Kentucky and South Carolina. Battles in which he participated include France, Moncont Woods and Rhineland Campaign. Discharged Oct. 25, 1945 with rank of sergeant.

Memorable experiences: Under dangerous conditions tried to save comrades twice, both died. Unable to get loose from barbed wire, under heavy fire. Considered best 60mm mortar man in 26th Div. Getting the only perfect score over 200.

Albert earned the EAME Campaign Medal, two Bronze Service Stars, WWII Victory Medal, Army of Occupation Medal w/Germany Clasp, Croix de Guerre, Good Conduct Medal and American Campaign Medal.

Married Etta Feb. 22, 1942. They were married 58-1/2 years until her death. He has one daughter, Marilyn and one granddaughter, Jayma. Civilian employment as a barber for many years, TV serviceman for 25 years and 10 years as deputy clerk of 6th District Court in Providence, RI. He has been retired since 1980, resides in Providence, RI and spends his winters in Florida.

ROY H. MATSUMOTO, born in Los Angeles, CA. Incarcerated at Internment Camp in Jerome, AR and on Nov. 12, 1942, volunteered to serve his country. He was sent to Military Intelligence Service Language School at Camp Savage, MN. Upon graduation sent to famed 442nd RCT at Camp Shelby, MS for basic infantry training.

Volunteered for hazardous duty with 5307th CUP, code name "Galahad" aka "Merrill's Marauders" and sent to CBI Theater. After completing long range penetrating tactics in India, was sent to Burma and assigned to Blue Combat Team I&R as intelligence NCO.

Awarded Legion of Merit by Gen. Frank Merrill for action at Walawbum, Burma in March 1944. Also participated in Siege of Nhpum-Ga and capture of airstrip at Myitkyina, Burma. Upon completion of mission was sent to Kunming, China and assigned to Det. 202, OSS, serving at French-Indo-China border area.

For Japanese surrender negotiation he acted as personal interpreter for Gen. Hayden Boatner at Chingkiang, China in August 1945. In September 1946 he escorted 24 Japanese war criminals from Shanghai, China to Sugamo Prison in Tokyo, Japan by air. Transferred to Japan for occupation and was assigned to GHQ, Allied Forces as undercover agent.

Returned to States in 1952, assigned to HQ 6th Army, Presidio of San Francisco and Oakland AB, CA. In 1958 he transferred to Fort Story, VA.

Retired as master sergeant in June 1963 after serving more than 20 years. He received numerous awards, medals, certificates, badges and citations wars and subsequent services. On July 19, 1993 he was inducted into U.S. Army Ranger Hall of Fame, Fort Benning, GA and on June 27, 1997 was inducted into Military Intelligence Hall of Fame at Fort Huachuca, AZ.

At present he lives with his wife, Kimiko, at Friday Harbor, WA; they have two daughters, Fumi and Karen; and three grandchildren.

DAVID MCALLISTER, born in Concord, MA graduated college at Stockbridge School of Agriculture in 1968. He was promptly drafted into the Army and completed basic training at Fort Gordon, GA and advanced infantry training at Fort Polk, LA. Arriving in Vietnam in June 1969 he was soon assigned to the First Inf. Div. (Big Red One), A Co., 2128th, 2nd Plt., Dau Tieng, Ben Chua, Saigon River, and Michelin Rubber Plantation were favorite hiking and camping spots, he particularly enjoyed the free helicopter rides. In March 1970 he was redeployed to the 199th Light Inf. Bde. 2/3rd (Old Guard) and spent the rest of his tour in Vietnam doing what an 11 Bravo does best. Back to the States in June 1970, he spent time at Fort Hood, TX with the First Armd. Div. before his discharge in January 1971.

Married in 1976 to the beautiful Wendy, he now operates an automotive repair shop with the help of his three boys in Chelmsford, MA.

His Air Medals, Purple Heart, Bronze Star, Vietnam Cross of Gallantry and Combat Infantry Badge are safely kept in the attic.

JOHN F. MCBURNEY, born Feb. 26, 1925 in Pawtucket, RI. Enlisted in the U.S. Army June 16, 1943 and served with the 103rd Inf. Div. Military locations/stations were Camp Grant, Jefferson Barracks and Camp Howze. He participated in battles at Rhineland, Ardennes and Central. Discharged Jan. 13, 1966 with rank of corporal.

Memorable experience: Dec. 7, 1944, E Co., 411th Regt. of the 103rd Div., under the command of Lt. William Kasper, was in a northeasterly advance in Alsace toward the German border. After crossing the Zintzel River near Griesbach, a unit of the enemy was observed in an open field about one mile away.

Lt. Kasper mistakenly believed they wished to surrender. He took the rifle from Pvt. John McBurney, age 19, and ordered him to go out and take their surrender although no white flag was displayed.

McBurney met with three of them in the middle of the field. They were armed and had no intention of surrendering. They believed instead the Americans were surrendering.

They ordered McBurney to join their unit but he refused. At that point their leader raised his rifle and fired point blank at McBurney but missed when McBurney dived behind a fallen tree stump.

Immediately, a heavy weapons platoon machine gunner opened fire and Kasper, St. Ralph McManus and Pvt. Conrad Hermann rushed out to rescue McBurney.

The enemy then retreated and that was the only shot they fired. On file, U.S. Army Military History Institute, Carlisle, PA.

He earned the EAME Theater Campaign Ribbon, Bronze Star, Victory Medal and American Theater Campaign Medal.

Married Ann Rivello and has six children and 17 grandchildren. Civilian employment as an electrical contractor, school teacher and attorney (52 years). He served as a senator for 16 years and elections commissioner for 14 years. McBurney is currently retired and resides in Pawtucket, RI.

WILLIAM R. MCCLAIN, born Feb. 15, 1929 in Dilliner, PA, grew up in Morgantown, WV. Enlisted into the U.S. Army in January 1950. Arrived in Inchon Korea. Was assigned to C Co., 1st Bn., 17th Inf. Combat Team.

He and his brother, Ted McClain, served together in C Co. at the same time. Not too many brothers were allowed to serve in the same combat company. William served in the 1st Plt. and Ted in the 4th Plt. in charge of the 60mm mortars. Ted took his discharge after returning to the States. William elected to make the Army his career.

While in Korea they fought battles in South and North Korea. He spent tours in Danang Vietnam with the 101st Abn. and Vont au Vietnam.

William was in the infantry 10 years and QMC for 18 years.

After leaving the infantry he managed NCO and officer clubs. He had assignments in Fort Polk, LA, Thailand, Vietnam and in Germany. He taught club management for three years at Fort Lee, VA.

His awards include the National Defense w/OLC, Korean Service Medal w/4 Campaign Stars, United Nations Service Medal, Combat Infantry Badge, Purple Heart w/OLC, Vietnam Service Medal, Vietnam Campaign Medal w/5 stars, Vietnam Cross of Gallantry w/ palm, Armed Forces Expeditionary Medal, Army Commendation Medal w/OLC, Bronze Star w/V, Presidential Citation w/OLC, Republic of Korea Presidential Unit Citation, Republic of Vietnam Presidential Unit Citation and Good Conduct Medal.

Retired from the U.S. Army in January 1977 as chief warrant officer.

Life member of the Combat Infantry Assn., Amvets, American Legion, Military Order of the Purple Heart, 17th Inf. Assn. and DAV.

Married Joy L. Riley Aug. 29, 1953. Has four children: Dana (deceased), Sierra, Shaun and Jeff; and six grandchildren: Shannon, Chilsea, Lindsey, Katelyn, Austin and Christian. Managed country clubs until retirement. The McClains reside in Columbus, OH.

JAMES MCGOUGAIN, born Sept. 11, 1950. Enlisted in the U.S. Army in April 1969 and served with the Comanche Co., Warriors Bn., 199th Inf. Bde. Light. Battles in which he participated include Operation Toan Thong and 1969-70 in Cambodia. Upon discharge his rank was private first class.

Memorable experiences: War Zone "D" on search and destroy battalion size base camp.

McGougain earned the Combat Infantry Badge and Gallantry Cross.

Civilian employment as a medical records clerk.

JAMES V. MCGOVERN, born in Providence, RI in 1945. He was inducted into the Army Sept. 7, 1965. After basic at Fort Dix, NJ he served with the Big Red One, 1st Inf. Div., A Co., 2nd Bn., 28th Inf. Black Lion of Cantigny out of Lai Khe Vietnam. He will always be proud to have served with the infamous Black Lions who engaged and were successful in numerous infantry operations in South Vietnam. He was honorably discharged in 1967.

In 1968 he married his wife, Nancy, and has two daughters, Kim and Kelly. Presently he has 35 years service with Massachusetts Electric Co. Has owned and operated a contract cleaning and property maintenance company since 1970. He resides with Nancy in Oxford, MA and is looking forward to retirement filled with travel and golf.

JOHN L. MCGUIRE, born Sept. 30, 1924 in Detroit, MI. Enlisted in the U.S. Army April 23, 1943 and served with E Co., 310th Inf., 78th Div. Military locations/stations include ASTP University of New Hampshire, Camp Pickett, VA and Fort Belvoir, VA. He participated in battles in Rhineland and Central Europe. Discharged Nov. 30, 1945 with rank of staff sergeant.

Memorable experiences: First combat patrol in December 1944; capture by German armor Dec. 14, 1946; RAT bombing of Stalag XII A Dec. 29, 1944; and liberation at Stalag XII A April 29, 1945.

Married to Muriel and has five daughters and 11 grandchildren. Civilian employment as manufacturing engineer, Ford Motor Co. Currently retired he resides in Pinckney, MI and spends his winters in Florida.

HERMAN H. MCLAWHORN, lieutenant colonel (Ret.), born in Kinston, NC. He attended school at Contentnea Elementary School and Hookerton High School. After returning from Korea, he entered East Carolina College and majored in accounting. He worked as a staff accountant for a CPA firm for 17 years and as controller of a pharmaceutical supply company for 22 years. He retired in 2001.

Drafted Jan. 10, 1952, sent to Camp Breckinridge, KY. After 16 weeks of infantry basic and advance training, he was assigned to eight weeks of Infantry Leadership School. Upon completion of

training he arrived in Korea on Aug. 14, 1951 and assigned to Co. G, Fifth Regimental Combat Team.

During the next nine months, he held the position of automatic rifleman to squad leader. Returned to the U.S. on July 4, 1952 and assigned to the Army Reserve.

Appointed as a second lieutenant in the NCNG on June 2, 1955. Held numerous assignments over the next 27 years. Most notable were battery commander, Btry. A, 690th FA Bn.; executive officer, 690th Maint. Bn.; and battalion commander, 730th Maint. Bn. Retired on June 29, 1982 with rank of lieutenant colonel.

Awards include the Combat Infantry Badge, Army Commendation Medal, Good Conduct Medal, Army Reserve Component Medal, National Defense Service Medal, Korean Service Medal, Armed Forces Reserve Medal, North Carolina Meritorious Service Medal, North Carolina Commendation Medal, United Nations Service Medal, Republic of Korea Service Medal, Korean Presidential Unit Citation, North Carolina Meritorious Unit Citation and North Carolina Distinguished Unit Citation.

Married to Bonnie Hall McLawhorn. Has two daughters, one stepdaughter, two stepsons and 13 grandchildren.

He is a life member of the Combat Infantryman's Assn., 24th Inf. Div. Assn., Reserve Officers Assn., American Legion, VFW, National Guard Assn. of the U.S. and the North Carolina National Guard Assn. He is also a member of the Korean War Veterans Assn. and the Fifth Regimental Combat Team Assn.

JAMES V. MCNICOL, born Feb. 4, 1925 to Harold V. and Artie May (nee Leigh) McNicol. He was inducted into the U.S. Army on Aug. 9, 1943, Akron, OH and joined the 42nd Rainbow Inf. Div. at Camp Gruber, OK on Sept. 6, 1943. A call came for combat replacements to the 20 infantry divisions that were training in the States. He was one of the 17,970 men that answered this call from the Rainbow Div. in this time frame.

Departed Camp Gruber May 5, 1944 for POE, Los Angeles, CA via Fort Ord and Camp Anza, CA. Joined the 33rd Golden Cross Div. at Finschhafen, New Guinea via Milne Bay, Oro Bay and Buena, New Guinea; prior to combat operations of the Golden Cross Div. in New Guinea, Dutch East Indies, Philippines and the eventual Occupation of Japan.

Returned to the Zone of Interior (ZI) via Pearl Harbor and arrived at Fort Lawton, WA. He was discharged at Camp Atterbury, IN on Feb. 11, 1946 with the rank of sergeant.

Enlisted in the USAF Nov. 21, 1950 and served under the Atomic Energy Commission and SAC under the umbrella of the Special Weapons Field. Zone of Interior stations included Lackland AFB, TX; Sandia Base, NM; Camp Kilmer, NJ; and Barksdale AFB, LA. Foreign stations were North Africa, Europe and England.

Discharged Nov. 20, 1954 with the rank of staff sergeant. Awards include the Bronze Star Medal, Combat Infantry Badge, Expert Infantryman's Badge, Expert Tank Weapons, Carbine, Sharpshooter Rifle, Marksman Pistol and Outstanding Airman, Strategic Air Command.

Memorable experiences: receiving the MacArthur Cup from the Rainbow Div. Veterans Memorial Foundation, Inc. in 1983 and presenting this cup to the Gen. Douglas MacArthur Memorial Foundation at Norfolk, VA in 1984 in appreciation for service with the 42nd Inf. Rainbow Div. and the MacArthur Crusade in the Pacific in WWII-a soldier and his commander. Also memorable was arriving at the Port of Seattle, WA on his 21st birthday, Feb. 4, 1946, receiving a birthday gift, courtesy of Uncle Sam. The Red, White and Blue had been good to this infantryman.

Married Eleanor Jean (nee McIntosh) on Dec. 13, 1952. He holds membership in the Rainbow Div. Veterans Assn., 33rd Inf. Golden Cross Div. Veterans Assn. and other major veterans organizations.

Worked as an electrician for 28 years. Retired in 1983 at the age of 58 years young, a forced retirement due to the policy of the government, closing down heavy industry in the rust belt to the States.

JOHN A. MENDEZ,
born June 24, 1944 in Fajardo, PR. He joined the U.S. Army Aug. 5, 1965; trained at Fort Dix, NJ; AIT at Fort Leonard Wood, MO; and Jump School at Fort Benning, GA. He served with A Co., 1/501 Inf., 101st Abn. Div. (1966); A Co., 4/503 Inf., 173rd Abn. Bde., Vietnam (1966-67); 711th AG (Postal) Co., 10th Mtn. Div. Somalia (1992-93).

He was on the USS *Pope* for 21 days to Vietnam. Participated in operations Aurora I and II, Toledo, Atlantic City, Sioux City, Robin Attleboro, Waco, Canary Duck, Cedar Falls, Big Spring, Junction City, Newark, Fort Wayne, Daytona, Cincinnati and Winchester.

He was wounded in Operation Junction City on March 1, 1967 and received an honorable discharge June 5, 1967.

Awards/medals include two Purple Hearts, Meritorious Service Medal, Good Conduct Medal, Meritorious Unit Emblem, National Defense Service Medal, Vietnam Service Medal, Armed Forces Reserve Medal, Army Reserve Achievement Medal, Combat Infantryman Badge, Republic of Vietnam Campaign Ribbon w/V (1960), Parachutist Badge, Marksman Badge w/Rifle Bar, Army Reserve Components Overseas Training Ribbon, Naval Presidential Unit Citation, Military Commendation Medal for Conspicuous Service, Armed Forces Expeditionary Medal, Overseas Service Ribbon and Army Service Ribbon.

MOS: 71L, administrative specialist; F-5, postal clerk; 11B, Infantryman; 12A, combat engine; 91B, medical specialist; 91S, preventive medical specialist; ITC, military instructor. Member of SWAT Team, Mogadishu, Somalia (1992-93).

Mendez has three daughters: Dora, Clarissa and Rocio. Employed by the U.S. Postal Service and is a licensed private investigator, security specialist and recovery agent.

SAMUEL HARVEY MERRITT,
born Oct. 2, 1932 in Pasadena, CA. When he was in the 10th grade and at the age of 16, he and several other guys joined the 40th Div. CANG. During his 11th year the Korean War broke out and as the 40th Div. was activated, he could not finish high school.

He was sent to Camp Cooke, CA (later Camp Cooke became Vandenburg AFB) for basic training. He had been promoted to corporal before the Korean War broke out so he was put in charge of close order drill (marching and the handling of rifles) and calisthenics, etc.

Before leaving for Japan he had one week's leave and he went home to visit with his family and neighbors.

He was shipped out on the *General M.C. Meigs* (operated by the Merchant Marines) and this was the first time that he had ever gone any place on a boat or a ship, and also he had never left California. For the most part, it was pretty much uneventful, except for the rough seas that hit them when they were a few days out of San Francisco and a few days out of Japan. The food onboard was handled by each unit's mess sergeant, as the food supplies were not the best, the mess sergeant had to be very creative. As they approached Japan they could see Mt. Fujiyama and that was a beautiful site.

Their first camp was Camp Younghans in the north part of Japan. The second camp was Camp Schimmelpenning located in the center of Japan near the town of Sendai. Their training continued on pretty much the same but with more hardships and emphasis, i.e., water and food rationing, climbing mountains with all of their equipment, engaged in many war games. Air lift training, real beach landings, classroom jump training, bayonet training, hand to hand combat training, Jujitsu, etc. The Aggressors used against them in the war games were Rangers.

On a three day pass they would go to Tokyo and see all of the sites, visit the various shops and buy souvenirs to send home. The Japanese were noticeably shorter than them. He did not see any aftermath of WWII.

They were shipped to Korea by naval ship, the *Sgt. Woodward*, and landed at Inchon Harbor on Jan. 2, 1952.

As soon as the ship was in Port, they got off and lined up to board a train. An interesting thing happened at that time. The sergeant called them to attention for an announcement. "He told us explicitly not to talk to or give any thing, i.e., food to the South Korean civilians that were watching us (there were women, children and old men all dressed in rags for clothes that I would not consider giving to the "Good Will")." The sergeant had a very good reason for this. Any way, somebody back in the ranks threw a candy bar out to the Koreans. He and everyone else could not believe their eyes at what happened, every Korean "dove" for that candy bar. Every man, woman and child. It looked like a bunch of "hyenas" stripping an animal. There was no consideration given to the women or children. They boarded the train.

They were shipped to Korea as a division and he kept his original rank and position, squad leader of HQ squad, Machine Gun Platoon, "H" Co., 2nd Bn., 223rd Regt., 40th Div.

From Inchon they took a Korean train northeast for several miles, then transferred to open trucks for several more miles, to the "Tent City" staging area and spent a couple of days there. They then packed up and marched to the rear area of the front line.

The regiment was located in the Kumsong area. At that time the MLR was stationary, not moving forward or backward. They, the machine gun platoon, were mainly supporting the rifle company's patrols as they made their rounds every day.

He was finally able to see what the "front line" was or looked like, he had no idea what to expect because a person's mind can not show him what it doesn't know.

Nothing was happening at that time, things were pretty quiet. Their artillery was constantly firing at the enemy as a "harassment" tactic. As far as he knows, this went on all of the time. The enemy, of course, returned fire.

One thing he did not expect was when the artillery shells were armed with "proximity fuses" they would sometimes explode when they came in contact with heavy moisture, etc., and sometimes this would happen right overhead and all of a sudden shrapnel would rain down on top of them.

He saw a lot of snow and ice and it was very, very cold, -30 to -40 degrees.

His "baptism of fire" was incoming barrages of mortar and artillery shells. This took place several times during his stay in Korea.

He was never injured by rifle bullets or artillery shells. But several time when the shells exploded, they covered him with dirt, knocked his helmet and other pieces of equipment off of him and twice, that he can recall, "duds" landed very close to him, one within inches of his right leg, so close that he could "feel" it.

Kumsong was his first position and it was generally quiet, even quieter when operation "Clam-up" came into effect, Feb. 10 to 15, 1952. Aside from that, his frostbite put him in the hospital during that same time frame.

The second position was the Kumhwa area. On their approach to that position was his first experience with incoming artillery. One shell knocked the "EE 8" field phone off of his back. After that attack they went up to their assigned position.

He received one Battle Star, Combat Infantry Badge, Army of Occupation Medal (Japan), Korean Service Medal w/Bronze Service Star and United Nations Service Medal. He is a life time member of the Combat Infantrymen's Assn. and a member of the Korean War Veterans Assn. and 40th Inf. Div. Assn.

He left Korea May 3, 1952 and held the rank of corporal. He was shipped home on the same vessel that he was sent to Korea on, the *M.C. Meigs*. They were then transported to Camp Stoneman for final processing out. His discharge was June 3, 1952.

He married Marian Pruett April 9, 1953. They have four children: Scott (48), David (46), Sandra (39) and Greg (32). David and Greg are both physicists. Civilian employment with Lockheed. He retired in 1987 and moved to Arizona.

RALPH E. METIVIER,
born Aug. 15, 1948 in Carlisle, MA. He was drafted in January 1969 and served in the U.S. Army. He went to Fort Gordon, GA for basic training. He then went to Fort Polk, LA for AIT. Then he went to Vietnam where he was with the Big Red One, 1st Inf. Div., A Co., 2nd and 28th (Black Lions). He worked out of fire support base Kein, along the Saigon River. He carried the M60 machine gun for about six month, then he got a break, a job interview within the base camp. Working in TOC had job interview with battalion Command Sgt. Maj. Robert M. Delia, Ralph is proud to say that he got the job and that he sees Command Sgt. Maj. Delia once a month at the CIA meeting and is proud to say that sergeant major is a great guy and good friend. Ralph made the rank of sergeant E-5.

He was awarded the Bronze Star, Air Medal, Combat Infantry Badge and Army Commendation Medal.

He went home to Carlisle in June 1970. Married Connie June 27, 1970. They went to Fort Riley, KS until Jan. 13, 1971, then Ralph and Connie moved back to Carlisle, MA. They have two children, Jessica (28) and Jason (26). Ralph has a sheet metal and welding company and like to play golf.

CHARLES I. MILLER,
Lieutenant Colonel, U.S. Army (Ret.), born in Millers, MD, Oct. 31, 1930. Graduated from Manchester High School in 1947. Enlisted in the Army in November 1947. Went to Japan in October 1949.

Served in Korea with the 24th Inf. Div., July

1950-September 1951. Graduated from Artillery OCS in 1955. Graduated from Command and General Staff College in 1963. Served in Vietnam during the Advisory Campaign 1964-65. Served two tours in Germany during the Cold War.

Retired from the Army in 1972. Awards include the Legion of Merit, Bronze Star w/OLC, Meritorious Service Medal w/OLC, Commendation Medal, Korea and Vietnam Campaign Medals, Parachutists Badge and Combat Infantrymen's Badge.

Married wife, Betty, and has three sons and four grandchildren. Currently retired and active in community and veterans affairs. Member of the Lineboro-Manchester Lions Club, Maryland Veterans Commission, Manchester War Memorial Committee, VFW, American Legion, DAV, AUSA, MOAA and Combat Infantrymen's Assn.

JOSEPH A. MINTO, born April 9, 1921 in Bridgeport, CT. Enlisted in the U.S. Army June 6, 1943 and served with the 71st Inf., Co. M, 48th Div. Basic training at Camp Blanding, FL. Overseas to France, Germany, Austria, Fern Pass, Brenner Pass, ending at Innsbruck Italy. Discharged Jan. 1, 1946 with rank of private first class.

Missions/battles participated in: Retook Maginot Line, fought across Rhine, Eller, Danube and Nectar rivers. Retook Ulm, Mannheim, Battle of Bulge.

Memorable experiences: In on captures of Werner von Braun and Gen. Wolfgang von Allstein (commander of 159th SS Grenadiers). Service under Gen. Dean who was later captured in Korea. Being blown out of the water while crossing the Eller River.

Minto was awarded the Combat Infantry Badge, two Bronze Stars, four Campaign Stars, ETO Ribbon, Victory Medal, Occupation of Germany Medal and Liberation of France Medal.

He is married and has two daughters. Civilian employment as vice president of sales for Jet Spray Corp., Waltham, MA. He is currently retired and resides in Bridgeport, CT. He is very active in the following military organizations: Commander and life member of Grosso-Seavey Post #167 American Legion, past Chef de Guerre 40&8 Assn., life member VFW, member Combat Infantrymen's Assn., member 44th Div. Assn. and member 71st Regt. Assn.

PHILIP J. MORANA, drafted Oct. 14, 1952 and took his basic training at Camp Breckinridge, KY. Arrived in Korea in February 1953 for one year and four and one-half months of war duty. He served in Co. E, 7th Regt., 3rd Div.

Memorable experience was when a short round (friendly fire) landed just outside of his trench, blowing him over and knocking off his helmet, but didn't get a scratch.

Discharged Oct. 13, 1954 at Fort Dix, NJ. After his discharge he became a Buffalo, NY, firefighter and retired 30 years later with the rank of battalion chief. He lives in Elma, NY.

FERD MORENO, Staff Sergeant, born Nov. 22, 1923 in Colorado Springs, CO to Ina F. Moreno. Taken into the service from high school June 28, 1943. Sworn into the Army in Forest Grove, OR. Taken into the Army at Fort Lewis, WA. Taken by train to Fort Knox, KY for basic training and assigned to the 717th Tank Bn. Became a tank driver for the proving grounds to test new types of tanks and equipment. Transferred to the Infantry when the call came for volunteers to help in the Battle of the Bulge. Sent to Fort Benning, GA for advanced infantry training and then joined the 5th Inf. Regt. They landed in Le Havre, France and attached to the 7th Army. When the allies started across Germany they were assigned to Patton's 3rd Army. Met up with the Russians near Styer, Austria. Worst day in Germany when on motorized patrol in Jeeps and was ambushed. Four were killed, four were seriously wounded and four of them received only cuts and scratches.

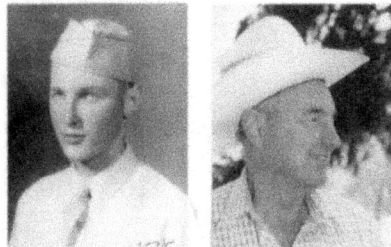

Awards: Combat Infantry Badge, two Bronze Stars, Victory Medal, American Theater Service Medal, EAME Medal and Good Conduct Medal.

Ranks held: T/5, corporal and staff sergeant. Discharged March 23, 1946.

Education: Graduated Laurelwood Academy 1943. Attended La Sierra College freshman year. Graduated in 1952 from Walla Walla College. One year graduate studies at University of Washington. BA degree in business administration. Employment with state of Oregon 12 years in workers compensation field, 17 years in private industry in industrial insurance field with last position as vice-president and general manager. Married to Jean Jutzy and has one son, Tony Moreno. Currently resides at 14430 SW McFarland Blvd., Portland, OR 97224. Phone: 503 620-8440.

ROCCO J. MORETTO, born June 20, 1924 in New York City, NJ. Inducted at Fort Dix, NJ on Feb. 12, 1942 and assigned to 1st Inf. Div., 26th Inf. Regt., Co. C. He had 13 weeks of infantry basic training at Camp Wheeler, GA. Joined 97th Div. for approximately two and one-half months at Camp Swift, TX. Left 97th Div. for overseas duty as a replacement, going first to Fort Meade, MD for clothing, equipment, etc.

POE was at Camp Myles Standish, Boston, MA where he boarded a train to Nova Scotia, Canada; then boarded the *Mauritania* and arrived in Liverpool, England, where he joined the 1st Inf. Div. He served with the Big Red One from October 1943-September 1945 without missing one day of service.

Campaigns: invaded France on June 6, 1944 at bloody Omaha Beach and fought through the campaigns of Normandy, Northern France, Ardennes, Rhineland and Central Europe.

Awards include the Bronze Star Medal w/OLC, Army Commendation Medal, Good Conduct Medal, American Campaign Medal, ETO Medal w/Bronze Arrowhead and five Campaign Stars, Victory Medal, Army of Occupation Medal w/Germany Clasp, New York State Conspicuous Service Cross, New York State Conspicuous Service Star, French and Belgium Fourragere, Combat Infantry Badge, Presidential Unit Citation, French Medaille Du Juliele and the French Croix De Combattant De L'Europe. SSgt. Moretto was discharged Oct. 19, 1945. On June 6, 2004, the 60th anniversary of D-Day, he was awarded the French Legion of Honor.,

Married Monica on May 8, 1949. They have one son, John, who is an engineer with the FAA. John is married to Ann and they have two daughters, Cara Ann and Jill Danielle.

WALTER H. MORRIS, born Jan. 12, 1934, Hazlehurst, MS. Entered military service March 19, 1951 and received basic training at Schofield Barracks, HI. He was sent to Korea as a replacement, assigned to Co. G, 2nd Bn., 27th Wolfhound Regt., 25th Inf. Div. and served in the Kumhwa Valley area until wounded Nov. 20, 1951 while on daylight combat patrol.

After a long stay in 343rd General Hospital, Japan, he returned to Co. G in late March 1952 on Heartbreak Ridge. Rotated out of Korea July 1, 1952 and spent the last 13-1/2 months service as a driver and smoke generator operator on an air base in England.

Awards include Combat Infantry Badge, Purple Heart, National Defense Service Medal. United Nations Service Medal, Korean Service Medal w/3 Bronze Stars, Good Conduct Medal and Presidential Unit Citation. PFC Morris was discharged at Fort Knox, KY March 10, 1954.

He received a BBA degree from Southern State College, Magnolia, AR in January 1960 and retired as a letter carrier from U.S. Postal Service on March 30, 1984; he also retired as captain of the Columbia County Sheriff's Reserve Deputies.

Presently he is the Columbia County Veteran's Service Officer and the county coordinator for the Salvation Army. He lives in Magnolia, AR with wife, Dorothy. They have three children: Denise, Dub and Doug; and five grandchildren.

DANIEL J. MUFFOLETTO, Private First Class, born April 12, 1925, in Baltimore, MD. Entered military service Feb. 16, 1944. Took basic training at Camp Blanding, FL. Assigned to 10th Mtn. Div., 87th Regt. HQ in Italy. Was a telephone lineman and jeep driver for CPT Joseph Hearst during WWII. Was honorably discharged Nov. 30, 1945.

Medals include American Theatre, European Theatre w/3 Battle Stars, Occupational Medal, WWII Victory Medal, Combat Infantry Badge, Good Conduct Medal, Rifle Sharpshooter Medal and three Bronze Star Citations and Medals with OLC and "V."

Spent 46 years with Chrysler dealers as body shop manager. Retired in 1987. Married Dorothy Rawlings April 12, 1947, and just celebrated their 50th anniversary. They now reside in Forest Hill, MD.

They have three children: Phyllis (Godwin), Daniel Jr. and Michael; and six grandchildren: Gail, Pamela, Jessica, Nicole, Kara and Samuel. Hobbies: Bowling, motorcycling, RC airplanes and boats.

CHARLES P. MURRAY, entered the Army from Wilmington, NC in 1942. Attended Infantry OCS and was commissioned second lieutenant in 1943. Served during WWII in France, Germany and Austria with 3rd Inf. Div. His final combat assignment was as brigade commander in Vietnam, where he served in the 196th Light Inf. Bde. and 9th Inf. Div. His awards include the Medal of Honor, Silver Star w/3 OLCs, Legion of Merit w/3 OLCs, Bronze Star w/OLC, Air Medal w/6 OLCs, Purple Heart, French Legion of Honor and Croix de Guerre, and various Republic of Vietnam, commendation and service medals. He attended National War College and has degrees from University of North Carolina and George Washington University.

Col. Murray retired after 30 years active service at Fort Jackson in 1973 and now lives with his wife in Columbia, SC. They have one daughter and two sons, both of whom are Vietnam veterans.

WESLEY E. MUTH, born Sept. 2, 1920 in Binghamton, NY. After serving two years in the CCCs (1938 and 1939) Wesley joined the Army in January 1940. He was assigned to Schofield Barracks in Hawaii.

After Pearl Harbor was attacked Wesley was sent back to Camp Gruber, OK to reactivate the 42nd Rainbow Div.

In August 1943 Wesley was sent to Europe on a noncom cadre as a platoon sergeant and assigned to the 4th Ivy Leaf Inf. Div. He was evacuated just prior to the Battle of the Bulge and returned after it was stopped.

Wesley was wounded and evacuated to England, given a medical discharge and left for the States soon after V-E Day.

Wesley was separated from the Army in Aug. 27, 1945 with rank of technical sergeant. He was awarded the Purple Heart.

Civilian employment: Mostly civil service retiring from USPS. He currently resides in Overgaard, AZ.

ROBERT NERNEY, born July 14, 1932 in Hammond, IN. Enlisted in the U.S. Army in August 1949 and served with the 3rd Inf., 29th, 7th Cav., 5th RCT and 2nd Inf. Military locations/stations include Fort Knox, Fort Benning, Okinawa, Japan, Korea and Fort Lewis. Missions/battles in which he participated were Korea from August 1950-July 1952. Discharged in 1954 with rank of sergeant.

Memorable experiences: Being in Alaska before it was a state. During the Korean War seeing how many different nations could help one nation.

Awarded the Combat Infantry Badge, CMB and Korean Service Medal w/7 Battle Stars.

Civilian employment: classified state employee, construction. He is currently retired and resides in Port Orchard.

RUDY PEZZARO, born June 23, 1926 in Washington, D.C. Enlisted in the U.S. Army Oct. 6, 1944 and served with the 81st CML Mort. Bn., 3rd Army, 71st Div. Military locations/stations include Camp Blanding, FL; England; France; Belgium; Luxembourg, Austria; Fort Benning, GA. He participated in two campaigns during the European Theatre of Operations, Central Europe and Germany. Discharged Feb. 16, 1946 with rank of private.

Memorable experiences: Liberation of concentration camps Ohrdruf, Buckenwald. Wounded taking Regensburg Germany in April 1945.

Awarded the Combat Infantry Badge, Presidential Unit Citation, Bronze Star, Purple Heart, French Diplome, New York Conspicuous Cross w/Silver Device, New York Conspicuous Star and New Jersey Distinguished Service Medal.

He is married to Edda and has one son, Edward and one grandson, Preston. Civilian employment as designer of ladies dresses. He is currently retired and resides in Fort Lee, NJ. He is an artist (a hobby).

CURTIS MERLE PILGRIM, born on a dairy farm near Edgewood, IA on Oct. 24, 1931 and graduated from Edgewood High School as salutatorian, class of 1949. Entered service at Des Moines on Feb. 21, 1951 with basic training at Camp McCoy, WI with the 114th Combat Engr. Bn. (MSNG), completed eight weeks of combat engineer training and eight weeks of infantry training.

In 1951 he volunteered for overseas replacement in Far East Command and departed on *General Black* to Yokohama, Honshu, Japan. Assigned to 1st Bn., 15th Inf. Regt., 3rd Inf. Div. in the vicinities of Yonchon and Chorwon; engaged in defensive and offensive battles

against Chinese Communist Forces. Wounded by shrapnel and re-assigned to HQ and Service Co., 15th Regt. Personnel, 3rd Inf. Div. Rear HQ south of Oijongbu.

Departed on troopship *General Hase* to Fort Mason, San Francisco, CA and released from active duty at Camp Carson, CO on Feb. 10, 1953. Awards include the Bronze Star for Valor, Purple Heart, Korean Service Medal w/4 Bronze Battle Stars and Bronze Arrowhead, United Nations Service Medal, Good Conduct Medal, National Defense Service Medal, Army Reserve Medal, Presidential Unit Citation, Korean Presidential Unit Citation, Meritorious Unit Commendation, Combat Infantry Badge, PB, EIB and Republic of Korea Hwa Rang Medal. He was honorably discharged April 22, 1957 from the Iowa USAR.

Received BS degree in agricultural from Iowa State University in 1956. Married Anna Margarethe Dona on June 23, 1957 and they have three children: David Alan (md. Naddene Mae Coziahr), Janice Kay (md. Mark David Winkler) and William Curtis; four grandchildren: Amanda Nichole and Jordan David Pilgrim; Nicole Margarethe and Benjamin Mark Winkler.

Was field foreman, Libby, MacNeil and Libby Pineapple Plantation, Molokai, Hawaiian Islands, 1954; high school vocational agriculture instructor; Future Farmers of America advisor; and adult farmer evening school instructor, 1956-60; crop and livestock farm owner and operator near Thomson, IL 1960-present.

Life member of the Korean War Veterans Assn. and the American Legion; charter member of the Korean War Veterans National Museum and Library; member of the Society of the 3rd Inf. Div., 15th Inf. Regt. Assn., Combat Infantryman's Brotherhood and the Non-Commissioned Officer's Assn., Sons of the American Revolution, the General Society of Mayflower Descendants and the Society of the War of 1812.

CHARLES PIPPITT, born Glenwood, IA, 1938. Joined IANG, 1955. Rank of staff sergeant before commissioned second lieutenant, 1961.

Active duty Army, 1966. Commander Basic Training Co., Fort Ord CA, 1967. Vietnam, 1967-68, 9th Inf. Div. 2/47(M), S-3 Air and Div. G-2 Air.

Married Deloma Hunt Hildebrand, 1968; two daughters, Shawna and Chri.

Instructor, Fort Benning, GA, 1968-69. Bootstrap UNO, 1970, BGS. Vietnam 1970-71, MACV advisor, 9th ARVN Div. Grafenwohr, Germany, 7th Army Training Center, director Public Affairs, 1971-74. Fort Bragg, NC, 4th PSYOPS Gp., assistant S-3, 1974-75.

Retired 1975, 20 years service, rank major. Awards: Combat Infantry Badge, three Bronze Stars, Air Medal, three Army Commendation Medals and Vietnamese Cross of Gallantry.

Moved to Colorado 1976, worked in real estate/ insurance business. Retired U.S. Postal Service, 2000. Life member: Veterans of Foreign Wars, Disabled American Veterans and Combat Infantrymen's Assn. Member: American Legion and Military Officers Assn. of America.

MEL POSNER, born June 21, 1924 in Syracuse, NY. Enlisted in the U.S. Army March 2, 1944 and served with Co. K, 14th Inf., 71st Div. Stationed at Camp Wheeler, GA and Fort Benning, GA.

Missions/battles participated in include Ardennes, Central Europe, Hartz Mountains, Siegfried Line and beyond.

Memorable experience was seeing England and France after the war.

Posner was discharged May 16, 1946 as technician 5. His awards include the Combat Infantry Badge and Bronze Star Medal.

As a civilian he worked in antique sales, jewelry and is still working part-time. He is married and lives in New York, NY.

RAY E. POYNTER, entered service as a draftee in 1943. After basic and advance training, he was sent to the Pacific where he served with the Americal Div., 1944-45, fought at Bougainville and Philippines and went on to Japan after the peace treaty was signed.

Discharged in 1945, re-enlisted in 1954 and served with the 1st Armd. Div. at Fort Hood, TX. He volunteered to go airborne and served in the 11th Abn. Div., 24th Inf., 82nd and 101st Airborne. Was assigned to the 1st Cav. Abn. Bde., 1st Bn., 8th Cav. where he served in the Vietnam war for a year.

Coming home he joined the 101st Abn. Div. and returned to Vietnam with them for a second tour. After Vietnam he was assigned as senior instructor at Tulane University before going to Korea for six months where he served with the 2nd Inf. Div.

Poynter retired as a first sergeant in 1972 and now lives in Arkansas. Awards include five Bronze Stars, National Defense Service Medal w/OLC, Good Conduct Medal (fourth award), Air Forces Expeditionary Medal (Korea), Combat Infantry Badge (second award), Purple Heart, Air Medal w/OLC, American Campaign Medal w/Bronze Star, Presidential Unit Citation, Asiatic-Pacific Campaign Medal w/3 Bronze Stars and Arrowhead, WWII Victory Medal, Army of Occupation Medal (Germany and Japan), National Defense Service Medal w/Bronze Star, Korean Service Medal, Armed Forces Expeditionary Medal (Korea), Vietnam Service Medal w/3 Bronze Stars and one Silver Star, Philippine Liberation Medal w/2 Bronze Stars, PIM, United Nations Service Medal, Republic of Vietnam Reserve Medal w/Device 1960 and Honorable Service Lapel Button (WWII).

He is a life member of DAV and VFW and is associate director of "The Jumping Mustangs" Abn., Air-Assault, Airmobile of the Vietnam War. With over 370 members, he has organized the chapter and made it one of the best organizations ever organized.

Served in combat as a pointman, BAR man, squad leader and first sergeant and is proud of his service.

Last but not least he is a member of the Combat Infantrymen's Assn.

LARRY K. PROCTOR, born Dec. 22, 1946 in Marietta, OH. Enlisted in the U.S. Army and served with the 196th LIB, 3/21 Inf. Military locations/stations include basic training at Fort Jackson, advanced infantry training at Fort Polk, Vietnam, Tam Ky, Chu Lai and DMZ. He participated in the Battle of Que Son, Tet

Offensive and Battle of Dong Ha. Discharged March 19, 1969 with rank of sergeant E5.

Memorable experiences: Bob Hope USO Christmas Show, 1967; R&R in Sydney, Australia; wounded July 9, 1968; LZ center S1 and S4 officer; diverted a sortie of beer and a sortie of ice cream during re-supply of line companies.

He was awarded the Combat Infantry Badge, Purple Heart, Bronze Star and USMC Unit Commendation.

Proctor has two daughters, Jennifer Paige and Stephanie Nichole. He is still employed as a veterans employment representative (LVER). He currently resides in Marietta, OH.

ALBERT RAMAS, born May 29, 1926 in Chicago, IL. Enlisted in the service Sept. 4, 1944 and served with K Co., 114th Inf., 44th Div. as a rifleman. Military locations/stations include Camp Hood, TX; Camp Chaffee, AR; and Fort Leavenworth, KS. He participated in battles in Rhineland and Central Europe. Discharged June 27, 1946 with rank of sergeant.

Memorable experiences: A German soldier saved his life near Gaildorf Germany (story too long to write). Meeting Gen. Dean, division commander.

Ramas earned the Combat Infantry Badge and Bronze Star.

He is married to Viola and has two daughters, Shari and Odette. Civilian employment as Chicago Park Dist. police officer (1947) and Chicago Police officer (1959). Ramas is currently retired and resides in Arlington Heights, IL.

ARTHUR WILLIAM REDDER, born Sept. 14, 1915, in Brooklyn, NY and was inducted into the Army July 14, 1941. After infantry training at Camp Croft, SC, was assigned to the 13th Inf. Regt., 8th Inf. Div., HQ Co. Received technician 5 rating after Radio School at Fort Benning, GA.

He was awarded the Bronze Star w/OLC, Combat Infantry Badge, Good Conduct Medal, etc.

The 13th Regt. sailed in a convoy from New York to Belfast, Ireland. Six months later, after intensive training, they were shipped to Normandy July 4, 1944. They fought their way through Normandy, Northern France, the Rhineland and Central Europe. The winter was extremely cold and fighting was tough, with a heavy loss of good men.

His brother served in an ambulance company, and

by chance, a wounded soldier directed him to Arthur at Cruzan, France. They had a great one day visit.

War ended in May 1945, at which time his outfit was east of the Elbe River, on the outskirts of Berlin, where they met their Russian allies. A short time later he was honorably discharged with the rank of technical sergeant.

Civilian employment with Benigan Essential Tremor. Redder is currently retired and resides in Pine Bush, NY. His wife passed away in November 1998.

SEWALL L. REYNOLDS, born May 1st, 1927 in Seattle, WA. Drafted into the Army Oct. 6, 1950 after completing five years of college at the University of Washington where he ran on the track team for four years.

He was trained at Camp Cook, CA with the 40th Div. National Guard, which was sent to Japan in March 1951. There they had further training and served as occupation forces.

They were sent to Korea in January 1952 and relieved the 24th Div. By that time Sewall was a rifle squad leader in the 1st Plt., A Co., 1st Bn., 223rd Inf. RCT.

Sewall was wounded March 13, 1952 during a night patrol when his squad was ambushed by a Chinese rifle platoon. For his actions that night he received the Bronze Star Medal w/V for valor and the Purple Heart Medal.

After five weeks on the hospital ship *Hope*, Sewall returned to his company on line and served as assistant platoon sergeant with the rank of sergeant first class. He returned to the States Sept. 24, 1952.

Sewall was married Nov. 16, 1952 to Emma Jelleberg and had four children: Larry, Karen, Karol and Jan. They celebrated their 50th anniversary in November 2002.

Sewall is a life member of the Combat Infantrymen's Assn. and a life member of the Disabled American Veterans.

Sewall taught and coached at both the junior high and high school level at Poulsbo, WA's North Kitsap school district for 30 years.

In his retirement he has enjoyed playing golf and tennis, fishing, traveling and making things for his 13 grandchildren and one great-grandchild.

CHURCHILL RIFENBURG, born June 24, 1917 in Tivoli, NY. Inducted in the Army Nov. 9, 1942 as corporal in 21st Coast Arty. stationed at Fort Miles, DE and Fort Monroe, VA. Joined 103rd Div., 410th Regt. Anti-Tank Co. later part of 1943 at Camp Howze, TX. Participated in European Theatre of Operation, landing at Marseilles and continued in combat through France, Germany and into Austria. Received American Defense Medal, European African Campaign Ribbon w/3 Battle Stars, Bronze Star, Army of Occupation and WWII Victory Medal.

Married on a three day pass March 4, 1943 to Miss

Catherine Postver and they have three sons. Retired from New York State Department of Transportation as engineering supervisor in 1980 after 30 years service.

PAUL R. ROCHFORD, born July 4, 1926 in Westfield, MA. Volunteered for U.S. Army after high school graduation in June 1944. Sent for tank destroyer basic training, Camp Hood, TX. Volunteered for parachute training and sent to Fort Benning, GA. In the 2nd Prcht. Training Regt.

He was a combat paratrooper in the 513th Prcht. Inf. Regt. of the 17th Abn. Div. for the Rhineland and Central Europe campaigns. Then he was transferred to the 460th Prcht. Pack Arty. of the 13th Abn. Div. headed for the invasion of Japan.

Graduated Middlebury College, Middle, VT with BA degree in 1950; Columbia University, New York City MA degree in 1951; and PD in 1953. Worked in all levels in education: elementary, secondary and college in guidance and counseling programs, college teaching (psychology) and college administration, psychology.

Married Patricia A. Clavin, New Bedford, MA and raised five children. Subsequently served four and one-half years in the 16th and 19th Special Forces groups, 1st Special Forces in 1960s.

He and Pat are now retired and live at 34 Bay Road, Barrington, RI 02806.

ROBERT S. RODDICK JR., born in East Highlands, CA. He left USC in his sophomore year to enlist in the Army. Served briefly in the 79th Inf. Div., then volunteered for the 10th Mtn. Div. (ski troops). Trained at Camp Hale, CO, then saw action in Italy (WIA) Discharged in January 1946.

Returned home to manage family citrus holdings and become reporter for the San Bernardino *Sun-Telegram*. He was county editor when he retired. At paper he met his wife, Jan, and married in 1947. They have two sons and two daughters and are still together! He is a life member of MOPH, DAV, Elks Lodge 836 and the CIA. He now plays a lot of cards at the Elks and an Indian casino.

MARTICA WILLIAM RUNYON, born in Logan, WV in 1922. After completing basic training in the 11th Inf., 5th Inf. Div. at Fort Benjamin Harrison, IN, he was transferred to Fort Custer, MI.

In April 1942 he landed in Iceland where he served for 16 months as a rifle platoon leader. He returned to the States and was assigned to the 63rd Inf. Div. Rangers.

In the spring of 1944 he landed in England and was assigned to the 30th Inf. Div. From there he served as a rifle platoon leader in Normandy and continued through France, Belgium, Holland and Germany.

Battles: St. Jean De Day, St. Lo, Mortain, Domfront, Tournai, Kerkrade, Aachen and Malmedy.

Medals: Bronze Star, Distinguished (Presidential) Unit Citation, Meritorious Unit Citation, Belgium Fourragere, American Campaign, Combat Infantry Badge, Expert Infantry Badge and EAME Campaign w/3 Battle Stars.

Upon discharge he attended college, earning a BS and MS degree and served as assistant headmaster in a military academy; college administrator, and then an assistant superintendent for the Charles County Board of Education.

Married, one son and four grandchildren and resides in La Plata, MD.

MIKE RUOFF SR., Sergeant, U.S. Army (Ret.), married to Vickie (32 years) and has one son, Sgt. Mike Ruoff Jr. who is active in the U.S. Army (Germany) with 1/77th Armd., 1st. Inf. Div. Ruoff entered the U.S. Army in April 1968. His state side units and duty include 1/63rd Armd., 1st Inf. Div.; 5/32nd Armd., 24th Inf. Div.; Reforger, Germany. Overseas tours: two tours Vietnam/Cambodian. First year with 11th Cav. Regt., B Troop, 1st and 3rd Plts., Vietnam (1969). Second year with 4th Inf. Div., Cambodia Campaign (1970).

Military locations: Vietnam and Cambodia, Xuan Loc, Ben Cat, An Loc, Loc Ninh, Quan Loi, Tay Ninh, Highway 13, Thunder 1,2,3 Fire Support. Luzon, Penn, Grant. Battles: "Contact areas."

His medals include the Vietnam Service Medal, Vietnam Campaign Medal, Combat Infantry Badge, Bronze Star Medal, two Army Commendation Medals and 1969 TET Offensive recognition.

Retired after 20 years as national park service road supervisor with Yosemite National Park, Wawona Dist. 100% disabled - service connected. Member of Combat Infantryman Badge Assn. and 11th Cav. Vietnam/Cambodia.

LORAN K. RUTLEDGE, born Oct. 31, 1925. Enlisted in the service Jan. 15, 1944 and served with Co. D, 410th Inf. Regt., 103rd Inf. Div. Military locations/stations include Fort Benjamin Harrison, Indianapolis, IN; Camp Blanding, FL; Camp Claiborne, LA; Camp Howze, TX; and Camp Shanks, NY. He participated in battles in Rhineland and Central Europe. When war ended he was transferred to a chemical mortar company. Volunteered to become a cook. Discharged April 19, 1946 with rank of technician 4.

Memorable experiences: Five months as a heavy machine gunner in the winter of 1944/45.

Rutledge earned the Combat Infantry Badge, Purple Heart, Bronze Star, Good Conduct Medal and WWII Victory Medal.

He is married and has one child and two grandchildren. Retired from a printing company after 43 years. He is currently a Montgomery County Veteran Service Office and resides in Crawfordsville, IN.

DANIEL R. SANKOFF, born Sept. 7, 1930 in Lackawanna, NY. Graduated from Lackawanna High

School in June 1948. Enlisted in the U.S. Army for three years on March 19, 1951. Took basic training at Fort Dix, NJ. After completion sent to Korea, arrived at Inchon on Aug. 30, 1951 and was assigned to the 31st RCT (Polar Bears) which was then attached to the 7th Inf. Div. (the Hourglass Div.).

Areas the 31st RCT participated in were Hill #700, #1073, #905 and various others, Hwachon Reservoir, Wyoming Line and Box Canyon. Was awarded the Combat Infantry Badge Sept. 21, 1951, just three weeks after arriving there. Promoted to the rank of sergeant in March 1952. On June 17, 1952, having enough points then, he rotated back to the USA.

Memorable experience was the day he rotated from Korea safe and sound.

After being permanently assigned to duty in the States in September 1952, of which two weeks was enough, he volunteered for duty in Europe. Arrived in Germany on Nov. 10, 1952. Assigned to 110th Regt., 28th Inf. Div. in Ulm, Germany. Met and married a German girl from Ulm (Maria deceased 1998). Rotated back to USA for an honorable discharge on April 13, 1954 with rank of sergeant.

In civilian life he worked as a clerk in the postal service for 17 years. He resigned from the post office in 1973 to open and operate his own travel agency. He founded Trade Winds Travel in Blasdell, NY and later opened a branch office in Springville, NY. Retired after 20 years as owner/president and moved to Lehigh Acres in Florida Dec. 27, 1993.

Awards: Combat Infantry Badge, Korean Service Medal w/3 Battle Stars, United Nations Service Medal, National Defense Medal, German Occupation Medal and Good Conduct Medal.

In February 2001 he heard about and became a member of the Combat Infantrymen's Assn., A Co., SW/FLA Fort Myers. Appointed to adjutant in April 2001 and on Aug. 23, 2001 was appointed as national membership officer. Both these positions keep him well occupied these days.

CALVIN "DOC" SAVAGE, born Feb. 24, 1933 in Rockaway, NJ. Enlisted in the U.S. Army April 1, 1950 and served with the 9th Inf. Div., 39th Inf. Regt., Co. C (basic). Military locations: Fort Dix, Hood, Bragg, Campbell, Stewart, Gordon and Monmouth. Missions/battles: Korea, Kumsong, 1951 summer and winter campaigns. Three Battle Stars, 24th Inf. Div., Co. C, 21st Inf. Regt.

Memorable experiences: 1953 married Elizabeth in Augusta, GA; two children, Deborah (b. 1960 at Fort Stewart, GA) and Calvin Joe (b. 1963 at Fort Huachuca). Service in Europe and Turkey with Army Security Agency as first sergeant. Retired at Fort Gordon in 1971 with 21 years service.

Awards: Silver Star, Purple Heart Combat Infantry Badge and Meritorious Service Medal.

Currently resides at 2529 Ivey Road, Augusta,

GA 30906. He is CEO and owner of Doc Savage Htg. & Air in Augusta, GA. Active with S.M.A.R.T. (Special Military Active & Retirement Travel Club), past president. Life membership with 24th Inf. Div., Combat Infantrymen's Assn. and Masonic Masons.

JAMES C. "JIM" SAVAGE III, Lieutenant Colonel, U.S. Army (Ret.), drafted in 1968 by Linden Local Board 72. Serving the Army with five active duty years and 17 active reserve years, he entered as a private and retired as a lieutenant colonel. In 2002, he retired from the Army's Soldier System Center after a 31 year civil service career as an Army chief counsel and chief of labor and General Law Team; Air Force foreign military sales attorney; contracts attorney and veterans attorney for the Veterans Administration General Counsel.

In Vietnam he served the 75th Rangers as a scout observer and operations/intelligence specialist. Following Law School, he re-entered the Army in 1973 as a JAG officer in Germany and Georgia serving as a prosecutor, defense counsel and claims judge advocate. In the Army Reserves, he was commander, New England Selective Service System; chief of Government Affairs for Civil Affairs units; trial counsel, production officer and personnel officer. LTC Savage is the recipient of 25 plus military citations, including the Bronze Star, nine Meritorious Service Medals, Combat Infantryman's Badge, Presidential Unit Citation and others.

Col. Savage received degrees from Austin Peay (BS), Memphis (JD), Georgetown (LLM), John Marshall Law (LLM) and Troy State (MSCJ). As an adjunct professor, he taught law school, university, and business school courses. He has served as president of the Massachusetts Chapter Federal Bar Assn. and the New England Judge Advocate Assn. and is a life member of the 75th Rangers Assn., Combat Infantrymen's Assn., Reserve Officer's Assn., Vietnam Veterans of America, American Legion, VFW, AMVETS, and has held association leadership roles, such as, state president, president, national and state judge advocate, and post commander. He is listed in several *Who's Who* editions, including ".. in the World, ..America, ..American Law* and was named by the Massachusetts Department of the American Legion as "Outstanding Citizen of Massachusetts."

The present Worcester, MA resident is married to Dr. Clara Parra Savage and is the father of four children: Sean, Catriona, Jimmy and Anthony; and is the eldest son of Mrs. Kitty Estes Savage of Clarksville, TN and the late James Savage.

ALFRED C. SEEBODE, born Nov. 6, 1924 in Philadelphia, PA. He graduated in June 1942 from Girard College, Philadelphia. Seebode was drafted in April 1943 and joined formation of 69th Div. at Camp Shelby, MS (this was very significant in possibly saving life later in his military career). The training cadre

were veterans of the North Africa Campaign. In a general discussion one day, their sergeant in answer to a question replied, "If you hear an artillery shell overhead like a train, or a bomb making a whistling sound, they are not going to get you. It is the one you don't hear that's big trouble."

In the spring of 1944, they broke up the 69th Div. and shipped them overseas as future replacements. After the invasion of France, Seebode went into Omaha Beach D+1 by landing craft as a replacement for the 1st Inf. Div. (Big Red One). He fought through the hedgerows of the Normandy Campaign until the break through at St. Lo on the night of July 31, 1944 while advancing to replace the front-line troops at Mortain. About midnight, while resting against an eight-foot high hedgerow on the side of the road, a bomb exploded just over the other side from them. He didn't hear anything but the explosion. The sergeant's remark back in basic training alerted his brain. He immediately changed from a sitting position to lying down in the very small depression, face down and cocked his helmet toward the road to protect him. Less than 15 minutes later, the antipersonal bombs exploded down the middle of the road. The one opposite him got him in the back of his right hand, but the six of the men around him, who were still in a sitting position, were killed. Who knows the answer, but he is certain the statement in basic training is the reason he is still here 59 years later.

Seebode was discharged in December 1945 with the Good Conduct Medal, European Theater Medal, Combat Infantry Badge, Purple Heart, Bronze Star, WWII Victory Medal, French Normandy Campaign Medal, New Jersey Meritorious Service Medal and the Burlington County Commemorative Medal.

He is still operating his own business of 39 years in the pattern and ship model field with the support of his lovely wife, Edna, and six loving cats as of May 2003.

JAMES P. SEIBERT SR., born Sept. 22, 1920 in Philadelphia, PA. Enlisted in the U.S. Army March 11, 1943 and served with the 7th Inf., Co. "F", 3rd Div. Basic training at Fort McClellan, AL and then to Camp Blanding, FL. Missions/battles in which he participated were Naples-Foggia and Rome-Arno. Discharged Dec. 19, 1945.

Memorable experiences: Captured 16 men in Cisterna, Italy May 25, 1944.

Seibert earned the Purple Heart, WWII Victory Medal, American Service Medal and EAME Campaign Medal w/2 Bronze Stars.

He married twice and has eight children (by his first wife), 26 grandchildren and two great-grandchildren. Civilian employment as a salesman. He currently resides in Reading, PA and is a volunteer at the VA Medical Center in Coatesville, PA.

ALBERT N. SEYMOUR, born Oct. 31, 1921 in Easthampton, MA. Enlisted in Army Infantry Sept. 2, 1942 and served in Co. F, 387th Regt., 97th Div. Stationed at Fort Leonard Wood, MO; San Luis Obispo, CA; Camp Cook, CA; Camp Kilmer, NJ; Germany; France; and Japan.

Missions/Battles participated in were Battle of the Ruhr Pocket (WWII), Germany and Czechoslovakia.

In early spring of 1945 in Cheb, Czechoslovakia, Co. F, 387th Inf. Regt., 97th Div. set up a defensive position preparing for the attack of the Germans

at midnight. One lone tank struck their forces. A nearby soldier took his bazooka, fired and knocked the tank out of action. He never knew who that soldier was until a few years later after the war ended. The soldier's brother said that he was Albert's neighbor in Florence.

Awards include the EAME, WWII Victory, Bronze Star, Good Conduct, American Campaign, Asiatic-Pacific, Combat Infantry Badge and AY w/Rifle Bar. PFC Seymour was discharged Feb. 14, 1946.

He and wife, Anna, have three children: Dennis, Edward and Joyce; four grandchildren; and three great-grandchildren. Their son-in-law, Francis, is a major in the U.S. Army. In civilian employment Seymour was a carpenter and is now retired and lives in Deerfield, MA. He enjoys golf and attends Co. F reunions.

ROBERT W. SHAUGHNESSY, born in Watertown, NY, March 8, 1920. From Jan. 3, 1939 to Dec. 15, 1942, he worked at the Florida Nation Bank and Trust Co., Miami, FL, as a teller, bookkeeper, custodian of the Safety Deposit Department.

From Dec. 15, 1942, after his induction at Camp Blanding, FL, he was transferred to USAAC as a private in Finance and HQ Co., Keesler Field, Biloxi, MS.

Next he was at Advance Combat Infantry Training, as a private, at Camp Livingston, LA, and then shipped overseas as a replacement to the 100th Div. and became first scout with a squad in Co. E, 397th Inf., 2nd Bn.

April 4, 1945, he crossed the Neckar River in a rubber boat and began the Battle of Heilbronn, as a corporal, and acting as first scout, came under intense sniper and machine gun fire, intense concentration of artillery and mortar shelling as well as small arms fire for seven consecutive days as his Co. "E", 397th Inf. forced its way forward, street by street, house by house, room by room, overcoming desperate enemy resistance repulsing counterclaim after counterclaim as the enemy struggled desperately to hold Heilbronn at all costs.

After taking Heilbronn, he, as point, led the unit on the road toward Backnang where he became "eye to eye" to a German "88" in the middle of the road pointed right at him, resulting in his diving to the right hand ditch. He proceeded to crawl toward the target, waded across a small stream and took his position on the left rear of a building adjacent to the stream. Being within distance, he began throwing his grenades at the "88." Within a short time, their unit appeared and made passable the damaged bridge and cleared the area for their procedure toward Stuttgart.

When the Germans surrounded, he was transferred to the Finance Office in Charlou, France, as technician 4, then transferred to 145th Finance Disbursing Section, Reims, France.

His awards, medals, badges: Bronze Star Medal, Combat Infantryman Badge and Distinguished Unit Citation.

Feb. 17, 1946, he was honorably discharged as technician 4, 64th FD Disb. Sect., Army of the U.S.

Presently he is broker/owner of Shaughnessy Realty, located at 1853 Marina Circle, N. Fort Myers, FL 33903. He is a licensed Real Estate broker and a licensed mortgage broker in the state of Florida.

He has lived with his daughter, Sandra Riley, in North Fort Myers, FL, for a number of years. Being very active in the community, he is a member of the Chamber of Commerce, Elks, VFW, American Legion, Delta Theta Phi Law Fraternity, The Southwest Alumni Club of the University of Miami, the Real Estate Investment Society and the Combat Infantrymen's Assn.

He is a member of the Realtor Assn. of Greater Fort Myers and the Beach, the Florida Assn. of Realtors and the National Assn. of Realtors.

CHARLES J. SHERMAN, went into the Army March 31, 1943 after two years service in the CCC. Service was at Camp Edwards, Fort Monmouth, Holabird, Fort Jackson, France, Rhineland, Central Europe and Valley Forge General Hospital.

Experiencing some frustration he volunteered for the infantry because he wished to feel like a soldier.

Greatest moments were being a replacement to Gen. Patton's Third Army; rowing across the Rhine River at midnight on March 21, 1945 at Oppenheim, Germany; and being awarded the Combat Infantry Badge.

Discharged July 11, 1947 with rank of sergeant. He earned the Combat Infantry Badge, Bronze Star and campaign ribbons.

Civilian employment as deputy probation officer. Currently retired and resides in Porterville, LA.

CARL W. SIEGEL, born in Chicago, IL in December 1919. Entered the service a month after Pearl Harbor taking his basic at Camp Hulen, TX before shipping overseas for additional training in England. His battery shipped to Oran when sniper fire still rang through the streets and participated in the entire North Africa expedition and then on to Italy for a total of five Campaign Stars.

Re-enlisted at the outbreak of the Korean War in 1950 and assigned to train troops at Camp Breckinridge, KY. Eventually shipping to Korea, but married Carol Fulwiler, his bride for the past 51 years, before his departure. Served as a first sergeant replacement in a line company of the 3rd Inf. Div. They were stationed on an OP along the Imjim River where he was wounded and lost much of his hearing from shellfire. Served the balance of his enlistment at Fort Ord, CA.

GERALD P. SIMAS, born Dec. 14, 1923 in Callahan, CA. Enlisted in the U.S. Army July 11, 1944 and served with the 96th Div. Military locations/stations include Camp Roberts, Philippines and Okinawa. He participated in battles at Leyte and Okinawa where he was a heavy machine gunner. Discharged Aug. 31, 1946 with rank of private first class.

Memorable experiences: Lots of mud and bullets, hard going. Lucky to have made it.

Gerald was awarded the Bronze Star, Asiatic-Pacific Campaign Medal, Philippine Liberation Medal and WWII Victory Medal.

He is married and has two children. Civilian employment: farming - timber faller. He is currently retired and taking it easy in Etna, CA.

ALLAN RICHARD SMITH, born May 22, 1926 in Springfield, IL. Enlisted in the service Aug. 14, 1944 and served with F Co., 30th Inf., 3rd Inf. Div. Military locations/stations include Camp Robinson, AR and Northeastern France. Missions/battles in which he participated were Colmar Pocket, Siegfried Line and Zweibruecken, Germany. Killed in action March 19, 1945 with rank of private.

Memorable experiences: Playing a large organ in a city in Eastern France before joining his division.

Smith was awarded the Presidential Unit Citation and French Fourragere. He is survived by his parents, Richard and Gladys Smith; and sister, Shirley Smith; all of Springfield, IL.

ROBERT PAUL SOLEY, born April 4, 1931. Entered Army Oct. 22, 1952 with basic training at Indiantown Gap, PA. C-R-B School, Eta Jima, Japan, Korea, Co. L, 15th Inf. Regt. and participated in Outpost Harry. Also at Camp Picket, Military Hospital, VA.

Awards include the Combat Infantry Badge, United Nations Service Medal, Korean Service Medal, Purple Heart, National Defense Service Medal and Bronze Service Star. He was discharged Feb. 28, 1954.

Soley is married and has one daughter, Bonita. He is retired and lives in Dallas, PA.

EVERETT L. SOWDEN, born June 30, 1920 in Providence, RI. Enlisted in the service in July 1942 and served with Co. E, 2nd Bn., 350th Regt., 88th Inf. Div. Military locations/stations include Camp Gruber, OK; Louisiana Maneuvers; Fort Sam Houston, TX; and Camp Wheeler, GA. Missions/battles participated in: Italy - Hitler - Gustav Lines - Gothic. Discharged Nov. 27, 1945 with rank of technical sergeant.

Memorable experiences: 88th Div. was the first all selective division to enter combat on any front in WWII; first to enter Rome Italy during combat; first selected to leave front line on rotation to USA; and first sergeant at Camp Wheeler, GA.

Sowden has been married for 55 years and has four children and seven grandchildren. Civilian employment was in automobile sales. He is currently retired and resides in Warwick, RI.

RAYMAN C. SPALSBURY, Colonel (Ret.), born in Mount Pleasant, MI on April 6, 1915. He enlisted April 23, 1941, assigned to AT Co., 126th Inf., 32nd Inf. Div., Camp Livingston, LA. Promoted to corporal, then sergeant. Attended OCS Fort Benning, GA and commissioned July 9, 1942. Served at IRTC Camp Wheeler, GA; Camp Butner, NC; Camp Phillips, KS; Camp Lugana, AZ (80th Div.); Fort McClellan, AL and Fort Lewis, WA.

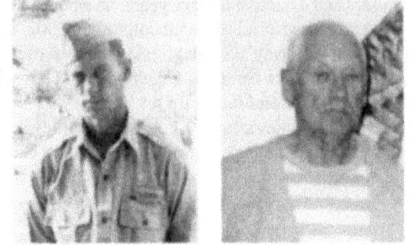

He went to the South Pacific in March 1944, landing at New Caledonia. Went to Guadalcanal and Bougainville and was assigned to the C Co., 145th Inf., 37th Div. He participated in landing on Luzon, battle of Manila as platoon leader and company commander, and was at Tuguegarao, Luzon on V-J Day. He served with 21st Inf., 24th Div. in Army of Occupation in Kyushu, Japan, 1947-48. Was wounded twice, Feb. 28, 1945 at Intramuros, Manila and May 7, 1945 at Mt. Pacwagon, Luzon.

He was awarded the Combat Infantry Badge, Bronze Star Medal w/OLC, Purple Heart Medal w/OLC, Good Conduct Medal, Army Reserve Achievement Medal, and the following service medals: American Defense, American Theater, Asiatic-Pacific Theater w/2 Bronze Service Stars, WWII Victory, Army of Occupation (Japan), Army Reserve w/2 Hour Glasses, Philippine Liberation w/1 Bronze Service Star, Philippine Independence and Philippine Presidential Unit Award.

He retired April 12, 1975 as colonel, AUS. Also retired as assistant postmaster, Lansing, MI. He has two daughters, two granddaughters, a grandson and one great-granddaughter.

He and his wife reside in Lansing, MI.

DAVID VINCENT STAHLEY, born Sept. 4, 1948 in Doylestown, PA. Inducted into the U.S. Army June 9, 1967 and served with Co. C, 1st Bn. 12th Cav. 1st Air Cav. Div. Basic at Fort Bragg, Advance Infantry at Fort Jackson and NCO Academy at Fort Benning. He served in Vietnam in 1968 at Base Camp Quang Tri.

His awards and medals include the National Defense Service Medal, Air Medal, Vietnam Service Medal, Vietnam Campaign Medal w/60 Device, Combat Infantry Badge, Purple Heart w/1 OLC, Sharpshooter Badge w/M60 Bar, Marksman Badge w/Rifle Bar (M-16).

Discharged from Valley Forge General Hospital, Phoenixville, PA April 18, 1969 with rank of sergeant E5.

Married his high school sweetheart, Bonnie Lee Krial. Latter had a baby girl, Stefanie, who grew up to be in the Army, 4th Inf. with a medical battalion. In Iraqi Freedom at the time of this publication. Excavation and heavy equipment was his life after his service. Now doing his heavy equipment operating at Fort Dix, NJ. Still calls Upper Black Eddy, PA his home.

ANGELO STALKOS, born Aug. 10, 1930 enlisted in the Army Infantry Oct. 7, 1947 and served with I Co., 5th RCT. Military locations/stations include Korea (four times), Berlin Germany and Alaska. He participated in the first four major battles of the Korean War and was on the beginning of Operation Ripper March 6, 1951. Discharged June 1, 1968 with rank of master sergeant E8.

Memorable experiences: First tour of duty in Korea 1948-49.

Angelo earned the Korean Service Medal, United Nations Medal, Korean Campaign Medal, Combat Infantry Badge, Army of Occupation Medal and Purple Heart.

Married Feb. 1, 1961 and has two daughters, Jo S. and Honey K. Civilian employment was in juvenile justice. He is currently enjoying retirement and resides in Leesville, SC.

BURTON STEINBERG, born on the lower east side of New York City on March 23, 1919. Raised on a farm in Connecticut, enlisted in the Army in 1950. Joined the 45th Inf. Div. "Thunderbirds" in Camp Polk, LA. Held all enlisted ranks through first sergeant with Hvy. Mortar Co. 279th. Received a battlefield commission in Korea in June 1952. Won Silver Star, Bronze Star, Purple Heart and Combat Infantry Badge. Wounded after jumping into a trench to take a prisoner during a patrol action on hill named "Dagmar." Served another four years as division training officer, Fort Dix, NJ. Married to Ann, a school teacher, one daughter, Jessica, also a school teacher.

Currently president of American Rod & Gun, Wholesale Division of Bass Pro Shops, Springfield, MO. Member of American Legion, VFW, 45th and 279th Assocs. National Order of Battlefield Commissions, Combat Infantrymen's Assn., Grand Lodge of Louisiana Masons and various Sporting Goods Assocs.

BARNEY STREETER, born June 10, 1923 in Astoria, OR. Enlisted in the U.S. Army in February 1943 and served with the 1st Armd. Div. Military locations/stations include Fort Knox, KY; Algeria; French Morocco; Italy; France; and Germany. The missions/battles in which he participated were Naples-Foggia, Anzio, Rome-Arno and Po Valley. He was discharged Dec. 8, 1945 with rank of technician 5.

Memorable experiences: Receiving the Combat Infantry Badge on Anzio.

He was in Co. F, 6th AIR with the 1st Armd. and Co. C, 11th AIB with the 1st Armd.

Streeter earned the Combat Infantry Badge, Silver Star and Bronze Star.

He married his wife, Louella, Aug. 7, 1954 in Odessa, WA. He has two daughters, Kim and Ellney, both born in Ritzville, WA. He is an apartment complex manager and resides in Spokane, WA.

DONALD L. STRUBING, born in Hicksville, OH March 17, 1967. He enlisted in the Army at age 20, after two years of college. He was stationed at Fort Hood, TX in 1987. In 1988 he married Robyn, his wife.

He deployed to the Persian Gulf in 1991, as a mortar platoon squad leader. He was assigned to 3/41st Inf., 2nd Armd. Div. as a corporal, at the time. He participated in Operation Desert Shield and Operation Desert Storm. Upon returning from the Persian Gulf, he left the Army and returned to school at Michigan State.

He earned the Combat Infantry Badge, Army Commendation Medal (2), Army Achievement Medal and Liberation of Kuwait Medal.

A daughter, Bryn, was born in 1997 after Don and Robyn moved back to Ohio, followed by a son, Evan, in 2000. Don is a computer technologist and a member of the American Legion, VFW, 2nd Armd. Div. Assn. and the Combat Infantrymen's Assn.

DONALD STUBBINGS, born on Sept. 13, 1931 in New York City, NY. He was inducted into the Army on Jan. 21, 1952 and assigned to the 9th Div. for basic training at Fort Dix, NJ. Received orders and arrived in Inchon, Korea on Dec. 3, 1952. Assigned to HQ Co. 1st Bn., 17th Inf. Regt., 7th Div. guarding POW on Kojedo Island. In January 1953, the regiment moved onto the MLR in I Corps where they were subjected to some of the heaviest fighting in the final months prior to the July 25, 1953 cease-fire.

Sgt. Stubbings received the following medals: Commendation Medal w/Metal Pendent, Korean Service Medal w/2 Bronze Stars, Combat Infantry Badge, United Nations Service Medal, National Defense Service Medal, Presidential Unit Citation, Good Conduct Medal, and was discharged on Dec. 11, 1953.

Married for 38 years, widowed in September 1995, he has two sons, one daughter, two grandsons and three granddaughters. He is a retired assistant mortgage officer and chief appraiser for a Savings Bank where he was employed for 45 years.

HIDEO SUGI, born Jan 3, 1930 in Hilo, HI. Drafted into the service in September 1951 and served with L Co., 224th Regt., 40th Div. in Korea. Missions/battles in which he participated were Kumhwa and Heartbreak Ridge. He was discharged in June 1953 with rank of private first class.

Memorable experiences: In May 1952 relocated to Cheju Island to guard North Korean POW. On reserve status. Hate spit and polish. Just like basic training. Went back to the Hills in July 1952. Better than Cheju Island.

Sugi earned the Combat Infantry Badge, National Defense Service Medal, Korean Service Medal, United Nations Service Medal and Korean War Service Medal.

He met and married his wife, Vicki, July 25, 1959. They have no children but many good friends. Civilian employment as a landscape engineer. He is currently enjoying retirement and resides in Kaneohe, HI. He is an active member with the Korean War Veterans Assn.

RAYMOND DARRELL SUMMERLOT, born May 29, 1925 in Bicknell, IN. Enlisted in the U.S. Army July 23, 1943 and served with Co. K, 317th Inf., 80th Div., 3rd Army. Military locations/stations include Fort McClellan, AL; Central Europe, Central England, Northern France and Rhineland. Discharged Nov. 22, 1945 with rank of private first class.

Memorable experiences: Sept. 24, 1944-May 5, 1945 POW Limburg Stalag XIIA, Neubranderburg Stalag IIA, Arbit Kommando, Glashutte, Germany.

He earned the Combat Infantryman Badge, Good Conduct Medal, Bronze Star, American POW Medal, American Theater Service Medal and EAME Theater Service Medal.

He married Naomi L. March 24, 1950 and has one son, Raymond L. (b. March 27, 1952). Earned his BS degree in mechanical engineering from Rose Hulman Institute of Technology. Civilian employment in design engineering for 41 years. Eight years of retirement spent enjoying golfing and computer games. He passed away Aug. 3, 1999 and is buried in Arlington National Cemetery. He lived in Terre Haute, IN for 52 years.

JOHN A. SUMMERS, born Jan. 4, 1927 at Prophetstown, IL and enlisted in the USMC at Moline, IL Feb. 1, 1944. He retired Feb. 1, 1972. He spent 28 years in the military. He was in the USMC in WWII, the Rangers in the Korean War and served with the 173rd Abn. in the Vietnam War. He held every rank from private to command sergeant major. He fought in 12 major campaigns and numerous battles. He was recommended for a battlefield commission during the Korean War. Three-war combat veteran.

Awards: Combat Action Ribbon, two Combat Infantrymen Badges, Presidential Unit Citation w/ Bronze Star, Republic of Korea Presidential Unit Citation w/Fram. Bronze star, Purple Heart, Air Medal w/4 OLCs, Marine Citation w/Combat V, Army Commendation Medal w/2 OLCs, Good Conduct Ribbon w/8 knots, Asiatic-Pacific Campaign w/Bronze Arrowhead and one Bronze Star, American Campaign Medal, WWII Victory Medal, V-J, WWII Occupation Medal w/bars from Japan and Germany, China Service Medal, Korean Service Medal w/6 Bronze Stars, Korean War Medal w/citation, Vietnam Service Medal w/4 Bronze Stars, Vietnam Campaign Medal w/date and bar, Vietnam Cross of Gallantry w/palm, National Defense Medal w/OLC, Cold War Medal w/ribbon, USMC Expert Rifle and Machine Gunners Badge, U.S. Army Expert Rifle Badge, 45-caliber Pistol Badge, Parachute Badge, U.S. Army Ranger Tab, 82nd Abn. Div. Raider Tab, 1st Marine Div. Patch and 8th Army Ranger Co. Patch. 173rd Abn., 25th Inf. Div. from the Korean War.

John and Gisela were married in December 1956 at Morrison, IL. They have four children: John R., Virgina, James M. and Patrica; six granddaughters; and four grandsons. His oldest son, John R., retired from the USAF. Civilian employment in construction trades. He is currently retired.

MARTIN L. TAHAKJIAN, born in Providence, RI. He graduated from Technical High School in 1928. Operated coal and wood company before entering the service on June 1, 1941.

Received his training at Camp Wheeler, GA, a member of the U.S. Army 37th Inf. Div. Was sent to Southwest Pacific and began duty on May 26, 1942. Served in Solomon Islands, Guadalcanal and Bougainville, and with Marine Raiders on New Georgia. Also served in the Philippines.

Is believed to be the first Rhode Islander to receive the Combat Infantry Badge. Was also awarded the Bronze Star, two Purple Hearts, Asia-Pacific Medal, among others. Was discharged Oct. 21, 1945 with rank of private first class.

Upon his return worked at USNAS, Quonset Pt., RI. Retired in 1970. Has been married to wife, Sharkey, for 56 years. They have three children: Martin T.L., Sharlene and Sheryl; and five grandchildren.

Is a member of the Combat Infantry Assn. and a life member of the Purple Heart, DAV and VFW.

JOHN REYNA TAPIA, JD, PhD, born in Ajo, AZ Jan. 29, 1922. WWII, ETO (1942-45): 862nd Engr. Avn. Bn.; 1A/60th Inf. Regt., 9th Inf. Div., platoon sergeant, 158th Inf., AZNG, 1947-48. Commissioned second lieutenant, Cavalry, ROTC, Univ. of Arizona, 1948. Active duty: 1948-65. 70th Tank Bn., Fort Knox/Korean War (1950). Non-line units: Chief, MP School, Fort Gulick, Canal Zone; chief, Army Section, MAAG, Chile; assistant professor MS&T, West Virginia State College; S3, Support Command, 4th Armd. Div. (Germany); Reserve advisor, Fort Douglas, UT. Retired as major, 1965.

Awards: Bronze Star w/V, two Bronze OLCs, Purple Heart Medal w/1 Silver and one Bronze OLCs, Army Commendation Medal, Republic of Korea Presidential Unit Citation, Bravery Gold Medal of Greece, Combat Infantry Badge, Parachute Badge and Scroll of Achievement. 4th Armd. Div. "DISTINGUISHED MEMBER" 70th Armd. Regt., by Order Secretary of the Army.

Academic degrees: BA, West Virginia State College, 1960; LLB, JD, Blackstone School of Law, 1960-61; MA, PhD, University of Utah, 1966-69. Professor: Western Michigan University, Kalamazoo; Southern Illinois University, Edwardsville; Fort Lewis College (10 years chairman), Durango, CO. Emeritus professor, FLC. Emeritus poetry editor, *Durango-Cortez Herald*; 3rd Colorado Congressional District "Certificate of Special Congressional Recognition" for 10 years service on the Academy (USMA; Navy; Air Force; Merchant Marine) Review Board.

Academic Honors: Scholarship, West Virginia State College; Sigma Delta Pi, Spanish; Phi Sigma Iota, Foreign Languages; Phi Kappa Phi, Graduate Studies; Order of Descubridores and Order of Don Quijote, SDP; Others: "Golden Laurel Leaf Crown" and "De-

cretum" as "Laureate Man of Letters", United Poets Laureate International; Honorable Order of Kentucky Colonels; Emeritus Professor, FLC; Emeritus Poetry Editor, *Durango-Cortez Herald*.

Life Memberships: Military Order of Purple Hearts, American Legion, VFW, 9th Inf. Div., 1st Cav. Div., MOAA; NAUS; NACCCA; Combat Infantrymen's Assn.

Books published: "*The Spanish Romantic Theater*", "*The Indian in the Spanish-American Novel*", "*Shadows in Ecstacy*"; "*La Tierra Comprometida...*" "*Alecia En Flowerland*".

Married to high school sweetheart, Bertha Cervantes Tapia. Resides in Prescott, AZ, where he has served on the Prescott Preservation Commission and chairman of the Yavapai County Republican Party, among a number of other leadership positions, including Yavapai County Special Deputy Sheriff.

RAYMOND H. TIMMER, born March 11, 1922, Chicago, IL. His education includes a bachelor's degree in commerce from DePaul University, Chicago and a MBA from Northwestern University, Evanston, IL. He enlisted in Co. D, 1st Inf. Regt., Illinois Reserve Militia in March 1942 and entered the Army on Dec. 10, 1942. He started at Fort Lewis, WA in the Mortar Section of Co. A. In November 1944 he was transferred to HQ Co., 1st Bn., 123rd Inf. Regt., 33rd Inf. Div. He was in the New Guinea and Luzon campaigns and the occupation of Japan at Takarazuka, Honshu.

Discharged as a staff sergeant in January 1946, he immediately enlisted in the Army Reserve. Was commissioned a second lieutenant, Infantry April 26, 1948. He was promoted to colonel April 3, 1969. After serving in a variety of assignments including commander, 3rd Bde. (AIT-INF) and chief of staff, 85th Div. (Training); commander 315th Field Depot and chief of staff, 86th U.S. Army Reserve Command; he retired from the Active Reserve in April 1977.

His decorations include the Legion of Merit, Bronze Star, Meritorious Service Medal and Combat Infantry Badge. He was placed on the Army of the U.S. retired list March 11, 1982.

He served as a member of the National Defense Executive Reserve 1981-90, president (1961) Department of Illinois, Reserve Officers Assn. of the U.S. and commander (1984) Chicago Chapter, The Military Order of the World Wars. He is a knight of the Military and Hospitaller Order of Saint Lazarus of Jerusalem and a knight grand officer of the Sovereign Military Order of the Temple of Jerusalem.

He and his wife, Dee, reside in Glenview, IL.

VICTOR J. TOMSKO, born Jan. 11, 1932 in Bairdford, PA. Served in the U.S. Army with 3rd Inf. Div., 15th Regt., 1st Bn., A Co. Basic training at Fort Knox, KY September 1949. Advance infantry train-

ing at Fort Benning, GA 1949-50. Missions/battles in which he participated include Wönsan Campaign, Chosin Reservoir Campaign and 1951 Spring Offensive. Enlisted for two years, one year extension due to war. After leaving Korea Victor trained recruits at Fort Leonard Wood, MO. Separated from service May 10, 1952. Transferred to Reserves and discharged July 25, 1956 with rank of sergeant.

Memorable experiences: Helping get wounded out of battlefield. Taking part in getting 7th Inf., 1st Marines out of Chosin Reservoir. Being evacuated from Hungnam Christmas Eve 1950.

His awards include the Silver Star, Bronze Star Valor, Combat Infantry Badge and four Bronze Battle Stars.

He and his wife, Elmira, have been married for 47 years. He has one son, Victor; one daughter, Kathleen; and six grandchildren. He is currently retired and resides in Gibsonia, PA. Interested in Native American history and is involved with veterans. Victor is a life member of DAV, VFW, American Legion, Korean War Veterans Assn. and 3rd Inf. Div. Society. He is also a member of the Combat Infantrymen's Assn. and Chosin Reservoir Org.

LAWRENCE TOPPI, born Aug. 27, 1947 in Cambridge, MA. Enlisted in the U.S. Army Dec. 12, 1967 and served with B Co., 413th Inf., 11th LIB, Americal Div. Military locations/stations include Fort Dix, NJ basic training; Fort Polk, LA advanced infantry training; Vietnam May 1968-69; Chu Lai (Duc Pho base camp). Missions/battles in which he participated were Counteroffensive Phase IV, V, VI and Tet 69 Counteroffensive (February-June 1969). Discharged Dec. 12, 1969 with rank of sergeant E-5.

Memorable experiences: When they went to Reserve Reconnaissance Platoon. It was a very sad experience and a sadder ending. But it is the most reoccurring memory he has of serving in the infantry in Vietnam.

Awarded the Combat Infantry Badge, Air Medal, Gallantry Cross, Army Commendation Medal, Vietnam Campaign Medal, Vietnam Service Medal w/4 Bronze Service Stars, Good Conduct Medal and National Defense Medal.

He is married to Sandy and has two children, Karl and Larry Jr. and two grandchildren, Kassandra and Kaitlyn. He just completed his 30th year with Raytheon Co. Toppi currently resides in Wilmington, MA.

GLENN H. TOWE, born in Walhalla, SC. He quit school and joined the USN at 17. Served in the Pacific in WWII, then went back to school in 1947 where he met his wife, Marian. He joined the Army in 1948 and went to Europe, Fort Benning, GA and Hawaii.

Went to Korea with the 5th RCT and was a first sergeant at Fort Jackson, SC when he and Marian mar-

ried. Their daughter, Glenda, was born there and son, Kevin was born at Fort Hood, TX. He retired in Augusta, GA on Nov. 30, 1973 with 30 years service.

Operated a home maintenance and handyman service until they returned to Walhalla in 1983. He is a member of the Oconee County Veterans Council, 5th Regt. Assn. and the 15th Inf. Assn.; life member of the Landing Ship Medium (LSM) Assn., 24th Inf. Assn. and Combat Infantrymen's Assn.

FREDERICK JOHN TREGASKES, born in

coal mining country in Yatesboro, PA, enlisted in 1953, took basic and advanced infantry training in Fort Jackson SC, where he attended Jr. Leadership School. He became an instructor in Fort Knox, KY and volunteered for Airborne School. He graduated from Jump School and served in numerous assignments in the 82nd Abn. Div. Served in Germany with 1/504th Abn. Inf., 1/509th Abn. (Mechanized) of the 1st Bde. Abn., 8th Inf. Div.

In January 1964 he returned to 82nd Abn. Div. at Fort Bragg and participated in numerous airborne operations to include testing the 11th Airmobile Div. Deployed with Aco 2/505 to the Dominican Republic in April 1964 with 82nd Abn. Div. Returned to Fort Bragg with 82nd Abn. Received orders in May 1966 for 1st Bde., 101st Abn. Div. in Vietnam and served with B Co, 2nd 327th Abn. Regt., the American Division and Advisor/Instructor with South Vietnamese Rangers. The last time he was wounded was June 27, 1967 north of Chu Lai. He was hit with a burst from an AK-47 rifle and a machine gun, through both hips, both buttocks and spine causing much destruction and paraplegia. After three hospitals in Vietnam, two years in Walter Reed Hospital, many years of recuperation and rehab at Womack Hospital, Fort Bragg and VA Hospitals this devoted paratrooper was medically retired. Through the years he continued to struggle to be normal. With braces on both legs, his back, and on crutches, he continued fighting a wheel chair, and eventually becoming bed bound. After being a squad leader, platoon sergeant, acting 1st sergeant, acting platoon leader, and running recon, he took his abilities into the veterans organizations. He assisted veterans as a service officer and a leader, he stayed active in the PTA and children with learning disabilities as a Charter and Board Member, served five years on Handicapped Advisor Council.

A life member of the Military Order of the Purple Heart, a Chapter Commander for 15 years and held numerous offices in state level including Judge Advocate, Americanism Officer (6 years), State Commander (twice) and Aide-de-Comp to National Commander. A life member of DAV serving in numerous offices including Commander, a life member of National Order of Trench Rat, a life member of VFW, Military Order of Cootie holding various offices. A life member of Keystone Paralyzed Veterans of America in Pennsylvania, he served 5 years on the Board of Directors, 5 years as Legislative Director, as president, and national director.

He is a member of Alleghenny-Kiski Valley Joint Veterans Committee, serving as chaplain 4 years and president 5 years. A life member of the Combat Infantryman's Association and Associations of International Paratroopers, 82nd Abn. Div. Assn., 101st Abn. Div. Assn., 1st Bde. (Sep.) 101st Abn. Div. and the American Division Assn. An active volunteer at VA Med. Center, Butler, PA, Aspinwall, PA, and S.W. Vet-

erans Home in Pittsburgh where he was appointed two terms by the governor to serve on the Advisory Committee. He served six years on Pennsylvania War Veterans Council and four years on the Pennsylvania Joint Veterans Commission.

He was awarded the Combat Infantry Badge, Expert Infantryman's Badge and Master Parachutist Badge. Among his numerous awards are the Silver Star, Bronze Star for Valor w/clusters, Purple Heart w/clusters, Commendation Medal for Valor w/clusters, Cross of Gallantry w/palm and numerous other medals and badges. He received a citation from the National President PVA, having 2,000 hours of volunteer service in the year 2001. He was awarded the Inspiration and Achievement Award by the President of Keystone Paralyzed Veterans of America.

In October 2001 he was inducted into the Hall of Valor at Soldiers Hall in Pittsburgh. On June 14, 2002 Fred was inducted into the 327th Inf. Regt., 101st Abn. Div. in Fort Campbell, KY as a distinguished member of the regiment. Unable to march he was wheeled in the formation by SFC Jonathan Tregaskes. That was the proudest most humble day of his life he stated. In April 2003 he was inducted and placed on the Wall of Valor in Southwestern Veterans Home in Pittsburgh. He was awarded the Pennsylvania State Commendation Medal by the Adjutant General for achievements and assistance to veterans.

When not at veterans meetings, functions or volunteering at the VA Hospitals or homes, you can find Fred at his beloved farm working in the fields on his tractor with hand controls. Hunting is good and corn grows well, air is clean and trout bite like hell. Married to Frieda Arlene for 46 years and has five daughters, two sons, and 18 grandchildren round out the family. He says, "A good wife, a good life, God has blessed me well. How can I complain?"

WALTER ALLEN TWYFORD, born June 15,

1944 in Kansas. Enlisted in the U.S. Army March 23, 1965 and served with the 25th Inf. Div. Military locations/stations were Fort Leonard Wood; Fort Polk; USAUR; Fort Benning; Fort Gulick; Republic of Vietnam; Fort Riley; and USMA. The missions/battles in which he participated include Task Force Oregon, I Corps, Republic of Vietnam 1967 and Tet Offensive 1968. Discharged in August 1968 with rank of first lieutenant infantry.

Memorable experiences: Being shot down during a helicopter combat air assault into a hot LZ by one "Charlie" with an AK-47.

He was awarded the Bronze Star w/V, Bronze Star w/OLC, Purple Heart, Combat Infantry Badge, Good Conduct Medal, Vietnam Campaign Medal, Vietnam Service Medal and Vietnam Cross of Gallantry.

He is married to Dietta and has one daughter, Marla and one stepson, Fred. Civilian employment: Teacher (retired). He is currently a consultant and resides in Chandler, AZ.

DAVID T. ULMER, Colonel, received the Air

Medal 10 years after his heroic deeds during Operation Desert Storm in his retirement ceremonies at Fort Bragg, NC Wednesday, Oct. 11, 2000. He was also awarded the Humanitarian Service Medal for actions associated with freeing Kuwaiti POWs in Iraq and providing humanitarian relief to citizens in Kuwait. Gen. Scales, Deputy Commanding General of the Special Forces Command, made the presentation. Col. Ulmer

was cited for flying highly classified combat missions into Iraq and Kuwait to locate enemy weaponry. In the same ceremony he was retired from the Army after an illustrious career which included over 30 years of service to include combat tours in Vietnam with the 173rd Abn. Bde. and Fifth Special Forces Group in Operation Desert Storm.

Col. Ulmer was initially assigned Deep Targeting missions in Iraq and trained Coalition Forces in the desert prior to the ground war in Operation Desert Storm. While leading Coalition Forces in the invasion and liberation of Kuwait he was wounded. It was during this action that he assaulted an Iraqi enemy position exposing himself to enemy fire enabling his assault group to advance to a strategic and safe position. He also pulled several wounded soldiers to safety and was awarded the Saudi Arabian Medal of Honor for his actions. Even though wounded himself he refused medical evacuation until five days later when he was flown back to Saudi Arabia where he was given medical treatment and awarded the Purple Heart for his wounds. In addition, he was awarded the Bronze Star Medal and Army Commendation Medal with "V" device for valor.

After the ground war he was credited with saving both civilian and military lives by volunteering and disarming hundreds of explosive devices at the risk of his own life. He served as the deputy chief, Coalition Warfare Branch (Task Force Freedom) and was attached to the 5th Special Forces Group during the invasion and liberation of Kuwait. He received special recognition by Gen. Schwarzkopf after the war. Col. Ulmer, then Maj. Ulmer, is recognized as being one of the most decorated combat soldiers in Operation Desert Storm.

Col. Ulmer is a native of Charleston, SC. He graduated from North Greenville College in 1962 with an AA degree and is a 1964 graduate of the University of South Carolina where he received his BS Degree in business administration. He is a graduate of the Army's Command and General Staff College.

His awards and decorations include: Combat Infantryman Badge, Master Parachutist Badge, High Altitude Military Freefall Parachutist Badge, Legion of Merit, Bronze Star with "V" device, Purple Heart, Saudi Arabian Medal of Honor, Meritorious Service Medal, Air Medal, Army Commendation Medal with "V" device for valor (4/OLCs), Army Achievement Medal (4/OLCs), Good Conduct Medal, National Defense Service Medal (second Award), Humanitarian Service Medal (second Award), Outstanding Volunteer Service Medal, Vietnam Service Medal, Vietnam Campaign Medal, Vietnam Cross of Gallantry, Southwest Asia Service Medal, Overseas Service Medal, the Saudi Arabian-Kuwait Liberation Medal and Liberation of Kuwait Medal awarded by the Kuwaiti government. He has been awarded foreign parachutist wings from Vietnam, Israel, Thailand, Germany, England, Australia and Italy.

Col. Ulmer has been married for the last 35 years to Patricia Ulmer, a media assistant at Central Davidson High in Lexington, NC. They have a son, Brian, who is an Eagle Scout and a graduate of Western Carolina University and works with Lowe's Home Improvement in Charlotte, NC. His daughter, Sherry, is a registered nurse who works in California.

HOMER T. UNDERWOOD, born Aug. 19, 1924.

Enlisted in the U.S. Army March 11, 1944. Military

locations include basic training at Camp Blanding, FL for 17 weeks. Joined 70th Inf. Div. in Fort Leonard Wood, MO. European Theater December 1944-May 1946. Battles and campaigns in which he participated were Rhineland and Central Europe. Discharged May 31, 1946 with rank of staff sergeant.

Memorable experiences: First day on front line was on Christmas day 1944; serving with Occupation Forces in Berlin, Germany after the war.

He was awarded the EAME Service Medal w/2 Bronze Stars, Combat Infantry Badge, Good Conduct Medal, Army of Occupation Medal and WWII Victory Medal.

Homer has two sons, Homer Underwood Jr. and Steve Underwood (wife, Kim); five grandchildren: Sarah, Amy, Kelly, Terril and Steven; and one great-granddaughter, Emily. Civilian employment as high school teacher and coach for 19 years, high school principal for 11 years and county schools supervisor for 10 years. He currently resides in Graceville, FL. Retired June 30, 1989 with 40 years service in public schools. Enjoying his time with his family, his friends, his church and fishing and going to University of Alabama football games.

WILLIAM G. WALKER, born July 18, 1947 in

Rosiclare, IL. Enlisted in the U.S. Army Infantry Aug. 8, 1966. Military locations/stations include Fort Lewis (basic), Fort Ord (AIT), Korea (7th Inf. Div.), Germany (3rd Inf. Div.), Vietnam (196th LIB Americal Div.), Korea (2nd Inf. Div.), Vietnam and Fort Campbell (101st Div.), Germany (7th Armd. Div.) and Fort Knox (Armor School as a drill sergeant). Missions/battles in which he participated were Fire Base Mary Ann Republic of Vietnam, Hiep Duc Valley Republic of Vietnam and A Shau Valley Republic of Vietnam. Retired from service Aug. 31, 1986 with rank of E-7.

Memorable experiences: Massacre of Fire Base Mary Ann Republic of Vietnam March 28, 1971.

He was awarded the Bronze Star Medal w/"V" and OLC, Meritorious Service Medal, Army Commendation Medal w/2 OLCs, Air Medal, National Defense Service Medal, Good Conduct Medal (six awards), Army Service Ribbon, Overseas Ribbon (two), Armed Forces Expeditionary Medal, Combat Infantry Badge, NCO Professional Development Ribbon, Republic of Vietnam Service Medal w/2 stars, Republic of Vietnam Campaign Medal w/60 device, Republic of Vietnam Civil Cross of Gallantry w/"Palm", Republic of Vietnam Civil Action Honor Medal, U.S. Valorous Unit Award and Republic of Korea Presidential Unit Citation.

He is married to Shannon and has two stepsons, Chris and J.W. William retired in 1996 from Asplund Tree Service. He currently resides in Vine Grove, KY and enjoys fishing, hunting, ATVing and RVing.

FREDERICK N. WASHINGTON, born in

Rochester, NY. Inducted in the U.S. Army April 3, 1962 and took basic training and AIT at Fort Dix, NJ. Assigned to Co. C, 1st Bn. (Mech), 5th Inf., 25th Inf. Div., Cu Chi, Vietnam, February 1966-February 1967. Returned to Vietnam in November 1969 and assigned to C Trp., 3rd Sqdn., 4th Cav., 25th Inf. Div. Participated in all operations with the units and returned stateside in November 1970.

Awards include the Combat Infantry Badge, three Bronze Stars (one w/V), Purple Heart, Army Commen-

dation Medal w/V, Valorous Unit Award, Republic of Vietnam Cross of Gallantry w/Palm Unit Award and Republic of Vietnam Civil Actions Award. Retired from the Army with the rank of sergeant first class (E-7) on Oct. 31, 1982.

Employed by South Carolina Department of Corrections. Married for 30 years and has two sons (one deceased). He is a member of the 25th Inf. Div. Assn., Military Order of Purple Hearts Assn., 1st Bn. (Mech), 5th Inf. Assn., 3rd Sqdn., 4th Cav. Assn. and is a life member of VFW Post #4262.

JOHN R. WASHNEY, born in Laflin, PA. Enlisted

in the Army, Jan. 9, 1951 went to Fort Dix, NJ. Volunteered for airborne service. Sent to Fort Bragg, NC for basic training with 82nd Abn. After 18 weeks training, shipped out to Fort Benning, GA for three weeks for parachute training. After five qualified jumps, assigned to 508th RCT. After 32 weeks of advanced training was promoted to corporal. Volunteered for service in Korea; shipped out from Fort Lewis, WA to Camp Drake, Japan. Assigned to "C" Co., 17th Regt., 7th Div. Wounded Oct. 9, 1952. Spent a couple of weeks in the hospital before getting back to outfit. Sent to Koje Island for November 1953. Returned to the front line in December 1952 around Old Baldy, Pork Chop Hill, Arsenal Hill, Erie Hill and Hill 327.

Promoted to sergeant in December 1953 and sergeant first class in February. Reinforced Pork Chop Hill March, April, July 1953. Wounded July 9th and returned to the U.S. in September at Fort Meade, MD. Received honorable discharge Jan. 9, 1954.

Received awards: Purple Heart w/OLC, Good Conduct Medal, National Defense Service Medal, Korean Service Medal w/3 Bronze Stars, Combat Infantryman Badge, United Nations Service Medal, Parachute Badge and Korean War Service Medal.

Married Gerry Mushinsky in 1955 and has five children: Noreen, Bruce, Robert, Nancy and Tina; and five grandchildren. Belongs to VFW, Korean War Vets of Wyoming Valley and Combat Infantrymen's Badge Assn. Lives in Plains, PA.

JOSEPH W. WEBBER JR., born May 29, 1931,

Columbus, OH. Entered active duty Dec. 4, 1952 with infantry basic training with the 101st Abn. at Camp Breckinridge, KY. Then to Pusan, Korea, to Yonchon,

Korea, 2nd Div. Replacement Center assigned to Baker Co., 1st Bn., 9th Inf. Regt., 2nd Div.

Served during the balance of war on line in the Kumhwa and Chorwon Valley areas until the cease fire was signed on July 27, 1953. He served in Korea one year, one month and one day, then assigned for remaining service at Fort Leonard Wood, MO, U.S. Army Hospital, 5th Army Med. Det.

Awards include Korean Service Medal w/Campaign Star, United Nations Medal, Combat Infantry Badge, National Defense Service Medal, Republic of Korea Presidential Unit Citation and Good Conduct Medal. He was discharged as sergeant on Dec. 3, 1954.

He is a life member of the Combat Infantry Assn., a member of the Ohio Legion and the 9th Inf. Regt. Manchu Assn. Retired as executive vice-president of Hadler Realty in June 1996 after 38 years of service. Presently resides in Columbus, OH with his wife, Audrey. He is semi-retired.

ARTHUR W. WELDON, born March 25, 1925

in San Pedro, CA. Enlisted in the Army Dec. 2, 1943 and served with F Co., 30th. Regt., 3rd. Inf. Div., Camp Shelby, MS. Served in Naples, Italy; Southern France; Germany; and Austria Aug. 4, 1944-Jan. 17, 1946.

The most memorable times came after the war. He returned to Europe in 1981 and again in 1994 with other vets. The welcome he received from the people was very emotional. They had parades, dinners, but the message made clear to him was their gratitude for freeing them from the oppression they had been under.

At the time of combat he never fully understood the reason for his being there, but after seeing the suffering at the Concentration Camps and the people going through his garbage for food, he understood!

Awarded the Combat Infantry Badge, Bronze Star, Purple Heart and Croix de Guerre. Discharged May 2, 1946 with rank of private first class.

Married high school sweetheart, Evelyn. Their daughter, Francine, was born nine days after he entered the service. Civil employment with the Department of Defense. Retired after 36 year as an aeronautical engineering technical supervisor, San Diego, CA. Volunteered at hospital, police patrol, Church Thrift Store.

JOHN A. WENDELL, born in Cambridge, MA

Sept. 29, 1944. He quit college and was drafted at 23. In 1968 he received BCT at Fort Dix, NJ and AIT at Fort Polk, LA (Tigerland). After AIT he was sent with 60 other infantrymen to NCO School at Fort Benning, GA.

Went to Vietnam from McGuire AFB as a replacement for C Co., 1/35th, 3rd Bde., 4th Inf. Div. operating near a Special Forces Camp (Duc Co). In 1969 after the battle of Chu Pa Mtn. and Search/Destroy mission in the Ia Drang Valley. He was transferred to HHC, 3rd Bde. (S-2).

After returning from Vietnam, he met Jo Ann and married. Their son, Bryan, was born at Hackensack, NJ. He is now married to Regina M. Vaccaro, MD. On June 1, 2001 he retired in Brooklyn from PG&E with 20 years of service. He is a life member of the 35th Inf. Regt. Assn. and New York/New Jersey Registrar for the 4th Inf. Div. Assn.

EDWIN D. WILLIAMS,
born in Brooklawn, NJ. Entered active duty in June 1944 and arrived in Europe December 1944. Assigned to Co. F, 22nd Regt., 4th Inf. Div. during the Battle of the Bulge. Though under strength from many casualties in the Hürtgen Forest, the unit went on the offensive in early January.

He was captured during heavy combat in early February and was a POW for five days then repatriated by the 9th Armd. Div. spearheading toward the one remaining bridge over the Rhine at Remagen. He stayed and fought with the unit until the end of hostilities.

Discharged as technical sergeant at Camp Grant, IL Feb. 6, 1946. Awards include the WWII Victory Medal, EAME Campaign Medal w/3 Battle Stars, Combat Infantry Medal, Presidential Unit Citation and Bronze Star.

He is a proud member of many veteran organizations. Retired in 1986 after over 45 years in the automobile field. Presently lives in Champaign, IL with his wife, Margaret. They have two daughters, Berta and Priscilla; one son, Steven; and three grandchildren.

FRANK J. WILLIAMS,
Chief Justice of the Supreme Court of Rhode Island was born in Cranston, RI where he attended public schools. He received his commission as a second lieutenant upon graduation from Boston University where he was a member of ROTC He served for three years in West Germany along the East/West German border with the 1st Recon. Sqdn., 2nd AC Regt. as a tank platoon leader, S3 Air, commanding officer C Troop and adjutant of the squadron.

He was transferred to Ban Me Thuot, Republic of Vietnam in December 1965 where he served with Adv. Tm. 33 and as an advisor to the 23rd Arvn. Inf. Div., MACV for one year. During this time he was promoted to captain.

His decorations include, in addition to the Combat Infantryman's Badge, the Bronze Star, three Air Medals, two Campaign Medals, the Army Commendation Medal, Aircraft Crewmen's Badge and from the Republic of Vietnam, the Gallantry Cross w/Silver Star for Valor and the Staff Service Medal - First Class.

He separated from the service in March 1967 and attended Boston University School of Law from which he graduated in 1970. He was in private practice for 25 years in Providence, RI and was selected as a Superior Court judge in December 1995. In February 2001, he was nominated by Gov. Lincoln Almond to be Rhode Island's 50th chief justice and was unanimously confirmed by the General Assembly.

RUSSELL "RUSTY" ZELENIAK,
born in Berlin, NH, on June 3, 1920. He gave up a deferment to enlist in the U.S. Army on Oct. 14, 1942 and took basic training at Fort Eustis, VA. In February 1943, he was sent to a replacement depot outside of Casablanca, French Morocco, from where he was assigned to 81mm mortar platoon, HHC, 1st Bn., 41st Armd. Inf. Regt., 2nd Armd. (Hell On Wheels) Div. which had made the D-Day landing at French Morocco on Nov. 8, 1942. He served in French Morocco, Algeria, Sicily, England, France, Belgium, Holland and Germany. He participated in five major battles: Sicily (D-Day), Normandy, Northern France, Rhineland and Ardennes/Alsace (Battle of the Bulge).

His awards include the Bronze Star Medal (Sicily), Combat Infantryman's Badge, Expert 81mm Mortar Badge, Marksman 45 Cal. Pistol Badge, Distinguished Unit Citation w/OLC, EAME Campaign Medal w/Bronze Arrowhead (D-Day Sicily) and a Silver Service Star for five major battles, Belgian Fourragere and Belgian Croix de Guerre which were awarded to all the men in the 2nd Armd. by the Belgium government for being the foremost division to liberate their country in September 4944, and for stopping the Germans' 60-mile advance into Belgium during the Battle of the Bulge by destroying their spearhead, the German 2nd Panzer Div., in a five day battle, Dec. 24-28, 1944, Good Conduct Medal, WWII Victory Medal, and the State of New Jersey's Distinguished Service Medal w/OLC. His division received two letters of commendation, one from Maj. Gen. J. Lawton Collins, commanding, U.S. Army VII Corps, and the other from Lt. Gen. Courtney H. Hodges, commanding, 1st U.S. Army, and Field Marshal Bernard

L. Montgomery. Gen. Collins commended the 2nd Armd. for its "remarkable dash and exceptional fighting spirit" in spearheading and expanding the breakout of Normandy at the end of July 1944, and Gen. Hodges and Field Marshal Montgomery commended the 2nd Armd. for its "outstanding and distinguished feat of arms" in defeating and destroying the German 2nd Panzer Div. during the Battle of the Bulge. Zeleniak served two years and seven months overseas. He received an honorable discharge at Fort Dix, NJ on Oct. 12, 1945, two days shy of a three-year hitch.

In January 1946, he enrolled under the GI Bill of Rights in the School of Journalism of the State University of Iowa, Iowa City, IA, where he was awarded the school's Johnson Memorial Award for feature writing (his stories were published in *The Daily Iowan,* a local college/city newspaper) and he received the university's bachelor of arts degree in August 1949. Among his jobs after graduation were reporter-news photographer for *The Linden News,* editor of the New Jersey *PDCA News,* a publication for painting and decorating contractors, and industrial office work. In March 2001 he retired from a nine-year part-time job at Trademark Plastics Corp., Linden, NJ, where he kept records of resin products purchased and sold to manufacturers of plastic products. He and his wife of 55 years, Pauline, reside in their ranch-style home in Edison, NJ, with their son, Mark. Their daughter, Mrs. Beth Ann Shipman, resides with her husband, Bruce, a building contractor, in the house he built outside of Gunnison, CO.

BURTON ZITKIN,
born in Providence, RI in 1925. He joined the Army in 1943. He was stationed at Fort McClellan, AL, for basic training and then was assigned to duty at Fort Meade, MD, and Camp Van Dorn, MS. He fought at Normandy, in the Rhineland, and in Ardennes and Central Europe. His most memorable experiences were fighting in Normandy and meeting the Russians in Czechoslovakia. He was awarded the Combat Infantry Badge, two Campaign Ribbons, four Battle Stars, and the Good Conduct Medal. He achieved the rank of private first class and was discharged in 1946.

Zitkin received a BSA from Bryant College and spent his career as a corporate accountant. He married Ellen Grilleches Weiss, a holocaust survivor in 1973, and helped to raise two stepchildren. Ellen died in 1996. Zitkin married Carolyn Livingston in 2000. He lives at Cranston, RI.

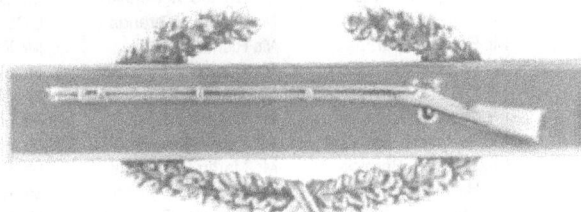

COMBAT INFANTRYMEN'S ASSOCIATION ROSTER

Mr. Harold P Aarhus
Mr. Daniel M Abbott
Mr. Frank E Abell
Hon. Richard B Abell
Mr. Abie Abraham
Mr. Edward G Abraham
Mr. Sidney B Abrams
Mr. Melvin Abramson
Mr. Robert D Ackerman
Mr. John E Ackermann
Mr. Harold H Ackles
Mr. Doyle F Acornley
Mr. John L Acre
Mr. Earl C Acuff
Mr. John C Adame
Mr. Gerald J Adamietz
Mr. Bill R Adams
Mr. Charles W Adams
Mr. Clarence M Adams
Mr. Conrad A Adams
COL Dwight L Adams (Ret)
Mr. Richard J Adams
Mr. Robert W Adams
Mr. Sidney G Adams
Mr. Thomas J Adams
Mr. William S Adams
Mr. Willie G Adams
Mr. Willie Addington
Mr. Peter E Addorisio
Mr. Walter Ade
LTC Jack I Aden
Mr. Grover C Adkins
Mr. James V Adkins
Mr. James M Adkinson
Mr. Harlan Adolphson
Mr. Matthew B Aitken
Mr. Neal A Akerlind
Mr. Dennis A Alba
Mr. Joseph H Albertson
Mr. Sam F Albertson Jr
Msg George A Albright Ret
Mr. Paul Alderete
Mr. Harold B Aldrich III
Mr. Arthur D Alexander Jr.
Mr. Richard O Alexander
Mr. William E Alexander
Mr. Ralph R Alexis Jr
COL Robert M Alford (Ret)
Mr. Duane E Alger Jr
Mr. Don A Alien
Mr. Gene Alien
Ltc Kirk T Alien
Mr. Michael Alien
Mr. Charles G Allen
Mr. Ralph R Allen
Mr. Willis G Allen
Mr. Arthur A Allender
Mr. Frank Allo
Mr. Norman L Alloway
Mr. Charles H Allwander
Mr. John M Almeida Jr
Mr. Kyle E Almond
Mr. Hector A Alonzo
Mr. William J Alpern
Mr. Charles W Alsterlund
Mr. John Alutto
Mr. David H Alva
Mr. Jose Alva
Mr. Richard S Alvarez
Mr. John R Amante

Mr. Charles J Ambrose
Mr. David H Amend
Mr. Eugene H Ames
Mr. Roland L Amlaw
Mr. Robert W Amos
Mr. Albert O Anctil
Mr. John H Andersen
Mr. John H Andersen
Mr. Andrew H Anderson
Mr. Carl A Anderson
Mr. Edward C Anderson
Mr. Erik C Anderson
Mr. Horace Anderson
Mr. Howard K Anderson
Mr. Jack M Anderson
Mr. Maltie Anderson
Mr. Merl G Anderson
Mr. Richard A Anderson
Mr. Virgil L Anderson
Mr. Norman E Andrew
Mr. Donald R Andrews
Mr. William M Andrews
Mr. Leonard L Andrzesewski
Mr. Joseph J Angi
Mr. Andrew G Anguiano
Mr. Richard R Angus
Mr. Edward R Anhalt
Mr. Charles E Anthony Jr
Mr. Alvaro Antone
Mr. Daniel P Antonino Sr
Mr. Orville A Antrim
Mr. Clayton E Apgar
Mr. Frank F Aplan
Mr. Raul Aquilar
Mr. Pablo R Aquirre
Mr. Robert Arbasetti
Mr. Benjamin J Arbuckle
Mr. John R Arend
Mr. Edward N Arendell
Mr. David L Argabright
Mr. Raleigh E Armentrout
Mr. James B Armstrong
Mr. Woodrow G Arndt
Mr. James H Arnett
Mr. Robert D Arnett
Mr. Edward R Arney
Mr. James L Arney II
Mr. Bill M Arnold
Mr. George L Arrollado
Mr. Edward T Arthur
Mr. Stephen M Artner
Mr. Thomas J Asaif Sr
Mr. Joseph W Ascolillo
Mr. Ralph E Ashcroft
Mr. Charles O Ashley
Mr. Clarence W Astleford
Mr. Dennar A Astyk
Mr. Denner Astyk
Mr. John D Atkinson
Mr. Ralph V Atkinson
LTC Hubert H Attaway (Ret)
Mr. Paul V Attaya Sr
Mr. Shelby Atwood
Mr. Thomas A Aubrey
Mr. Aaron Augustus
Mr. James M Auletto
Mr. Ralph E Aull
Mr. Howard D Ault
Mr. William H Ault
Mr. Royce V Austin
Mr. Alexander J Austin III

Mr. Vincent A Autuori Jr
Mr. Dudley S Averill
Sgm Victor V Aviles Ret
Mr. Norman E P Aweau
Mr. Fred D Ayer
Mr. James L Ayers
Mr. John M Ayers
Mr. Tayyar Aymelek
Mr. Armondo C Azzinaro
Mr. Arnold L Babbit
Col William P Babcock Ret
Mr. Carroll W Baber
Mr. Luis J Baca
Mr. Miguel Bach
Mr. Elroy F Backlund
Mr. William S Bacon
Mr. Paul W Baehr
Mr. John Bage
Mr. John F Bagienski
Mr. Harry A Baij
Mr. Paul D Bailey
Mr. William H Bailey Sr
Mr. John E Bakach
Mr. Gary H Baker
1SG Gerald J Baker Sr
Mr. James O Baker
Mr. Milton B Baker
Mr. Paul N Baker
Mr. Roy L Baker
Mr. Wayne M Baker
Mr. Russell A Bakken
Mr. George F Balas
Mr. Joseph Balcazar
Mr. Louis Baldovi
Mr. Richard C Baldwin
Mr. Lloyd W Ballard
Mr. David A Balint
Mr. Jay W Ball
Mr. Joseph W Ball
Mr. Leslie F Ball III
Mr. Ronald W Ball
Mr. Samuel W Ballinger
Mr. Bernard K Banach
Mr. Leo Bank
Mr. James D Bankes
Mr. Joseph A Baptista
Mr. George J Baranski Jr
Mr. George A Barber
Ssg James C Barber Ret
Mr. Clifton L Barbieri
Mr. Louis H Barbone
Mr. Fred M Barbosa
Mr. Rocco J Barbuto
Mr. Angelo Barca
Mr. Joseph S Barca
Csm James T Barker Ret
Mr. William S Barker
Mr. Joseph T Barna
Mr. Joseph S Barnes
Mr. Robert K Barnes
Mr. William M Barnes
Mr. Walter L Barnett
Mr. Jesse C Barnhardt Jr
Mr. Bernard C Barnhart
Mr. Stephen Barnick
Mr. Harry L Barr
Mr. Angelo Barresi
Mr. Daniel R Barrett
Mr. Donald L Barrett
Mr. Joseph J Barrett

Sgm Raymond C Barrett Ret
Mr. Frank M Barrows
Mr. Michael J Barry
Mr. James M Bartholomew
Mr. Joseph F Bartholomew
Mr. Harold W Bartig
Mr. John R Bartlett
Mr. Kenneth L Bartlett
Mr. Michael K Barton
Mr. Stanley E Baska
Mr. Larry D Bass
Col Archie F Bassham Ret
Mr. Benton E Bastian
CSM Robert Bates (Ret)
Mr. William Y Bath
Mr. George W Bauer
Mr. John L Bauer
Mr. Stephen L Bauer
Mr. Arnold R Baum
Mr. Harry A Baumann
Mr. William S Baumgardner
Mr. Marvin C Baumgardt
Mr. Ray A Baumgarner
Mr. Harold Baumgarten
Mr. Frederick H Bayer
Mr. Raymond A Bayer
Mr. William R Bayless
Mr. Andrew Baysura
Mr. Matthew B Beacher
Mr. Claud P Beal
Mr. William L Beal
Mr. Lynne O Beall
Mr. Harold V Bean
Mr. Loren E Bean
Mr. Herbert E Bearce
Mr. Rutlend D Beard Jr
Mr. Daniel L Beardsley
Mr. James Beattey
Mr. Paul J Beauchaine
MSGT Charles F Beazley
Mr. Harold H Bechtoid
Mr. Joseph W Beckenbach
Mr. Albert H Becker
Mr. Valloyd B Becker
Mr. Alvin P Bedgood
Mr. Basil B Beeken
Mr. Benjamin R Beeman
Mr. Edwin W Beers
Mr. Clarence W Begole
Mr. Martin M Behan
Mr. Charles T Behler
Mr. Richard A Behlman
Mr. William D Behlmer
Mr. Donald W Behnke
Mr. John F Behrends
Mr. Richard R Beil
Mr. Donald E Beilinson
Mr. Alfred E Beinemann
Mr. William J Beitz
Mr. Paul F Belardino
Mr. Martin S Belefant
LTC Frank C Belitsky
Mr. Clarence D Bell Jr
Mr. John L Bellini
Mr. Frank Bellomo
Mr. Frederick A Bellows

Mr. Joseph S Belonos
Mr. Marvin E Bendel
Mr. Richard J Benedict
Mr. John F Benko
Mr. James A Bennett
Mr. Lawrence E Bennett
Msg Norman M Bennett Ret
Mr. Paul H Bennett
Mr. Arvin W Bennington
Mr. Jesse W Bennington
Mr. Burtis W Bensinger
Mr. Ernest J Benting
Cpt Anthony E Berardesca
Mr. Gordon F Berg
Mr. Arthur C Berger
Mr. John H Berger
Mr. John T Berger
Mr. Perry J Bergeron Jr
Mr. Theodore W Berghoff
Mr. Samuel M Bergin
Mr. Rick G Bergman
Mr. Richard S Bergquist
Mr. Albert S Bergstrom
Mr. Lawrence H Beringer
Mr. P Ott Bernard
PSG Rick A Bernardi
Mr. William J Bernardini
Mr. Francis C Bernas
Mr. Charles Bernat Jr
Mr. Frank W Bernschein
Mr. Joe K Berry
Mr. Merle K Berry
Mr. Michael D Berry
Mr. Robert I Berry
Mr. Roger J Berry
Mr. Earl Bertenshaw Jr
Mr. Gerald J Berto
Mr. Richard O Bertoli
Mr. Dale B Besom
Mr. Thomas E Bessler
Mr. Ray V Bethel
Mr. William L Bevan
Mr. Alden C Beverly
Mr. Carl J Bevilacqua Sr
Mr. John G Beville
Mr. Edward J Bialobok
Mr. Joseph R Bianculli
Mr. Joseph Bielski
Mr. Edward S Bierce
Mr. Richard O Biering Jr
Mr. Bernard L Billing
Mr. James E Billman
Mr. Michael G Birdsale
Mr. Raymond L Birsen
Mr. Wilbur C Bishof
Mr. Joseph G Bishop
Mr. Lee Bishop
Mr. Leroy F Bishop
Mr. Lester B Bishop
COL Thomas B Bishop
Mr. Walter M Bishop Jr
Mr. John C Bitler
Mr. Sheldon Bitner
Mr. Howard E Bjerke
Mr. Harold D Black
Mr. Patrick F Black Jr
Mr. Edward J Blackburn
Mr. Laban C Blackburn
Mr. William D Blackburn
Mr. Allan F Blackmar
Mr. Paul D Blackmer

Mr. Jack V Blackwell
1 Sg Woodrow T Blair Ret
Mr. Joseph P Blake
Mr. Richard J Blake
Mr. Roland F Blanchard
Mr. Willis C Blanchette
Mr. William R Blankenberg
Mr. Donald Blankenship
Mr. Martin Bleile
Mr. Arlen H Bliefernight
Mr. Wayne H Blessinf
Mr. Alfred E Block
Mr. Henry D Block
Mr. Herbert Blondheim
Mr. Willard A Bloom
Mr. Richard A Blowers
Mr. Douglas Blue Jr
Mr. Cecil Blumenstein
Mr. James P Boardman
Mr. James S Boardman
Mr. Aram A Bobigian
Mr. Theodore J Bocci
Mr. Raymond H Bockleman
Mr. Charles G Boelkins
Mr. Alan E Boers
Mr. Frank S Boffa
Mr. Richard H Bogard
Mr. Frederick W Bohnberger Sr
Mr. John W Boicourt
Mr. William D Boleman
Mr. Tom F Boles
Mr. Richard W Bolin
Bg Philip L Bolte Ret
Mr. Thomas N Bompensa
Mr. George Bonchulo
Mr. Norbert J Bonn
Mr. Robert M Bookbinder
COL Joseph A Bookhamer
Mr. Donald W Booth
Mr. Larry D Booth
Mr. Roland J Bordeleau
Mr. John E Boren III
Mr. George F Borjes
Mr. Jim F Bork
Mr. Lawrence A Borsari
LTC Charles H Borsom (Ret)
Mr. Samuel Bosch
Mr. Eugene S Boss
Mr. Edwin J Boss Jr
Mr. Robert J Botash
Mr. Warren C Bouchard
Mr. Lyle J Bouck Jr
Mr. Robert J Bouldin
Csm James A Bourgeois Ret
Mr. Archille O Bourque
Mr. Fredric A Bourne
Mr. Charles W Bowar
Mr. Charles B Bowen
Mr. Arthur M Bowen Jr
Mr. James M Bower
Mr. Robert Bowles Jr
Mr. David J Bowman
Mr. James F Bowman
Mr. John A Bowman
Mr. Thomas J Bowns

100

Mr. Warren H Bowser
Mr. Michael A Boxer
Mr. Edward F Boyce
Mr. John Boyce
Mr. Hugh L Boyd
Mr. William E Boyd
Mr. William Y Boyd II
Mr. Walter F Boyda
Mr. Frank Boyko Jr
Mr. John D Boyle
Mr. Joseph F Boyle
Mr. James W Bozeman
Mr. Richard D Bradbury
Mr. William D Braddock
Mr. William C Bradford
Mr. William W Bradford
Mr. Harvey D Bradford Jr
Mr. Richard W Bradley
Mr. William F Bradley
COL Wray E Bradley (Ret)
Mr. William T Brady
Mr. Isador Bragger
Mr. Charles E Brainard
Maj Russell M Brami Ret
Mr. Oscar R Braman
Mr. Robert L Bramley
Mr. Ellis S Branch
Mr. Sol R Brandell
Mr. Jerall D Branson
Mr. William R Brant
Mr. William W Braswell
Mr. Saul Brechner
Mr. James F Breen
Mr. Vernon C Breen
Mr. Marvin F Breighner
Mr. Alfred H Breninger
Mr. James F Brennan
Mr. John W Brennan
Mr. Daniel A Brescia
Mr. Harry F Brett
Mr. Kermit W Brey
Mr. Leroy C Bricker
Mr. Franklin H Bridenbeck
Mr. George H Bridges
Mr. William C Bridges
Mr. Robert V Bridwell
Mr. Elmer F Bright
Mr. Don I Brillhart
Mr. Charles V Brinkley
Mr. Henry J Briscoe
Mr. Donald L Brittain
Mr. Andrew J Britten
Dr. Joseph P Broccolo
Mr. Joseph T Broccoli
Mr. Eugene P Broderick
Mr. George G Brocherding
Mr. Theodore N Broeckling
Mr. Thomas Bromley
Mr. Larry F Brooks
Mr. Robert C Brooks
Mr. Thomas A Brooks
Mr. William F Brooks
Mr. Michael E Brophy
Mr. Larry A Brotman
Mr. James W Broughton
Mr. George R Brouse
Mr. Byron J Brower
Mr. Arthur W Brown
Mr. Carl H Brown
Mr. Carl R Brown
Mr. Chris N Brown
Mr. Franklin L Brown
Mr. George J Brown
Mr. George W Brown
Mr. Gerald B Brown
Mr. Glenn C Brown

Mr. James A Brown
Mr. James L Brown
Mr. Jerome F Brown
Mr. Jesse M Brown
Mr. Joseph E Brown
Mr. Kenneth E Brown
Mr. Milt Brown
Mr. Morris Brown
Mr. Raymond H Brown
Mr. Raymond L Brown
Mr. Robert E Brown
Mr. William P Brown
MAJ James L Brown (Ret)
Mr. Kermit E Browning
Mr. Michael F Browning
Mr. Paul L Brubaker
Mr. Henry J Brudis
Mr. Robert Bruns
LTC William F Brustman
Mr. James V Bryan
Mr. Kenneth V Bryan
Mr. Lynn G Bryan
Mr. Melvin L Bryant
MSG Paul J Bryan (Ret)
Mr. Ross R Bryant
Mr. Anthony S Bubbico
Mr. Richard S Bucca
Mr. Robert C Buchanan
Mr. Marvin G Bucher
Mr. Harold A Buchler
Mr. Clarence W Buck
SSG Henry E Buck (Ret)
Mr. Dennis P Buckingham
Mr. James C Buckle
Mr. Douglas E Buckley
Mr. Roger L Bucy
Mr. Robert J Buege
Mr. Paul W Buell
Mr. S Bill Buemi
Mr. William H Bumgarner
Mr. Jean D Bundy
Mr. Albert A Buonanno
Mr. Benedict A Bur
Mr. Lowell W Burchett
Mr. Louis J Bures
Mr. David M Burke
Mr. Donald M Burke
Mr. G Lee Burke
Mr. James W Burke
Ltc Patrick W Burke Ret
Mr. Thomas J Burke
Mr. Francis T J Burkett
Mr. Lucius W Burkett
Csm Royce D Burkett Ret
Mr. Robert S Burkey
Mr. Albert Burl
Mr. Joseph A Burnett
Mr. Joseph M Burnette
Mr. Ernest H Burns
Mr. Coy D Burton
Mr. Douglas P Burton
Mr. William L Burton
Mr. James N Bury
Mr. Robert H Buse
Mr. Clayton F Bush Jr
Mr. Ernest W Busha Jr
Mr. Joseph F Buss
Mr. George M Bussey
Mr. William G Bustin
Mr. Stephen J Butko
Mr. Clarence M Butler
Mr. Joseph R Butler
Mr. Lloyd W Butler
Mr. Michael R Butler
Mr. Russell S Butler
CSM Robert G Button
Mr. John J Butts

Mr. David Butvinik
Mr. Bredan M Byrne
Mr. John Byrne
Mr. Vincent F Byrnes
Mr. Earl J Bytell
Mr. Louis A Caccioppoli
WO1 Robert G Cadena Ret
Mr. Damian E Caffrey
Mr. Carl T Cain
Mr. Dale W Cain
Mr. Chester A Caine Jr
Mr. Charles C Caldera
Mr. Willard C Calkins Jr
Mr. Edward J Callahan
Mr. Paul L Callahan
Mr. Robert E Callahan
Mr. Joseph P Calvi
Mr. Charles A Camadra
Mr. Antonio J Camasso
Mr. Arthur D Cameron
Mr. Hugh M Cameron
Mr. Dennis W Camp
Mr. Jurl D Camp
Mr. Frank L Campanaro
Mr. Charles Campawella
Mr. Thomas G Campanella
Mr. John T Campbell
Mr. Haywood Campbell
Mr. Roger E Campbell
Mr. Terry E Campbell
Ltc Robert B Campbell Ret
Mr. Patrick G Camunes
Mr. Frank W Camunes Jr
Mr. Martin K Canape
Mr. James V Cancellaro
Mr. Peter Cannell
Mr. Sal Cannizzaro
Mr. Malcolm B Canon
Mr. Paul Cantor
Mr. Alfred Capiz
Mr. Henry T Capiz
Mr. Joseph T Capone
Mr. Leonard J Capoziello
Mr. Allen D Cappella
Mr. Martin A Cappelli
Mr. Michael R Cappiello
Mr. George P Cappos
Mr. Anthony B Caproni
Mr. Charles R Capsalors
Mr. Louis T Capuano
Mr. Dominic J Caraccilo
Mr. Anthony J Carachilo
Mr. Angelo L Carbone
Mr. Joseph Carbone
Mr. Larry J Carbone
Mr. Walter E Card Jr
Mr. Paul M Cardinale
Mr. Martin Caretto
Mr. James A Carey
Mr. Richard G Carey
Mr. Arthur B Carle
Mr. Harold R Carle
Mr. Robert W Carlson
Mr. Russell W Carlson
Mr. Terry J Carlson
Mr. Carl Carlton
Mr. Carl Carlton
Mr. John J Carney
Mr. Anthony F Caroli
Mr. Donald G Carpenter
Mr. William E Carpenter
LTC Loring R. Carper
Mr. David A Carr
Mr. Wendell M Carr
Mr. Edward J Carrara Jr
Mr. Calvin H Carrier
Mr. John T Carrig Jr

Mr. Henry R Carrizosa
Mr. Thomas D Carroll
Mr. David D Carter
Mr. Edward Carter
Mr. Jack E Carter
Mr. John H Carter
Mr. Raymond K Carter Jr
Mr. Hassel E Cartwright
Mr. John W Carty
Mr. Raymond T Carty
Mr. Edward L Caruso
Mr. Patrick J Caruso
Mr. Jules Carvalho
Mr. Pasquale J Casanova
Mr. Edward G Casazza
Mr. Edgar H Case II
Mr. Ernest J Casey
Mr. Joseph T Casey
Mr. William L Casey
Mr. Thomas P Cashin
Mr. Edward D Casper
Mr. Erwin D Casper
Mr. Patrick Cassalia Sr
Mr. John I Cassidy
Mr. Edward Castillo-Rubio
Mr. Nicholas Castoro
Mr. Carl J Cataldo
Mr. Billy S Cater
Mr. Harold J Catt
Mr. James E Caudle
MAJ Arthur P Cebull
Mr. E Wayne Ceder
Mr. Louis A Cerce
Mr. Ciro E Cerra
Mr. Vincent L Cerreta
Mr. Andrew W Chabra
Mr. Antonio Chacon
Mr. James E Chaddock
Mr. Harold Chalet
Mr. Joseph J Chalkis
Mr. Robert L Chamberlain
Mr. Alton B Chamberlin
Mr. Howard J Chambers
Mr. Clifton Chamblin
Mr. Louis N Champagne
Mr. James G Chaney
Mr. Marshall W Chaney
Mr. Charles V Chapman
Mr. Charles A Charbeneau
Mr. William F Charboneau Jr
Mr. Harvey E Charbonneau
Mr. Jay Charles
Mr. Raymond M Charleston
Mr. Ralph E Charnley
Mr. Irwin J Chase
Mr. James P Chassie
Mr. Edward W Chastain
Mr. Gus E Chavalas
Mr. Gary J Chenett
Mr. James W Chernesky
Mr. A W Cherkes
Mr. Sam G Cherone
Mr. Giovanni J Chianese
Mr. Frank R Chibbaro
Mr. Paul J Childress
Mr. Jessie Childress
Mr. Donald L Childs Sr
Mr. Austin C Chiles
Mr. Edward C Chirdon
Mr. Frank A Chironno
Mr. Peter T Chokola
Mr. Ronald R Choquette

Mr. Randolph N Christensen
Mr. Harold W Christenson
Mr. Dennis E Christian
COL Charles R Christian (Ret)
Mr. Thomas R Christy
Mr. Carlton D Chuman
Mr. Donald C Chumley
Mr. Andrew Chundock Jr
Mr. Ron A Chura
Mr. Frank T Cichocki
Mr. Felix J Cistolo
Mr. Sylvio P Ciummo
Mr. Duain F Claiborne
Mr. Harold H Clark
Mr. Harry L Clark
Mr. James F Clark
Mr. James L Clark
Mr. Oather H Clark
Mr. Ralph M Clark
Mr. Reginald R Clark
Mr. Richard C Clark
Mr. Robert L Clark
Mr. Roy E Clark
Mr. Shelby T Clark Sr (Ret)
Mr. William E Clark Jr
Mr. Finley K Clarke
Mr. Robert N Clarke
Mr. John E Clarkin
Mr. Royle C Clausen
Mr. Arthur J Clauter Jr
Mr. Emanuel Claver
Mr. James R Claypole
Mr. Daniel G Claypool
Mr. Robert M Cleary
Mr. Wayne E Cleary
Mr. Glenn D Clegg
Mr. Norman S Clegg
Mr. Karl W Clemen
Mr. Morris W Clemen
Mr. Dennis A Clements
Mr. Calvin L Clemmer
Mr. Kevin J Cleveland
Mr. Frank Cline
Mr. Alvin M Clouse
Mr. Leo E Clune
Mr. Richard E Coate
Mr. Grant T Coates
Mr. Phillip W Cochrane
Mr. Michael A Codella
Mr. James E Cody
Mr. William C Coe
Mr. Alvin M Cohen
Mr. Bernard B Cohen
Mr. Don M Cohen
Mr. Harold Cohen
Mr. Irving Cohen
Mr. Samuel Cohen
Mr. Hensil S Cohron
Mr. John J Coine
Mr. Bernard Cokeley
Mr. Thomas F Colburn
Mr. Arthur G Cole
Mr. David L Cole
Mr. William Cole
Mr. Christopher Cole Jr
Mr. Anthony J Colello
Sgm Charles L Coleman
Mr. William A Coleman Jr
Mr. James R Colignon
Mr. Clarence A Collette
Mr. Edward J Collins
Mr. Harry Collins
Mr. John F Collins
Mr. Michael L Collins
Mr. Stanley F Collins
Mr. Dominic E Cologgi

Mr. Robert Colombi
Mr. Francisco Colon
Mr. Rocco A Colucci
Maj Howard J Coman Ret
MSG John P Comejo (Ret)
Mr. Joseph S Comley
Mr. Jack W Compau
Mr. Roger F Conger
Mr. Edward H Conklin
Mr. John L Conley
Mr. Douglas A Connaher
Mr. William C Conner
Mr. Joseph M Connolly
Mr. Patrick J Connolly
Mr. Edward E Connors
Mr. Lawrence Connors
Ltc Lawrence P Connors Ret
Mr. Frederick K Conrad
Mr. Edward J Conroy
Mr. John J Considine
Mr. Alfred J Conti
Mr. Dominick Conti
Mr. Melvin E Coobs
Mr. Donald M Cook
Mr. George N Cook
Mr. Melborne D Cook
PSG Grant E Cook (Ret)
Msg Arnon W Cool Ret
Mr. Harrison S Coolidge
Mr. William Coombs
Mr. Robert Cooney
Mr. Harvey Cooper
Mr. Thomas L Cope
Mr. William J Copel
Mr. Salvadore J Coppola
Mr. John R Corbett
Mr. Leroy L Corbin
Mr. Charles E Corcoran
Mr. Charles C Cornell
Mr. Robert L Cornett Jr
Mr. William M Cornwell
Mr. Raymond Cornyn
Mr. Bill Corwin
Mr. John T Costa
Mr. Glynn S Coster
Mr. James D Costley
Mr. Joseph Costo
Mr. John M Cotey
Mr. Harry W Cottell
Mr. John W Cotter
Mr. Thomas J Cotter
Mr. Emil Coudenys
Mr. John H Courtet
Mr. Sidney D Cousin
Mr. John J Covai Sr
Mr. C William Cowan
Mr. Austin H Cox
Mr. Charles R Cox
Mr. Homer Cox
Mr. Michael E Cox
Mr. Michael K Cox
Mr. Paul M Cox
Mr. Russell H Cox
Mr. Randall L Coyne
Mr. Truman G Crabbe
Mr. Charles R Craddock
Mr. Chester S Cramer
Mr. Ronald E Cramer
Mr. Henry E Crandall
Mr. Albert E Crane
Mr. William A Cravener
Mr. Douglas J Crawford
Mr. Paul A Crawford
Mr. Hunt D Crawford Sr
Mr. John J Crimmins
Sfc Milton D Crippin Ret
Mr. Charles W Cripps

Mr. Joseph A Crist
Mr. David C Crocker
Mr. Andrew L Crockett
Mr. Donald G Cronan
Mr. Julian L Cronce
Mr. Thomas E Crosby
Mr. Lonnie E Cross
Mr. Robert E Cross
Mr. Willard D Crossen Sr
Mr. Walter P Croswell
Mr. George R Crothers
Mr. Robert A Crowl
COL Donald O Crutchley
CSM Jose T Cruz (Ret)
Mr. Charles A Ctibor
Mr. William P Cucco
Mr. James B Cuddihy
Mr. Lynn B Cuddy
Ltc Robert F Cudworth Ret
Mr. Edgar Cuebas
Mr. John P Cullen
Mr. Joseph A Culotta
Mr. Charles A Culp
Mr. Robert L Cummings
Mr. Russell Cummins
Mr. Van B Cunningham
Mr. Vincent J Cupo
Mr. Wesley A Cureton
Mr. Frank A Curiel Sr
Mr. Arthur B Curle
Mr. John T Curren
Mr. Oscar J Curry
LT Angelo A Cursio
Mr. Richard D Curtis
Mr. Robert E Cushing
Mr. Richard E Cushman
Mr. Leonard M Cusson
Mr. Bernard L Cutler
Mr. Dwight W Cutler
Mr. Billy K Cutlip
Mr. Clyde E Cutrell
Mr. John J Cylkowski Jr
Mr. William H Cyrs
Mr. David W Cyrulik
Mr. Roy A D 'Agnosca
Mr. James J D Agostino
Mr. Antonio J D Ambrosia
Mr. Anthony M D Amore
Ltc Gregory M D Arbonne
Mr. Joseph J Dabbs
Mr. William J Dabe
Mr. William R Dabel
Mr. Ralph B Dabkiewicz
Mr. Larry J Dachille
Mr. Anthony J Dagnelli
Mr. Andrew J Dagoumas
Mr. Harlan C Dahl
Mr. William H Dailey
Mr. Thomas W Daley
Mr. Michael J Daly
Mr. Thomas M Daly
Mr. Edward T Damaso
Mr. Louis E D'Ambrosia
Mr. Larry A Danforth
Mr. William L Danforth
Mr. John W Danforth Jr
Mr. Gateley N Daniel
Mr. Gene E Daniels
Mr. Fred A Daniels Jr
Mr. Louis J Danolfo
Mr. Robert F Daragan
Mr. Fred A Darden
Mr. Henry J Darnaud
Mr. Rouglas J Datcher
Mr. Frederick W Dates
Mr. Alfred O Dault Sr
Mr. Gene C Davenport
Mr. Harold G Daves

Mr. Roger A Davids
Mr. Harold E Davidson
Mr. Harry C Davidson
Mr. Sherwood Davidson
Mr. Robert Davies
Mr. Thomas C Davies
Mr. Arnold E Davis
Mr. Bernard L Davis
Mr. Carl P Davis
Mr. Carl W Davis
Mr. Charles G Davis
Mr. Francis X Davis
Mr. Gordon L Davis
Mr. Henry T Davis
Mr. Jack D Davis
Mr. James M Davis
Mr. Leonard W Davis
Mr. Michael G Davis
Mr. Thomas D Davis Sr
Mr. W D Davis
Mr. William F Davis
Mr.Willie Davis Jr
Mr. Prentice C Dawkins
Mr. Thomas N Dawson Jr
Mr. James E Day
Mr. Robert W Day
Mr. William C Day
Mr. Anthony De Angelis Jr
Mr. Victor L De Cosmis
Mr. John F De Fazio Jr
Mr. Henry C De Ford
Mr. Michael P DeFrancesco
Mr. Joseph J De Fulvio
Mr. Charles W De Gregorio
Mr. Richard T De Genaro
Mr. Donald J De Haven
Mr. Harold E DeHoff
Mr. Percy E De Lanoy
Mr. Millard L De Lauder
Mr. John R De Lay
Mr. Leonard L De Luca
Mr. Joseph De Luca Jr
Mr. Joseph De Martino
Mr. Vincent A De Martino
Mr. Atthue J De Matteo
Mr. Gustav De Mauro
Mr. Gaetano De Mayo
LTC Dante G De Mio (Ret)
Mr. Paul J De Nicola
Mr. Richard F De Nise
Mr. Louis J De Ole
Mr. Frank A De Rosa
Mr. Nick L De Shullo
Mr. Richard De Thomas
Mr. John A De Wire
Mr. Paul E Deadrich
Mr. Michael P Deal
Mr. Ellis W Dean
Mr. William LDearen
Mr. Ronald Decker
Mr. Robert W Decker II
Mr. James F Deegan
Mr. Michael J Deel
MSG Gerard A Defelica (Ret)
Mr. Peter R Deipome
Mr. Robert I Del Conte
Mr. Angel Dela Cruz Jr
Mr. Edward J Delaloye
Mr. Richard A Delaney
Mr. Charles C Delaney Jr
CSM Robert M Delia (Ret)
Mr. Charles H Dellangelo
Mr. Alex J Dely
Mr. Jack W Dempsey
Mr. John P Dempsey

Mr. James A Denam
Mr. Frank Dennis
Mr. John C Dennis
Mr. Benjamin P Denny
Mr. Allen E Denton Jr
Mr. Andrew Denton
Mr. David C Derry
Mr. Carl Desendorf
Mr. David F Desjardins
Mr. Leroy A Desmond
Mr. John L Desormean
Mr. Roy J Dettrner
Mr. Irving Deutsch
Mr. Rudolph A Deutsch
Mr. Costantino DeViio
Mr. Donald F Devine
Mr. Nathan H Devine
Mr. Robert R Devins
Mr. Gerald J Devlin
Mr. Todd P Dexter
Mr. Michael Di Bella Sr
Mr. Pat D Di Giammerino
Mr. Joseph J Di Grovanni
Mr. Joseph M Di June
Mr. James Di Lorenzo
Mr. Dary D DiMaio
Mr. Anthony R Di Pierro
Mr. Nicholas F DiStasio
Mr. Thomas A Dials
Mr. Jack M Diamondstein
Mr. David T Diaz
Mr. E Tucker Dickerson
Mr. Monroe P Dickey
Mr. Robert K Dickey
Mr. Joseph Dickinson
Mr. Frank E Dickman
Mr. Terry D Dickson
Mr. Donald A Diefenbach
Mr. John P Diefenbaker
Mr. Richard W Dielen
Mr. John E Dier
Mr. William C Dierker
Mr. Anton J Dietrich Jr
Mr. Randy E Dillenbeck
Mr. Eric Diller
Mr. Donald J Dilley
Mr. James E Dillon
Mr. Robert Dillon
Mr. William J Dillon Jr
Mr. Pat A Dilonardo
Mr. Alfred A Dilorio
Mr. Raymond Dimas
Mr. Marino Dimengo
Mr. William A Dinges
Mr. JamesA Dinofa
Mr. Henry V Diodati
Mr. James A Disarro
Mr. Ralph E Dittmann
Mr. Walter J Diver
Mr. Charles R Dixon
Mr. John J Dixon Jr
COL Robert E Doak (Ret)
Mr. John A Dobbins
Mr. Kim Dobbins
Mr. Frank A Dobry
Mr. John V Doherty
Mr. Edwin S Dojka
Mr. James R Dolan
Mr. William D Dolce
LTC James W Dollar (Ret)
Mr. Thomas A Dombek
Mr. Robert F Dominicus
Mr. George M Donaldson
Mr. Steven L Donaldson
Mr. Steven F Donarski
Mr. Robert M Dondero
Mr. William A Dondero
Mr. Roger H Donlon

Mr. Clarence C Donnel
Mr. Thomas J Donnelly
Mr. Arthur J Donoghue Jr
Mr. Joseph E Donohue
Mr. Joseph W Donovan
Mr. Philip W Dooley
Mr. Robert W Dooley
Mr. James E Dorety
Mr. Frank J Dorko
Mr. Andrew P Doro
Mr. Milton E Dorr
Mr. Thomas B Dorrian
Mr. William R Dorsett
Mr. George A Dorsey
Mr. Robert L Doub
Mr. Robert E Dougan
Mr. Charles W Dougherty
Mr. James J Dowd
Mr. Thomas H Dowd
Mr. William H Dowell
Mr. William T Dower
Mr. George T Doyle
Mr. George W Doyle
Mr. John F Doyle
Mr. Steven Doyle
Mr. Charles L Drago
Mr. Anthony C Drago
Mr. Lester J Dreesen
Mr. John T Driver
Mr. Stephen J Drovick
Mr.Hugh W Drudy
Mr. John L Drugan
Mr. Ralph S Drum
Mr. Billy D Drumm
Mr. Kenneth D Drumm
Mr. Frank M Drummond
Mr. Larry J Du Bois
Mr. Edward N Dubey
Mr. Harold L Dubick
MAJ John T Ducket (Ret)
Mr. Thomas W Duckworth
Mr. Douglas R Duda
Mr. John M Duda
Mr. John Dudeck Jr
Mr. Roger R Dufek
Mr. Edward G Duff
Mr. James F Duffy
Mr. William R Duffy
Mr. John T Dugan
Mr. Roy E Dukovac
Mr. Ralph C Dula
Mr. Joseph L Dulio
Mr. James S Duncan
Mr. Lee A Duncan
Mr. Wade A Duncan
Mr. Arlo L Dundas
Mr. Donald G Dunn
Mr. Robert J Dunn
Mr. James B Dunnigan
Mr. Lawrence Duplechan
Mr. Delbert F Duppenhaler
Mr. Joseph E Duraski
Mr. Gerald R Dusel
Mr. Barry J Dussault Sr
Mr. Frank J Dwyer
Mr. Delmar J Dyer
Mr. Robert F Dygos
Mr. Gerald E Dzierawski
Sgm Edward E Eaglin
Mr. Allan W Earley
COL Curtis D Earp Jr
Mr. Van A Easley
Mr. Wilbert (Shorty) R East
Mr. Paul P Eaton
Mr. Peter B Eaton
Mr. Bryan F Eaves Sr

MAJ Herman J Eberle (Ret)
Mr. Cleon C Eckler
Mr. Larry H Eckard
Mr. Michael G Eckert
Mr. Cliff Eckmann
Mr. Harold Eckman
Mr. Michael L Eddington
1SG Robert L Eddy (Ret)
Ltc John D Edgerton Ret
Mr. Richard J Edlebeck
Mr. Allen B Edwards
Mr. Dwight D Edwards
Mr. Harold Edwards
Mr. Woodrow P Edwards
Mr. Carl R Edwards Jr
Mr. Kenneth W Egan
Mr. Robert J Eggle Jr
Mr. William P Egri
Mr. Norman J Ehlinger
Mr. Roberts E Ehrgott
Mr. Sheldon Ehrlich
Mr. Alfonso S Eitmant
Mr. James W Eikner
Mr. Leonard I Einhorn
Mr. James Elleby
Mr. Alfred L Elliott
Mr. Charles Elliott
Mr. Loy M Ellis
Mr. Wilbur G Ellis
Mr. Donald F Ely
SGT Rodney R Emerson
Mr. Harold E Emery
Mr. Patrick L Emery
Mr. Samuel E Emmons
Mr. Billy H Endress
Mr. Manuel A Eneriz
Mr. Charlie D Engel Jr
Mr. Louis H Englert
Mr. Robert F English
Mr. Robert E Enkelmann
Mr. John E Enkemann
Mr. Emil A Ercolono
Mr. August C Erdbrink
Mr. Howard C Erickson
Mr. Samuel Erlick
Mr. Nelson B Ernest
Mr. William M Enright
Mr. Robert J Ernmert
Mr. Ronald E Ernst
Mr. James F Ervin
Mr. J Willis Erwin
Mr. Joseph Esmond
Ltc Willard B Esplin Ret
Mr. Dominic N Esposito
Mr. Neil A Esposito
Mr. Vincent J Esposito
Mr. Gilbert R Esquer
Mr. Gilbert R Esquer
Mr. James M Estepp
Mr. William F Etherington
Col Christos J Evangelos Ret
PSG Donald E Evans (Ret)
Mr. Gary W Evans
Mr. Richard D Evans
Mr. Thomas E Evans
Mr. Warren M Evans
Mr. Louis E Eve
Mr. Charles E Everett
Mr. Warren E Everett Jr
Mr. Harold B Everham
Mr. Edgar P Everhard
Mr. Carroll G Everist
Mr. John D Evert
Mr. Thomas P Eviston
FSGT John P Faass Sr
Mr. Sarge J Fagan
Mr. Allan N Fagley

Mr. Robert J Faione
Mr. John B Fairchild
Dr. Kenneth A Falber
Mr. Harry T Falck
Mr. George F Fanning
Mr. Ray C Fanning
Mr. Walter J Farmer
MSGT Lee M Farmer (Ret)
Mr. John L Farnsworth
Mr. Dudley H Farquhar
Mr. Raymond P Farrell
Mr. Jeremiah L Farrell (Ret)
Mr. Carl A Farren
Mr. Malcolm E Farris Sr
Mr. Roger E Farris
Mr. Warren C Farris
Mr. Robert H Fass
Mr. Wayne W Faucett
Mr. Raymond E Faucher
Mr. Robert J Faught
Mr. Charles D Faulkner
MAJ Glenn D Faulks (Ret)
Mr. Michael D Favata
Mr. Melvin L Faw
Mr. Richard L Fear
Mr. Richard T Feddersen
Mr. Henry J Feigenheimer
Mr. Edward L Feistl
Mr. Paul S Feldheim
Mr. Donald Feldman
Mr. Gerald J Feldman
Mr. Walter C Felty
Mr. David J Fennessey
Mr. John E Fenwick
Mr. Arthur J Ferguson
Mr. William K Ferguson
Mr.Paul M Ferla
Mr. Anthony J Fernandes
Mr. Robert J Fernandez
Mr. Cecil Fernandez Jr
Mr. Joseph Ferrara
Mr. Andrew P Ferreira
Mr. Raymond P Ferreira
Mr. Joseph M Ferrell Jr
Maj Vincent A Ferrero Ret
Mr. Louis A Ferris
Mr. Leo Ferstenberg
Mr. Stephen R Feudner
Mr. David R Fey
Mr. George A Fichtenbaum
Mr. Frank Fidler
Mr. Ralph O Field
Mr. Donald L Fielder
Mr. William A Fielder
Mr. Arthur T Fieldsend
Mr. Anthony F Fierro
Mr. Manuel Figueroa
Mr. Filipelli L Filippo
Mr. Leroy M Finch
Mr. Solomon S Fineblum
Mr. Robert R Finger
Mr. Clayton F Fink
Mr. Murray Finkelstein
Mr. John Finn
Mr. Ralph M Finnerty
Mr. Thomas P Finnerty
LTC Michael N Fiore (Ret)
Mr.John P Firestone
Mr. Louis P Fischer
Mr. Stanley Fishbein
Mr. Albert R Fisher
Mr. Cebren P Fisher
Mr. George Fisher

Mr. Marvin K Fisher
Mr. Waldo G Fisher
Mr. Walter H Fisher
Mr. Robert M Fisk
Hugh H Fite
Mr. William R Fitts
Mr. Edward J Fitzgerald
Csm Larry L Fitzgerald Ret
Mr. Lawrence V Fitzgerald
Mr. Ralph D Fitzgerald
Mr. Robert P Fitzgerald
Mr. Anthony J Fitzgibbons
Mr. Thomas F Fitzpatrick
Csm Thomas E Fitzpatrick
Mr. Donald E Flagg
Mr. Bruce J Flaherty
Mr. Douglas J Flanagan
Mr. Donald A Flatt
Mr. Donald E Fleck
Mr. Antonine G Fleming
Mr. J Morrell Fleming
Mr. Charles M Fletcher
Mr. Joe G Floees
Mr. Robert N Flohre
Mr. Dominick S Florio
Mr. Jackie L Floyd
Mr. Thomas M Floyd
Mr. David N Fluti
Mr. Daniel F Flynn
Mr. Paul J Flynn
Mr. Richard T Flynn
Cpt Winston E Flynn
Mr. Harold C Foley
Mr. Joseph F Foley
Mr. James H Follensbee
Mr. Kendrick H Folsom Sr
Mr. Robert F Foor
Mr. Vernon E Foraker
Ltc William A Forbes Ret
Mr. Robert E Forcier
Mr. Reavis S Ford
Mr. Mathew C Ford Jr
Mr. Donald G Foreman
Mr. Mack B Forgey
Mr. Randolph Foriest
Mr. Patrick J Forkin
Mr. Edwin F Forrest
Mr. Charles A Forrester
Mr. Harold L Forrester
Mr. William E Fortier
Mr. Francis K Fortson
Sgm Gary P Fortunate Ret
Mr. Albert D Fosco
Mr. Herbert Foster
Mr. Philip E Foster
Mr. Wayne D Foster
Mr. James C Foushee Sr
Mr. Herbert C Fowle
Mr. John D Foy
Mr. Duward B Frampton Jr
Mr. Wilmer H France
Mr. James J Francis Jr
Mr. Henry D Franey
Mr. Arthur L Frank
Mr. Thomas S Frank
Mr. Stanley A Frankel
Mr. James E Franks Jr
Mr. Thomas Franz
CWO Francis J Franze (Ret)
Mr. Virgil E Franzen
Mr. Salvatore V Frascello
Mr. Bernard A Frati
Mr. Donald S Freeberg

Mr. Alfred J Freeman
Mr. Robert L Freeman
Mr. Joseph G Freilick
Mr. Ernest S Frerichs
Mr. Ellsworth E Freshno
Mr. Frank Frieb
Mr. Bernard L Friedman
Mr. Walter B Fries
Mr. Floyd E Fritz
Mr. James R Fritz Sr
Mr. George W Frode
Mr. James C Froman
Mr. James N Froome
Mr. Bob R Frothingharn
Mr. John Fuccello Jr
Mr. Earl D Fuerst
Mr. Dwight R Fuhrman
Mr. Peter J Fuino
COL Charles W Fulkerson
Mr. Charles R Fuller
Mr. Frank Fulton
Mr. Gerald J Fulton
Mr. Carl J Fumando
Mr. Gennaru J Fumando
Mr. Lester Funk
Mr. Darrell L Furan
LTC Charles T Furgeson
Mr. George L Furman
Mr. Arthue J Fusco Jr
Mr. Charles J Fusco
Mr. Mario M Fusto
Mr. Joseph Gaborsky Jr
Mr. John M Gabri
Rev. Eugene V Gaetzke
Mr. Robert M Gage
Mr. Charles A Gagne
Mr. Harvey Gagnon
LTC Raymond H Gaier (Ret)
Mr. William J Gaither
Mr. Michael A Galanda
Mr. Stanley J Galazin
Mr. Armand L Galdi
Mr. Clair R Galdonik
Mr. Joseph D Galinski
Mr. Leo D Gallagher
Mr. Michael J Gallagher
Mr. James Gallas
Mr. Nicholas G Gallo
Mr. Peter L Gallo
Mr. Salvatore G Gallo
Mr. Franklin D Galloway
Mr. John H Galloway
Sfc Joseph A Galluccio Ret
Mr. Vincent H Gannon
PSG Geraldo Gapol (Ret)
CPL Walter E Garceau
Mr. Jose S Garcia
Mr. Margarito M Garcia
Mr. Thomas Garcia Jr
SGM Vicente Garcia (Ret)
Mr.Ken J Gardellis
Mr. Kenneth W Gardiner
MAJ Donald P Gardner (Ret)
Mr. Paul R Garland
Mr. Raymond L Gardner
Mr. Roderick G Garlitz
Mr. Gale E Garman
COL Floris M Garner (Ret)
Mr. John C Garrett
Mr. Orlow F Garrett
Mr. Gilbert Garshman
Mr. Gonzalo Garza
Mr. Donald H Gastorf

Mr. Joseph E Gates
Col Harold B Gatslick Ret
Mr. Raymond J Gaudet
Mr. John J Gaumer
Mr. James J Gavin
Mr. Roger A Geary
Mr. William H Geary
Mr. Ronald J Gebo
Ltc Bradley W Gebott
Sfc Albert A Gecide Ret
Mr. Rocco N Gedaro
Mr. Charles W Geerz
Mr. Roy L Geigen
Mr. Raymond E Geisser
Mr. Frank J Gelish
Mr. Earl C Gellenbeck
Mr. Robert A Gelwick
Mr. Richard J Gendek
Mr. Laurent E Gendron
Mr. Salvatore Genova
Mr. Herman W Genrich
Mr. Edward H Gensel
Mr. Anthony M Gentile
Mr. Hans J Gentile
Mr. Henry J Geodde Jr.
Mr. Donald W George
Mr. Richard M George
Mr. Theodore E George
Mr. Warren H George
Mr. Martin R Gerhardt
Mr. Eddie L German
Mr. Andrew Gerrier
Mr. Edward J Gerrity Jr
Mr. Victor C Gerst Jr
Mr. Roy Gersten
Mr. Victor N Gerue
Mr. John V Gerze
Mr. Joseph Gethers
Mr. William Getman
Mr. Charles B Gettings
Mr. Duane F Getzmeyer
Mr. James W Geygan
Mr. William J Gianelli
Mr. Anthony R Giangrande
Mr. Alfred L Gibbs
Mr. Edward M Gibbs
Mr. John J Giberson
Mr. Robert J Giberson
Mr. John Giboney
Mr. Donald T Gibson
Mr. John W Gibson
Mr. Loral A Gibson
Mr. Raymond L Gibson
Mr. Samuel T Gibson
Mr. William G Gibson
Mr. Roland T Gignac
1SG Lawrence R Gilbert (Ret)
CSM Robert F Gilbert (Ret)
Mr. Malcolm R Giles
Mr. Frederick J Gill
Mr. Jesse M Gill Jr
Mr. Thomas M Gill Sr
Mr. Melvin C Gillenwater
Mr. Eugene P Gillespie
Mr. William C Gilliam
Mr. Charles L Gilliland
COL Thomas D Gillis
Mr. Bruce A Gilman
Mr. James E Gilmer
Mr. James R Gilreath
Mr. Theodore C Gilroy
Mr. Robert R Giordano
Mr. John F Giovanniello
Mr. Anthony R Giralico
Mr. Joseph A Girard
Mr. Marcel Gladu

Mr. Robert G Glans
Mr. Donald M Gleason
Mr. P Earle Gleason
Mr. Harry Glenchur
Mr. Albert B Glenn
Mr. Harry Glickman
Mr. Don L Glover
Mr. Emory J Glover
Mr. Janet Glover
Mr. Robert L Glover Sr
Mr. Ernest S Goard
Mr. Carl Gochman
Mr. John H Gochnour
Mr. Erwin J Godawa
Mr. Earl E Goddard
Mr. Paul E Goddu
Mr. Gary T Godfrey
Mr. Robert W Godshall
Mr. Paul T Goebel
Mr.Hugh K Goerner
Mr. Louis R Goetz
Mr. BufordF Goff Sr
Mr. Robert W Goff Jr
Mr. Thomas M Goff
Mr. William H Goff Jr
Dr. Alan J Golden
Mr. Edward M Golden
Mr. Herb I Goldenberg
Mr. Lawrence Goldgeier
Mr. Robert E Golosov
Mr. Jesus Gonzales
Mr. Richard A Gonzales
Mr. Joseph Gonzalez
Mr. Joseph J Good
Mr. Leroy D Good
Mr. William Goode
CSM James H Gooden
Mr. Norman R Goodfarb
Mr. Jay G Goodman
Mr. George W Goodwin
Mr. John J Goodwin
Mr. Robert W Goodwin Sr
Mr. Edward P Gorczyca
Mr. Dale E Gordon
Mr. Marvin F Gordon
Mr. Richard A Gordon
Mr. Virgil M Gordon
Mr. Hugh P Gorman
Mr. John T Gorman
Mr. William J Gorman
Mr. Kenneth Gormley
Mr. Michael F Gorry
Mr. Thomas B Gorse
Mr. William R Goshorn
Mr. Orien R Gossett
Mr. Donald L Gottschall
Mr. Frederick M Gould
Mr. Clyde R Grabb
Mr. Kenneth J Grabner
Mr. Larry F Grace
Mr. Wilbur R Gradin
Mr. Francis Grady
Mr. Vincent A Graf
Mr. Harold W Graff
Mr. Gerald L Grafsgaard
Mr. Arthur R Graham
Mr. David L Graham
Mr. Merlin S Graham
Mr. James A Graham Sr
Mr. James E Graham
Mr. John C Graham
Mr. Manuel J Grajeda
Mr. Charles R Gramc
Mr. Malcolm A Grant
Mr. Allan A Grarnlich
Mr. Louis E Grasser
Mr. Lloyd W Gratz
Mr. Gerald R Graves
Mr. Robert W Graves
Mr. Eugene W Gray

Mr. Johnny D Gray
Mr. Harry T Graykowski
Mr. Joseph M Greaney
Mr. Robert L Greb
Mr. Harry J Greco
Mr. Edward W Green
Mr. Kenneth M Green
Mr. Thomas M Green
Mr. Vernard C Green
Mr. Charles C Greene
Mr. James A Greene
Mr. Mark F Greene
Mr. Richard R Greene
Mr. Vernon E Greene
Mr. Melvin P Greenwald
Mr. Donald G Greenwood
Mr. Carl L Greenwood
Mr. Blaine H Greer
Mr. Curtis J Greer
Mr. Homer B Greetham
Mr. Jay Grefe
Mr. Edward W Gregory
Sfc Michael O Gregory Sr
Mr. Walter A Gressick
Mr. Shirley D Griebe
Mr. Victor C Grieco
Mr. Francis V Grifasi
Mr. Daniel Griffin
Mr. JesseL Griffin Jr
Mr. Julian F Griffith
Mr. Kermit D Griffith
Mr. Trevor J Griffith
Mr. Louis A Griffith Jr
Mr. Harold V Grimm
Mr. Donald C Grise
Mr. Gerald Griswald
Mr. Robert R Gritzke
Mr. Sidney I Grodsky
LTC Fred A Grohgan Jr
Mr. James M Groom
Mr. Frederick H Grooms
Mr. Milton G Groonitzky
Mr. David H Gross
Mr. James F Grossman
Mr. Robert E Grote
Mr. Lyle F Groundwater
MSGT Ted M Groupe (Ret)
Mr. Walter J Grover
Pfc David Groves
Mr. James F Gruber
Mr. Jay Gruenfeld
Mr. Julius J Grunauer
Mr. T Raymond Gruno
Mr. John J Gruss
Mr. Edward A Grygier
Mr. Edward R Grygier
Mr. Thomas J Guadagno
MAJ Albert Guarnieri Jr (Ret)
Mr. Frank J Gubala
Mr. Gerald A Guess
Mr. Solomon J Guevara
Mr. Donald M Guldin
Mr. John W Gullen
Mr. William B Gundrum
Mr. Chester H Gursky
Mr. George Gutch
Mr. A Ray Guthrie
Mr. Abelardo Guzman
LTC Stanley T Gwiazdowski (Ret)
Mr. John F Gwizdak
Mr. Henry F W Haas
Mr. Robert F Haas
Mr. Conrad P Habermann Jr
Mr. Lawrence J Hackett Jr
Mr. Thomas M Hackler

Mr. Richard M Hadad
Mr. Joseph E Hafer Jr
Mr. Clayton J Hagemann
Mr. Earl S Hagen
Mr. Keith Hagen
Mr. Leonard B Hagen
Mr. Michael H Hagen
Mr. Norris L Hagen
Mr. Dennis E Haines
Cpt Richard W Hale Ret
Mr. Michael Halik
Mr. David L Hall
Mr. Joe B Hall
Mr. Oliver V Hall
Col John W Halladay Ret
Mr. Joseph E Hallemann
Mr. Louis E Hallett
COL Sanford B Halperin
Mr. Donat J Hamel
Mr. Eugene A Hametner
Mr. Robert V Hamilton
Mr. Robert E Hamlett
Mr. Clark K Hamm
Mr. Grover L Hamm
Mr. Sidney M Hammer
Mr. Donald G Hammond
Mr. Donald J Hammond
Mr. Donald L Hammond
Csm Thomas R Hammond Ret
Mr. Guy A Hamrick
Mr. Frank E Hancock
Mr. William L Hancock
Mr. Richard D Hanft
Mr. Joseph Hanko
Ltc James A Hanlon Ret
Mr. Leo J Hannan
MAJ Jack H Hansel
Mr. Donald F Hansen
Mr. Allen E Hanson
1LT Guerdon A Hanson
Mr. John B Hanson
Mr. Myron J Harband
Mr. Philip F Harbour
Mr. Arthur S Harburger
Mr. Ernest A Hardy
Mr. Gary W Hardy II
Mr. Jesse E Hare Sr
Mr. Frank E Harget
Mr. John F Harlow
Mr. Earl C Harmeyer
Mr. John J Harrington
Mr. Kenneth R Harmon
Mr. Thomas J Harmon Jr
Mr. Roy C Harms
Mr. William P Harnack
Mr. William C Harned
Mr. George W Harold
Mr. Charles E Harp
Mr. Stephen S Harper
LTC James A Harps (Ret)
Mr. Wallace L Harrier
Mr. Ashley S Harrington
Mr. Herman G Harrington
Mr. Martin J Harrington
Mr. Melvin A Harrington
Mr. Albert F Harris
Mr. Philip M Harris
Mr. Thurman R Harris
Mr. Frank B Harris II
Mr. Howard C Harris
Mr. Ronald J Harris
Mr. Edward S Harrison
Mr. Jimmy L Harrison
Mr. John A Harrison
Mr. Willie J Harry
Mr. George W Harstedt III
Mr. James G Hart

Mr. William F Hartman
Mr. Michael L Hartness
Mr. Andre M Hartzell
Mr. George E Harvey
Mr. Howard F Harvier
Mr. William P Harvill
Mr. Roger W Haskins
Mr. William E Haste
Mr. Garland S Hastings
Mr. Clay W Hatler
Mr. Frederick D Hatter
Mr. Harold J Hauberg
MSG Larry L Hauck
    USAF (Ret)
Mr. Gary P Hauser
Mr. Werner Hauser
Mr. John D Hawk
Mr. Roger A Hawk
Mr. Harry Hawkey
Mr. Ronald C Haxer
Mr. Armender Hayes
Mr. Ernest R Hayes
Mr. John M Hayes
Mr. Michael T Hayes
Mr. Richard C Hayes
Mr. Richard J Hayes Sr
Mr. Joseph A Haymes Jr
SGT Lawrence S Haynes
Mr. Robert C Hays
Sfc Richard W Haywood
Sfc Kenneth D Head Ret
Mr. Howard R Head
Mr. Robert E Heath
Mr. John A Hebert
Mr. Theodore Hebert Jr
Mr. John E Heck
Mr. Robert L Hedstrom
Mr. Wilbert A Hegel
LTC George D Heib
Mr. James M Hein
Mr. William J Heinlein
Mr. Robert S Heintz
Mr. Elwood Heinz
Mr. Arland C Heistand
Mr. Warren C
    Heisterkamp
Mr. Paul J Heles
Mr. Ora E Hellemn
Mr. Fred A Heller
Mr. Kermit G Heller
Mr. William F Helm
Mr. Joseph Helton
Mr. Robert E Helton Jr
Mr. Robert L Hemphill
COL William R Hemphill
Mr. Robert C
    Hendershott
Mr. Albert V Henderson
Mr. Howard W
    Henderson
Mr. James A Henderson
Mr. Russell F
    Henderson
Mr. Ulysses G
    Henderson
Mr. Vaughn K Hendricks
Mr. Woodrow
    Hendrickson
Mr. Rodney E Hendrix
Mr. David Hendry III
Mr. William Hendry
Mr. Charles A Henne
Mr. Billy W Hensley
Mr. James D Hensley
Mr. Billy Henson
Mr. Charles E Henry
Mr. Elmer L Herbaly
Mr. John J Herman
Mr. James A Herman Sr
Mr. Richard W Herman

Mr. Paul M Hermessey
Mr. Leo N Hernandez
Sgm Richard Hernandez
    Ret
Mr. David W Herold
Mr. Thomas E Herring
Mr. Gerald E Herron
Mr. Hugh J Herron
Mr. Patrick J Herward
Mr. Leonard G Hess
Mr. James W Hester
Mr. Thomas F Heston
Mr. Robert W Hettiger
Mr. Leo A Hetzler
Col Newton J Heuberger
    Ret
Mr. Erail W Heugatter Jr
Mr. Carl D Hewitt III
Mr. Sidney S Heyman
Mr. Omega G Hibbert
Mr. Paul F Hickey
Mr. Robert W Hickey
Mr. David L Hicks
Mr. William (Bill) R Hicks
Mr. Dale E Higbee
Mr. Edward H Hightower
Mr. James A Hildebrandt
Cwo Raymond J Hilgart
    Ret
Mr. Blake Hill
Mr. Harold D Hill
1LT James W Hill
Mr. Major H Hill
Mr. Michael E Hill
Mr. Robert M Hill
Mr. William O Hill Jr
Mr. Donald Hillard
Mr. Robert M Hilleque
Mr. Lawrence R Hilliard
Mr. Roy J Hilliard
Mr. Keith O Hills
Mr. Maurie Hillson
Mr. Joe Hindle
Mr. Herbert L Hines
Mr. William J Hinson
Mr. Glenn R Hintsala
Mr. Thomas W Hipp Sr
Mr. Garry W Hippe
Mr. John I Hipson
Mr. Henry J Hirlemann
Mr. Fred C Hirner
Mr. Jack L Hisey
Mr. Daniel J Hissey
Mr. Joseph N Hite III
LTC Frederick G
    Hitzman
Mr. George A Hitzman
Mr. William R Hoag
Mr. John J Hoback
Mr. Robert T Hock
Mr. Charles B Hoessel
Mr. Norman L
    Hoewischer
Mr. Joseph J Hofelder Jr
Mr. Charles L Hoffman
Mr. Harlan M Hoffman
Mr. Richard M Hoffman
Mr. Robert L Hoffman
Mr. Audie C Hogan
Mr. John I Hogan
Mr. Richard E Hogan
Mr. William P Hogan
Sfc Laurence D Hogan
    Ret
Mr. Richard F Hogue
Mr. J B Holden
Mr. John C Holdredge
Mr. Roger D Holiday
Mr. Gordon K Holiey
Mr. Elwyn Hollenbeck

Mr. Curtis H
    Hollingsworth
Mr. David F
    Hollingsworth III
Mr. Erwin O Hollmann
Mr. William Hollos
Msg Nathan Holloway
    Ret
Mr. Arthur F Holly
Mr. Paul W Holm
Mr. Jeff G Holman
Mr. Cleve W Holmes
Mr. Robert B Holmes
Mr. Arnold Holt
Mr. Eric M Holt
LTC Frank E Holt (Ret)
Mr. Herman J Holthaus
Mr. Robert M Holzinger
Mr. James A Hontz Jr
Mr. Frank D Hood
Mr. John H Hoogasian
Mr. John H Hooper
Mr. Ralph K Hoover
Mr. Robert A Hoover
Mr. Robert W Hope
Mr. David P Hopkins
Mr. Allen B Hopkinson
Mr. Phillip G Horan
2Lt William J Horan Ret
Mr. John M Homey
Mr. James T Horns
Mr. Jacob J Horowitz
Mr. Herbert J Horton
Mr. Joseph J Horton
Mr. Reginald J Horton
Mr. Robert L Horton Sr
SGT Roger K Horton
Mr. Steve Horvath Jr
Mr. Carroll E Hose
Mr. Gerald E Hosick
Mr. William C Hosier
Col Donald L Hoskin Ret
Mr. Harold L Hoss
Mr. Maurice E
    Houckes Sr
Mr. Jack L Houser
Mr. Alfred D Houston
Mr. Russell E Houston
Mr. Wayne J Houston
Mr. Vincent G Houten
Mr. John D Houze
Mr. Francis E Howard
Mr. Glenn A Howard
Mr. James R Howard
Mr. Norman L Howard
Psg Theodore R Howard
    Ret
Mr. Albert L Howell
Mr. Johnnie G Howell
Mr. Peter K Howenstein
Mr. Joseph Hricko
Mr. Glenn H Hubenette
Mr. Joseph F Huber
Mr. Robert L Huber
Mr. Theodore L Huberts
Mr. George E Hudiburg
Mr. Claudie B Hudson
Mr. Curtis H Hudson
Mr. Halbert A Hudson
Mr. Leslie E Hudson
Mr. Walton M Hudson
Mr. Glenn R Huesgen
Mr. Steven P Huff
Mr. George T Hufford
Mr. John J Hufford
Mr. Jack E Hughes
CSM James L Hughes
Mr. Paul W Hughes
Mr. Tony W Hughes
Mr. Henry R Huizar Jr

Mr. Albert J Humphrey
Mr. Frederick G
    Hundheim Jr
Mr. John A Hundt
Mr. Henry C Huneken
Mr. Robert Hunnewell
Mr. Cecil W Hunnicutt
Col Alexander H Hunt
    Ret
Mr. Jeffery E Hunt
Mr. John E Hunt
Mr. Lewis R Hunter
Mr. Dana C Hunton
Mr. Gerald F
    Huntsbarger
Mr. James H Huntsman
Mr. Victor W Hurlbert
Mr. Arthur J Hurley
Mr. Lawrence J Hurley
Mr. Stephen Husak
Mr. Harry L Husberg Jr
Mr. James A Husing
Mr. Warren H Hutchens
Mr. Thomas D Hutt
Mr. Allen L Huttig
Mr. Kenneth D Hutton
Mr. John J Hyland
Mr. Ralph Iagulli
Mr. Bernard A Iammatteo
Mr. Robert C Ianazzi
Mr. Peter Iannone
Mr. Mario Iezzoni
Mr. Norman S Ikari
Mr. William G Ilg
Mr. George L Illingworth
Mr. Vincent Impallomeni
Mr. Joseph J Indovina
Mr. Richard A Ingersoll
Mr. Addison A Ingles
Mr. Ernest C Ingles
Mr. Warren W Inglese
Mr. John D Ingram
Mr. Paul T Ingram
Mr. Harold L Irving
Mr. Uno Isaacson
Mr. Paul L Isbell
Mr. Gerald C Isham Jr
Mr. Homer H Isham
Mr. Daniel Islas
Mr. Louis Ivery
Mr. Lawrence N Izzo
Mr. Robert E Jablonski
Mr. Robert P Jack
Mr. Bobby J Jackson
Mr. Grover J Jackson
Mr. Jack Jackson
Mr. Joshaway Jackson
Mr. Spencer B Jackson
Mr. Robert B Jackson
Mr. Robert G Jackson
Mr. Robert H Jackson
Mr. Robert L Jacobs
Mr. George F
    Jagodowski
Mr. Harry J James
Mr. Robert Jamison
Mr. Roy F Janota
Mr. Edmund H
    Janiszewski
Mr. Walter Janus
Mr. Francis J
    Januszewski
Mr. William F Jarasinski
Mr. Kenneth Jarman
Mr. Michael A Jaroche
Mr. Walter S Jarosick
Mr. Barney F Jasek Jr
Mr. Robert Jaworski
Mr. Alfred W Jay
Mr. Charles R Jeffery

Mr. Carl W Jefrers
Mr. Wesley C Jeffrey
Mr. Elbert S Jemison Jr
Mr. Paul P Jendral
Mr. Dennis G Jenkins
Ltc Homer R Jenkins Ret
Mr. Larry Jenkins
Csm Samuel D Jenkins
    Ret
Mr. Joe T Jennings
Mr. Wayne E Jens
Mr. Carl J Jensen
Mr. Jerry E Jensen
Mr. Robert N Jensen
COL Edward M Jentz
Mr. Richard L Jepsen
Mr. Leo S Jereb
Mr. Helmuth M Jeremias
LTC Robert B Jerrell
Mr. Wilburn C Jeschke Jr
Mr. John H Jessen
Mr. Robert P Jett
Mr. Donald E Jewell
Mr. John Jigliotti
CPT Joseph W Jimenez
Mr. Bradley N Jimerson
Mr. Ronald L Jochum
Mr. William A Johns Jr
Mr. Albert J Johnson
Mr. Arthur C Johnson
Mr. Charles D Johnson
Mr. Clifford S Johnson
Mr. David Johnson
Mr. David L Johnson
Mr. Donald R Johnson
Mr. Douglas Johnson
Mr. Franklin D Johnson
Mr. Harris E Johnson
Mr. Harris E Johnson
Mr. Jimmy M Johnson
Mr. Joel L Johnson
Mr. John D Johnson
Mr. Le Roy E Johnson
Mr. Lowell G Johnson
Mr. Ralph T Johnson
Mr. Robert D Johnson
Mr. Robert H Johnson
Mr. Robert V Johnson
Mr. Thomas A Johnson
Mr. Walter H Johnson
Mr. Wesley L Johnson
Mr. William B Johnson
Mr. William L Johnson
Mr. Harry Johnson Jr
Mr. Jesse J Johnson
Mr. Harry D Johnson Sr
Mr. William T Johnson
Mr. Dave Jolly Jr
Mr. Carnie L Jones
Mr. George T Jones
Mr. Howard R Jones
Mr. Lewis B Jones
Mr. Lloyd E Jones
Mr. Lloyd L Jones
Mr. Richard L Jones
Mr. Ricky W Jones
Mr. Robert F Jones
Mr. Robert H Jones
Mr. Robert L Jones
Mr. Ronald L Jones
Mr. Simon E Jones
Mr. Vincent Jones
Mr. Wilbur D Jones
Mr. William J Jones
Col Richard L Jones Ret
Cpt Thomas A Jones Ret
Mr. Ronald L Jordan
Mr. Stephen P Joyce
Mr. Raymond F Joyce Jr
Mr. Oakley S Joyner

Mr. David Y Juarez
Mr. Pasqual Juarez
Mr. Robert F Julian
Mr. Stanley Jurczyk
Mr. George L Justice
Mr. Glenn M Justice
Mr. Robert H Justice
Mr. Leonard P Justofin
Mr. Theodore J
    Kachelmeier
Mr. Bernard L
    Kaczmarek
Mr. Robert Kahler
Mr. Myron T Kaiser
Mr. Sam Kaiser
Mr. William Kalinowski
Mr. Phillip G Kallas
Mr. Bill J Kaltenbach
Mr. Thomas B Kanawyer
Mr. George H Kane
Mr. Leon W Kania
Mr. Morris B Kantor
Mr. Norman S Kantor
Mr. George Kantor Jr
Mr. John S Kapior
Mr. Casimir B Kaplan
Mr. Renold Kappra
Mr. Steven N Kapsick
LTC Daniel G Karis
Mr. Edward J Karl
Mr. George P Karlis
Mr. James S Karmeris
Mr. Joe T Karpel
Mr. Lester N Karr
Mr. Roy E Karvo
Mr. Frank R Kasee
Mr. George J Kasko
Mr. Paul E Kasprzyk
Dr. John A Kassay
Mr. William N Kasson
Mr. William E Kast
Col Richard J Kattar Ret
Mr. Abe Katz
Mr. David Katz
Mr. David J Katz
Mr. Harry Katz
Mr. Kevin D Kavanaugh
Mr. Kenneth L Kean
Mr. Robert E Kearce
Mr. Merlin F Keck
Mr. Marvin J Keefer
Mr. James C Keele
Mr. Robert L Keffner
Mr. John C Kehoe III
Mr. Lyle L Keiser
Mr. Howard R Keithan
Mr. Richard J Kelcourse
Mr. Raymond C Keller
Mr. William J Keller
Mr. Charles L Kellerman
Mr. Clifton Kelley
Mr. Edward J Kelley
Mr. Timothy W Kelley
Mr. James L Kelly
Mr. John B Kelly
Cpt Paul F Kelly
Mr. Robert Kelly
Mr. Russel R Kelly
Mr. Timothy J Kelly
Mr. William P Kelly
Mr. Eugene T Kelly Jr
Mr. Fred W Kemmer Jr
Mr. David W Kemple
Mr. Joseph X Kenavan
Rev. William F Kenneally
Mr. John M Kennedy
Mr. Robert E Kennedy
Mr. Willie J Kenner
Mr. Thomas E Kenney
Mr. Willie J Kenney

Mr. Eugene R Kennington
Mr. Paul E Kent
Mr. Charles R Ker
Mr. Edward E Kerkhoff
Dr. William H Kern
Mr. Ronald Kernberg
Mr. Peter J Kerner
Mr James F Kerschner
Mr. Robert C Kess
Mr. George L Kessel
Mr. Surnner W Kesselman
Mr. Marion D Kessler Sr
Mr. Irvine J Kessler Jr
Mr. Donald B Kibbee
Mr. Leo E Kibble
Mr. Richard G Kibble
Mr. George E Kibler
MSGT Donald E Kidd
Mr. Nelson D Kidder
Mr. Frederic T Kielsgard
Mr. Thomas J Kielty Jr
Mr. James R Kiely
Mr. Arthur V Kierstead
Mr. William G Kiker
Mr. Henry L Kil
Mr. Richard R Kilgen
Mr. Earl E Killen
Mr. Samuel Kimbarow
Mr. James H Kimmer
Mr. James T Kiney
Mr. Charles D King
Mr. Charles P King
Mr. Eugene T King
Mr. Gilbert A King
Mr. James W King
Mr. John R King
Priest Kale F King
Mr. Norman L King
Mr. William A Kingston
Mr. Daniel L Kinsey
Mr. Ernest E Kintler
Mr. Robert J Kippert
Mr. Bobby L Kirby
Mr. Raymond P Kirchmer
Mr. Robert E Kirk
Mr. Charles E Kirkman
Mr. Fred W Kirkpatrick
Mr. Paul E Kiser
Mr. William G Kishler
Mr. David P Kiska
Mr. Charles R Kistier
Mr. Paul C Kitchen
Mr. Walter C Kitelinger
Mr. George O Kjeldahl
Mr. Francis L Klamik
Mr. Matthew T Klaritch
Mr. Loyd J Klassen
Mr. S J Klava
Mr. Scott M Klawinski
Mr. Edwin F Klawitter
Mr. Lamar W Klawitter
Mr. Norman H Klayman
Mr. Otis Kleaver
Mr. Frank S Klecha
Mr. Charles E Klenklen
Mr. George F Kline
Mr. John W Kline
Mr. Thomas L Kline
Mr. Karl R Klinger
Mr. William J Klink
Mr. Kenneth R Klinsky
Mr. Perrin A Klumpp
Mr. Shephen E Kmush
Mr. David G Knapp
Mr. Robert V Kneedler
Mr. Curley B Knepp
Mr. John S Knewell

Ssg Joseph Knickerbocker Sr
Mr. George Knight
Mr. James G Knight
Mr. John R Knight
Mr. Roger P Knight
Mr. Richard R Knight Jr
Mr. Arthur K Knudsen
Mr. James F Knudsen
Mr. Wesley Ko
Mr. R Kenneth Kochel
Mr. William M Koczwara
Mr. Lawrence J Koesters
Mr. Thomas L Kohl
Mr. Robert W Kohler
Mr. Rae L Kohn
COL James T Kolb
Mr. Melvin B Kolker
CSM Edward F Komac
Mr. Edwrd C Koneski
Mr. Charles C Konesky
Mr. Thomas J Konopka
Mr. Marshall W Koontz
Mr. Ronald D Koontz
Mr. Allen R Koops
Mr. William L Korbel
Mr. John F Korosec
Mr. John P Korsan
Mr. Reginald H Korte
Mr. Thomas J Koskie
Mr. Martin W Kotel
Mr. Christopher A Kotz
Mr. Julius F Kovalaski
Mr. John F Kowalewski
Mr. Robert A Koznecki
Ltc Leonard J Kraft Ret
Mr. Daryl E Kramer
Mr. Roger H Kramer
Mr. Jack R Krashin
Mr. Edward Krasovich
Mr. Edward J Kraus
Mr. Richard L Kraus
Mr. Robert L Kresbaugh
Mr. Mark Krofek
Mr. John J Krokosky
Mr. Marvin C Kruse
Mr. Raymond A Krylowski
Mr. Bernard J Krzywulak
Mr. Robert W Kuenzli
Mr. Charles R Kues
Mr. Wallace F Kuhner
Mr. David A Kuitunen
Mr. Frank V Kulczak
Mr. Joseph E Kuligoski Sr
Mr. Edward M Kulsa
Mr. Henry E Kulwicki
Mr. Robert Kummins
Mr. Michael D Kupchick
Mr. Robert Kurlander
Mr. Ed F Kurth
Mr. Arden J Kurtz
Mr. Eugene A Kuta
Mr. Michael Kutzmonich
Mr. Edward P Kysar
Mr. Thomas H Kysor
Mr. Edmund L L' Heureux
Mr. Frank La Creta
Mr. Robert W LaDu
Mr. Bernard W La Due
Mr. ClarksW LaFlamme
Mr. Joseph M La Fatch
Mr. Hilton M LaFontain
Mr. Bertrand E La France
Mr. Arthur E La Jeunesse
Mr. Jack I LaMar
Mr. Lawrence L LeMay
COL Paul M La Pierre (Ret)
Col Kenneth A LaPlante Ret

Mr. Anthony F La Rosa
Mr. Theodore N La Rue
Mr. Joseph P Labay
Mr. Mark L Labbe
Mr. William D Labbe
Mr. Robert A Labrie
Mr. Marlay E Lacey
Mr. Edwin J Ladlee
Mr. Richard G Ladlee
Mr. Gaylen F Lael
1SG Eugene S Lael (Ret)
Mr. William C Lagos
Mr. Robert L Lagree
Mr. Octavio Laguna
Mr. George J Lai
Mr. Douglas M Laidlaw
Mr. John E Laird
Mr. Arthur E Lajeunesse
Mr. Richard M Lake
Mr. Norman H Lambert
Mr. John E Lamle
Mr. Normand R Lamoureux
Mr. John A Lanaro Jr
Mr. James A Land
Mr. Terril D Landers
Mr. Titus E Landis
Mr. Donald H Landry
Mr. Norman J Landry
Mr. Edward J Landshof Sr
Mr. James G Lane
Mr. Otis A Lane
Mr. Peter A Lang
Mr. Robert V Lange
Mr. Leo E Langenback
Mr. Jonas C Lanham
Mr. Vincent D Lapadula Jr
Mr. Nicholas Lapenna
Mr. Thomas F Lapins
Mr. Colby S Laplace
Mr. Ray Larribas
Mr. Alan W Larsen
Mr. Clifford Larsen
Mr. Melvin O Larsen
Mr. Robert R Larsen
Mr. Alfred Lee Larson
Mr. Craig S Larson
Mr. Ivan A Larson
Mr. Thedore C Larson
Mr. Abraham I Lashin
Mr. Paul J Laskowski
Mr. Joseph D Lasky
Mr. Floyd Lasure Jr
Mr. George R Laswell
Mr. Glenn M Latimer
Mr. Charles G Laufer
Mr. V W Laughlin
Csm Waiter J Laverry Ret
Mr. Leonard J Lavnder
Mr. Ival V Lawhon Jr
Mr. Harry H Lawrence
Mr. Jack T W Lawrence
Mr. Paul J Lawrence
Mr. Albert E Lawson
Mr. Burt Lawson
Mr. Dennis J Lasowski
Mr. Harry A Layman
Mr. John J Lazos
Mr. Ralph J Le Blanc
Mr. David R LeFebvre
Mr. Paul E Le Guenec
Mr. Carl F Le Mier Sr
Mr. G A Le Vasser
Mr. John H Leavitt
Mr. James E Leach
Mr. David G Leaton
Mr. Kenneth W Leavens
Col Donald B Leazott Ret

Mr. Thomas E Lebo
Mr. Till D Lecian
Mr. William L Lederer
Mr. Benjamin F Lee
Mr. Dewey E Lee
Mr. Harrison Lee
Mr. Jack E Lee
Rev. William H Lee
Mr. William W Lee
Mr. Edward W Leeming
Mr. Leo F Lefevre
Mr. Gilbert E Leggett
Mr. George T Legros
Mr. Robert Lehmann
Mr. Raymond Lehrer
Mr. Martin R Leidig
Mr. Martin B Lein
Mr. George M Leiner
Mr. Lester H Leistikow
Mr. Raymond L Lemoine
Mr. Michael J Lendino
Mr. John G Leninger
Mr. Ron A Lenk
MSGT Darryl G Lentini (Ret)
Mr. John A Lenz
Mr. Alfred J Leo
Mr. David R Leon
Mr. Francis A Leonard
Mr. John E Leonard
Mr. Earl A Leonelly
Mr. Sergei Leonink
Mr. Robert L Leslie
Mr. Michael J Lester
Mr. James Levatino
Mr. Arthur J Levesque
Mr. Herbert N Levin
Mr. John Levinski
Mr. Larry R Lewis
Mr. Wayne B Lewis
SGM James W Lewis (Ret)
Mr. Bernard P Liberatore
Mr. Fred R Liberman
Mr. Robert J Liberty
Mr. Seymour L Lichtenfeld
Mr. James A Lidderdale
Mr. William J Liell
Mr. Russell W Light
Mr. Joseph L Liles
Mr. James M Lill
Mr. John V Lilyea
CWO Roy E Liming
Mr. Charles L Linden
Mr. Donald J Lindgren
Mr. Lloyd Lindsay
Mr. Gerald W Linekin
Mr. Edward B Linert
Mr. Bill Tushka - Chito Lingo
Mr. Robert W Linhart
Cwo Billy R Linker Ret
Mr. Donald J Linktewicz
Mr. Lloyd M Lippman
Mr. Paul Lippman
Mr. Joseph Lischinsky
Mr. Anthony T Lisi
Mr. Richard A Lisiecki
Mr. Richard H List
Mr. Stanley J Liszka
Mr. Chester S Litchfield
Mr. John G Litterer
Mr. James C Litz
Mr. Joseph J Livingston
Mr. Neil F Livingston
Mr. Albert Llauger
Mr. George W Lock
Mr. Philip Lockwood Jr
Mr. Vincent J Lodato

Mr. Dwaine A Loest
Mr. Rudolph A Loffel
Mr. Dwayne S Logan
Mr. Gilbert M Logan
Mr. Vincent J Logiudice
LTC Richard V Lohrens (Ret)
Mr. Carl E Lombard
Mr. Domenic J Lombardi
Mr. Nicholas P Lombardi
Mr. William W Lomnicki
Mr. David E Long
Mr. George C Long
Mr. Milton J Long
Mr. Robert L Long
Mr. William H Longenecker Jr
Mr. Dominic Loperfido
Mr. Albino A Lopez
Mr. Apolinar (Paul) Lopez
Mr. Richard Lopez
Mr. Camelo Lopez - Estevas
Mr. Laverne M Losee
Mr. William Losito
Mr. Richard J Lother
Mr. James Loucks
Mr. James R Loughrey
Mr. Benjamin E Loup
Mr. Thomas P Love
Mr. William J Love
Mr. Wayne C Love Sr
Msg Augustus F Lover Jr Ret
Mr. Robert A Lovering
Mr. Frank A Loveso
Mr. Joseph A Lovetro
Mr. Chris J Lovrovich
Mr. Henry I Lowder
Mr. John P Lowery
Mr. John C Lowman
Mr. Frank A Lowry
Mr. James M Lowry
Mr. John P Lubera
Mr. Charles B Lucas
Mr. Michael Lucas
Mr. Roger A Lucas
Mr. Charles F Luce
Mr. Iglo A Luci
Mr. Theodore L Luciani
Mr. Robert M Ludwig
Mr. Roger J Lueckenhoff
Mr. Anthony Lugo
Mr. Lloyd J Lukas
Mr. Clifton S Luke
Mr. Edwin S Lukemire
Mr. Frank Lukes
Mr. Milton A Lukken
Mr. Albert Lumpkin
Mr. John J Lupetin
MSG Randall L Lusk (Ret)
Mr. Charles J Lussier
Mr. Nicholas G Luxon
Mr. Peter Luyk
Mr. Harry R Luzader
Mr. Billy Lycans
Mr. William H Lynn
Mr. Dale W Lynton
Mr. Dwight W Lyon
Mr. George R Lyon
Mr. Kenneth W Lyon
Mr. Brendan F Lyons
Mr. John J Lyons Jr
Mr. John T Lypowy
Mr. Lothar A Maaser
Mr. Jerome E Mac Donald
Mr. Kenneth W MacDonald

Mr. Roderick A MacKenzie
Mr. John C MacKinnon
Mr. Richard A Mac Leod
Mr. Thomas M MacNeil
Mr. William F Mac Swain
Mr. Armando Macaruso
Mr. Francis M Macey
Mr. William Mach
Mr. Frank J Mack
Mr. William J Mack
Mr. Edward L Madaris
Mr. Eddie L Madaris
Mr. Richard T Madden
Mr. Charles W Maddox
Mr. William J Mader
Mr. Mark P Madrid
Mr. Joseph E Maes
Mr. Robert H Magar
Mr. John T Magazzu
Mr. Angelo R Magli
Mr. Paul D Magro
Mr. Jethro C Mahaffey
Csm Cyril G Maher Ret
Mr. George J Mahr
Mr. Howard T Maki
Mr. Francisco A Maldonado
Mr. John P Maleiko
Mr. Anthony L Malek
Mr. James R Mallard
Mr. Gene C Mallette
Mr. John J Mallon
Mr. Fernand J Malo
Mr. Harold E Malone
Mr. Anthony F Malvaso
Mr. Anthony Manca
Mr. Michael A Mandac
Mr. Carmine V Mandarano
CSM Juan M Manibusan
Mr. George A Manizza
1Sgt Hilbert J Manley Ret
Mr. Charles G Mankin
Mr. Jerome A Manley
Mr. Howard R Mann
Mr. Joseph H Mann Jr
Mr. James W Manning
Mr. Joseph Manoni
Mr. Charles S Mansell
Mr. Nicholas W Mansolillo
Mr. Raymind A Manz
Mr. John L Maracle
Mr. Nicholas L Marasco
Mr. Frank Marcan
Mr. James E Marceron
Mr. Anthony D Marchesani
Mr. Michael L Marcukaitis
Mr. Frank J Marek
Mr. Richard D Marez
Mr. Richard Margolin
Mr. Kenneth J Mari
Mr. Alfred J Mariani
Mr. Michael A Marinelli
SSGT Antonio Marinello
Mr. Earl L Marion
Mr. Richard F Mariot
Mr. Henry J Mark
Mr. John F Markham
Mr. Robert L Marks
Mr. Edward P Markunas
CWO Patrick A Marotta
Mr. Richard M Marowitz
Mr. Elmer M Marple
Mr. Daniel P Marquardo
Mr. Armand J Marques

Mr. Frederick D Marrin
Mr. Louis R Marrone
Mr. Edward S Marsh Sr
Mr. Russell Marsh Jr
Mr. Vance Marsh
Mr. John Marshalek
CPT John H Marshall
Mr. James Marshall Jr
Mr. Daniel E Martelli
Sgm David T Martin Ret
Mr. Edward J Martens
Mr. George K Martin
Mr. John F Martin
Mr. Joseph A Martin
Mr. Morry H Martin
Mr. Richard W Martin
PSG Robert O Martin (Ret)
Mr. Wayne D Martin
Mr. William F Martin
Mr. Louis V Martina
Mr. Ernest Martinez
Mr. Guadalupe L Martinez
Mr. Hector L Martinez
Mr. Manuel Martinez Rivera
Mr. Santos M Martinez
Mr. Louis G Martino
Mr. Harold N Martling
Mr. Clayton L Marvin
Mr. Daniel Marvin
Mr. Howard L Mason
Mr. Felice J Massa
Mr. Albert Masso
Mr. George T Masters
Mr. John L Mastromarino
Mr. Charles E Mateer
Mr. Allen R Mathews
Mr. Albert A Matlak
Mr. Paul H Matranga
Mr. Merrill R Matson
Mr. James Masullo
Mr. Arthur P Masur Jr
Bg Ted C Mataxis Ret
Mr. Roy H Matsumoto
Mr. Aaron M Matheny
Mr. Thomas L Mathews
Mr. Charles W Mattes
Mr. Christopher Mattiace
Sfc Andrew T Matoes Ret
Mr. Rudolph R Matuscsak
Mr. Glenn W Maundorf
Mr. Roger J Maurice
Mr. Richard C Maxfield
Mr. Larry T Maxwell
Mr. Norris K Maxwell
Mr. John M May
Mr. Samuel M May
Mr. William C May
Mr. Bernardo Mayeda
Mr. Kenneth A Mayer
Mr. Egbert A Mayers
Mr. William G Mayti
Mr. Donald G Mayvilie
Mr. Eugene A Maziarz
Mr. David A McAllister
Mr. Victor L Mc Allister
Mr. John E Mc Auliffe
Mr. John F McBurney
Mr. David L Mc Cabe
Mr. Francis P McCabe
Mr. Charles D McCall
Mr. Harold K Mc Call
Mr. William Mc Call
Mr. Joseph P Mc Callion
Mr. James G Mc Cann
Mr. Robert L Mc Cann

Mr. Theodore R McChin
Mr. William R Mc Clain
Mr. Gene E Mc Clure
COL Chester B Mc Coid (Ret)
Mr. William T Mc Collum
Mr. Donald R Mc Conahay
Mr. Everett L McConnell
Mr. Fred Mc Conville
Mr. Frank McCord
Mr. Martin A Mc Coy
Mr. William E Mc Cullough Jr
Dr. Bailey B Mc Cune
Mr. Lavon T Mc Daniel
Mr. Terrance M Mc Daniel
Mr. Thomas J Mc Darby
Mr. Paul C Mc Dermott
Mr. Raymond A Mc Dermott Jr
Mr. Bradley L Mc Donald
Mr. Edmund A Mc Donald
Mr. Lee E Mc Donald
Mr. Norvel A McDonald
Mr. Walter R Mc Donald
Mr. Wilford D McDonald
Mr. John E Mc Donough
Mr. Joseph P Mc Donough
Mr. James A Mc Dougal
Mr. William B Mc Dougal
SGM William Mc Dougall (Ret)
Mr. William D Mc Elfish
Mr. Nealie C McElhany
Mr. John F Mc Elmeel
Mr. James A McElroy
Mr. Thomas D Mc Enerney
Mr. Steward H Mc Fadden
Mr. James M Mc Farlane
Mr. James C Mc Farlen
Mr. Douglas C Mc Garraugh
Mr. Vincent J Mc Gavisk
Mr. Fred B Mc Gee Sr
Mr. Robert L Mc George
Mr. James A Mc Ginnes
Mr. John A Mc Glone Jr
Mr. John J Mc Glue
Mr. James W Mc Gougain
Mr. James O McGovern
Mr. James V McGovern
Mr. Thomas H Mc Gowan Jr
Mr. Anthony A Mc Grath
Mr. Bobby J Mc Gregor
Mr. Leonard R Mc Guffey
Mr. Edward M McGuire
Mr. James J Mc Guire
2Lt John L McGuire
Mr.Rolin E McGuire
Mr. Joseph P Mc Henry
Mr. William P Mc Henry
Mr. William F Mc Hugh
Mr. William M Mc Ilvain
Mr. Bruce R Mc Kaba
Mr. Jeffry C Mc Keague
Mr. Charles Mc Kean
Mr. Charles L Mc Kee
Mr. Frank E McKee
Ssg John W McKee Ret
Mr. Robert L Mc Kee Jr
Mr. John T Mc Keil
Mr. William J Mc Kenna
Mr. Charles W McKinky

Mr. James O Mc Kinley
Mr. John E McKinnon
Mr. Edward J Mc Kitrick
Mr. Thomas N Mc Lauchlin
Mr. Leland J Mc Laughlin
Mr. George E Mc Laughlin Jr
Mr. Walter A McLaughlin
Mr. Herman H Mc Lawhorn
Mr. Arthur T McLellan
Mr. David D Mc Leod
Mr. Laurin R Mc Leod
Mr. Russell E McLogan
Mr. Harold E Mc Mackin
Mr. Hubert F McMaster
Bg John J J McMullan Ret
Mr. John P Mc Mullen
Mr. James H McNally
Ltc Paul K McNamara Ret
Mr. John R Mc Neese
Mr. Richard J Mc Neil
Mr. James V Mc Nicol
Mr. Edward Mc Phail
Mr. Norman R McQuade
Mr. Gordon McWade
Mr. John A McWatters
Mr. Sherman McWilliams
Mr. Grant A Mead
Mr. Norman E Mead
Mr. Lawrence G Meades
Mr. Wayne A Meadowa
Mr. Jack A Measley
Mr. Dillard E Medford
Mr. Raymond E Meece
Mr. Thomas D Meier
Mr. Thomas C Meinhardt
Mr. Thomas L Mekolites
Mr. Manuel S Mello
Mr. Charles D Melucci
Mr. Wayne G Melvin
Mr. Elsworth H Melzer
Mr. John A Mendez
Mr. R Edward Mengak
Mr. George S Mentzer
Mr. G Jerry Merges
Mr. Joseph J Merlino
Mr. Joseph A Merola
Mr. David J Merrick
Mr. Samuel H Merritt
Mr. Richard J Mertes
Mr. John A Mesa
Mr. Dennis A Mesaros
Mr. George Meschwitz
Mr. John Mesich
Mr. George F Messer
Mr. Ralph E Metivier
Cpt Raymond H Metternich
Mr. Robert H Meuser
Mr. Donald C Meyer Jr
Mr. Henry W Meyers
Ltc James F Meyer Ret
Mr. Morris J Meyers
Mr. John F Micciche
Mr. Joseph G Micek
Mr. August H Michaels
Mr. Thomas E Michalik
Mr. Arthur G Michel
Mr. Clarence E Middlekauff
Mr. Bryant E Middleton
Mr. Ross D Middleton
Mr. Kenneth F Midkiff
Mr. James R Mihr
Mr. Robert J Mikus
Mr. Fidencio Milanes

Mr. Charles E Miles
Mr. Paul Milhofer
Mr. Paul Milich
Ltc Charles I Miller Ret
Mr. Edmund E Miller
Mr. Elwyn H Miller
Mr. Frank Miller
Mr. Frank J Miller
Mr. James H Miller
Mr. John N Miller
Bg Judson F Miller Ret
Mr. Mark A Milier
Mr. Paul B Miller
Mr. Ralph A Miller
CWO Raymond D Miller
Mr. Robert W Miller
Mr. Roger H Miller
Mr. William L Miller
Mr. Howard S Milligan
Mr. Chester C Milliken
Mr. James H Mills
Mr. Donald J Mills
Mr. Billy L Mims Sr
COL Philip S Minges Jr (Ret)
Mr. Arthur Mings
Mr. Louis P Minicucci
Mr. Julius Minkoff
Mr. Joseph A Minto
Mr. Fred J Miscisz
Mr. Remus (Ray) J Miserendino
Mr. Robert Mishkin
Mr. Everett J Miskimens
Mr. David S Mitchell Sr
Mr. William E Mitchell
Col William L Mitchell Ret
Mr. Edward Mize
Mr. John P Mizzoni
Mr. Daniel H Mock
Mr. Jesse A Moffett
Mr. Henry G Mohr
Sfc Kenneth Mohr Sr Ret
Mr. Thomas R Mohar
Mr. Joseph Molczan
Mr. James M Moloney
Mr. John E Monaco
Mr. Adrian L Monday
Mr. Ferdinand A Moniz
Mr. Edward Monks
Mr. Lawrence F Monroe
Mr. Paul A Mons
Mr. Ralph H Monsees
Mr. Angelo G Montaglione
Mr. Tony Montagnese
Mr. Jerome H Montagnino
Mr. Gillesoie V Montgomer
Mr. Joseph A Montana
Mr. Donald J Monterosso
1SG Manuel Montezdeoca (Ret)
Mr. Henry G Montgomery
Mr. Joseph Montigney Jr
Mr. Charles T Mooney
Mr. David P Mooney
Dr. J William Mooney
Mr. Brady J Moore
Ltc David R Moore Ret
Mr. Edward R Moore
Mr. Fred J Moore
Mr. George L Moore
Mr. Jack M Moore
Mr. Jimmie L Moore
1SG John L Moore
Mr. Ray E Moore Jr
Mr. Robert E Moore

Mr. Robert H Moore
Mr. Ronald C Moore
Mr. William T Moore Jr
CSM Phillip D Moore (Ret)
Mr. Mike Morado
Csm Pete Morakon Ret
Mr. Raul Morales
Mr. Harold R Moran
Mr. Philip J Morana
Mr. George Moranian
Mr. Richard J Moravek
Mr. Dominick J Morelli
Mr. John C Morelli
Mr. Edward Morend Jr
Mr. Ferd A Moreno
Mr. John F Moreno
Mr. Mario Moreno
Mr. Rocco J Moretto
LTC Ernest H Morgan
Mr. Kenneth R Morgan
Mr. Ronald S Morgan
Mr. Walter E Morgan
Hon. Gregory L Morgan US Congress
Mr. William G Mori
Mr. Louis J Morinelli
Mr. James P Morio
Mr. David R Morris
Mr. Melvin C Morris
Mr. Walter H Morris
Sfc Baxter T Morrison Ret
Mr. Samuel J Morrison
Mr. Thomas D Morrissey
Mr. Frank M Morrow
COL Ray Mortensen
Mr. Arthur D Morton
Mr. Nelson A Morton
Mr. Ralph A Morton
Mr. Ernest V Morton Jr
Mr. George L Moscardini
Mr. Richard A Moscatel
MAJ Richard J Moser Sr
Mr. Eugene C Mosher
Mr. Robert L Moss
Mr. Emil W Motzny
Mr. James F Moulds
Maj Wm Bird Mounsey Ret
Mr. John K Moyer
Mr. Ralph W Moyer
Mr. William A Mrkvicha
Mr. Edmond J Mrowczynski
Mr. Thomas V Mucciariello
Mr. Richard P Mueller
Mr. William P Mueller
MSG Kenneth H Mueller (Ret)
Mr. Richard L Muffins
Mr. Daniel J Muffoletto
Mr. David E Muhlenbruch
Mr. Homer M Muir
Mr. Thomas J Mulcahey
CSM Joseph E Mulcahy
Mr. Paul T Mulcahy
Mr. Robert F Mulcahy
Mr. Donald J J D Mulkerne
Mr. Joseph W Mullaney
Mr. William A Mullens
Mr. George W Muller
Mr. Bill L Mullins
Mr. Theodore W Mulqueen
Mr. James P Mulvey
Mr. William P Mulvey
Mr. Mc Coy Mumphrey

Mr. Millard E Mundew
Mr. Joseph Munoz
Mr. James D Munroe
Mr. Joseph V Muraca'
Mr. Paul H Murdoch
SGM Paul J Murman (Ret)
Mr. Anthony J Murphy
Mr. Charles B Murphy
Mr. David E Murphy
Mr. Eugene H Murphy
Mr. George H Murphy
Mr. Leo J Murphy
Mr. William C Murphy
Mr. William V Murphy
Col Charles P Murray Jr Ret
Mr. Michael S Musich
Mr. Wesley E Muth
Mr. Benjamin N Myers
Mr. Bobby L Myers
Mr. Joseph F Myers
Mr. Lewis Myers
Mr. William L Myers
Mr. Edward R Naccari
Mr. Lawrence E Nagel
Mr. Herman Nagora Jr
Mr. Walter K Nakata
Mr. Mike Nalbandian
Mr. John J Nangle
Mr. James B Nannini
Mr. E Ray Nasser
Mr. Glenn W Naundorf
Mr. Robert Nava
Mr. Paul A Nazer
Mr. Danny L Neely
Mr. Victor R Neiland
Mr. August Neitzel
Mr. Eugene N Nelsen
Mr. Berwin H Nelson
Mr. Robert E Nelson
Mr. Robert E Nerney
Mr. Victor A Nerone
Mr. Richard L Nestor
Mr. Glen C Neuhard
Mr. Arthur Neukrug
Mr. Archibald E Nevitt
Mr. Bennie R Newcomb
Mr. C Lum Newbum III
Mr. Albert H Newman
Mr. Davis E Newman
Mr. James Newman
Mr. Louis Newman
Mr. Mark A Newman
Mr. Paul E Newman
Mr. John W Newsham
Mr. Denver E Newsom
Mr. James D Newsome Sr
Mr. John W Newsham
Mr. Edward L Newton
LTC Joseph W Newton
Mr. Charles R Nichols
Mr. David L Nichols
Mr. Warren E Nichols
Mr. John A Nicholson
Mr. Thomas E Nicholson
Mr. Nicholas Nickas
Mr. Frank B Niehaus
Mr. Ted R Niess Sr
Msg Stanley J Nikulski Ret
Mr. John M Nipper
Mr. David M Nisbet
Mr. Roger H Nitchman
Mr. Andrew W Nix Jr
Mr. Robert B Nixon
Mr. Stephen O Noble
Mr. David C Noe
Mr. Dennis M Noel
Mr. Arthur E Nolan

Mr. James V Nolan
Mr. Gary L Noller
Mr. Ralph A Nolletti
Mr. Paul J Nordone
Mr. Richard W Nordquist
Mr. Fredrick E Nordt
Mr. Gerald R Norman
Mr. Joseph B Normile
Mr. Jim Norris
Mr. Charlie O Norris
Mr. Lawrence R Northcutt
Mr. Christopher B Norton
Mr. Paul M Nowaczewski
Mr. John R Nowak
Mr. Duane E Noyes
Mr. Thomas F Nugent
Mr. Russell J Nunamaker
Mr. Rosalio S Nunez
Mr. Carlo I Nybergh
Mr. Henry R Nylan
Mr. John W O'Brien
Mr. Robert L O ' Brien
Mr. Kevin J O' Brien
Mr. Richard M O' Brien
Mr. Thomas J O' Connor
Mr. Thomas P O'Cornell
Mr. Joseph M O' Donnell
Mr. Robert B O' Donnell
Mr. Eswin E O' Donoghue
Mr. Robert D O' Hara
Mr. Lawrence H O' Keeffe
Mr. Robert J O'Malley
Mr. William J O'Malley
Mr. John R O'Malley
Mr. John J O'Neil
Mr. William E O' Neil
Mr. Daniel P O' Neill
Mr. James T O' Neill
Mr. Walter F O' Quinn
Mr. Edwin M Oberdorf
Mr. Salvatore A Occhipinti
1 Sg Morgan J Odom Ret
Mr. William J Ogden
Mr. Keith S Oja
Mr. Lawrence D Okendo
Mr. Jose D Olea
Mr. Lloyd E Oler Sr
Mr. Christopher Oliveira
Mr. Charles P Oliver
Mr. Clay D Oliver
Mr. Walter E Oliver
Mr. Thomas B Olney
Mr. Ernest R Olsen
Mr. John E Olson
Mr. Robert A Olson
Mr. Theodore Onukiewech
Mr. Andrew Oravecz
Mr. Frank A Oriolo
Mr. Anthony V Orlando
Mr. Carlo J Orlando
Mr. Louis L Orlando
Mr. Albert S Orr Jr
Mr. Rafael Orta - Delgado
Mr. Lorenzo G Ortega
Mr. Daniel M Ortiz
Mr. Andres Ortiz Jr
Mr. Edwart T Osowski
Mr. Floyd C Oster
Mr. Robert K Osterman
Mr. James Osterman II
Mr. Laurence W Ostling
Mr. Glendon L Oswalt
Mr. Floryan B Oszuscik

Mr. Robert G Ott
Mr. John F Ottersberg
Mr. Francis H Otterstedt
Dr. Merle L Otto
Mr. Michael F Ottomano
Mr. Buford T Otwell
Mr. Donald P Oulton
Mr. Reynold H Overroeder
Mr. Andrew Pace
Mr. John R Pacheco
Mr. Samuel D Pagan
Mr. Federico Pagani
Mr. Paul D Pagliaro
Mr. Arthur D Painter
Mr. Arthur J Paiva
Mr. Joseph Palachick
Mr. Robert K Palassou
Mr. Peter P Paldino
Mr. James P Paleologos
Mr. Angelo M Palermo
Mr. Rosario J Palermo
Mr. Cecil R Palmer
Mr. Riley F Palmer
Mr. William S Palmer
Mr. Michael Palmeri Jr
Mr. Thomas J Panke
Mr. Joaquin Paniagua Jr
Mr. Nicholas J Paolicelli
Mr. Michael J Pape
Mr. Gordon J Papin
Mr. Richard R Papp
Mr. Charles Pappas
Mr. Richard J Paraboschi
Mr. Elmer L Pargen
Mr. Caesar J Parise
Mr. Joseph W Parisi
Mr. Stephen Parisi
Mr. Desmond R Parker
Mr. Donald E Parker
Mr. Edward D Parker
Mr. Horace T Parker
Mr. James M Parker
Mr. Leslie R Parker
Mr. Vernon M Parker
Mr. William P Parker
Mr. Esward W Parks
Mr. Maxwell H Parrish
Mr. William T Parsons
Mr. William O Partington
Mr. Kenneth J Partoyan
Mr. Joseph H Parzy
Mr. Edward L Paschal
Mr. Harry E Paschall
Mr. Jack A Pascoline
Mr. Modesto J Pasella
Mr. Daniel J Passafiume
Mr. Arden N Passaro
Mr. Dennis S Passell
Mr. Dennis E Passwater
Mr. Michael A Patalano
Mr. Francis E Patenaude
Mr. Chester L Pater
Mr. Frank M Patnaude
Mr. Earl L Patterson
Mr. Leland C Patterson
Mr. Loran E Patterson
Mr. Michael N Patterson
Mr. Olon R Patterson
Mr. Paul A Patterson
Mr. Earl W Patto
Mr. Jack L Patton
Mr. George Paul
Maj Skevos G Pavlou
Mr. Nicholas A Pavone
Mr. Arthur J Pawelkop Jr
Mr. Stanley L Pawlinski
Mr. Gene Payne
Mr. Robert R Payne
Mr. Jack Payton

Mr. Sidney B Pearce Jr
Mr. Dick W Pearl
Mr. James E Pearson
Mr. Roy G Pearson
Mr. Walter D Pearson
Mr. Richard S Peckham
Mr. Paul P Pederzani Jr
Mr. Lawrence B Peet
Mr. Norwood M Peirson Jr
Mr. Michael S Pejakovich
Mr. Anthony A Pellegrino
Mr. Francis J Pelletier
Mr. Raymond N Pelletier
Mr. James C Pemberton
Mr. Morris Penermon
Mr. Samuel T Pennington
Mr. Pete L Penoff
Mr. Robert D Penoyer
Mr. Edward J Penrose
Mr. John T Pepper
Mr. Archie B Perea
Mr. Daniel G Perkins
Mr. George P Peroni
Mr. Creston F Perrin
Mr. Ralph Perroncello
Mr. Charles Perry
Mr. Edward Perry
Mr. Edward W Perry
Mr. Frank Perry Jr
Mr. Melvin D Perttunen
Mr. Robert H Pessin
Mr. William M Pestana
Mr. Zigmund Pesti
Mr. George Petcoff
Mr. Ronald A Peters
Mr. Thomas E Peters
Mr. Bruce W Peterson
Mr. Maurice E Peterson
Mr. Richard W Peterson
Mr. William E Peterson
Mr. Norman S Petit
Mr. Michael Petock
Mr. Grover R Petrie
Mr. Rocco J Petrillo
Mr. Joseph Petrucci
Mr. Ray O Pettit
Mr. James T Pettus
Mr. Warren R Petty
Mr. Lawrence Pezza Jr
Mr. Rudy Pezzaro
Mr. Walter J Pezzei
Mr. Gilbert C Pfleger
Mr. Warren E Phalen
Mr. Paul A Phelan
Ltc Julian H Philips Ret
Mr. Bernard G Phillips
Mr. Cecil D Phillips
Mr. Clifford G Phillips
Mr. Clifford R Phillips
Mr. Daniel P Phillips
Mr. Frank C Phillips
Mr. Lewis G Phillips
Mr. Okie S Phillips
Mr. Paul S Phillips
Mr. Robert L Phillips
Mr. Stanley Phillips
Mr. Jodie E Phipps
Mr. Phillip B Piazza
Mr. Thomas Pickering
Mr. Thomas F Pienta
Mr. John Piepowski
Mr. Burton Pierce
Mr. Donald R Pierce
Mr. James E Pierce
Mr. Walter A Pierce
Mr. John E Pierson
Mr. Joseph Pietroforte
Mr. Kirk A Pietsch
Mr. Victor B Pigoga
Mr. Mathew R Pike

PSG Curtis M Pilgrim (Ret)
Mr. Albert E Pilson
Sfc Leonard A Pimentel
Mr. Robert B Piner
Mr. John D Pinezaddleby
1SG Lionel F Pinn Sr
Mr. John E Pinkham
Mr. Frank P Pinto
Mr. Charles R Pippitt
Mr. George Pires
Mr. Frederick M Pirl
Mr. William F Pirro
Mr. Joseph A Pisack
Mr. Frank Pistecchia
Mr. Frank J Pistone Sr
Mr. John D Pitman
Mr. William M Pitt
Mr. James A Pius
Mr. Lawrence R Plaatje
Mr. Eldon J Plante Sr
Mr. John R Platt
Mr. Pete Plaza
Mr. Rick L Plett
Mr. Walter R Ployer
Mr. Richard R Plum
LTC Gerrell V Plummer (Ret)
Mr. Charles F Platz
Mr. Michael L Plemens
Mr. Rick L Plett
Mr. Theodore B Podkul Jr
Ltc Phitlip W Poe Ret
Mr. Paul F Poepperling
Mr. Joseph M Poggi
Mr. Aldo J Poggio
Mr. Paavo E Pogue
Mr. Stephen P Polander
Mr. Robert R Polaski
Mr. Anthony F Polemeni
Mr. Sidney Pollock
Mr. Casimer J Pomianek
COL Lewington S Ponder
Mr. George B Poochigian
Mr. Jack J Poole
Mr. Homer O Poorman
Mr. Fred J Pope
Mr. Peter Popolizio
Mr. Donald W Popp
Sfc Peter D Porata
Mr. Joseph R Porcarelli
Mr. Albert A Porfirio Jr
Mr. George F Porod
Mr. Carl H Porter
Mr. George E Porter
Mr. George L Porter
Dr. Lester L Porter
Mr. Phillips E Porter Jr
Mr. Robert W Porter
Mr. Alfred W Porterfield
Mr. James R Posey
Mr. Mel Posner
Mr. Lawrence W Post
Mr. Ernamiel F Poston Jr
Mr. Joseph E Potestio
Mr. Richard H Potter
LTC Franklin E Potter (Ret)
Mr. Terry L Potter
Mr. Ralph G Potts
Mr. Charles Pou
Mr. Gerald J Pouliot
Mr. Eugene M Powell
Mr. Henry E Powell
Mr. Russell T Powell
Mr. Charles F Powers
Mr. Lyle A Powers
Mr. Terrance R Powers
1SG Ray E Poynter (Ret)

Sgm Raul V Prado Ret
Mr. Frank N Prano J
Mr. Benny W Prater
Mr. Arnold W Prather
Mr. Charles N Pratt
Mr. Mark A Praught
Mr. Delmer R Presley
Mr. Basil P Presti
Mr. John H Pribnow
Mr. George H Price
MSG Johnnie S Price (Ret)
Mr. Michael R Price
Mr. Bruce W Price Sr
Mr. Francis J Priest
Mr. Edward J Principe
Mr. Michael Prochko
Mr. Dewey R Proctor
Mr. Joseph D Proctor
Mr. Larry K Proctor
Mr. Joseph R Proeller
Mr. James A Proie
Mr. Woodrow Prokosch
Mr. Gaetano A Proto
Mr. Charles O Provow
Mr. Charles J Prusik
Mr. Robert J Pryor
Ltc John J Przybylski Ret
Mr. John F Pullo Jr
Mr. Chester A Pulst
MSG Laverne G Pulvermacher (Ret)
Mr. Woodrow F Purcell
Mr. Willard Purdy
Mr. Robert W Purple
Mr. James R Puryear
Mr. William K Putney Jr
Mr. David L Quaid
Mr. Jessie F Qualls
Mr. James W Quigley
Mr. Harold J Quinn
Mr. Hillman P Rabalais
Mr. Joseph Raccosta
Mr. James E Rachau
Mr. Kevin C Rachford
Mr. Roy J Radke
Mr. Robert M Ragan
Mr. Thomas E Ragland
Mr. Sylvester P Ragnone
Mr. Joseph G Rahie
Mr. Emil V Raimondi
Mr. Allan W Rainsberry
Mr. Anton F Rajer
Mr. Michael E Raleigh
Mr. Jack W Ralls
Mr. Albert W Ramas
Mr. Andres Ramirez
Mr. James A Ramsden
Mr. Thomas N Ramsey
Mr. Bruce J Randall
Mr. Thomas E Randell
Mr. William M Randle Sr
Mr. Robert R Randlett
COL George H Rankin
Mr. Alfred B Ranzenbach
Mr. Justin Raphael
Mr. Robert N Rasmus
Mr. Clarence R Rasnake
CSM Ronald H Rath
Mr. Frederick H Raymer
Mr. Robert V Re
Mr. Richard S Reahard
Mr. Michael G Rebar
Mr. Richard W Rebban
Mr. William B Record
Mr. Arthur W Redder
Mr. Joseph T Reddington
Mr. Frank A Redin
Mr. Robert C Redman
Mr. Wayne E Redmon

Mr. Dean T Redmond
Mr. Leon W Reece
Mr. Gareth D Reed
PSG Jeffrey S Reed (Ret)
Mr. Lloyd H Reed
Mr. Karl R Reemsen
Mr. Jacob L Rees
Mr. Elwood M Reese
Mr. Russell P Rego
Mr. Henry L Rehn Jr
Mr. Robert F Reichel
Mr. Calvin C Reichert
Mr. George Reichert
Mr. Thomas A Reiches
Mr. Richard M Reid
Mr. Howard F Reiff
Maj Chris Reilly Ret
Mr. James P Reilly
Mr. Frederick A Rein
Mr. Edward Reinhard
Mr. Raymond Reis
Mr. Christian F Reischauer
Mr. Wilfred G Reist
Mr. Joseph T Reiter
SGM Salvatore A Rende (Ret)
Mr. Cyril B Renner
Mr. David T Renolds
Mr. James M Renton
Mr. Joseph Resende
Mr. Freeman S Revels
Mr. Robert B Revere
Mr. Amado B Reyna Jr
Mr. Andrew E Reyna
Mr. Fred L Reynolds
Mr. Joseph M Reynolds
Mr. Kenneth E Reynolds
Mr. Sewall Reynolds
Mr. John R Reynoldson
Mr. Robert J Rezek
Mr. Melvin L Rhiel
Mr. Herbert J Rhodes
Mr. Robert E Rhodes
BG Douglas A Riach
Mr. Joseph A Ricciardi
Mr. Edward C Rice
Mr. Franklin D Rice
Mr. Gary E Rice
Mr. Marvin L Rice
COL Rex T Rice Sr (Ret)
Mr. Edward Rich
Mr. Donald Richard
Mr. Robert O Richard
Mr. Dal R Richards
Mr. Jerry R Richards
Mr. Kenneth R Richards
Mr. Raymond L Richards
Mr. Bruce D Richardson
Mr. Warren Richart
Mr. Herbert L Richey Jr
Mr. Elgin Richie
Mr. Duncan B Richman
Mr. Melvin A Richmond MD
Mr. Arden Riddle
Mr. Dale H Riden
Mr. Herbert C Riedel
Mr. Norman J Riegler
Mr. Richard T Riehle
Mr. Christopher G Riendeau
Mr. Churchill Rifenburgh
Mr. John A Riggs
Mr. John F Riley
Mr. Chester A Riley Jr
Mr. Lee R Rimbey
Mr. Peter M Rinaudo
Mr. Daniel W Rinehart

Mr. Charles W Rinek
Mr. James E Ringquist
Mr. Larry J Ritter
Mr. Maurice A Ritter
Mr. Miguel Rivera
Mr. John J Rivers
Mr. David R Rives
Mr. Philip Rmims
Mr. Donald W Roach
Mr. Francis B Roach
Mr. Robert M Roach
Mr. Loy L Robb
Mr. Norbert F Robben
Mr. William P Robbins Jr
Mr. Robert A Roberge
Mr. Michael Roberta
Mr. James L Roberts
Mr. Ralph Roberts
Mr. James C Robertson
Mr. William J Robertson
Mr. Wolfgang F Robinow
Mr. Cecil D Robinson
Mr. James F Robinson
Mr. John T Robinson
SGT Marion M Robinson
Mr. Walter I Robinson
Mr. Carl D Robison
Mr.Paul R Rochford
Mr. Arthur H Rochefort
Mr. Robert S Roddick Jr
Mr. Edward R Rode
Mr. Mervin G Rodgers Sr
Mr. Ernest Rodriguez
Mr. Edmund L Roeder
FSGT Laurence B
    Rogers
Mr. Karl R Rohde
Mr. James E Rohr
Mr. Daniel T Rohrer
Mr. Arthur W. Rohweder
Mr. Stanford L Roland
Mr. Milan A Rolik
Mr. Gregory A Rollinger
Mr. Bruce E Rollins
Mr. Earl T Roman
Mr. Michael Romano
Mr. Paul G Rombaut
Mr. Craig D Romeo
Mr. William J Romz
Mr. Walter L Ronaghan
Mr. Philip Roncari
Mr. Robert R Ronning
Mr. Thoralf I Ronninger
Mr. Bennie R Rooks Jr
Mr. John J Rooney
Mr. Joseph A Ropel
Mr. Jose F Rosa
Mr. Richard C Rosa
Dr. Samuel Rosa
Mr. Thomas F Rosa
Mr. Edwin G Rosado
Mr. Pedro R
    Rosado-Valazq
Mr. Maurice C Rosch
Mr. Harvey A Rose
Mr. Kenneth H Rose
Mr. Leonard Rose
Mr. Samuel F Rosella
Mr. Herman Rosen
Mr. Seymour N Rosen
Mr. Martin Rosenbaum
Ltg Donald E Rosenblum
    Ret
Mr. Russell J Rosener
Mr. Jerome Rosenfeld
Mr. Geoffrey B
    Rosengarten
Mr. Benjamin Rosenthal
Mr. Alvin D Rosenzweig
Mr. Stanley Rosenzweig

Mr. Kenneth G Roskey
Mr. John M Ross
Mr. John R Ross
Mr. Lloyd R Ross
Mr. Louis Ross Jr
Mr. Sanford E Ross
Mr. James D Rosselli
Mr. Philip A Rossetti
Mr. William F Roth
Mr. Ralph E Rotruck
Mr. James J Rotunno
Mr. Robert H Rounsefell
SGM Delbert A Routh Sr
    (Ret)
Mr. Thomas J Rowan
Mr. Robert D Rowe
Mr. Willis C Rowe
Mr. Sheldon C Royal
Mr. James Rozanski
Mr. Sidney Rubenstein
Mr. Anthony Rubinstello
Mr. Earl A Rubley
Mr. Robert A Rue
Mr. Wilbur C Rugg
Mr. Thomas M Ruggeri
Mr. Arthur W Ruhl
Mr. Jose E Ruiz
Mr. William E Rumbold
Mr. Edward J Rumsey
Mr. Martica W Runyon
Mr. Myron D Runyon
Mr. Michael L Ruoff
Mr. Raymond L Rushing
Mr. Robert W Russ
Mr. Thomas W Russ
Mr. Alfred A Russo
Mr. Eugene L Russell
Mr. Ivan L Russell
Mr. Ivan W Russell
Mr. Kent E Russell
Mr. Peter A Russell
Mr. Raymond B Russell
Mr. Robert J Russell
Mr. Smith Russell Jr
Mr. Vito J Russo
Mr. John J Rutkowski
Mr. Jack L Rutledge
Mr. Loran K Rutledge
Mr. Ralph R Rutledge
Mr. Daniel E Ryan
Mr. Eugene F Ryan
Mr. John P Ryan
Mr. Peter P Ryan
Mr. Robert E Ryan
Mr. Roger S Ryan
Mr. Richard D Ryder
Mr. William J Ryland
Mr. Wesley Rylander
Mr. John W Sacca
Mr. William H Sachau
Mr. Andrew Sackela
Mr. Ervin P Sacra
Mr. John M Sadler
Mr. Paul F Sadler
Mr. Andrew J Sager
Mr. Gordon L Saint
Mr. Charles A Salas
Mr. Gene C Salay
Mr. Armando M Salazar
Mr. Thomas W Sale
Mr. Stevano Salerno
Mr. Thomas J Salerno
Mr. Robert L Sales
Mr. Wilfredo Salgado
Mr. James O Salladay
Mr. Stanley R Sallee
Mr.Jess E Salley
Mr. Alphonse C
    Salvaggio
Mr. Michael J Salvo Jr

Mr. Carl T Salyers
Mr. Robert P Salzman
Mr. Michael Samberg
Mr. George Samios
Mr. Maynard H Sampson
Mr. William M Sampson
Mr. Paul F Samuel
Mr. Arthur G Samuelsohn
Mr. Lester E Samuelson
Mr. Kenneth A San
    Soucie
Mr. Benjamin Sanchez
Mr. Donaid L Sanchez
Mr. Jeffery L Sanchez
Mr. Robert Sanchez
Mr. Ronald Sanchez
Mr. Clinton L Sanderfer
Mr. Fred W Sanders
Mr. Cecil T Sandifer
Mr. Billy D Sandlin
Mr. Glenn H Sandlin
Mr. Daniel R Sankoff
Mr. David W Sanshuck
Mr. John J Santangelo
Mr. Luis A Santiago
Mr. Thomas Santiago Jr
Mr. Juan Santiago-Seda
Mr. John P Santini
Mr. Louis E Santucci
Mr. Michael E Sapara
Mr. Vincent Saporito
Mr. Frenando R Sarabia
Mr. Louis G Sardina
Mr. John E Sargent
Mr. Roy W Sargent
Mr. Wellington H Sargent
Mr. Paul F Satterthwaite
Mr. Jesse M Saunders
Mr. Frank J Sauer Jr
Mr. Harold E Saunders Jr
Mr. Robert Sauter
Mr. Raymond P Sautter
1Sgt Calvin Doc Savage
    Ret
Mr. Joseph P Savage
Mr. Jamoo O Oavage III
Mr. Charles T Sawyer Jr
Mr. Edward J Saviski
Mr. Nick T Savko Sr
Mr. Anthony R Saxton
Mr. Robert D Saxton
Mr. Noel J Say
Dr. Richard H Sayers
Mr. William H Sayers
COL Daniel T Saylor
Mr. Gerald B Saylor
Mr. Charles Saylor Jr
Mr. John Sbaffi
Mr. Frank Scafidi
Mr. Patsy J Scarpato
Mr. Charles F Scarpone
Cpt George M
    Schabacker
Mr. Arthur G Schaefer Sr
Mr. Harold Schaefer
Mr. David M Schaff
Mr. George W Schaffler
Mr. George C Schakow
Mr. Robert E Schatz
Mr. Stephen J Schawang
Mr. Howard A Scheinhoiz
Mr. Robert F Schell
Mr. Woodrow T
    Schellenberg
Mr. Henry L Schenck
Mr. Robert G Scheppan
Mr. Walter C Scherar
Mr. Vincent A Schettino
Mr. Leo Schildhouse
Mr. Eugene F Schildman

Mr. Wendell H Schillinger
Mr. Louis A Schindler
Mr. Robert C Schindling
Mr. Richard W Schirr
Mr. Frank T Schleicher
Mr. Richard C Schlenker
LTC Otto A Schludecker
Mr. Fredrick F Schmidt
Mr. George Schmidt
Mr. Gerald M Schmidt
Mr. Leonard T Schmidt
Mr. Neils I Schmidt
Mr. Vernon N Schmidt
Mr. Fred Schmitt
Mr. Virgil U Schnatis
Mr. Howard C Schneider
Mr. John J Schneider III
Mr. Jacob W Schock
Mr. Richard H Schofield
Mr. Edward F Schooner
Mr. Charles B
    Schoonmaker
Mr. Walter C Schrank Jr
LTC Francis R Schreiber
Mr. William H Schreiber
Mr. Malcolm R Schreiner
Mr. Richard L Schreiner
Mr. Frederick W
    Schroeder
Mr. Kenneth M
    Schroeder
Mr. Milburn C Schubert
Mr. Frank L Schulgen
Mr. Dale L Schumacher
Mr. Ronald L
    Schumacher
Mr. Ernest R Schumann
Mr. Harold H Schuster
Mr. Gene W Schutt
Mr. Edward Schwartz
Mr. Herbert Schwartz
Mr. Leroy Schwartz
Mr. George M
    Schwemmer
Mr. Sal J Scialo
Mr. Ernest A Sciascia
Mr. Alastair D Scott
Mr. Charles S Scott
Mr. Curtis R Scott
Mr. James E Scott
Mr. Orvan W Scott
Mr. Robert D Scott
Mr. William A Scott
Mr. Charies L Scranton
Mr. George J Seaman
Mr. James R Searcy
Mr. Fred C Searles
Mr. George L Seaver
Mr. Edward C Sedberry
Mr. George O Sedgwick
Mr. Michael J Sedlock
Mr. Joseph A Sedor Sr
Mr. Leonard Sedorovitz
Mr. Alfred C Seebode
Mr. William F K Seefeld
Mr. James E Segal
Mr. Amadito G Segura
Mr. James P Seibert Sr
Mr. Robert M Seibert
Mr. Joseph J Seid
Mr. Lloyd M Seifert
Mr. Gerald R Seifer
Mr. George H Seifert
Mr. Francis B Selby
Mr. John Seleway
Mr. Clair V Sellers
Maj Wilbur R Sellers Ret
Mr. Louis Selmi Jr
Mr. Richard H Semans
Mr. Anthony L Semrau

Mr. Michael J Seneca
Mr. George E Senft
Mr. William T Senn Jr
Mr. Dale E Sensabaugh
Mr. James Serano
Mr. Theodore F Sershen
Mr. Eugene Settles
Mr. Martin L Sever
Mr. Walter W Seyfferth
Mr. Albert N Seymour
Mr. Calvin E Seymour
Mr. Sidney Shaenfield
Mr. Charles W Shaffner
Mr. Hyman F Shakin
Mr. Raymond J
    Shallbetter
Mr. Walter A A Shamp
Mr. Edwin B Shannon II
Mr. Harold M Shapiro
Mr. Erwin L Sharp
Mr. Karl W Sharples
Mr. Robert Sharpnack
Mr. Robert L Sharrow
Mr. David J Shattuck
Mr. Robert W
    Shaughnessy
Mr. Harry G Shaul
Mr. Elmer C Shaw
Mr. Harvey J Shaw
Mr. Thomas W Shaw
Mr. Robert B Shea
Mr. Martin B Shedd
Mr. Robert J Sheehy Sr
Mr. Edwin F Sheets
Mr. Robert A Sheipe
Mr. Marlan H Shepard
ILt William G Shephard
    Ret
Mr. Emmett D Shepherd
Mr. Hubert C Sheppard
Mr. Charles J Sherman
Sgm Thomas Sherrer
Mr. Thomas E Sherry
Mr. Edward L Shields
Mr. James L Shields
Mr. John J Shields
Mr. John R Shields
Mr. Clyde W Shinault
Mr. Thomas W Shipp Sr
Mr. Edward L Shives
Mr. Harry W Shoemaker
Mr. Albert J Shook
Mr. Harry V Shoop
Mr. Terry E Shoopman
Mr. Thomas E Showalter
Mr. Thomas A Shtogren
Mr. William E Shubin
Mr. Don C Shuffstall
Mr. Paul W Shugar
Mr. Ottis G Shull
Mr. Stephen L Shull
Mr. Mervyn M Shuman
COL Leonard E Shupp
    USA (Ret)
Mr. Raymond O
    Shurson Sr
Mr. Frank P Sicari
Mr. Stephen A Siciliato
Mr. Wilbur A Sidney
Mr. Anthony J Siegel
Mr. Carl W Siegel
Mr. Joseph Siegel
CWO Eugene C
    Siegfried (Ret)
Mr. Harold E Sigman
Mr. John H Sikes Jr.
Mr. Robert H Siler
Mr. Himes M Silin
Mr. Harry Silk
Mr. Daniel E Silla

Mr. Al J Silvano
Mr. Paul Silver
Mr. Gerald P Simas
Mr. Ralph Simeone
Mr. Frank Simko
Mr. James E Simmerman
Mr. Raymond H
    Simmons Jr
Mr. Richard W Simmons
Mr. Earl L Simo
Mr. Seymour Simon
Mr. John C Simons
Mr. Bobby K Simpson
Mr. Joseph B Simpson Jr
Mr. Randall L Sims
Mr. Edward F Sinclair
Mr. Gary W Sinclair
Mr. Robert C Sinclair
Mr. Douglas O Singletary
Mr. Donald Singleton
Mr. Everett W Singleton
Mr. James E Singleton
Mr. Leo R Sinnett
Mr. Anthony F Sirica
Mr. Robert D Sisson
Cpt Charies T Sizemore
    Ret
Mr. Stewart E Sizemore
Mr. Gary C Skaggs
Mr. George Skiba
Mr. Johnny C Skidmore
Mr. John J Skiffington III
1Sgt Terrance A Skipper
    Ret
Mr. Lynn Skocdopole
Mr. Vincent A Skowronski
Mr. Michael F
    Skrzypczak
Mr. Marion F Skwarek
Mr. Frank J Slagle
Mr. Maurice R Slaney
MAJ Marion R Slater
Mr. John F Slattery
Mr. William J Slaughter Jr
Mr. Raymond A Slavik
Mr. Garland L Slayton
Mr. Charles W Slentz Sr
Mr. Robert C Slingerland
Mr. Ronald S Sloat
Mr. Thomas R Slusarz
Mr. Richard S Smacher
Mr. Adam J Smagala
Mr. Edward J Smagala
Mr. Edward L
    Smaldone Sr
Mr. Roger W Smalley
Mr. William H Smalley
Mr. Allen R Smartt
Mr. James Smit
Mr. Albert H Smith
Mr. Charles J Smith
Mr. Charles M Smith Jr
Mr. David C Smith
Mr. David C Smith
Mr. David E Smith
Mr. Edward J Smith
Mr. Francis W Smith
Msg Fred L Smith Ret
Mr. Geoffrey S Smith Jr
Mr. Harry R Smith
Mr. Howard A Smith
Mr. Howard N Smith
Mr. James C Smith
Mr. John D Smith
Mr. Joseph P Smith
Mr. Kingsley J Smith
Mr. Lee F Smith
Mr. Loyd A Smith
Mr. Norman O Smith
Mr. Mark W Smith

Mr. Oscar H Smith
Mr. Richard B Smith
Mr. Robert A Smith
Mr. Robert J Smith
Mr. Robert L Smith
Mr. Robert M Smith
Mr. Robert W Smith
Mr. Ronald L Smith
Mr. Stanley R Smith
MAJ Todd D Smith
Mr. William E Smith
Mr. William G Smith Sr
Mr. Irwin C Smoler
Mr. Garland B Snedegar
Mr. Eddie L Sneed
Mr. Edwin M Sneed Jr
Mr. Lee C Snidow
Mr. Olgerts P Sniedze
Mr. Morton D Snow
Mr. Carl D Snyder
Mr. Clifford W Snyder
Mr. Denis E Snyder
Mr. Gilbert J Snyder
Mr. William E Snyder
Mr. William L Snyder
Mr. Allen L Snyder Jr
COL Clinton W Snyder
    (Ret)
Mr. Carlyle Sobel
Mr. Herman E Soblick
Mr. Ronald E Soder
Mr. John E Soderberg
Mr. Richard S Soja
Mr. Lyle D Solchenberger
Mr. Robert P Soley
Mr. Clyde H Solmon
Mr. Frank U Solomon Jr
Mr. Peter A Soltysiak
Mr. Stanley J Soltysiak
Mr. John W Sonley
Mr. Albert O Sonnenberg
Mr. Thomas J Soppeland
Mr. Gustave R Sorenson
Mr. William F Sorgie
Mr. Steve A Sosnowski
Mr. Cody C Souders
Mr. Herbert M Soule Jr
Mr. Charles B Soules
Mr. Charles Southern
Mr. Kenneth N
    Southworth
Mr. Richard A Sover
Mr. Everett L Sowden
Mr. Robert V Sowin
Mr. Rayman C Spalsbury
Mr. Irwin B Spandau
Mr. Roy Spanower
Mr. Beriram L Sparks
Mr. William D Sparks
Mr. William V Sparks
Col Anse Ed H Speairs
    Ret
Mr. Robert Spearing III
Mr. Donald E Spears
Mr. Ralph W Spears
Mr. Thomas G Spegar
Mr. Thomas C Spence
Mr. Clifford J Spencer
Mr. Joe E Spencer
Mr. John D Spencer
Mr. Russell Spencer
Mr. Allen B Sperling
Mr. John J Sperry
Mr. Reinhold L Spicker
Mr. Louis A Spiegler
Mr. Oren W Spilker
Mr. David T Spillane
Mr. Harold W Spillman
Mr. James M Spillman Sr
Mr. Sidney B Spiro Jr

Mr. Ronald F Spivak
Mr. Theodore E Spohn
Mr. William S Spriggs
Mr. Robert E Springer
Mr. James G Sproul
Mr. Donald H Sprowls
Mr. Kenneth J Spry
Mr. Robert A Sroka
Mr. Albert R St Clair
Mr. Leo W St John
Mr. E Larry St Laurent
Mr. Dale W St Louis
Mr. Patsy J Staffiera
Mr. Rohland R Stager
Mr. Dave V Stahley
Mr. Angelo J Staikos
Mr. Robert H Stallwood
Mr. Max E Stambach
Mr. William P Stambaugh
Mr. Elmer J Stamp
Mr. Robert M Standerfer
Mr. Michael D Standt
Mr. Edward W
    Stankowski
Mr. Edwin W Stanton
Mr. Glenn E Starcher
Mr. Gary J Stark
Mr. Everette E Starnes
Mr. Henry Starr Jr
Mr. Robert M Starr
Mr. James A Staton
Mr. Robert E
    Stauffeneger
Mr. Carlton H Stauffer
Mr. Kim R Stavis
Mr. John D Stavola
LTC Kenneth A
    Steadman (Ret)
Mr. Wayne R Stebold
Mr. Robert E Stecker
Mr. Earl D Steele
COL Howard M Steele Jr
Mr. Robert C Steele
Mr. William Steele
Mr. John H Steenberg
Mr. James A Stefani
Mr. Bruno J Stefanoni
Mr. Arthur H Steffensen
Mr. George J Steggerda
Mr. Burton Steinberg
Mr. Anthony W Steiner
Mr. Joseph A Steiner Jr
Mr. Nicholas C Stella
Mr. John A Stenmo
Mr. Jude C Stenson
Mr. Dock W P Stephens
Mr. Larry O Stephens
Mr. Larry D Steponik
Mr. Richard L Sterr
Mr. James W Sterriker
Mr. Lawrence Steubing
Mr. Joseph H K Stevens
Mr. Roy A Stevens
Mr. John J Stevenson
Mr. Charles L Stewart
Mr. Earl C Stewart
COL Matthew C Stewart
Mr. Richard R Stewart
Mr. Richard S Stewart
Mr. James P Stidham Sr
Mr. William R Stiles
Mr. Charles J Stitz Sr
Mr. Michael C Stockton
Mr. Lester J Stoddard
Mr. Karol T Stofka
Mr. James R Stokely
Mr. Andrew L Stone
Mr. James R Stone III
Mr. Richard B Stone Sr
Mr. Jerry H Stone

Mr. Walter R Stone
Mr. James M Stoner
Mr. Richard L Storey Jr
Mr. Wayne A Stouffer
Mr. Harold V Stout
Mr. Larry J Stovall
Mr. Billy D Stover
Mr. Charles L Stowe
Mr. Stephen L Strahan
Mr. Andrew J Straka
Mr. Ashley M Stranahan
Mr. Alfred E Strangfeld
Mr. David L Straten Sr
Mr. Charles D Stratton
Mr. John J Strauser
Mr. Barney Streeter
Mr. Charles L Streetman
Mr. David Streger
Mr. William T Strish
Mr. William L Strong
Mr. Melvin E Strople
Mr. Donald L Strubing
Mr. Harold L Strunk
Mr. Robert W Stryker
Mr. Charles L Stuart
Mr. Donald Stubbings
Mr. James M Stubbs
Mr. Richard A Stuben
Mr. Frederick Stumpf
Mr. Robert J Stumpf
Mr. Arthur W Sturgeon
SGM Bobby L Sturgill
    (Ret)
Mr. Joseph R Sturm
Mr. Stanley Stypulkowski
Mr. David J Suehring
Mr. Henry J Suffoletto
Mr.Hideo Sugi
Mr. Frederick J Suhr
Mr. Robert E Suhr
Mr. Daniel J Sullivan
Mr. John W Sullivan
Mr. Paul J Sullivan
Mr. Sidney M Sultzbaugh
Mr. Robert I Sulzer
Mr. Raymond D
    Summerlot
Sgm John A Summers
    Ret
Mr. Robert W
    Sundermann
Mr. Norman Superstein
Mr. Dominick Suppa
Mr. Kernig Bo Surabian
Mr. John J Surash
Mr. Eurias C Sutton
Mr. Michael K Sutton
Mr. Roy L Swagler
Mr. James A Swan
Mr. George L Swanson
Mr. William M Swartz
Mr. Charles R Sweeney
Mr. James H Sweeney
Mr. John F Sweeney
Mr. John J Sweeney
MAJ Charles P Sweeney
    (Ret)
Mr. Carl Swenson
Mr. Richard E Swing
Mr. Robert E Swords
Mr. Scott M Sylvester
Mr. Bernard R Symczak
Mr. Damian B Szumski
Mr. Arthur J Szymanski
Mr. Joseph M Szymanski
Mr. Peter J Taddeo
Mr. Martin L Tahakjian
Mr. Patrick J Tajak
Mr. Edwin J Takala
Mr. Kenneth E Talbert

Mr. Thomas H Talbert
Mr. Neil C Talcott
Mr. Vincent Tallarico
Mr. George F Tallent
Mr. Harold R Tallent
Mr. Donald E Tallon
Mr. Gary S Talman
Mr. Ruben Tamariz
1Sgt Joe Tamayo Ret
Mr. Bruce W Taneski
Mr. John Tango Jr
Mr. Paul H Tanner
Mr. Joseph V Tanyer
Mr. John R Tapia
Mr. Robert D Tapscott
Mr. Frank A Taraburelli
Mr. Raymond A Tarabusi
Mr. Joseph L Tarallo
Mr. Anthony M Taschler
Mr. Albert E Tartaglia
Mr. Coy L Tate
Mr. David P Tatum
Mr. Gregory A Tavarone
Mr. Anthony Tavilla
Mr. Saul Taxon
Mr. Acie W Taylor
Mr. Bobby Taylor
Mr. Bobby G Taylor
Mr. Charles E Taylor
Mr. David B Taylor
Mr. Donald E Taylor
Mr. Doug P Taylor
Mr. Harold W Taylor
Mr. Kenneth M Taylor
Mr. Lewis C Taylor
Mr. Roscoe L Taylor
Mr. Frederick A Taylor Jr
Mr. Herschel M Teach
Mr. Lloyd V Teale
Mr. Ronald D Tears
Mr. Leroy R Tecube
Mr. Louis Tedone
Mr. Carl T Teegarden
Mr. Robert W Teeples
Mr. Graham K Tefft
Mr. Robert N Tegelman
Mr. Edward Teixeira
Mr. Rocco A Telese
Mr. Patrick A Teora
Mr. Frederick J Terhune
Sgm Morris J Terrebonne
    Jr
Mr. Vincent D Terrible
Mr. J C Terry
LTC Bruno C Terlizzi
    (Ret)
Mr. Charles Thackara
Mr. Harry A
    Thambounaris
Mr. Albert C Thomas
Mr. Bill W Thomas
Mr. Charles R Thomas
Mr. Edward F Thomas
Mr. Jack Thomas
Mr. John A Thomas
Mr. John J Thomas
Psg John L Thomas Ret
Mr. Michael Thomas Sr
Sgm William E Thomas
    Ret
Mr. Lewis A Thomason
Ssg James Thompson
    Ret
Mr. James E Thompson
Mr. Richard L Thompson
Mr. Robert L Thomson
Mr. Winfred M Thompson
Mr. John E Thomson
MSGT Marion F Throne
Mr. James L Tilley

Mr. Charles Timm Jr
Mr. Rraymond H Timmer
Mr. James R Tinkle
MSG Edward J Tinney
    (Ret)
Mr. George C Tips
Mr. George Tirro
Mr. Michael Tkalcevic
Mr. James A Tobias
Mr. Steve Tobolski
Ssg Walter L Tokamori
    Ret
Mr. Robert D Tokar Sr
Mr. Manual Toledo
Mr. Charles V Tomasella
Mr. Philip J Tomasetti
Mr. William A
    Tomaszewski
Mr. Charles S Tomlin
Mr. David S Tomlin
Mr. Edward L Tomlinson
Mr. Herbert E Tomlinson
Mr. Paul F Toms
Mr. Victor J Tomsko
Mr. Lawrence S Toppi
Mr. Edward S Tooma
Mr. Robert T Toomey
Mr. Roy F Torey
Mr. Salvatore D Tormello
Mr. Juan (Skip) M Torres
Mr. Anthony Torrieri
Mr. Fred S Tortello
Mr. John P Toscano
Mr. Bertalan J Toth
CSM Glenn H Towe (Ret)
Mr. Joseph T Towler
Mr. Eugene P Towles
Dr. Robert L Towles
Mr. James D Townsend Jr
Mr. William H Townsend
Mr. Ernest D Townsley
Mr. Robert J Tracey
Mr. William J Tracey Sr
Mr. Michael Tragoutsis
Mr. Harry H Traitz
Mr. Charles J Trant Jr
Mr. Joseph K Trant
Mr. Richard A Travali
Mr. Syl Treaster
Sfc Frederick J
    Tregaskes
Mr. Robert E Trego
Mr. Joseph L Tremblay
Mr. Emil M Trgala
Mr. Allan A Tribett
Mr. Donald D Trickel
Mr. George L Trimble III
Col Orfeo Trombetta Ret
Mr. Alfred F Trotola
Mr. Charles D Trotter
Mr. Thomas B Trousdell
Mr. Fielding D Tucker
Mr. John A Tujague
Mr. John A Tunney
Mr. Dennis M Turk
Mr. Joseph J Turk
Mr. Bernard L Turner
Mr. David L Turner
Mr. James W Turner
Mr. Joe R Turner
Mr. Richard E Turner
Mr. Leon Turner
Mr. Patrick L Turner
Mr. John P Tutini
Mr. Jack S Tuttle
Mr. Walter A Twyford
Mr. Edmund S Tyksinski
Mr. George F Tyson Jr
Mr. Donald A Uccello
Mr. Robert I Uhl

Mr. Stephen R Uhl
Mr. Gary W Uirich
Mr. Gerald H Ulm
Mr. Merle E Ulm
LTC David T Ulmer
Mr. Jack L Ulmer
Mr. Samuel J Umbriac
Mr. Paul A Umbstead
Mr. Lee R Umlauf
Mr. Herbert L Underwood
Mr. Homer T Underwood
Mr. Michael Unger
Mr. Timothy S Ungurean
Mr. Arnold W Unterseher
Csm Raymond H Upp
    Ret
Mr. William A Uricchio
Psg Ray C Utley Sr Ret
Mr. Rodney E Utley
Mr. Edward Uttian
Mr. Christopher J Uzzi
Mr. William P Vadovich
Mr. James A Vagnier
Mr. Philip A Valenti
Mr. Frank Valentin
Mr. Terry M Valentine
Mr. Joseph C Valerie
Mr. John Valerio
Mr. Ezio J Vallese
Mr. Raymond L Valley
Mr. Burton C Van Buren
Msg Elmer R
    Van Cleave Ret
Mr. Robert M Van Dam
Mr. Jack F Van Eaton
Mr. Donald H Van Engen
Mr. John A Van Haften
Mr. Donald E Van Hooser
Mr. James H Van Matre
Mr. Edward L Van
    Nordheim
Mr. Clement C
    Van Wagoner
Mr. Samuel O
    Van Wegen
Mr. James H Van Winkle
Mr. Harry C Van Zandt
Mr. Kenneth E Vance
Mr. Varlan D Vancil
Mr. William H
    Vandenbergh
Mr. Herbert C
    Vander Horst
Mr. Kenneth W
    Vander Molen
Mr. Joe C Vanderlip
Mr. Michael D
    Vanderputten
Mr. Harold A Vanderwall
Mr. Michael L Vanihel
Mr. Billy E Vansiclde
Mr. Anthony Varbavo
Mr. Albert R Vargas
Mr. Jimmy S Vargas
Mr. Robert J Vargas
Mr. Joseph M Vas Dias
Mr. Stephen J Vasco
Mr. John J Vaughan
Mr. Kenneth M Vaughan
Mr. Gordon E Vaughn
Mr. James G Vaughn
Mr. William T Vazal
Mr. Bienvenido Vazquez
Mr. Wendell Vega
MAJ Thomas C Veit
    (Ret)
Mr. Johnny Velasquez
Mr. William T Venderford
Mr. Arsanio Vendiola
Mr. John M Vera

Mr. Arthur J Vera - Martinez
Mr. Joseph C Vicari
Mr. Jesse I Vicera
Mr. Ellison B Vickery Jr
Mr. Raoul Vidal
Mr. Elric R Vieau
Mr. Ernest A Vigna
Mr. Joseph A Villabol
Mr. Lois M Villalpando
Mr. Anthony J Villani
Mr. Jesse E Vincent
Mr. Sherwin Vine
Mr. Harold R Visser
Mr. Louis J Vita
Mr. Frank L Vlach
Mr. James B Vogels
Mr. Carl Vogt
Mr. Harold G Void
Mr. Stanley Volens
Mr. Alvin E Von Holle
Mr. Dale T Von Stein
Mr. Glendon W Voorhees
Mr. Henry V Voorhees
Mr. Robert M Vorphal
Mr. Joseph R Vucich
Mr. Spyros Vutetakis
Mr. Joseph V Wachtler
Mr. Henry H Wadahara
Mr. Robert W Wadington
Mr. Harold J Wagner
Mr. John F Wagner
Mr. John R Wagner
Mr. Melvin H Wagner
Mr. Richard F Wagner
Mr. Charles H E Wahl
Mr. Dwight E Wahlberg
Mr. Albert Wahnon
Mr. Frank J Waideck
Sfc Lewis E Waik
Mr. Clayton F Waldron
Mr. Raymond A Waldron
CPT David P Walker
Mr. George G Walker Sr
Mr. Gregory C Walker
Mr. Jim H Walker
Mr John A Walker
Mr. Larry L Walker Jr
Mr. Lawrence E Walker
Mr. Leo W Walker
Mr. Robert L Walker
Mr. Stephen J Walker Sr
Mr. William G Walker
Mr. Earl N Wall
Mr. Gene R Wall
Mr. Dennis A Wallot
Mr. Dale L Walls
Mr. Robert N Wallworth
Mr. David L Walsh
Mr. George H Walsh
Mr. William J Walsh
Mr. Robert E Walter

Mr. Charles E Walters
Mr. Donald E Walters
Mr. Robert L Walters
Mr. John C Walton
Mr. James K Wambold
Mr. Peter R Wandrie
LTC Stan W Wapinski (Ret)
Mr. Wilbur O Wardle
Mr. William C Ware
Mr. Louise R Warman
Mr. Robert L Warner
Mr. Ralph W Warnock
Mr. Floyd D Washburn
Mr. Harold S Washburn
Mr. Frederick N Washington
Mr. John R Washney
Mr. John F Waterman
Ltc Douglas T Waters Ret
Mr. James F Waters
Mr. James L Watkins
Mr. Keith A Watkins
Mr. John F Watson Sr
Mr. Larry J Watson
Mr. Donald J Watts
Mr. Wayne E Watts
Mr. Sam Waxman
Mr. Richard E Wayman
Mr. William K Wayne
Mr. Alen R Webb
Mr. John R Webb
Mr. Edward C Webber
Mr. Edwin J Webber
Mr. Joseph W Webber Jr
Mr. Gerald C Weber
Mr. Glenn G Weber
Mr. Carroll M Webster
Mr. Wesley D Webster
Mr. Millard F Weddel
Mr. Edward J Weeks
Mr. Thomas H Weidensaul
Mr. Earl H Weigel
Mr. Richard C Weil
Mr. George E Weiland
Mr. Harry D Weiland
Mr. John H Weimer
Mr. Stanley Weiner
Mr. Lester Weinstein
Mr. James M Weir
Mr. John H Weir
Mr. John W Weiss
Mr. Arthur W Weldon
Mr. Andrew Wells Jr
Mr. Dennis M Wells
Mr. Jack R Wells
Mr. Raymond C Wells
Mr. Joseph J Welsh Jr
Mr. Chester C Wenc
Mr. John A Wendell

Mr. Irving R Wendt
Sgm Dennis J Wenthe Ret
Mr. John W Wenzel
Mr. William F Werckman
Mr. Benjamin F Werner
Mr. Anthony B Werthmann
COL John E Wesbrook
Mr. Arthur E Wessels Sr
Mr. Harrison West
Mr. James W West
Mr. Max L West
Mr. Robert A West
Mr. Verle E West
Mr. Ivar S Westerback
Mr. Curtis D Weston
Mr. Thomas G Weston
Mr. Donald C Weyer
Mr. Carroll M Weyrich
Mr. John L Whalen
Mr. Mark A Whaley
LTC Robert E Whaley (Ret)
Mr. Jackson B Wharton
Mr. Edward A Wheeler
Mr. Ray Wheeler
Mr. Charles (Chuck) T Whit
Mr. James E Whitaker
Mr. David J Whitaker Jr
Mr. Charles I White
Mr. David M White
Mr. Joseph P White
Mr. Robert E White
1SG George A White (Ret)
Mr. Hiram H Whitehead Jr
Mr. Everett P Whitehouse
Mr. Charles V Whitlock
Mr. James H Whitman
Mr. William H Whitman
Mr. Donald R Whitner
Mr. Leo G Whitney
Mr. Richard G Whitson
Mr. Otto W Whittington
Mr. Jerry E Wholaver Sr
Mr. Edward L Wiegand
Mr. Darrell K Wiegert
Mr. Daniel K Wiggins
LTC Richard A Wiggins (Ret)
Mr. J David Wilcher
Mr. Charles J Wilcox
Msg Alfred J Wild Ret
Mr. George A Wild
Mr. Wilson B Wilder
Mr. William R Wilds
Mr. George A Wilfong
Mr. Charles S Wilke
Mr. Roger J Wilkins

Mr. Mc Gruder G Wilkinson
Mr. Francis Wilkish Jr
Mr. Clarence E Will
Mr. Ernest L Willey
Mr. Albert Williams
Mr. Alfred D Williams
1Sgt Benjamin Williams Jr
Mr. Carl A Williams
Mr. Donald Williams
Mr. Edwin D Williams
Mr. Frank J Williams
Mr. Gary P Williams
Mr. Harold S Williams
Mr. James B Williams
Mr. Kenneth D Williams
PSG Kenneth E Williams
Mr. Norval R Williams
Mr. Richard E Williams
Mr. Thomas E Williams
Mr. Thomas L Williams
Mr. Warren L Williams
Mr. William J Williams
CSM Jesse W Williams Jr
Mr. Carl E Williamson
Mr. Emerson S Williamson
Mr. James C Williford Sr
Mr. Michael J Willis
LTC Albert T Willis (Ret)
Mr. William C Willmot
Mr. Charles E Wilson
Mr. Eugene K Wilson
Mr. Fenton M Wilson
Mr. George C Wilson
Mr. George M Wilson
Mr. Jesse R Wilson
Mr. John S Wilson
Mr. Michael R Wilson
Mr. Scott D Wilson
Mr. Van R Wilson
Mr. William K Wilson
Mr. Rerry A Wilt
Mr. Russell L Wincentsen
Mr. Fred Winchester
Mr. John S Winchock
Csm Frederick D Wingate Ret
Mr. Charles R Winder
Mr. Helmer R Winger
Mr. Martin W Winkle
Mr. Eugene P Winters
MAJ Ray D Wire Ret
Mr. Roy Wireman
Mr. Joseph W Wirthman
Mr. Frank N Wise
Mr. Robert W Wisecup
Mr. John J Witmeyer Jr
Mr. Clarence J Witt
Mr. Michael Witt
Mr. Ralph F Witt
Mr. Harold H Wittig

Mr. Clem H Wittebort
Mr. Stephen J Wittenberg
Mr. Robert E Witter
MSGT William Witts Jr
Mr.Leslie A Woepple
Mr. Stanley A Wojtusik
Mr. Stanley J Wolczyk
Mr. Alfred R Wolf
Mr. Burton E Wolf
Mr. Handy B Wolf
Mr. Richard F Wolf
LT Vincent E Wolf
Mr. William Wolf
Mr. Gene T Wolff
Mr. Theodore H Wolff
Mr. Maurice Wolfson
Mr. Garson Wolitzky
Mr. John C Wolke
Mr. James P Wollner
Sgm Curtis D Womack Ret
Mr. T E Womack
Mr. John W Wondra
Mr. Ercell Wood
Mr. Robert Q Wood
Mr. Wallace E Wood
Mr. Willard E Wood
Mr. Morton Wood Jr
Mr. Richard F Woodhouse Jr
Mr. Robert W Woodhouse Sr
Mr. Gene H Woods
Mr. Kenneth G Woods
Mr. William J Woods
Mr. Lloyd W Wooley
Mr. Robert T Wooten
Mr. Robert D Work
Mr. John W Worley
Mr. Kenneth S Worrasll
Mr. Ivan G Worrell
Mr. Harvey W Worrell
Mr. Herbert W Worthington
Mr. Steven A Wowk
Mr. Richard S Wren
Mr. Brace M Wright
Mr. Charles R Wright
Mr. Donald R Wright Jr
COL Edward P Wright
CSM John L Wright (Ret)
Mr. Robert C Wright
Mr. William E Wright
Mr. Edward D Wubben
Mr. Clarence H Wulff
Mr. Walter S Wyand Jr
Mr. Richard C Wyckoff
Mr. Russell L Wyckoff
Mr. Joseph A Wydra
Mr. Thomas W Yadouga
Mr. Robert H Yancey Sr

Mr. Robert L Yancy
LTG William P Yarborough (Ret)
Mr. Edward L Yarbrough
Mr. Wayne Yarbrough
Mr. Paul N Yeckel Jr
Mr. Frank I Yerks
Mr. Steven C Yevich
Mr. Frank R Yocum
Mr. Carl M Yoders
Mr. Lawrence L Yohe
Mr. Souvenir W Yonkers
Mr. James O York Jr
Mr. Robert E York Jr
Mr. Arthur H Young
Mr. Hobert E Young
Mr. James L Young
Mr. Michael W Young
Mr. Ofa S Young
Mr. Philip W Youngstrum
COL David T Zabecki
Mr. George L Zaiger
Mr. Angelo C Zarra
Mr. Carl J Zarzyski
Mr. Leonard Zatorski
Mr. Adolfo Zavala
Mr. Bernard Zavislak
Mr. Joseph R Zawacki
Mr. Thaddeus J Zawacki
CWO Robert N Zaza (Ret)
Dr. Edward J Zebrowski
Mr. Frank J Zeccola
Mr. Lee P Zeddies
Mr. Robert S Zeeman
Mr. Russell V Zeleniak
Mr. Frederick H Zellmer
Mr. Albert G Zentko
Mr. Herman Zerger Jr
Mr. Andrew J Zeyer
Mr. John L Ziebell
Cwo Charles F Ziegler
Mr. Matthew Z Ziemak
Mr. Frederick C Ziemer
Mr. Eugene A Zientek
Mr. David Zifkin
Mr. George H Zimmer
Mr. Joseph F Zimmer
Mr. Dominic F Zinnie
Mr. Robert J Zinsmeister
Mr. Mark L Zissler
Mr. Burton Zitkin
Mr. Frank Zito
Mr. Philip T Zito
Mr. Prosper Zito Jr
Mr. Harry C Zourdos
Mr. Jack L Zuker
Mr. Rene Zwick
Mr. Joseph B Zych

INDEX

The Biographies and the Roster are not included in this index since they are in alphabetical order in their respective sections.

INFANTRYMEN IN VIETNAM

www.ingramcontent.com/pod-product-compliance
Lightning Source LLC
Chambersburg PA
CBHW050354110426
42812CB00008B/2460